BANGLADESH

INVESTMENT AND BUSINESS GUIDE

VOLUME 1

STRATEGIC AND PRACTICAL INFORMATION

International Business Publications, USA
Washington DC, USA - Bangladesh

BANGLADESH

BUSINESS AND INVESTMENT OPPORTUNITIES YEARBOOK

VOLUME 1 STRATEGIC, PRACTICAL INFORMATION AND OPPORTUNITIES

UPDATED ANNUALLY

Cover Design: **International Business Publications, USA**

We express our sincere appreciation to all government agencies and international organizations which provided information and other materials for this yearbook

2016 Edition Updated Reprint International Business Publications, USA
ISBN 1-4387-7622-5

This yearbook provides basic information for starting or/and conducting business in the country. The extraordinary volume of materials covering the topic, prevents us from placing all these materials in this yearbook. For more detailed information on issues related to any specific investment and business activity in the country, please contact Global Investment Center, USA Please acquire the list of our business intelligence and marketing reports and other business publications. We constantly update and expand our business intelligence and marketing materials. Please contact the center for the updated list of reports on over 200 countries.

in the USA: **Global Investment Center, USA.**
P.O.Box 15343, Washington, DC 20003
Phone: (202) 546-2103, Fax: (202) 546-3275, E-mail: rusric@erols.com

For additional analytical, marketing and other information please contact Global Investment Center, USA

Printed in the USA

BANGLADESH

BUSINESS AND INVESTMENT OPPORTUNITIES YEARBOOK

VOLUME 1

STRATEGIC, PRACTICAL INFORMATION AND OPPORTUNITIES

TABLE OF CONTENTS

STRATEGIC AND DEVELOPMENT PROFILES

BASIC PROFILE

Capital and largest city	Dhaka 23°42′N 90°21′E23.700°N 90.350°E
Official languages	Bengali
Other languages	English
Ethnic groups (2014[2])	• 98% Bengali • 2% other
Religion	Islam
Demonym	Bangladeshi
Government	Unitary parliamentary constitutional republic
- President	Abdul Hamid
- Prime Minister	Sheikh Hasina
- Speaker of the House	Shirin Sharmin Chaudhury
- Chief Justice	Surendra Kumar Sinha
Legislature	Jatiyo Sangshad
	Formation
- Partition of British India	14 August 1947
- Declaration of Independence	26 March 1971
- Liberation of Bangladesh	16 December 1971
- Constitution	4 November 1972
	Area
- Total	147,570 km^2 (94th) 56,977 sq mi
- Water (%)	6.4
	Population
- March 2013 estimate	156,594,962[4] (8th)
- Density	1,033.5/km^2 (12th) 2,676.8/sq mi
GDP (PPP)	2013 estimate
- Total	$496 billion[5] (36th)
- Per capita	$3,167[6] (144th)
GDP (nominal)	2013 estimate
- Total	$161.76 billion (58th)
- Per capita	$1,033 (155th)
Gini (2010)	32.1 medium
HDI (2013)	▲0.558[8] medium · 142nd
Currency	Taka (৳) (BDT)
Time zone	BST (UTC+6)
Date format	• dd-mm-yyyy • BS ব (CE−594)
Drives on the	left
Calling code	+880

ISO 3166 code	BD
Internet TLD	.bd

Bangladesh officially the **People's Republic of Bangladesh** is a country in South Asia. It is bordered by India to its west, north and east; Burma to its southeast and separated from Nepal and Bhutan by the Chicken's Neck corridor. To its south, it faces the Bay of Bengal. Bangladesh is the world's eighth-most populous country, with over 160 million people, and among the most densely populated countries. It forms part of the ethno-linguistic region of Bengal, along with the neighbouring Indian states of West Bengal and Tripura.

The present-day borders of Bangladesh took shape during the Partition of Bengal and British India in 1947, when the region used to be known as East Pakistan, as a part of the newly formed state of Pakistan. It was separated from West Pakistan by 1,400 km of Indian territory. Due to political exclusion, ethnic and linguistic discrimination and economic neglect by the politically dominant western wing, nationalism, popular agitation and civil disobedience led to the Bangladesh Liberation War and independence in 1971. After independence, the new state endured poverty, famine, political turmoil and military coups. The restoration of democracy in 1991 has been followed by relative calm and economic progress. In 2014, the Bangladeshi general election was boycotted by major opposition parties, resulting in a parliament and government dominated by the Awami League and its smaller coalition partners.

Bangladesh is a unitary parliamentary republic with an elected parliament called the Jatiyo Sangshad. The native Bengalis form the country's largest ethnic group, along with indigenous peoples in northern and southeastern districts. Geographically, the country is dominated by the fertile Bengal delta, the world's largest delta. This also gives Bangladesh a unique name tag "The land of rivers".

Bangladesh is a Next Eleven emerging economy. It has achieved significant strides in human and social development since independence, including in progress in gender equity, universal primary education, food production, health and population control.[9][10][11] However, Bangladesh continues to face numerous political, economic, social and environmental challenges, including political instability, corruption, poverty, overpopulation and climate change.

Bangladesh is a founding member of SAARC, the Developing 8 Countries and BIMSTEC. It contributes one of the largest peacekeeping forces to the United Nations. It is a member of the Commonwealth of Nations, the Organization of Islamic Cooperation and the Non-Aligned Movement.

Bangladesh has been aptly described as a new state in an ancient land. Much has been written about the past glory of Bangladesh, notably in old records like the evidence of Pliny and Periplus of the Erythrean Sea (first century AD). It was drawn in Ptolemy's map. These indicate that from the earliest times Bangladesh was known to the West, particularly for its Muslin, the finest fabric the world has ever produced. Travellers and scholars who were attracted by the charms and fame of Bangladesh since time immemorial had showered effusive epithets on its bounties and wealth, affluence and prosperity, craftsmanship and cultural advancement.

They include the Chinese travellers Fa-hien (fourth century AD), Hue-an-tsung (seventh century), Ma-hoen and Fei-shin (fifteenth century), Ibne Batuta (fourteenth century) from Africa, Nicola Kanti (fifteenth century) and Ceasar the Frederik (sixteenth century) from Venice, Verthema, an Italian in the sixteenth century, Barbosa and Sebastin Manric (sixteenth century) from Portugal, Travernier and Bernier from France (seventeenth century) and Queen Elizabeth-the First's ambassador Ralf Fish.

Location:	Between 20°34' N and 26°38' N latitude and between 88°01' E and 92°41' E longitudes. Altitude between zero and 1,200 metres.
Area:	147,570 km^2
Land boundaries:	Total of 4,246 km
Population:	131.2 (2002 estimate, source: BOI)
	Female: 49 per cent
Population density:	889 inhabitants per km^2
	Urban population 25 per cent
Capital:	Dhaka
Administrative Division:	Six administrative divisions and 21 regions
Time zone:	Add six hours to Greenwich Mean Time
Principal languages:	Bangla (95 per cent), dialects (5 per cent)
	English widely used
Principal religions:	Muslim (88 per cent), Hindu (10 per cent), Bhuddhist (1 per cent) and Christian (1 per cent)
Information technology:	15.32 Internet users per 10,000 inhabitants (2002)
	0.34 estimated PCs per 100 inhabitants (2002)
Education and literacy:	Adult literacy rate stands at 41.1 per cent (UNESCO 2000-2004)
	Female: 31.4 per cent
	Male: 50.3 per cent
Currency:	Taka (Tk), 1 Tk = 100 poisha
Measures:	Metric system
Business hours:	From 0900 to 1600, Friday non-working day
Holidays:	1 January: New Year's Day
	21 February: Shaheed Day
	26 March: Independence and National Day
	14 April: Bengali Solar New Year
	1 May: Labour Day
	1st Monday in July Bank Holiday
	15 August: National Mourning Day
	7 November: National Revolution Day
	16 December: Victory Day

	25 December: Christmas Day
	26 December: Boxing Day
	31 December: Bank Holiday
Credit cards:	VISA, MasterCard, American Express
Airlines:	Biman Bangladesh Airlines < www.bimanair.com >
Airports:	Three International airports in Dhaka, Chittagong and Sylhet
Railway network:	2,733.51 km
Road network:	About 20,799 km (13,000 km are paved)
Shipping:	8,046 km
Exchange rate:	US$ 1 = 58.87 taka (average February 2004)

To Ibne Batuta, Bangladesh was a 'hell full of bounties and wealthiest and cheapest land of the world.' So great were the attractions of Bangladesh that to quote Bernier 'it has a hundred gates open for entrance but not one for departure.' Ladies of Imperial Rome were literally crazy for Bangladesh's Muslin and luxury items, which according to Pliny, resulted in serious drain of gold of the Empire. Because of its location, Bangladesh served as a flourishing entry port and intermediary in trade and commerce between South Asia and the Far East. The region also played a seminal role in disseminating its belief art and architecture in the wider world of Asia. Ancient Bangladesh took great pride as a coveted seat of learning and education and scholars from far away countries regularly flocked to its numerous universities and monasteries.

Etymologically, the word Bangladesh is derived from the cognate Vanga which was first mentioned in Aitarey Aranyaka, a Hindu scripture composed between 500 BC and 500 AD. Literally it means a wetland. Muslim merchants of Arab origin used to refer it as Bangalah from which its present nomenclature is believed to have gradually evolved.

Geological evidence indicates that much of Bangladesh was formed 1 to 6.5 million years ago during the tertiary era. Human habitation in this region, therefore, is likely to be very old with the evidence of Palaeolithic civilization dating back to about 1,00,000 years.

Bangladesh has an area of 148,393 sq km and occupies the apex of the arch formed by the Bay of Bengal into which all the rivers flowing through the country drain. Bangladesh has one of the most complex river systems in the world numbering about 230 with their tributaries having a total length of about 24,140 km. The climate of Bangladesh is characterised by high temperature and high humidity, heavy rainfall and marked seasonal variation. Daily temperature ranges from 10° C to 12° C in the cool months and in the other months it varies between 28° C and 40° C. Soil of Bangladesh may be divided into three main categories, namely hill soils (Chittagong and Sylhet regions), terrace soils (Barind and Madhupur tracts) and alluvial and flood plain soils.

Bangladesh contains greater biodiversity than that of many countries taken together. Indeed few countries in the world can match its rich and varied flora and fauna which are not only a unique biological phenomenon but are also a great natural resource of the country. Bangladeshis are historically descendants of various races and nationalities. An Austro-Asian race first inhabited this region followed by Dravidians and Aryans. There was also an influx of the Mongolians from Tibet and Mayanmar. The Arab Muslims started coming here in the early ninth century AD. Persians, Armenians, Turks, Afghans and lastly the Mughals came in quick succession.

As per the census of 1991 Bangladesh has a population of 111.5 million with an average density of 755 people per sq. km. It is the second largest Muslim country. Traditionally a land of communal harmony, followers of other religions enjoy full freedom of worship. The economy is mainly agrarian. Recently there is a spurt in industrialisation with the utilisation of country's available natural resources and manpower. Trade and commerce are increasing and widening. Bangladesh is a repository of rich cultural heritage and tradition.

Long colonial exploitation has largely denuded Bangladesh of its past affluence and wealth. Independence has, however, opened new vistas of prospects and opportunities. In the final analysis, Bangladesh is a land made splendid by natural grace - a veritable mosaic in green, verdant and boisterous, with its dedicated and creative people adding colour and vibrancy to it.

THE LAND

The landscape of Bangladesh, as if, looks like a magical tapestry in green woven intricately by nature. Across the tropic of cancer it lies in the north-eastern part of South Asia between latitudes 20° - 34' and 26° 38' north and longitudes 88° 01' and 92° 41' east. The country is fenced by India on the west, north and the Northeast, Myanmar on the Southeast and the Bay of Bengal on the south. Strategically located Bangladesh is virtually a bridge between south and Southeast Asia. It has a landmass of 1,48,393 sq. km criss-crossed by a network of several major rivers, their numerous tributaries and canals forming a lace of interconnecting channels. In fact, Bangladesh is the largest riverine delta in the world. The extensive river systems are fundamental to the country's economy and the people's way of life. Its low flat alluvial deltaic plains present an enchanting vista of vast verdant green fields sweeping the horizon. Bangladesh has some of the world's most fertile agricultural lands accounting for abundant growth of various crops.

The north-eastern and south-eastern parts of the country are dotted with small hills and ridges, their average elevations being 244m and 610m respectively. The highest peak Keokradong in the south-east end of Bandarban district 1230 meters above the sea level. Thus with its variegated topographical features Bangladesh appears like a vibrant motif splashed with enchanting beauty and serenity.

Bangladeshis are essentially simple in nature. Since time immemorial they are noted for their valour and resilience as well as hospitality and friendliness. Bangladeshis are also equally known for their creativity. They have an innate quality of open mindedness. Communal or ethnic feeling is alien to them and despite diverse racial mix from pre-historic days they are, by and large, a homogeneous group.

Almost all the people speak and understand Bangla, a language which occupies an exalted position because of the richness of its literature. Generally speaking, fish, rice and lentils constitute the main diet of the masses, the vast majority of whom live in the country's villages. A cotton lungi and a jersey called kurta are the common attire for men in rural areas. The urban people have, however, largely adapted to western costume. Sari is women's universal dress, both in the cities and countryside.

Bangladeshi women are traditionally adored for their charm, beauty and elegance. They are now increasingly adapting themselves to changing needs of time; working shoulder to shoulder with the men-folk in fields, factories and offices. In fact, they can be found in all professions and there is no exclusive male domain. Agriculture and its related fields still provide the main livelihood of the people. The expanding industrial and service sectors together with trade and commerce offer increasing alternate occupations for the people.

GEOGRAPHY

Location: Southern Asia, bordering the Bay of Bengal, between Burma and India

Geographic coordinates: 24 00 N, 90 00 E
Map references: Asia

Area:
total: 144,000 sq km
land: 133,910 sq km *water:* 10,090 sq km

Area—comparative: slightly smaller than Wisconsin

Land boundaries:
total: 4,246 km
border countries: Burma 193 km, India 4,053 km

Coastline: 580 km

Maritime claims:
contiguous zone: 18 nm
continental shelf: up to the outer limits of the continental margin
exclusive economic zone: 200 nm *territorial sea:* 12 nm

Climate: tropical; cool, dry winter (October to March); hot, humid summer (March to June); cool, rainy monsoon (June to October)

Terrain: mostly flat alluvial plain; hilly in southeast

Elevation extremes:
lowest point: Indian Ocean 0 m *highest point:* Keokradong 1,230 m

Natural resources: natural gas, arable land, timber

Land use:
arable land: 73% *permanent crops:* 2%
permanent pastures: 5% *forests and woodland:* 15% *other:* 5%

Irrigated land: 31,000 sq km

Natural hazards: droughts, cyclones; much of the country routinely flooded during the summer monsoon season

Environment—current issues: many people are landless and forced to live on and cultivate flood-prone land; limited access to potable water; water-borne diseases prevalent; water pollution especially of fishing areas results from the use of commercial pesticides; intermittent water shortages because of falling water tables in the northern and central parts of the country; soil degradation; deforestation; severe overpopulation

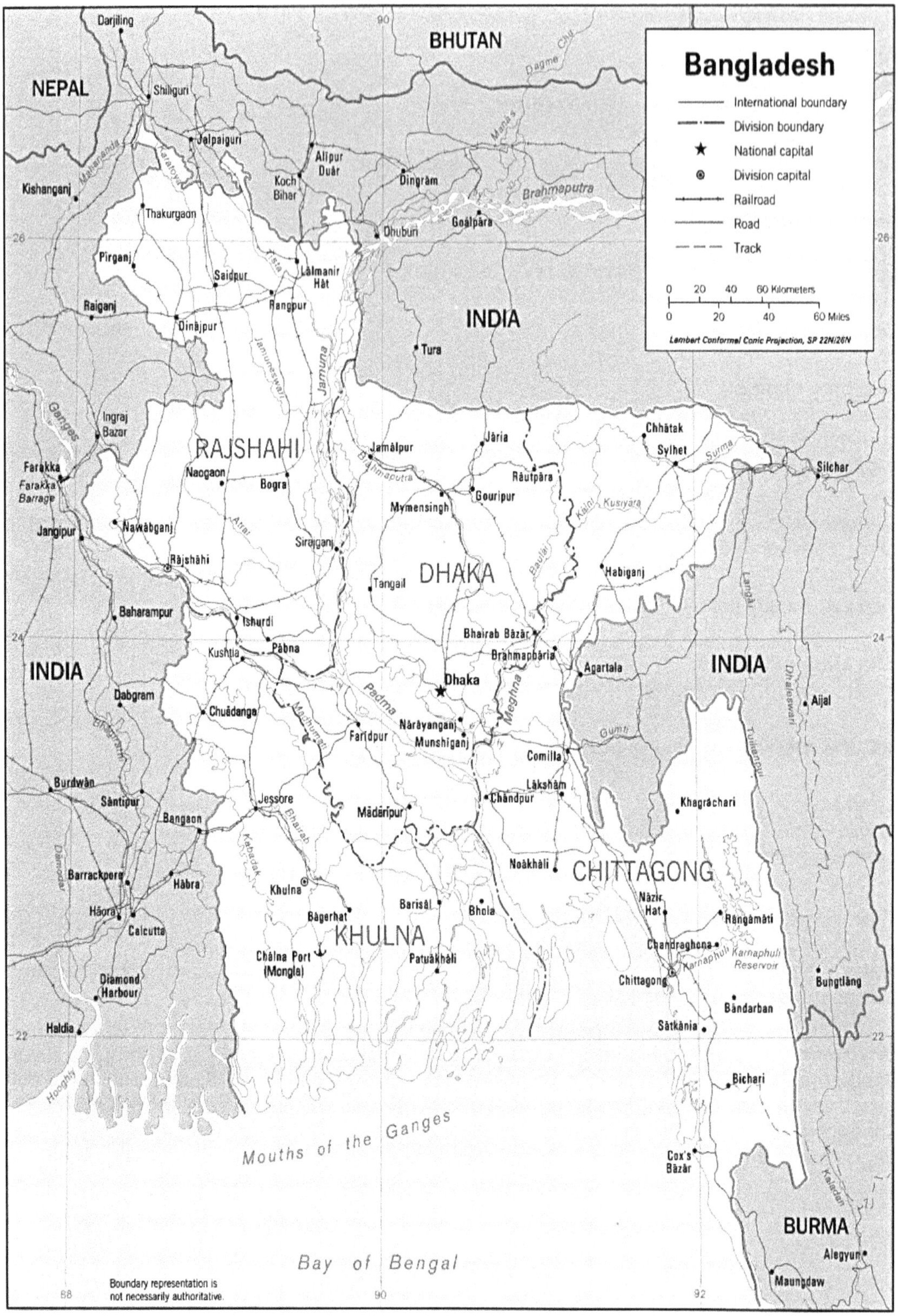

Base 802490 (544488) 5-96

Environment—international agreements:
party to: Biodiversity, Climate Change, Desertification, Endangered Species, Environmental Modification, Hazardous Wastes, Nuclear Test Ban, Ozone Layer Protection, Wetlands
signed, but not ratified: Law of the Sea

PEOPLE

Population: 127,117,967

Age structure:
0-14 years: 38% (male 24,516,722; female 23,346,904)
15-64 years: 59% (male 38,441,064; female 36,586,743)
65 years and over: 3% (male 2,303,613; female 1,922,921)

Population growth rate: 1.59%
Birth rate: 25.2 births/1,000 population
Death rate: 8.5 deaths/1,000 population
Net migration rate: -0.79 migrant(s)/1,000 population

Sex ratio:
at birth: 1.06 male(s)/female
under 15 years: 1.05 male(s)/female
15-64 years: 1.05 male(s)/female
65 years and over: 1.2 male(s)/female
total population: 1.06 male(s)/female

Infant mortality rate: 69.68 deaths/1,000 live births

Life expectancy at birth:
total population: 60.6 years
male: 60.73 years
female: 60.46 years

Total fertility rate: 2.86 children born/woman

Nationality:
noun: Bangladeshi(s)
adjective: Bangladesh

Ethnic groups: Bengali 98%, Biharis 250,000, tribals less than 1 million
Religions: Muslim 88.3%, Hindu 10.5%, other 1.2%
Languages: Bangla (official), English

Literacy:
definition: age 15 and over can read and write
total population: 38.1%
male: 49.4%
female: 26.1%

GOVERNMENT

Country name:

conventional long form: People's Republic of Bangladesh
conventional short form: Bangladesh
local long form: Gana Prajatantri Bangladesh
local short form: Bangladesh
former: East Bengal, East Pakistan

Government type:

parliamentary democracy

Capital:

name: Dhaka
geographic coordinates: 23 43 N, 90 24 E
time difference: UTC+6 (11 hours ahead of Washington, DC, during Standard Time)

Administrative divisions:

7 divisions; Barisal, Chittagong, Dhaka, Khulna, Rajshahi, Rangpur, Sylhet

Independence:

16 December 1971 (from West Pakistan)

National holiday:

Independence Day, 26 March (1971); Victory Day; note - March 1971 is the date of the Awami League's declaration of an independent Bangladesh, and 16 December, known as Victory Day, memorializes the military victory over Pakistan and the official creation of the state of Bangladesh

Constitution:

previous 1935, 1956, 1962 (preindependence); latest enacted 4 November 1972, effective 16 December 1972, suspended March 1982, restored November 1986; amended many times, last in 2011 (2011)

Legal system:

mixed legal system of mostly English common law and Islamic law

International law organization participation:

has not submitted an ICJ jurisdiction declaration; accepts ICCt jurisdiction

Suffrage:

18 years of age; universal

Executive branch:

chief of state: President Abdul HAMID (since 24 April 2013); note - Abdul HAMID served as acting president following the death of Zillur RAHMAN in March 2013; HAMID was subsequently elected by the National Parliament and was sworn in 24 April 2013
head of government: Prime Minister Sheikh HASINA (since 6 January 2009; reelected 5 January 2014)
cabinet: Cabinet selected by the prime minister and appointed by the president
elections: president elected by National Parliament for a five-year term (eligible for a second term); last election held on 29 April 2013 (next must be held by 2018)
election results: President Abdul HAMID was elected by the National Parliament unopposed

Legislative branch:

unicameral National Parliament or Jatiya Sangsad; 300 seats (45 reserved for women) elected by popular vote from single territorial constituencies; members serve five-year terms
elections: last held on 5 January 2014 (next to be held by January 2019); note - the 5 January 2014 poll was marred by widespread violence, boycotts, general strikes, and low voter turnout
election results: percent of vote by party - AL-led Alliance 79%, JP 34%; seats by party - AL 234, JP 34, other 32

Judicial branch:

highest court(s): Supreme Court of Bangladesh (organized into the Appellate Division with 7 justices and the High Court Division with 99 justices)
judge selection and term of office: chief justice and justices appointed by the president; justices serve until retirement at age 67
subordinate courts: civil courts include: Assistant Judge's Court; Joint District Judge's Court; Additional District Judge's Court; District Judge's Court; criminal courts include: Court of Sessions; Court of Metropolitan Sessions; special courts/tribunals; Metropolitan Magistrate Courts; Magistrate Court

Political parties and leaders:

Awami League or AL [Sheikh HASINA]
Communist Party of Bangladesh or CPB [Manjurul A. KHAN]
Bangladesh Nationalist Front or BNF [Abdul Kalam AZADI]
Bangladesh Nationalist Party or BNP [Khaleda ZIA]
Bikalpa Dhara Bangladesh or BDB [Badrudozza CHOWDHURY]
Islami Oikya Jote or IOJ [multiple leaders]
Jatiya Party or JP (Ershad faction) [Hussain Mohammad ERSHAD]
Liberal Democratic Party or LDP [Oli AHMED]
National Socialist Party or JSD [KHALEQUZZAMAN]
Tarikat Foundation [Syed Nozibul Bashar MAIZBHANDARI]
Workers Party or WP [Rashed Khan MENON]

Political pressure groups and leaders:

Advocacy to End Gender-based Violence through the MoWCA (Ministry of Women's and Children's Affairs)
Ain o Salish Kendro (Law and Order Center)
Bangladesh Rural Advancement Committee or BRAC
Bangladesh Center for Worker Solidarity
Federation of Bangladesh Chambers of Commerce and Industry
Odikhar (Human Rights)
other: associations of madrassa teachers; business associations, including those intended to promote international trade; development and advocacy NGOs associated with the Grameen Bank; environmentalists; Islamist groups; labor rights advocacy groups; nongovernmental organizations focused on poverty, alleviation, and socioeconomic international trade; religious leaders; tribal groups and advocacy organizations; union leaders

International organization participation:

ADB, ARF, BIMSTEC, C, CD, CICA (observer), CP, D-8, FAO, G-77, IAEA, IBRD, ICAO, ICC (national committees), ICRM, IDA, IDB, IFAD, IFC, IFRCS, IHO, ILO, IMF, IMO, IMSO, Interpol, IOC, IOM, IPU, ISO, ITSO, ITU, ITUC (NGOs), MIGA, MINURSO, MINUSMA, MONUSCO, NAM, OIC, OPCW, PCA, SAARC, SACEP, UN, UNAMID, UNCTAD, UNESCO, UNHCR, UNIDO, UNIFIL, UNISFA, UNMIL, UNMISS, UNMIT, UNOCI, UNWTO, UPU, WCO, WFTU (NGOs), WHO, WIPO, WMO, WTO

Diplomatic representation in the US:

chief of mission: Ambassador Akramul QADER (since 1 September 2009)
chancery: 3510 International Drive NW, Washington, DC 20008
telephone: [1] (202) 244-0183
FAX: [1] (202) 244-7830/2771
consulate(s) general: Los Angeles, New York

Diplomatic representation from the US:

chief of mission: Ambassador Dan W. MOZENA (since 11 November 2011)
embassy: Madani Avenue, Baridhara, Dhaka 1212
mailing address: G. P. O. Box 323, Dhaka 1000
telephone: [880] (2) 885-5500
FAX: [880] (2) 882-3744

Flag description:

green field with a large red disk shifted slightly to the hoist side of center; the red disk represents the rising sun and the sacrifice to achieve independence; the green field symbolizes the lush vegetation of Bangladesh

National symbol(s):

Bengal tiger, water lily

National anthem:

name: "Amar Shonar Bangla" (My Golden Bengal)

ECONOMY

Bangladesh's economy has grown roughly 6% per year since 1996 despite political instability, poor infrastructure, corruption, insufficient power supplies, slow implementation of economic reforms, and the 2008-09 global financial crisis and recession. Although more than half of GDP is generated through the service sector, almost half of Bangladeshis are employed in the agriculture sector with rice as the single-most-important product. Garment exports, the backbone of Bangladesh's industrial sector and 80% of total exports, surpassed $21 billion last year, 18% of GDP. The sector has remained resilient in recent years amidst a series of factory accidents that have killed over 1,000 workers and crippling strikes that shut down virtually all economic activity. Steady garment export growth combined with remittances from overseas Bangladeshis, which totaled almost $15 billion and 13% of GDP IN 2013, are the largest contributors to Bangladesh's current account surplus and record foreign exchange holdings.

GDP (purchasing power parity):

$324.6 billion
country comparison to the world: 44
$307 billion (2012 est.)
$289.2 billion (2011 est.)
note: data are in 2013 US dollars

GDP (official exchange rate):

$140.2 billion

GDP - real growth rate:

5.8%
country comparison to the world: 42
6.1% (2012 est.)
6.5% (2011 est.)

GDP - per capita (PPP):

$2,100
country comparison to the world: 194
$2,000 (2012 est.)
$1,900 (2011 est.)
note: data are in 2013 US dollars

Gross national saving:

28.3% of GDP
country comparison to the world: 34
27% of GDP (2012 est.)
25% of GDP (2011 est.)

GDP - composition, by end use:

household consumption: 75.3%
government consumption: 5.7%
investment in fixed capital: 25.6%
investment in inventories: 3.6%
exports of goods and services: 24.5%
imports of goods and services: -34.7%

GDP - composition, by sector of origin:

agriculture: 17.2%
industry: 28.9%
services: 53.9%

Agriculture - products:

rice, jute, tea, wheat, sugarcane, potatoes, tobacco, pulses, oilseeds, spices, fruit; beef, milk, poultry

Industries:

jute, cotton, garments, paper, leather, fertilizer, iron and steel, cement, petroleum products, tobacco, pharmaceuticals, ceramics, tea, salt, sugar, edible oils, soap and detergent, fabricated metal products, electricity, natural gas

Industrial production growth rate:

9%
country comparison to the world: 20

Labor force:

78.62 million
country comparison to the world: 7
note: extensive export of labor to Saudi Arabia, Kuwait, UAE, Oman, Qatar, and Malaysia; workers' remittances were $10.9 billion in FY09/10

Labor force - by occupation:

agriculture: 47%
industry: 13%
services: 40% (2010 est.)

Unemployment rate:

5%
country comparison to the world: 48

5% (2012 est.)
note: about 40% of the population is underemployed; many persons counted as employed work only a few hours a week and at low wages

Population below poverty line:

31.5% (2010 est.)

Household income or consumption by percentage share:

lowest 10%: 4%
highest 10%: 27% (2010 est.)

Distribution of family income - Gini index:

32.1 (2010)
country comparison to the world: 106
33.6 (1996)

Budget:

revenues: $17.19 billion
expenditures: $24.02 billion

Taxes and other revenues:

12.3% of GDP
country comparison to the world: 203

Budget surplus (+) or deficit (-):

-4.9% of GDP
country comparison to the world: 164

Public debt:

30.9% of GDP
country comparison to the world: 118
32.2% of GDP (2012 est.)

Fiscal year:

1 July - 30 June

Inflation rate (consumer prices):

7.6%
country comparison to the world: 191
6.6% (2012 est.)

Central bank discount rate:

5% (31 December 2010 est.)
country comparison to the world: 69
5% (31 December 2009 est.)

Commercial bank prime lending rate:

13% (31 December 2013 est.)
country comparison to the world: 58
13% (31 December 2012 est.)

Stock of narrow money:

$17.11 billion (31 December 2013 est.)
country comparison to the world: 67
$14.85 billion (31 December 2012 est.)

Stock of broad money:

$85.61 billion (31 December 2013 est.)
country comparison to the world: 58
$70.87 billion (31 December 2012 est.)

Stock of domestic credit:

$93.38 billion (31 December 2013 est.)
country comparison to the world: 53
$79.32 billion (31 December 2012 est.)

Market value of publicly traded shares:

$NA (February 2014 est.)
country comparison to the world: 60
$17.48 billion (31 December 2012)
$23.55 billion (31 December 2011 est.)

Current account balance:

$3.541 billion
country comparison to the world: 32
$1.754 billion (2012 est.)

Exports:

$26.91 billion
country comparison to the world: 68
$24.92 billion (2012 est.)

Exports - commodities:

garments, knitwear, agricultural products, frozen food (fish and seafood), jute and jute goods, leather

Exports - partners:

US 18.7%, Germany 15.8%, UK 10.2%, France 6.2%, Spain 4.6%, Canada 4.3%, Italy 4%

Imports:

$32.94 billion
country comparison to the world: 64
$32.29 billion (2012 est.)

Imports - commodities:

machinery and equipment, chemicals, iron and steel, textiles, foodstuffs, petroleum products, cement

Imports - partners:

China 21.7%, India 16.3%, Malaysia 5.2%, Republic of Korea 4.5%, Japan 4.1%

Reserves of foreign exchange and gold:

$15.74 billion (31 December 2013 est.)
country comparison to the world: 68
$12.75 billion (31 December 2012 est.)

Debt - external:

$30.69 billion (31 December 2013 est.)
country comparison to the world: 72
$29.53 billion (31 December 2012 est.)

Stock of direct foreign investment - at home:

$7.04 billion (31 December 2013 est.)
country comparison to the world: 88
$6.64 billion (31 December 2012 est.)

Stock of direct foreign investment - abroad:

$110.1 million (31 December 2013 est.)
country comparison to the world: 85
$108.1 million (31 December 2012 est.)

Exchange rates:

taka (BDT) per US dollar -
78.19
81.863 (2012 est.)
69.649 (2010 est.)
69.04 (2009)
68.554 (2008)

ENERGY

Electricity - production:

40.08 billion kWh
country comparison to the world: 58

Electricity - consumption:

38.89 billion kWh
country comparison to the world: 55

Electricity - exports:

0 kWh
country comparison to the world: 105

Electricity - imports:

500,000 kWh
country comparison to the world: 108

Electricity - installed generating capacity:

10.26 million kW
country comparison to the world: 55

Electricity - from fossil fuels:

97.7% of total installed capacity
country comparison to the world: 59

Electricity - from nuclear fuels:

0% of total installed capacity
country comparison to the world: 48

Electricity - from hydroelectric plants:

2.3% of total installed capacity
country comparison to the world: 135

Electricity - from other renewable sources:

0% of total installed capacity
country comparison to the world: 157

Crude oil - production:

5,452 bbl/day
country comparison to the world: 97

Crude oil - exports:

0 bbl/day
country comparison to the world: 85

Crude oil - imports:

23,620 bbl/day
country comparison to the world: 66

Crude oil - proved reserves:

28 million bbl
country comparison to the world: 82

Refined petroleum products - production:

22,710 bbl/day
country comparison to the world: 90

Refined petroleum products - consumption:

108,900 bbl/day
country comparison to the world: 74

Refined petroleum products - exports:

3,288 bbl/day
country comparison to the world: 97

Refined petroleum products - imports:

84,490 bbl/day
country comparison to the world: 54

Natural gas - production:

20.11 billion cu m

country comparison to the world: 32

Natural gas - consumption:

19.91 billion cu m
country comparison to the world: 35

Natural gas - exports:

0 cu m
country comparison to the world: 65

Natural gas - imports:

0 cu m
country comparison to the world: 160

Natural gas - proved reserves:

183.7 billion cu m
country comparison to the world: 47

Carbon dioxide emissions from consumption of energy:

58.81 million Mt

COMMUNICATIONS

Telephones - main lines in use:

962,000
country comparison to the world: 78

Telephones - mobile cellular:

97.18 million
country comparison to the world: 15

Telephone system:

general assessment: inadequate for a modern country; introducing digital systems; trunk systems include VHF and UHF microwave radio relay links, and some fiber-optic cable in cities
domestic: fixed-line teledensity remains only about 1 per 100 persons; mobile-cellular telephone subscribership has been increasing rapidly and now exceeds 50 telephones per 100 persons
international: country code - 880; landing point for the SEA-ME-WE-4 fiber-optic submarine cable system that provides links to Europe, the Middle East, and Asia; satellite earth stations - 6; international radiotelephone communications and landline service to neighboring countries

Broadcast media:

state-owned Bangladesh Television (BTV) operates 1 terrestrial TV station, 3 radio networks, and about 10 local stations; 8 private satellite TV stations and 3 private radio stations also broadcasting; foreign satellite TV stations are gaining audience share in the large cities; several international radio broadcasters are available

Internet country code:

.bd

Internet hosts:

71,164 (2012)
country comparison to the world: 87

Internet users:

617,300
country comparison to the world: 112

TRANSPORTATION

Airports:

18
country comparison to the world: 139

Airports - with paved runways:

total: 16
over 3,047 m: 2
2,438 to 3,047 m: 2
1,524 to 2,437 m: 6
914 to 1,523 m: 1
under 914 m: 5

Airports - with unpaved runways:

total: 2
1,524 to 2,437 m: 1
under 914 m:
1 (2013)

Heliports:

3

Pipelines:

gas 2,950 km

Railways:

total: 2,622 km
country comparison to the world: 65
broad gauge: 946 km 1.676-m gauge
narrow gauge: 1,676 km 1.000-m gauge

Roadways:

total: 21,269 km
country comparison to the world: 106
paved: 1,063 km
unpaved: 20,206 km

Waterways:

8,370 km (includes up to 3,060 km of main cargo routes; the network is reduced to 5,200 km in the dry season)
country comparison to the world: 17

Merchant marine:

total: 62
country comparison to the world: 64
by type: bulk carrier 25, cargo 28, chemical tanker 1, container 5, petroleum tanker 3
foreign-owned: 8 (China 1, Singapore 7)
registered in other countries: 10 (Comoros 1, Hong Kong 1, Panama 5, Saint Vincent and the Grenadines 1, Sierra Leone 1, Singapore 1)

Ports and terminals:

major seaport(s): Chittagong
river port(s): Mongla Port (Sela River)
container port(s): Chittagong (1,392,104)

Transportation - note:

the International Maritime Bureau reports the territorial waters of Bangladesh remain a risk for armed robbery against ships; attacks against vessels have decreased over the last few years in response to improved local security

MILITARY

Military branches:

Bangladesh Defense Force: Bangladesh Army (Sena Bahini), Bangladesh Navy (Noh Bahini, BN), Bangladesh Air Force (Biman Bahini, BAF)

Military service age and obligation:

16-19 years of age for voluntary military service; Bangladeshi birth and 10th grade education required; initial obligation 15 years

Manpower available for military service:

males age 16-49: 36,520,491

Manpower fit for military service:

males age 16-49: 30,486,086
females age 16-49: 35,616,093

Manpower reaching militarily significant age annually:

male: 1,606,963
female: 1,689,442

Military expenditures:

1.35% of GDP
country comparison to the world: 76
1.44% of GDP (2011)
1.35% of GDP (2010)

TRANSNATIONAL ISSUES

Disputes - international:

Bangladesh referred its maritime boundary claims with Burma and India to the International Tribunal on the Law of the Sea; Indian Prime Minister Singh's September 2011 visit to Bangladesh resulted in the signing of a Protocol to the 1974 Land Boundary Agreement between India and Bangladesh, which had called for the settlement of longstanding boundary disputes over undemarcated areas and the exchange of territorial enclaves, but which had never been implemented; Bangladesh struggles to accommodate 29,000 Rohingya, Burmese Muslim minority from Arakan State, living as refugees in Cox's Bazar; Burmese border authorities are constructing a 200 km (124 mi) wire fence designed to deter illegal cross-border transit and tensions from the military build-up along border

Refugees and internally displaced persons:

refugees (country of origin): 231,125 (Burma) (2013)
IDPs: up to 280,000 (violence, human rights violations, religious persecution, natural disasters)

Illicit drugs:

transit country for illegal drugs produced in neighboring countries

IMPORTANT INFORMATION FOR UNDERSTANDING BANGLADESH

OFFICIAL NAME: People's Republic of Bangladesh

Geography
Area: 147, 570 sq. km. (55,813 sq. mi.); about the size of Wisconsin.
Cities: *Capital*--Dhaka (pop. 10 million). *Other cities*--Chittagong (2.8 million), Khulna (1.8 million), Rajshahi (1 million).
Terrain: Mainly flat alluvial plain, with hills in the northeast and southeast.
Climate: Semitropical, monsoonal.

People
Nationality: *Noun and adjective*--Bangladeshi(s).
Population: 144 million.
Annual growth rate: 2.09%.
Ethnic groups: Bengali 98%, tribal groups, non-Bengali Muslims.
Religions: Muslim 88.3%; Hindu 10.5%; Christian 0.3%, Buddhist 0.6%, others 0.3%.
Languages: Bangla (official, also known as Bengali), English.
Education: *Attendance*--55.9%. *Literacy*--53.9% for males; 31.8% for females; a total of 43.1% literacy.
Health: *Infant mortality rate*--62.6/1,000. *Life expectancy*--62.13 years (male), 62.02 years (female).
Work force (60.3 million): *Agriculture*--60%; *manufacturing and mining*--7.8%; *others*--28.5%.

Government
Type: Parliamentary democracy.
Independence: 1971 (from Pakistan).
Constitution: 1972; amended 1974, 1979, 1986, 1988, 1991, 1996, 2004.
Branches: *Executive*--president (chief of state), prime minister (head of government), cabinet. *Legislative*--unicameral parliament (300 members). *Judicial*--civil court system based on British model.
Administrative subdivisions: Divisions, districts, subdistricts, unions, villages.
Political parties: 30-40 active political parties: largest ones include Bangladesh Nationalist Party (BNP), the Awami League (AL), the Jatiya Party, and the Jamaat-e-Islami Party.
Suffrage: Universal at age 18.

GEOGRAPHY

Bangladesh is a low-lying, riverine country located in South Asia with a largely marshy jungle coastline of 710 kilometers (440 mi.) on the northern littoral of the Bay of Bengal. Formed by a deltaic plain at the confluence of the Ganges (Padma), Brahmaputra (Jamuna), and Meghna Rivers and their tributaries, Bangladesh's alluvial soil is highly fertile but vulnerable to flood and drought. Hills rise above the plain only in the Chittagong Hill Tracts in the far southeast and the Sylhet division in the northeast. Straddling the Tropic of Cancer, Bangladesh has a subtropical monsoonal climate characterized by heavy seasonal rainfall, moderately warm temperatures, and high humidity. Natural calamities, such as floods, tropical cyclones, tornadoes, and tidal bores affect the country almost every year. Bangladesh also is affected by major cyclones--on average 16 times a decade.

Urbanization is proceeding rapidly, and it is estimated that only 30% of the population entering the labor force in the future will be absorbed into agriculture, although many will likely find other kinds of work in rural areas. The areas around Dhaka and Comilla are the most densely settled. The Sundarbans, an area of coastal tropical jungle in the southwest and last wild home of the Bengal Tiger, and the Chittagong Hill Tracts on the southeastern border with Burma and India, are the least densely populated.

PEOPLE

The area that is now Bangladesh has a rich historical and cultural past, combining Dravidian, Indo-Aryan, Mongol/Mughul, Arab, Persian, Turkic, and west European cultures. Residents of Bangladesh, about 98% of whom are ethnic Bengali and speak Bangla, are called Bangladeshis. Urdu-speaking, non-Bengali Muslims of Indian origin, and various tribal groups, mostly in the Chittagong Hill Tracts, comprise the remainder. Most Bangladeshis (about 88.3%) are Muslims, but Hindus constitute a sizable (10.5%) minority. There also are a small number of Buddhists, Christians, and animists. English is spoken in urban areas and among the educated.

Sufi religious teachers succeeded in converting many Bengalis to Islam, even before the arrival of Muslim armies from the west. About 1200 AD, Muslim invaders established political control over the Bengal region. This political control also encouraged conversion to Islam. Since then, Islam has played a crucial role in the region's history and politics, with a Muslim majority emerging, particularly in the eastern region of Bengal.

HISTORY

Bengal was absorbed into the Mughul Empire in the 16th century, and Dhaka, the seat of a nawab (the representative of the emperor), gained some importance as a provincial center. But it remained remote and thus a difficult to govern region--especially the section east of the Brahmaputra River--outside the mainstream of Mughul politics. Portuguese traders and missionaries were the first Europeans to reach Bengal in the latter part of the 15th century. They were followed by representatives of the Dutch, the French, and the British East India Companies. By the end of the 17th century, the British presence on the Indian subcontinent was centered in Calcutta. During the 18th and 19th centuries, the British gradually extended their commercial contacts and administrative control beyond Calcutta to Bengal. In 1859, the British Crown replaced the East India Company, extending British dominion from Bengal, which became a region of India, in the east to the Indus River in the west.

The rise of nationalism throughout British-controlled India in the late 19th century resulted in mounting animosity between the Hindu and Muslim communities. In 1885, the All-India National Congress was founded with Indian and British membership. Muslims seeking an organization of their own founded the All-India Muslim League in 1906. Although both the League and the Congress supported the goal of Indian self-government within the British Empire, the two parties were unable to agree on a way to ensure the protection of Muslim political, social, and economic rights. The subsequent history of the nationalist movement was characterized by periods of Hindu-Muslim cooperation, as well as by communal antagonism. The idea of a separate Muslim state gained increasing popularity among Indian Muslims after 1936, when the Muslim League suffered a decisive defeat in the first elections under India's 1935 constitution. In 1940, the Muslim League called for an independent state in regions where Muslims were in the majority. Campaigning on that platform in provincial elections in 1946, the League won the majority of the Muslim seats contested in Bengal. Widespread communal violence followed, especially in Calcutta.

When British India was partitioned and the independent dominions of India and Pakistan were created in 1947, the region of Bengal was divided along religious lines. The predominantly Muslim eastern half was designated East Pakistan--and made part of the newly independent Pakistan--while the predominantly Hindu western part became the Indian state of West Bengal. Pakistan's history from 1947 to 1971 was marked by political instability and economic difficulties. Dominion status was rejected in 1956 in favor of an "Islamic republic within the Commonwealth." Attempts at civilian political rule failed, and the government imposed martial law between 1958 and 1962, and again between 1969 and 1972.

Almost from the advent of independent Pakistan in 1947, frictions developed between East and West Pakistan, which were separated by more than 1,000 miles of Indian territory. East Pakistanis felt exploited by the West Pakistan-dominated central government. Linguistic, cultural, and ethnic differences also contributed to the estrangement of East from West Pakistan. Bengalis strongly resisted attempts to impose Urdu as the sole official language of Pakistan. Responding to these grievances, Sheikh Mujibur Rahman in 1948 formed a students' organization called the Chhatra League. In 1949, Maulana Abdul Hamid Khan Bhasani and some other Bengali leaders formed the East Pakistan Awami Muslim League (AL), a party designed mainly to promote Bengali interests. This party dropped the word Muslim from its name in 1955 and came to be known as Awami League. Mujib became president of the Awami League in 1966 and emerged as leader of the Bengali autonomy movement. In 1966, he was arrested for his political activities.

After the Awami League won almost all the East Pakistan seats of the Pakistan national assembly in 1970-71 elections, West Pakistan opened talks with the East on constitutional questions about the division of power between the central government and the provinces, as well as the formation of a national government headed by the Awami League. The talks proved unsuccessful, however, and on March 1, 1971, Pakistani President Yahya Khan indefinitely postponed the pending national assembly session, precipitating massive civil disobedience in East Pakistan. Mujib was arrested again; his party was banned, and most of his aides fled to India and organized a provisional government. On March 26, 1971, following a bloody crackdown by the Pakistan Army, Bengali nationalists declared an independent People's Republic of Bangladesh. As fighting grew between the army and the Bengali mukti bahini ("freedom fighters"), an estimated 10 million Bengalis, mainly Hindus, sought refuge in the Indian states of Assam and West Bengal.

The crisis in East Pakistan produced new strains in Pakistan's troubled relations with India. The two nations had fought a war in 1965, mainly in the west, but the refugee pressure in India in the fall of 1971 produced new tensions in the east. Indian sympathies lay with East Pakistan, and in November, India intervened on the side of the Bangladeshis. On December 16, 1971, Pakistani forces surrendered, and Bangladesh-- meaning "Bengal country"-- was born; the new country became a parliamentary democracy under a 1972 constitution.

The provisional government of the new nation of Bangladesh was formed in Dhaka with Justice Abu Sayeed Choudhury as President, and Sheikh Mujibur Rahman ("Mujib")--who was released from Pakistani prison in early 1972--as Prime Minister.

Sheikh Mujibur Rahman, 1972-75

Mujib came to office with immense personal popularity but had difficulty transforming this popular support into the political strength needed to function as head of government. The new constitution, which came into force in December 1972, created a strong executive prime minister, a largely ceremonial presidency, an independent judiciary, and a unicameral legislature on a modified Westminster model. The 1972 constitution adopted as state policy the Awami League's (AL) four basic principles of nationalism, secularism, socialism, and democracy.

The first parliamentary elections held under the 1972 constitution were in March 1973, with the Awami League winning a massive majority. No other political party in Bangladesh's early years was able to duplicate or challenge the League's broad-based appeal, membership, or organizational strength. Relying heavily on experienced civil servants and members of the Awami League, the new Bangladesh Government focused on relief, rehabilitation, and reconstruction of the economy and society. Economic conditions remained precarious, however. In December 1974, Mujib decided that continuing economic deterioration and mounting civil disorder required strong measures. After proclaiming a state of emergency, Mujib used his parliamentary majority to win a constitutional amendment limiting the powers of the legislative and judicial branches, establishing an executive presidency, and instituting a one-party system, the Bangladesh Krishak Sramik Awami League (BAKSAL), which all members of Parliament (and senior civil and military officials) were obliged to join.

Despite some improvement in the economic situation during the first half of 1975, implementation of promised political reforms was slow, and criticism of government policies became increasingly centered on Mujib. In August 1975, Mujib, and most of his family, were assassinated by mid-level army officers. His daughter, Sheikh Hasina, was out of the country. A new government, headed by former Mujib associate Khandakar Moshtaque, was formed.

Ziaur Rahman, 1975-81

Successive military coups resulted in the emergence of Army Chief of Staff Gen. Ziaur Rahman ("Zia") as strongman. He pledged the army's support to the civilian government headed by President Chief Justice Sayem. Acting at Zia's behest, Sayem dissolved Parliament, promising fresh elections in 1977, and instituted martial law.

Acting behind the scenes of the Martial Law Administration (MLA), Zia sought to invigorate government policy and administration. While continuing the ban on political parties, he sought to revitalize the demoralized bureaucracy, to begin new economic development programs, and to emphasize family planning. In November 1976, Zia became Chief Martial Law Administrator (CMLA) and assumed the presidency upon Sayem's retirement 5 months later, promising national elections in 1978.

As President, Zia announced a 19-point program of economic reform and began dismantling the MLA. Keeping his promise to hold elections, Zia won a 5-year term in June 1978 elections, with 76% of the vote. In November 1978, his government removed the remaining restrictions on political party activities in time for parliamentary elections in February 1979. These elections, which were contested by more than 30 parties, marked the culmination of Zia's transformation of Bangladesh's Government from the MLA to a democratically elected, constitutional one. The AL and the Bangladesh Nationalist Party (BNP), founded by Zia, emerged as the two major parties.

In May 1981, Zia was assassinated in Chittagong by dissident elements of the military. The attempted coup never spread beyond that city, and the major conspirators were either taken into custody or killed. In accordance with the constitution, Vice President Justice Abdus Sattar was sworn in as acting president. He declared a new national emergency and called for election of a new president within 6 months--an election Sattar won as the BNP's candidate. President Sattar sought to follow the policies of his predecessor and retained essentially the same cabinet, but the army stepped in once again.

Hussain Mohammed Ershad, 1982-90

Army Chief of Staff Lt. Gen. H.M. Ershad assumed power in a bloodless coup in March 1982. Like his predecessors, Ershad suspended the constitution and--citing pervasive corruption, ineffectual government, and economic mismanagement--declared martial law. The following year, Ershad assumed the presidency, retaining his positions as army chief and CMLA. During most of

1984, Ershad sought the opposition parties' participation in local elections under martial law. The opposition's refusal to participate, however, forced Ershad to abandon these plans. Ershad sought public support for his regime in a national referendum on his leadership in March 1985. He won overwhelmingly, although turnout was small. Two months later, Ershad held elections for local council chairmen. Pro-government candidates won a majority of the posts, setting in motion the President's ambitious decentralization program. Political life was further liberalized in early 1986, and additional political rights, including the right to hold large public rallies, were restored. At the same time, the Jatiya (National) Party, designed as Ershad's political vehicle for the transition from martial law, was established.

Despite a boycott by the BNP, led by President Zia's widow, Begum Khaleda Zia, parliamentary elections were held on schedule in May 1986. The Jatiya Party won a modest majority of the 300 elected seats in the National Assembly. The participation of the Awami League--led by the late President Mujib's daughter, Sheikh Hasina Wajed--lent the elections some credibility, despite widespread charges of voting irregularities.

Ershad resigned as Army Chief of Staff and retired from military service in preparation for the presidential elections, scheduled for October. Protesting that martial law was still in effect, both the BNP and the AL refused to put up opposing candidates. Ershad easily outdistanced the remaining candidates, taking 84% of the vote. Although Ershad's government claimed a turnout of more than 50%, opposition leaders, and much of the foreign press, estimated a far lower percentage and alleged voting irregularities.

Ershad continued his stated commitment to lift martial law. In November 1986, his government mustered the necessary two-thirds majority in the National Assembly to amend the constitution and confirm the previous actions of the martial law regime. The President then lifted martial law, and the opposition parties took their elected seats in the National Assembly.

In July 1987, however, after the government hastily pushed through a controversial legislative bill to include military representation on local administrative councils, the opposition walked out of Parliament. Passage of the bill helped spark an opposition movement that quickly gathered momentum, uniting Bangladesh's opposition parties for the first time. The government began to arrest scores of opposition activists under the country's Special Powers Act of 1974. Despite these arrests, opposition parties continued to organize protest marches and nationwide strikes. After declaring a state of emergency, Ershad dissolved Parliament and scheduled fresh elections for March 1988.

All major opposition parties refused government overtures to participate in these polls, maintaining that the government was incapable of holding free and fair elections. Despite the opposition boycott, the government proceeded. The ruling Jatiya Party won 251 of the 300 seats. The Parliament, while still regarded by the opposition as an illegitimate body, held its sessions as scheduled, and passed a large number of bills, including, in June 1988, a controversial constitutional amendment making Islam Bangladesh's state religion and provision for setting up High Court benches in major cities outside of Dhaka. While Islam remains the state religion, the provision for decentralizing the High Court division has been struck down by the Supreme Court.

By 1989, the domestic political situation in the country seemed to have quieted. The local council elections were generally considered by international observers to have been less violent and more free and fair than previous elections. However, opposition to Ershad's rule began to regain momentum, escalating by the end of 1990 in frequent general strikes, increased campus protests, public rallies, and a general disintegration of law and order.

On December 6, 1990, Ershad offered his resignation. On February 27, 1991, after 2 months of widespread civil unrest, an interim government oversaw what most observers believed to be the nation's most free and fair elections to that date.

Khaleda Zia, 1991-96

The center-right BNP won a plurality of seats and formed a government with support from the Islamic fundamentalist party Jamaat-I-Islami, with Khaleda Zia, widow of Ziaur Rahman, obtaining the post of prime minister. Only four parties had more than 10 members elected to the 1991 Parliament: The BNP, led by Prime Minister Begum Khaleda Zia; the AL, led by Sheikh Hasina; the Jamaat-I-Islami (JI), led by Golam Azam; and the Jatiya Party (JP), led by acting chairman Mizanur Rahman Choudhury while its founder, former President Ershad, served out a prison sentence on corruption charges. The electorate approved still more changes to the constitution, formally re-creating a parliamentary system and returning governing power to the office of the prime minister, as in Bangladesh's original 1972 constitution. In October 1991, members of Parliament elected a new head of state, President Abdur Rahman Biswas.

In March 1994, controversy over a parliamentary by-election, which the opposition claimed the government had rigged, led to an indefinite boycott of Parliament by the entire opposition. The opposition also began a program of repeated general strikes to press its demand that Khaleda Zia's government resign and a caretaker government supervise a general election. Efforts to mediate the dispute, under the auspices of the Commonwealth Secretariat, failed. After another attempt at a negotiated settlement failed narrowly in late December 1994, the opposition resigned en masse from Parliament. The opposition then continued a campaign of marches, demonstrations, and strikes in an effort to force the government to resign. The opposition, including the Awami League's Sheikh Hasina, pledged to boycott national elections scheduled for February 15, 1996.

In February, Khaleda Zia was re-elected by a landslide in voting boycotted and denounced as unfair by the three main opposition parties. In March 1996, following escalating political turmoil, the sitting Parliament enacted a constitutional amendment to allow a neutral caretaker government to assume power and conduct new parliamentary elections; former Chief Justice Mohammed Habibur Rahman was named Chief Adviser (a position equivalent to prime minister) in the interim government. New parliamentary elections were held in June 1996 and were won by the Awami League; party leader Sheikh Hasina became Prime Minister.

Sheikh Hasina, 1996-2001

Sheikh Hasina formed what she called a "Government of National Consensus" in June 1996, which included one minister from the Jatiya Party and another from the Jatiyo Samajtantric Dal, a very small leftist party. The Jatiya Party never entered into a formal coalition arrangement, and party president H.M. Ershad withdrew his support from the government in September 2007. Only three parties had more than 10 members elected to the 1996 Parliament: The Awami League, BNP, and Jatiya Party. Jatiya Party president, Ershad, was released from prison on bail in January 2007.

Although international and domestic election observers found the June 1996 election free and fair, the BNP protested alleged vote rigging by the Awami League. Ultimately, however, the BNP party decided to join the new Parliament. The BNP soon charged that police and Awami League activists were engaged in large-scale harassment and jailing of opposition activists. At the end of 1996, the BNP staged a parliamentary walkout over this and other grievances but returned in January 2007 under a four-point agreement with the ruling party. The BNP asserted that this agreement was never implemented and later staged another walkout in August 2007. The BNP returned to Parliament under another agreement in March 2007.

In June 1999, the BNP and other opposition parties again began to abstain from attending Parliament. Opposition parties staged an increasing number of nationwide general strikes, rising from 6 days of general strikes in 2007 to 27 days in 1999. A four-party opposition alliance formed at the beginning of 1999 announced that it would boycott parliamentary by-elections and local government elections unless the government took steps demanded by the opposition to ensure electoral fairness. The government did not take these steps, and the opposition subsequently boycotted all elections, including municipal council elections in February 1999, several parliamentary by-elections, and the Chittagong city corporation elections in January 2000.

In July 2001, the Awami League government stepped down to allow a caretaker government to preside over parliamentary elections. Political violence that had increased during the Awami League government's tenure continued to increase through the summer in the run up to the election. In August, Khaleda Zia and Sheikh Hasina agreed during a visit of former President Jimmy Carter to respect the results of the election, join Parliament win or lose, foreswear the use of hartals (violently enforced strikes) as political tools, and if successful in forming a government allow for a more meaningful role for the opposition in Parliament. The caretaker government was successful in containing the violence, which allowed a parliamentary general election to be successfully held on October 1, 2001.

Khaleda Zia, 2001-2006

The four-party alliance led by the BNP won over a two-thirds majority in Parliament. Begum Khaleda Zia was sworn in on October 10, 2001, as Prime Minister for the third time (first in 1991, second after the February 15, 1996 elections).

Despite her August 2001 pledge and all election monitoring groups declaring the election free and fair, Sheikh Hasina condemned the election, rejected the results, and boycotted Parliament. In 2002, however, she led her party legislators back to Parliament, but the Awami League again walked out in June 2003 to protest derogatory remarks about Hasina by a State Minister and the allegedly partisan role of the Parliamentary Speaker. In June 2004, the AL returned to Parliament without having any of their demands met. They then attended Parliament irregularly before announcing a boycott of the entire June 2005 budget session.

On August 17, 2005, near-synchronized blasts of improvised explosive devices in 63 out of 64 administrative districts targeted mainly government buildings and killed two persons. An extremist Islamist group named Jama'atul Mujahideen, Bangladesh (JMB) claimed responsibility for the blasts, which aimed to press home JMB's demand for a replacement of the secular legal system with Islamic sharia courts. Subsequent attacks on the courts in several districts killed 28 people, including judges, lawyers, and police personnel guarding the courts. A government campaign against the Islamic extremists led to the arrest of hundreds of senior and mid-level JMB leaders. Six top JMB leaders were tried and sentenced to death for their role in the murder of two judges; another leader was tried and sentenced to death in absentia in the same case.

In February 2006, the AL returned to Parliament, demanded early elections, and requested significant changes in the electoral and caretaker government systems to stop alleged moves by the ruling coalition to rig the next election. The AL blamed the BNP for several high-profile attacks on opposition leaders and asserted the BNP was bent on eliminating Sheikh Hasina and the Awami League as a viable force. The BNP and its allies accused the AL of maligning Bangladesh at home and abroad out of jealousy over the government's performance on development and economic issues. Dialogue between the Secretaries General of the main ruling and opposition parties failed to sort out the electoral reform issues

CARETAKER GOVERNMENT, OCTOBER 2006-JANUARY 2009

The 13th Amendment to the constitution required the president to offer the position of the Chief Adviser to the immediate past Chief Justice of the Supreme Court, Justice K.M. Hasan, once the previous parliamentary session expired on October 28, 2006. The AL opposed Justice Hasan, alleging that he belonged to the ruling BNP in the past and that the BNP government in 2004 amended the constitution to extend the retirement age for the Supreme Court judges to ensure Justice Hasan became the Chief Adviser to help BNP win the elections. Justice Hasan declined the position, and after two days of violent protests, President Iajuddin Ahmed also assumed the role of Chief Adviser to the caretaker government.

On January 3, 2007, the Awami League announced it would boycott the January 22 parliamentary elections. The Awami League planned a series of country-wide general strikes and transportation blockades.

On January 11, 2007, President Iajuddin Ahmed declared a state of emergency, resigned as Chief Adviser, and indefinitely postponed parliamentary elections. On January 12, 2007, former Bangladesh Bank governor Fakhruddin Ahmed was sworn in as the new Chief Adviser, and ten new advisers (ministers) were appointed. Under emergency provisions, the government suspended certain fundamental rights guaranteed by the constitution and detained a large number of politicians and others on suspicion of involvement in corruption and other crimes. In January 2008, a reshuffle of the caretaker government took place, which included the appointment of special assistants to help oversee the functioning of the administration.

On July 16, 2007 the government arrested Awami League president and former Prime Minister Sheikh Hasina on charges of extortion during her tenure as Prime Minister. Hasina was released on parole in June 2008 and allowed to travel to the United States for medical treatment. The cases against her continue. On September 3, 2007, the government arrested BNP chairperson and former Prime Minister Khaleda Zia on charges of corruption. Sheikh Hasina returned from abroad and Khaleda Zia was released from prison to lead their respective parties in the parliamentary election campaign in the fall of 2008.

Municipal elections were held in thirteen city corporations and municipalities on August 4, 2008. These elections were judged free and fair by international and domestic observers. The Election Commission registered over 80 million voters in preparation for parliamentary elections, which were held December 29, 2008. The Awami League swept to a landslide victory in what domestic and international observers declared a free, fair and credible election. The caretaker government ended on January 6, 2009 when Awami League President Sheikh Hasina became Prime Minister.

Sheikh Hasina, 2009-Present

Despite hopes that the new government would reject the highly partisan politics of the past, it soon became clear little had changed. Prime Minister Sheikh Hasina and opposition leader Khaleda Zia attacked one another over matters substantive and petty. The opposition Bangladesh Nationalist Party boycotted Parliament over the chamber's seating chart and launched demonstrations over Awami League efforts to force Khaleda Zia out of her Dhaka cantonment home.

The Awami League also failed to make good on promises to enact into legislation democratic-reform ordinances approved by the caretaker government. The ruling party rejected caretaker government measures to decentralize government and to clearly separate judicial functions from the executive branch. Parliament did enact, however, caretaker government measures to fight terrorism and money-laundering that received strong support from the U.S. Government and other countries that provide Bangladesh counterterrorism assistance.

The government was rocked by a mutiny by border guards on February 25-26, 2009 in which more than 50 army officers were murdered. Sheikh Hasina faced strong opposition within the military for not ordering an immediate attack on the mutinous guards. The political situation appeared to have stabilized several weeks after the mutiny, and the U.S. Federal Bureau of Investigation sent teams to Dhaka to provide technical assistance to Bangladesh authorities responsible for the probe into the incident.

GOVERNMENT

The president, while chief of state, holds a largely ceremonial post; the real power is held by the prime minister, who is head of government. The president is elected by the legislature (Parliament) every 5 years. The president's circumscribed powers are substantially expanded during the tenure of a caretaker government. Under the 13th Amendment, which Parliament passed in March 1996, a caretaker government assumes power temporarily to oversee general elections after dissolution of the Parliament. In the caretaker government, the president has control over the Ministry of Defense, the authority to declare a state of emergency, and the power to dismiss the Chief Adviser and other members of the caretaker government. Once elections have been held and a new government and Parliament are in place, the president's powers and position revert to their largely ceremonial role. The Chief Adviser and other advisers to the caretaker government must be appointed within 15 days after the current Parliament expires.

The prime minister is appointed by the president. The prime minister must be a Member of Parliament (MP) who the president feels commands the confidence of the majority of other MPs. The cabinet is composed of ministers selected by the prime minister and appointed by the president. At least 90% of the ministers must be MPs. The other 10% may be non-MP experts or "technocrats" who are not otherwise disqualified from being elected MPs. According to the constitution, the president can dissolve Parliament upon the written request of the prime minister.

The legislature is a unicameral, 300-seat body. All of its members are elected by universal suffrage at least every five years. Parliament amended the constitution in May 2004, making a provision for 45 seats reserved for women to be distributed among political parties in proportion to their numerical strength in Parliament. The AL did not take its share of the reserved seats, arguing that it did not support the indirect election or nomination of women to fill these seats. Several women's groups also demanded direct election to fill the reserved seats for women.

Bangladesh's judiciary is a civil court system based on the British model; the highest court of appeal is the appellate court of the Supreme Court. At the local government level, the country is divided into divisions, districts, sub districts, unions, and villages. Local officials are elected at the union level and selected at the village level. All larger administrative units are run by members of the civil service.

Principal Government Officials

Minister	Secretariat and Executive offices	State Minister and Deputy Minister
Abul Hasan Mahmood Ali	Ministry of Foreign Affairs	Shahriar Alam
Abul Maal Abdul Muhith	Ministry of Finance	MA Mannan
Akm Mojammel Haque	Ministry of Liberation War	
Amir Hossain Amu	Ministry of Industries	
Anisul Islam Mahmud	Ministry of Water Resources	Muhammad Nazrul Islam

Minister	Secretariat and Executive offices	State Minister and Deputy Minister
		Abdullah Al Islam Jacob (Deputy Minister)
Anwar Hossain Manju	Ministry of Environment and Forest	
Asaduzzaman Noor	Ministry of Cultural Affairs	
Barrister Anisul Haque	Ministry of Law, Justice and Parliamentary Affairs	
Begum Matia Chowdhury	Ministry of Agriculture	
Emaz Uddin Pramanik	Ministry of Textiles and Jute	Mirza Azam
Hasanul Haq Inu	Ministry of Information	
Khandaker Mosharraf Hossain	Ministry of Expatriates' Welfare and Overseas Employment	
Md Qamrul Islam	Ministry of Food	Jahangir Kabir Nanak
Mofazzal Hossain Chowdhury Maya	Ministry of Disaster Management and Relief	
Mohammed Nasim	Ministry of Health and Family Welfare	Jahid Malek Swapan
Mohammed Sayedul Haque	Ministry of Fisheries and Livestock	Narayan Chandra Chan
Mosharraf Hossain	Ministry of Housing and Public Works	
Motiur Rahman	Ministry of Religious Affairs	
Mujibul Haq Mujib	Ministry of Railways	
Mujibul Haque Chunnu	Ministry of Labour and Employment	Md. Mojibul Haque Chunnu
Mustafa Kamal	Ministry of Planning	
Mustafizur Rahman	Ministry of Primary and Mass Education	
Nurul Islam Nahid	Ministry of Education	
Obaidul Quader	Ministry of Road Transport and Bridge	
Rashed Khan Menon	Ministry of Civil Aviation and Tourism	
Shahjahan Khan	Ministry of Shipping	
Shamshur Rahaman Sherif	Ministry of Land	Saifuzzaman Chowdhury
Sheikh Hasina	Prime Minister Ministry of Public Administration Cabinet Division Ministry of Defence Ministry of Power, Energy & Mineral Resources Armed Forces Division	Ismat Ara Sadeq (Public Administration) Nasrul Hamid (Power, Energy & Mineral Resources)
Syed Ashraful Islam	Ministry of Local Government and Rural Development & Co-operatives	

Minister	Secretariat and Executive offices	State Minister and Deputy Minister
Syed Mohsin Ali	Ministry of Social Welfare	Promod Mankin
Tofael Ahmed	Ministry of Commerce	
Vacant	Ministry of Home Affairs	Asaduzzaman Khan
vacant	Ministry of Posts, Telecommunications & Information Technology	Junaid Ahmed Polok

Bangladesh maintains an Embassy in the United States at 3510 International Drive NW, Washington, DC 20008 (tel: 202-244-0183; fax: 202-244-5366). Bangladesh has Consulates General in New York and Los Angeles.

POLITICAL CONDITIONS

Despite serious problems related to a dysfunctional political system, weak governance, and pervasive corruption, Bangladesh remains one of the few democracies in the Muslim world. Bangladeshis regard democracy as an important legacy of their bloody war for independence, and they vote in large numbers. However, democratic institutions and practices remain weak. Under the state of emergency, political activities were restricted. Bangladesh is generally a force for moderation in international forums, and it is also a long-time leader in international peacekeeping operations. Its activities in international organizations, with other governments, and its regional partners to promote human rights, democracy, and free markets are coordinated and high profile. In May 2005, Bangladesh became a member of the United Nations Human Rights Council.

Bangladesh lies at the strategic crossroads of South and Southeast Asia. Potential terrorist movements and activities in or through Bangladesh pose a potentially serious threat to India, Nepal, Bhutan, and Burma, as well as Bangladesh itself. The Bangladesh Government routinely denies Indian allegations that Indian insurgents in northeast India operate out of Bangladesh and that extremist Islamist forces are overwhelming Bangladesh's traditionally moderate character. It also denies there is any international terrorist presence in Bangladesh. The Bangladesh Government, however, banned a number of Islamic extremist groups in recent years. In February 2002, the government banned Shahdat al Hiqma, in February 2005 it banned Jagrata Muslim Janata, Bangladesh (JMJB) and Jama'atul Mujahideen Bangladesh (JMB), and in October 2005 it banned Harkatul Jehad Al Islami (HUJI). Following the August 17, 2005 serial bombings in the country, the government launched a crackdown on extremists. In 2006, seven senior JMB leaders were sentenced to death for their role in the 2005 murder of two judges. Six of the seven were executed in March 2007; another leader was tried and sentenced to death in absentia in the same case. In March 2008, the U.S. Government listed Harkatul Jihadi Islami (HUJI)-Bangladesh a foreign terrorist organization. Given its size and location, a major crisis in Bangladesh could have important consequences for regional stability, particularly if significant refugee movements ensue.

ECONOMY

Currency	৳ Bangladesh Taka (BDT)
Fiscal year	1 July - 30 June
Trade organizations	WTO, SAFTA, BIMSTEC, Developing 8 Countries, BCIM, IOR-ARC
	Statistics
GDP	$655 billion (PPP) 35th;

	$175.52 billion (nominal) 35th;
GDP rank	35th (PPP) / 56th (nominal)
GDP growth	6.2%
GDP per capita	$3,385 (PPP) $1,190 (nominal; 2014)
GDP by sector	Agriculture: 19%; industry: 30%; services: 51% (2013 est.)
Inflation (CPI)	6.2%
Population below poverty line	26.0%
Gini coefficient	32.1
Labour force	87.9 million
Labour force by occupation	agriculture: 40%, industry: 30%, services: 30% (2013)
Unemployment	4.5%
Main industries	textiles, food processing, steel, pulp and paper, jute, shipbuilding, pharmaceuticals, electronics, automotive parts, ceramics, fertilizer, construction materials, leather, natural gas, renewable energy
Ease-of-doing-business rank	117th
	External
Exports	$30.1 billion
Export goods	textiles, leather goods, processed and frozen food, porcelain, bone china, ocean-going ships, medicine, software, consumer appliances, jute, jute products, tea
Main export partners	European Union 53.3% United States 21% Canada 4.2% Turkey 2.7% Japan 2.2%
Imports	$29.37 billion
Import goods	petroleum, machinery and equipment, foodstuffs, iron and steel, automobiles, cotton, palm oil
Main import partners	Thailand 22.8% India 11.2% China 8.8% European Union 6.6% Indonesia 6%
Gross external debt	$36.21 billion
	Public finances
Public debt	22.8% of GDP
Revenues	$14.67 billion
Expenses	$22.15 billion
Credit rating	BB - (domestic) BB - (foreign) BB -(T&C assessment) Outlook: Stable (Standard & Poor's)
Foreign reserves	$22.327 billion

The **Economy of Bangladesh** is a market-based economy. The country is classified as a Next Eleven emerging market and one of the Frontier Five. According to a recent opinion poll, Bangladesh has the second most pro-capitalist population in the developing world.

Between 2004 and 2014, Bangladesh averaged a GDP growth rate of 6%. The economy is increasingly led by export-oriented industrialization. The Bangladesh textile industry is the second-largest in the world. Other key sectors include pharmaceuticals, shipbuilding, ceramics, leather goods and electronics. Being situated in one of the most fertile regions on Earth, agriculture plays a crucial role, with the principal cash crops including rice, jute, tea, wheat, cotton and sugarcane. Bangladesh ranks fifth in the global production of fish and seafood. Remittances from the Bangladeshi diaspora provide vital foreign exchange.

The Bangladesh telecoms industry has witnessed rapid growth over the years and is dominated by foreign investors. The government has emphasized the development of software services and hi-tech industries under the *Digital Bangladesh* scheme. Bangladesh has substantial reserves of natural gas and coal; and many international energy companies are involved in production and exploration activities, including in the Bay of Bengal. Regional neighbours are keen to use Bangladeshi ports and railways for transhipment. Located at the crossroads of SAARC, BIMSTEC, the ASEAN+3 and the Indian Ocean, Bangladesh has the potential to emerge as a regional logistics hub.

In 2014, per-capita income stood at USD 1,190. While achieving significant macroeconomic stability, Bangladesh continues to face challenges such as infrastructure deficits and energy shortages.

Although one of the world's poorest and most densely populated countries, Bangladesh has made major strides to meet the food needs of its increasing population, through increased domestic production augmented by imports. The land is devoted mainly to rice and jute cultivation, although wheat production has increased in recent years; the country is largely self-sufficient in rice production. Nonetheless, an estimated 10% to 15% of the population faces serious nutritional risk. Bangladesh's predominantly agricultural economy depends heavily on an erratic monsoonal cycle, with periodic flooding and drought. Although improving, infrastructure to support transportation, communications, and power supply is poorly developed. Bangladesh is limited in its reserves of coal and oil, and its industrial base is weak. The country's main endowments include its vast human resource base, rich agricultural land, relatively abundant water, and substantial reserves of natural gas.

Since independence in 1971, Bangladesh has received more than $30 billion in grant aid and loan commitments from foreign donors, about $15 billion of which has been disbursed. Major donors include the World Bank, the Asian Development Bank, the UN Development Program, the United States, Japan, Saudi Arabia, and west European countries. Bangladesh historically has run a large trade deficit, financed largely through aid receipts and remittances from workers overseas. Foreign reserves dropped markedly in 2001 but stabilized in the $3 to $4 billion range (or about 3 months' import cover). In January 2007, reserves stood at $3.74 billion, and they increased to $5.39 billion by January 2008, according to the Bank of Bangladesh, the central bank.

MOVES TOWARD A MARKET ECONOMY

Following the violent events of 1971 during the fight for independence, Bangladesh--with the help of large infusions of donor relief and development aid--slowly began to turn its attention to developing new industrial capacity and rehabilitating its economy. The static economic model adopted by its early leadership, however--including the nationalization of much of the industrial sector--resulted in inefficiency and economic stagnation. Beginning in late 1975, the government gradually gave greater scope to private sector participation in the economy, a pattern that has continued. A few state-owned enterprises have been privatized, but many, including major portions of the banking and jute sectors, remain under government control. Population growth, inefficiency in the public sector, resistance to developing the country's richest natural resources, and limited capital have all continued to restrict economic growth.

In the mid-1980s, there were encouraging, if halting, signs of progress. Economic policies aimed at encouraging private enterprise and investment, denationalizing public industries, reinstating budgetary discipline, and liberalizing the import regime were accelerated. From 1991 to 1993, the government successfully followed an enhanced structural adjustment facility (ESAF) with the International Monetary Fund (IMF) but failed to follow through on reforms in large part because of preoccupation with the government's domestic political troubles. In the late 1990s the government's economic policies became more entrenched, and some of the early gains were lost, which was highlighted by a precipitous drop in foreign direct investment in 2000 and 2001. In June 2003 the IMF approved 3-year, $490-million plan as part of the Poverty Reduction and Growth Facility (PRGF) for Bangladesh that aimed to support the government's economic reform program up to 2006. Seventy million dollars was made available immediately. In the same vein the World Bank approved $536 million in interest-free loans.

Efforts to achieve Bangladesh's macroeconomic goals have been problematic. The privatization of public sector industries has proceeded at a slow pace--due in part to worker unrest in affected industries--although on June 30, 2002, the government took a bold step as it closed down the Adamjee Jute Mill, the country's largest and most costly state-owned enterprise. The government also has proven unable to resist demands for wage hikes in government-owned industries. Access to capital is impeded. State-owned banks, which control about three-fourths of deposits and loans, carry classified loan burdens of about 50%.

The IMF and World Bank predict GDP growth over the next 5 years will be about 6.0%, well short of the 8%-9% needed to lift Bangladesh out of its severe poverty. The initial impact of the end of quotas under the Multi-Fiber Arrangement has been positive for Bangladesh, with continuing investment in the ready-made garment sector, which has experienced annual export growth of around 20%. Downward price pressure means Bangladesh must continue to cut final delivered costs if it is to remain competitive in the world market. Foreign investors in a broad range of sectors have been increasingly frustrated with the politics of confrontation, the level of corruption, and the slow pace of reform. While investors viewed favorably steps by the interim government to address corruption, governance, and infrastructure issues, most believed it was too early to assess the long-term impact of those developments.

AGRICULTURE

Most Bangladeshis earn their living from agriculture. Although rice and jute are the primary crops, maize and vegetables are assuming greater importance. Due to the expansion of irrigation networks, some wheat producers have switched to cultivation of maize which is used mostly as poultry feed. Tea is grown in the northeast. Because of Bangladesh's fertile soil and normally ample water supply, rice can be grown and harvested three times a year in many areas. Due to a number of factors, Bangladesh's labor-intensive agriculture has achieved steady increases in food grain production despite the often unfavorable weather conditions. These include better flood control and irrigation, a generally more efficient use of fertilizers, and the establishment of better distribution and rural credit networks. With 28.8 million metric tons produced in 2005-2006 (July-June), rice is Bangladesh's principal crop. By comparison, wheat output in 2005-2006 was 9 million metric tons. Population pressure continues to place a severe burden on productive capacity, creating a food deficit, especially of wheat. Foreign assistance and commercial imports fill the gap. Underemployment remains a serious problem, and a growing concern for Bangladesh's agricultural sector will be its ability to absorb additional manpower. Finding alternative sources of employment will continue to be a daunting problem for future governments, particularly with the increasing numbers of landless peasants who already account for about half the rural labor force.

INDUSTRY AND INVESTMENT

Fortunately for Bangladesh, many new jobs--1.8 million, mostly for women--have been created by the country's dynamic private ready-made garment industry, which grew at double-digit rates through most of the 1990s. The labor-intensive process of ship-breaking for scrap has developed to the point where it now meets most of Bangladesh's domestic steel needs. Other industries include sugar, tea, leather goods, newsprint, pharmaceutical, and fertilizer production. The country has done less well, however, in expanding its export base--garments account for more than three-fourths of all exports, dwarfing the country's historic cash crop, jute, along with leather, shrimp, pharmaceuticals, and ceramics.

Despite the country's politically motivated general strikes, poor infrastructure, and weak financial system, Bangladeshi entrepreneurs have shown themselves adept at competing in the global garments marketplace. Bangladesh exports significant amounts of garments and knitwear to the U.S. and the European Union (EU) market. As noted, the initial impact of the end of quotas on Bangladesh's ready-made garment industry has been positive. Downward price pressures, however, mean Bangladesh must continue to cut final delivered costs if it is to remain competitive in the world market.

The Bangladesh Government continues to court foreign investment, something it did fairly well in the 1990s in private power generation and gas exploration and production, as well as in other sectors such as cellular telephony, textiles, and pharmaceuticals. In 1989, the same year it signed a bilateral investment treaty with the United States, it established a board of investment to simplify approval and start-up procedures for foreign investors, although in practice the board has done little to increase investment. Bangladesh also has established export processing zones in Chittagong (1983), Dhaka (1994), Comilla (2000), Mongla (2001), Iswardi (2005), Uttara (2006), and Karnafully (2007).

The most important reforms Bangladesh should make to be able to compete in a global economy are to privatize state-owned enterprises (SOEs), deregulate and promote foreign investment in high-potential industries like energy and telecommunications, and take decisive steps toward combating corruption and strengthening rule of law.

DEFENSE

The Bangladesh Army, Navy, and Air Force are composed of volunteer military members. In addition to traditional defense roles, the military is frequently called on to provide support to civil authorities for disaster relief and internal security. During the period of emergency rule from January 2007 to December 2008, the military played a central role in the formulation and execution of key government strategies, including the anti-corruption campaign and voter registration. The army is modeled and organized along British lines, similar to other armies on the Indian subcontinent. However, the army is attempting to adopt U.S. Army tactical planning procedures, training management techniques, and noncommissioned officer educational systems. The Bangladesh military continues to improve its peacekeeping operations capabilities and receives such training from the U.S. military, UN, and other nations. The United States provided the Bangladesh Air Force four U.S. C-130 B transport aircraft in 2001 under the Excess Defense Article (EDA) program. These aircraft have improved the military's disaster response and peacekeeping capabilities. The Bangladesh Navy is mostly limited to coastal patrolling within the Bay of Bengal and participates in international exercises. A Coast Guard exists under the Ministry of Home Affairs (MOHA) to address anti-smuggling, anti-piracy, and protection of offshore resources. The Bangladesh Rifles (BDR), also under the MOHA, addresses anti-smuggling and other missions along the land border. With 9,234 peacekeepers deployed around the world as of March 2009, Bangladesh is the second-largest troop contributor to international peacekeeping operations.

FOREIGN RELATIONS

Bangladesh pursues a moderate foreign policy that places heavy reliance on multinational diplomacy, especially at the United Nations.

Participation in Multilateral Organizations
Bangladesh was admitted to the United Nations in 1974 and was elected to a Security Council term in 1978 and again for a 2000-2001 term. Then Foreign Minister Choudhury served as president of the 41st UN General Assembly in 1986. The government has participated in numerous international conferences, especially those dealing with population, food, development, and women's issues. In 1982-83, Bangladesh played a constructive role as chair of the "Group of 77," an informal association encompassing most of the world's developing nations. It has taken a leading role in the "Group of 48" developing countries and the "Developing-8" group of countries. It is also a participant in the activities of the Non-Aligned Movement.

Since 1975, Bangladesh has sought close relations with other Islamic states and a role among moderate members of the Organization of the Islamic Conference (OIC). In 1983, Bangladesh hosted the foreign ministers meeting of the OIC. The government also has pursued the expansion of cooperation among the nations of South Asia, bringing the process--an initiative of former President Ziaur Rahman--through its earliest, most tentative stages to the formal inauguration of the South Asian Association for Regional Cooperation (SAARC) at a summit gathering of South Asian leaders in Dhaka in December 1985. Bangladesh hosted the SAARC summit in November 2005, and Prime Minister Khaleda Zia reassumed its chairmanship. Bangladesh has participated in a wide range of ongoing SAARC regional activities. The head of the then-caretaker government participated in the April 2007 SAARC summit in India.

In recent years, Bangladesh has played a significant role in international peacekeeping activities. Several thousand Bangladeshi military personnel are deployed overseas on peacekeeping operations. Under UN auspices, Bangladeshi troops have served or are serving in Sierra Leone, Somalia, Rwanda, Mozambique, Kuwait, Ethiopia-Eritrea, Kosovo, Timor Leste, Georgia, Congo, Cote d'Ivoire and Western Sahara, Bosnia, and Haiti. Bangladesh responded quickly to President Clinton's 1994 request for troops and police for the multinational force for Haiti and provided the largest non-U.S. contingent.

Bilateral Relations With Other Nations
Bangladesh is bordered on the west, north, and east by a 2,400-kilometer land frontier with India, and on the southeast by a land and water frontier (193 kilometers) with Burma.

India. India is Bangladesh's most important neighbor. Geographic, cultural, historic, and commercial ties are strong, and both countries recognize the importance of good relations. During and immediately after Bangladesh's struggle for independence from Pakistan in 1971, India assisted refugees from East Pakistan, intervened militarily to help bring about the independence of Bangladesh, and furnished relief and reconstruction aid.

Indo-Bangladesh relations are often strained, and many Bangladeshis feel India likes to play "big brother" to smaller neighbors, including Bangladesh. Bilateral relations warmed in 1996, due to a softer Indian foreign policy and the new Awami League government. A 30-year water-sharing agreement for the Ganges River was signed in December 1996, after an earlier bilateral water-sharing agreement for the Ganges River lapsed in 1988. Bangladesh remains extremely concerned about a proposed Indian river linking project, which the government says could turn large parts of Bangladesh into a desert The Bangladesh Government and tribal insurgents signed a peace accord in December 2007, which allowed for the return of tribal refugees who had fled into India, beginning in 1986, to escape violence caused by an insurgency in their homeland in the Chittagong Hill Tracts. The implementation of most parts of this agreement has stalled, and the army maintains a strong presence in the Hill Tracts. Arms smuggling and reported opium poppy cultivation are concerns in this area. Occasional skirmishes between Bangladeshi and Indian border forces sometimes escalate and seriously disrupt bilateral relations. Much to Bangladesh's displeasure, India has erected a barbed-wire fence on part of its border with

Bangladesh to prevent alleged illegal migration of Bangladeshis into India.

The BNP and other political parties view the Indian Government as a major benefactor of the Awami League and blame negative international media coverage of Bangladesh on alleged Indian manipulation. Former Prime Minister Khaleda Zia, however, visited the Indian capital in March 2006 and reviewed bilateral relations with her Indian counterpart. Two agreements--the Revised Trade Agreement and the Agreement on Mutual Cooperation for Preventing Illicit Drug Trafficking in Narcotic Drugs and Psychotropic Substances and Related Matters--were signed between the two countries during this visit. Indian Foreign Minister Pranab Mukherjee met with the Chief Adviser in Dhaka on February 26, 2007. Mukherjee invited Ahmed to the April 3-4, 2007, SAARC summit in Delhi, and both sides pledged to put Bangladesh-India relations on "an irreversible higher trajectory." Mukherjee again visited Bangladesh after Cyclone Sidr hit the southwestern coastal districts on November 15, 2007 and offered help to rebuild 10 of the devastated villages. Bangladesh Army Chief General Moeen U. Ahmed paid a six-day visit to India beginning late February 2008 at the invitation of his Indian counterpart. He met with Mukherjee and the Chief Minister of West Bengal province, besides meeting military officials. During this visit, Ahmed announced that passenger trains could start running between Dhaka and Kolkata by April 14.

Pakistan. Bangladesh enjoys warm relations with Pakistan, despite the strained early days of their relationship. Landmarks in their reconciliation are:

- An August 1973 agreement between Bangladesh and Pakistan on the repatriation of numerous individuals, including 90,000 Pakistani prisoners of war stranded in Bangladesh as a result of the 1971 conflict;
- A February 1974 accord by Bangladesh and Pakistan on mutual recognition followed more than two years later by establishment of formal diplomatic relations;
- The organization by the UN High Commissioner for Refugees (UNHCR) of an airlift that moved almost 250,000 Bengalis from Pakistan to Bangladesh, and non-Bengalis from Bangladesh to Pakistan; and
- Exchanges of high-level visits, including a visit by Prime Minister Benazir Bhutto to Bangladesh in 1989 and visits by Prime Minister Zia to Pakistan in 1992 and in 1995.
- President Pervez Musharraf visited Bangladesh in 2002.
- Prime Minister Shaukat Aziz visited Bangladesh in 2004.
- Prime Minister Khaleda Zia visited Pakistan in 2006.

Still to be resolved are the division of assets from the pre-1971 period and the status of more than 250,000 non-Bengali Muslims (known as "Biharis") remaining in Bangladesh but seeking resettlement in Pakistan.

Burma. Bilateral ties with Burma are good, despite occasional border strains and an influx of more than 270,000 Muslim refugees (known as "Rohingya") from predominantly Buddhist Burma. As a result of bilateral discussions, and with the cooperation and assistance of the UNHCR, most of the Rohingya refugees have now returned to Burma. As of 2007, about 20,000 refugees remained in camps in southern Bangladesh. Thousands of other Burmese, not officially registered as refugees, are squatting on the bank of the river Naaf or living in Bangladeshi villages in the southeastern tip of the country. Bangladesh and Burmese officials are negotiating a deal to establish a road link between the capitals of the two countries.

Russia. The former Soviet Union supported India's actions during the 1971 Indo-Pakistan war and was among the first to recognize Bangladesh. The U.S.S.R. initially contributed considerable relief and rehabilitation aid to the new nation. After Sheikh Mujib was assassinated in 1975 and replaced by military regimes, however, Soviet-Bangladesh relations cooled.

In 1989, the U.S.S.R. ranked 14th among aid donors to Bangladesh. The Soviets focused on the development of electrical power, natural gas and oil, and maintained active cultural relations with Bangladesh. They financed the Ghorasal thermal power station--the largest in Bangladesh. Russia conducted an aggressive military sales effort in Dhaka and won a $124-million deal for eight MIG-29 fighters. Bangladesh began to open diplomatic relations with the newly independent Central Asian states in 1992.

China. China traditionally has been more important to Bangladesh than the former U.S.S.R., even though China supported Pakistan in 1971. As Bangladesh's relations with the Soviet Union and India cooled in the mid-1970s, and as Bangladesh and Pakistan became reconciled, China's relations with Bangladesh grew warmer. An exchange of diplomatic missions in February 1976 followed an accord on recognition in late 1975.

Since that time, relations have grown stronger, centering on trade, cultural activities, military and civilian aid, and exchanges of high-level visits, beginning in January 1977 with President Zia's trip to Beijing. The largest and most visible symbol of bilateral amity is the Bangladesh-China "Friendship Bridge," completed in 1989 near Dhaka, as well as extensive military hardware in the Bangladesh inventory and warm military relations between the two countries. In the 1990s, the Chinese also built two 210-megawatt power plants outside of Chittagong; mechanical faults in the plants cause them to shut down frequently for days at a time, heightening the country's power shortage. In April 2005, Bangladesh and China signed nine memoranda of understanding on trade and other issues during the visit to Dhaka of Prime Minister Wen. The opening of a Taiwanese trade center in Dhaka in 2004 displeased China, but the Bangladesh government moved quickly to repair the crack and closed the trade center. In August 2005 former Prime Minister Khaleda Zia visited China.

Other countries in South Asia. Bangladesh maintains friendly relations with Bhutan, Maldives, Nepal, and Sri Lanka and strongly opposed the Soviet invasion of Afghanistan. Bangladesh has cordial relations with the government of Afghan President Hamid Karzai, and Bangladeshi non-governmental organizations (NGOs) are active in Afghan reconstruction efforts. Bangladesh and Nepal recently agreed to facilitate land transit between the two countries. Bangladesh is considering importing electricity from Bhutan through India to meet its energy shortfall.

U.S.-BANGLADESH RELATIONS

Although the U.S. relationship with Bangladesh was initially troubled because of strong U.S. ties with Pakistan, U.S.-Bangladesh friendship and support developed quickly following Bangladesh's independence from Pakistan in 1971.

U.S.-Bangladesh relations are excellent. These relations were boosted in March 2000 when President Clinton visited Bangladesh, the first-ever visit by a sitting U.S. President, when Secretary of State Colin Powell visited in June 2003, as well as when Secretary of Defense Donald Rumsfeld visited in June 2004. A centerpiece of the bilateral relationship is a large U.S. aid program, totaling about $110 million for fiscal year 2008. U.S. economic and food aid programs, which began as emergency relief following the 1971 war for independence, now concentrate on long-term development. U.S. assistance objectives include stabilizing population growth, protecting human health, encouraging broad-based economic growth, and building democracy. In total, the United States has provided more than $4.3 billion in food and development assistance to Bangladesh. Food aid under Titles I, II, and III of PL-480 (congressional "food-for-peace" legislation) has been designed to help Bangladesh meet minimum food requirements, promote food production, and moderate fluctuation in consumer prices. Other U.S. development assistance emphasizes family planning and health, agricultural development, and rural employment. The United States works with other donors and the

Bangladesh Government to avoid duplication and ensure that resources are used to maximum benefit.

Since 1986, with the exception of 1988-89, when an aircraft purchase made the trade balance even, the U.S. trade balance with Bangladesh has been negative, due largely to growing imports of readymade garments. Jute carpet backing is the other major U.S. import from Bangladesh. Total imports from Bangladesh were about $2.6 billion (excluding services) in FY 2005, up from $2.1 billion in 2002. In 2007 total imports reached $3.4 billion. U.S. exports to Bangladesh (some $333 million--excluding services--in 2005, and $456 million in 2007) include wheat, fertilizer, cotton, communications equipment, aircraft, and medical supplies, a portion of which is financed by the U.S. Agency for International Development (USAID). A bilateral investment treaty was signed in 1989.

Another trade related issue between the two countries involves the export processing zones (EPZs). The government provides several tax, foreign exchange, customs and labor incentives to investors in the EPZs. One such incentive provided in recent years was an exemption from certain labor laws, which had the practical effect of prohibiting trade unions from the zones. The U.S. Generalized System of Preferences (GSP) law requires the beneficiary country to satisfy certain conditions relating to labor rights. On July 13, 2004, the government passed a bill allowing limited trade unionism in the EPZs effective November 1, 2006. Implementation of the law has been slow, however, and a U.S. labor organization has filed a petition with the U.S. Government to suspend Bangladesh's GSP privileges in the absence of progress on labor rights issues.

Relations between Bangladesh and the United States were further strengthened by the participation of Bangladesh troops in the 1991 Gulf war coalition, and alongside U.S. forces in numerous UN peacekeeping operations, including Haiti in 1994, as well as by the assistance of a U.S. naval task force after a disastrous March 1991 cyclone in Bangladesh. The relief efforts of U.S. troops are credited with having saved as many as 200,000 lives. In response to Bangladesh's worst flooding of the century in 2007, the United States donated 700,000 metric tons of food grains, helping to mitigate shortages. In July 2006, the U.S. Navy's hospital ship Mercy visited Bangladesh and U.S. personnel worked with Bangladeshi medical personnel to provide medical treatment to Bangladeshi patients. Between 2005 and 2008, the United States obligated $2.2 million in grant aid funding (Foreign Military Financing) to purchase Defender class small boats for the Coast Guard of Bangladesh, and allocated $934,000 in IMET (International Military Education and Training) for 2007. In addition to heavy flooding at the end of summer 2007, Cyclone Sidr hit the country on November 15, causing widespread devastation and affecting the lives of millions of people. Following the cyclone, U.S. troops and two U.S. naval vessels assisted in the delivery of relief supplies to cyclone victims. USAID provided approximately $36.5 million in food and relief items to Cyclone Sidr-affected people and has continued its support through rebuilding houses for people in the cyclone-affected areas. An additional $80 million will be provided to rebuild livelihoods, strengthen local government, generate economic recovery through income-generation activities, and to plan and construct cyclone shelters in the disaster-prone areas.

Additionally, Bangladesh has become a valuable United States ally in our global efforts to defeat terrorism. As part of these efforts, the Government of Bangladesh has begun to address problems of money laundering and weak border controls to ensure that Bangladesh does not become a terrorist safe-haven.

Principal U.S. Officials
Chargé d'affaires - David Meale

David Meale became the Deputy Chief of Mission at the U.S. Embassy in Dhaka, Bangladesh, in August 2014. He has been acting as Chargé d'affaires, a.i. since the departure of former Ambassador Dan Mozena on December 21, 2014.

Deputy Chief of Mission--Geeta Pasi; Nicolas Dean (incoming)
Political/Economic Counselor--Jon F. Danilowicz
USAID Mission Director--Denise Rollins
Consular Chief--Robert Dreesen (acting); Sandi Ingram (incoming)
Management Counselor--David Sarisky (acting); Adam Lamoreaux (incoming)
Regional Security Officer--Dax Landry (acting); David Koczot (incoming)
Public Affairs Officer--Amy Vrampas; Lauren Lovelace (incoming)

The U.S. Embassy in Dhaka is located at Madani Avenue, Baridhara, Dhaka 1212, Bangladesh; tel: (880) (2) 885-5500, fax: (880) (2) 8823744. Hours of Operation: Sunday to Thursday (08:00 a.m.-16:30 p.m.), except holidays.

TRAVEL AND BUSINESS INFORMATION

The U.S. Department of State's Consular Information Program advises Americans traveling and residing abroad through Country Specific Information, Travel Alerts, and Travel Warnings. **Country Specific Information** exists for all countries and includes information on entry and exit requirements, currency regulations, health conditions, safety and security, crime, political disturbances, and the addresses of the U.S. embassies and consulates abroad. **Travel Alerts** are issued to disseminate information quickly about terrorist threats and other relatively short-term conditions overseas that pose significant risks to the security of American travelers. **Travel Warnings** are issued when the State Department recommends that Americans avoid travel to a certain country because the situation is dangerous or unstable.

For the latest security information, Americans living and traveling abroad should regularly monitor the Department's Bureau of Consular Affairs Internet web site at http://www.travel.state.gov, where the current Worldwide Caution, Travel Alerts, and Travel Warnings can be found. Consular Affairs Publications, which contain information on obtaining passports and planning a safe trip abroad, are also available at http://www.travel.state.gov. For additional information on international travel, see http://www.usa.gov/Citizen/Topics/Travel/International.shtml.

The Department of State encourages all U.S. citizens traveling or residing abroad to register via the State Department's travel registration website or at the nearest U.S. embassy or consulate abroad. Registration will make your presence and whereabouts known in case it is necessary to contact you in an emergency and will enable you to receive up-to-date information on security conditions.

Emergency information concerning Americans traveling abroad may be obtained by calling 1-888-407-4747 toll free in the U.S. and Canada or the regular toll line 1-202-501-4444 for callers outside the U.S. and Canada.

The National Passport Information Center (NPIC) is the U.S. Department of State's single, centralized public contact center for U.S. passport information. Telephone: 1-877-4-USA-PPT (1-877-487-2778); TDD/TTY: 1-888-874-7793. Passport information is available 24 hours, 7 days a week. You may speak with a representative Monday-Friday, 8 a.m. to 10 p.m., Eastern Time, excluding federal holidays.
Travelers can check the latest health information with the U.S. Centers for Disease Control and Prevention in Atlanta, Georgia. A hotline at 800-CDC-INFO (800-232-4636) and a web site at http://wwwn.cdc.gov/travel/default.aspx give the most recent health advisories, immunization recommendations or requirements, and advice on food and drinking water safety for regions and

countries. The CDC publication "Health Information for International Travel" can be found at http://wwwn.cdc.gov/travel/contentYellowBook.aspx.

STRATEGIC INFORMATION FOR TRADE, BUSINESS AND INVESTMENTS

ECONOMY AND ECONOMIC DEVELOPMENT

MAJOR EXPORTING INDUSTRIES AND BUSINESS OPPORTUNITIES

CERAMICS

The art of pottery is perhaps as old as human civilisation. Initially, it started with clay and then passed through various media like wood, stone, shell, and metal before reaching the age of ceramic and porcelain. Bangladesh can proudly claim to have passed through all these stages so to land successfully in the ceramic age.

Till the other day export market of ceramic tablewares was exclusively the domain of china, Japan and South Korea in the East and France, Germany, Italy and the UK in the West. But those days are gone and the old order has started yielding place to the new through the process of competition. That is how Bangladesh has emerged as one of the successful manufacturing and exporting countries of quality ceramic tablewares. With the traditional skill and craftsmanship handed down from generation to generation and the favorable environment created for investment and export, Bangladesh has now reached such a stage of development that she is second to none in respect of manufacturing and exporting ceramic tablewares. The secret of this success is quality. Bangladeshi ceramic tableware is rated as one the best in the world. Almost all the producing units have succeeded in establishing their brand names in the international ceramic tableware market. As for example, when you say Manno, you need not say ceramic.

To ensure proper quality and goodwill, the ceramic tableware producing units use high quality raw materials. The machinery and equipments are also modem and conform to the latest technology and standard. Each of the units has its own in-house laboratory facility and quality control and testing mechanism. All these arrangements have contributed to the production of world class ceramic tablewares in Bangladesh. The types of products presently being marketed are : dinner sets, tea sets coffee sets, soup sets, fruit sets, plates, bowls, flower vases, mugs and various types of souvenir items. Most of the ceremic products are oven-proof, chill-proof and dishwasher-proof and free from any chemical hazards. This enables the user to rely on ceramic tablewares from Bangladesh with confidence.

At present, Bangladesh is exporting ceramic tablewares to more than 30 countries, the most important of which are the USA, the UK, Italy, Spain, France, New Zealand, the Netherlands, Australia and Sweden. The preferential tariff treatment available under the GSP schemes are contributing to the growth of export of this merchandise to these markets. Efforts are underway to diversity the market base beyond these GSP-giving countries and in the process export to non-GSP countries has also started developing. Argentina, Chilli, South Africa represent some such markets where Bangladesh has already succeeded in making a dent with the ceramic tableware's. Along with the market diversification, product diversification efforts are also being consolidated and strengthened.

All said and done, Bangladesh offers a great opportunity for international consumers looking for high quality, fashionable and hygienic ceramic tablewares at a reasonable price tag.

ELECTRONICS

There have been profound and sweeping changes in the world of high technology in the past few decades and Bangladesh has prepared itself to meet the challenges of these changes and take a reasonable share of the business they will generate. The information technology has come upon us swiftly and suddenly and Bangladesh is emerging as a reliable and able exporter of electronics and computer software. At present, Bangladesh has diversified into many areas which include electronic and electro-mechanical assembling/manufacturing and computer software and data entry services.

The Govermment is now offering opportunities for highly efficient export-oriented activities at an ectremely low cost for any profitable joint venture. Bangladesh enjoys GSP status and with a value addition of 35% and above, all exports will have the advantage of duty free entry in the USA. Similar facilities are also available in the EU countries.

In this situation, Bangladesh, with its excellent geographical location, adapatable skills for technological development and the availability of a vast pool of cheap labour has realized the immense benefits it can reap by conscientious commitment to electronics and computer based industries.

Bangladeshi workers are said to be among the best in the world. They have proved their worth by demonstrating various manufacturing skills and proficiencies in a remarkably short time.

Bangladeshi female workers have shown high skill in a very successful, hundred percent Japanese-owned electronic unit called Miniplo Electric Company. Their Proficiency in the micro elecronic assesmbly (IC Bonding) operations where their higher output and lower rejection rate were found to be of international standard was very laudable.

Bangladeshi software engineers have developed a world class computer software for swedish car manufacturer Volvo. As a result, any new Volvo that is seen on the road to day has more than a touch of Bangladeshi software.
The present democratic Govermment is very much suportive of any industrial initative(s) which will generate new jobs and promote export. Thus the Govermment has taken up a very liberal policy for foreign private investment. Joint venture projects are actively encouraged and no pror approval of the Govermment is necessary. The Export Processing Zones (EPZ) in Chittagong and Dhaka provide necessary fiscal and infrastructural facilities, such as duty-free import of capital machinery raw materials, factory buildings, ware-housing, roads, power, water and telecommunications. Foreign investment to the tune of 100% ownership is also allowed in and outside the EPZ in many sectors, return on investments can be as high as 100% in less than three years.

There has been a consistent growth in the export of electronic components over the last decade and one can certainly anticipate a higher growth rate in the future. Bangladesh's electronic industry can develop into a major world supplier in the years to come.

In the telecommunication sector, E-mail and Internet have already been activated and Bangladesh is slowly getting into the sophisticated method of electronic data communication.

LIST OF EXPORTERS OF ELECTRONIC AND COMPUTER SOFTWARE PRODUCTS	
1. M/s Mas Industries Ltd., House 8, Road 16 (Old 27) Dhanmondi R/A. Dhaka-1209	**2. M/s Micro Electronics Ltd.,** 59/C, Darus Salam, Mirpur Road Dhaka. Bangladesh

Bangladesh Tel : 815967-8, 884628 Fax : 88-02-811138	Tel : 802288, 802244, 862555 Fax : 88-02-802244
3. M/s. Marsha Audio Video Service 28, Prassanga podder Lane, Tati Bazar Dhaka-1000, Bangladesh Tel : 238631, 832631 Fax : 88-02-863797, 88-02-863307 Tlx : 632170 BJSSR BJ (Att: Marsha)	**4. M/s. Tanin Bangladesh Co. Ltd.,** 43, Rankin Street, Wari Dhaka-1203, Bangladesh Tel : 238414, 243054 Fax : 88-02-863023
5. M/s. Limo Electronics Ltd., 12-13, Motijheel C/A Dhaka-1000, Bangladesh Tel : 862219, 237773, 211620 Fax : 88-02-863947 Tlx : 632157 MTT BJ	**6. M/s. Facto yamagon Electronics Ltd.,** 218/C, Tejgaon I/A Dhaka-1208, Bangladesh Tel : 881504 Fax : 88-02-863667
7. M/s. Singer Bangladesh Ltd., 39, Dilkusha C/A, Dhaka-1000 Dhaka-1000, Bangladesh Tel : 8686652-6, 234221, 863704 Fax : 88-02-863682 Tlx : 675637 SGR BJ	**8. M/s. Cybernetic Systems** 515/1, Malibagh Dhaka, Bangladesh Tel : 413377 Fax : 880-2-413377
9. M/s. Rahim Afrooz (Bangladesh) Ltd., 104, Motijheel C/A Dhaka-1000, Bangladesh Tel : 865270-4, 233208 Fax : 880-2-863432 Tlx : 642814 LVTF BJ	**10 M/s. Pacific Industries Ltd.,** 14, Mohakhali C/A, Pacific Centre Dhaka, Bangladesh Tel : 884869, 882761-65 Fax : 880-2-883266 Tlx : 642665 FCF BJ

COMPUTER SOFTWARE

M/s. Telephone Shilpa Sangstha Ltd., Tongi, Dhaka, Bangladesh Tel : 892701, 892233, 891188 Fax : 880-2-891188	
1. M/s. Applied Computer Tech Ltd., 23, New Eskaton Dhaka, Bangladesh Tel : 833647 Fax : 880-2-833647	**2. M/s. Bangladesh Export Import Co. Ltd.,** 17, Dhanmondi R/A Road No. 2, Dhaka-1205 Bangladesh Tel : 500151, 861891-5, 863266 Fax : 880-2-863470, 880-2-867647 Tlx : 675848 BEXIM BJ

FISH EXPORT

As a riverine deltaic country Bangladesh with its warm tropical climate is ideally located and offers a vast reserve of fresh brackish water fish, including the sea- food/shrimps. Bangladesh has .33

million hectors of inland water and 480 km coast line. During 1996-97 fiscal year about 1.5 million metric ton of fish including shrimp were produced from different sources.

Fisheries sector plays a vital role in the economic development of Bangladesh contributing about 4.7% of the countries GDP. About 1.2 million people directly and 10 million people indirectly are associated with this sector for their livelihood.

The development of fisheries sector is one of the top priorities of the Government and hence included in the 'thrust sector' of our export policy. Planned culture of shrimp and fish has been encouraged in the country through the private sector with adequate financial and technical support of the government. The exuberance of the entrepreneurs coupled with the given support, resulted in the rapid development of the sector and helped emerge Bangladesh as potential supplier of shrimp and fish within a short span of time. During the last 25 years, number of fish processing plants increased from 15 to 128 and export earning increased from US$ 3.17 million to US$ 314 million. Export of shrimp generally accounts 85% of this export earning. The existing processing plants in the country have a total capacity of processing 200,000 metric tons of fishery products.

The country exported 76.05 million pounds fishery products in the year 1997-98. Bangladesh is exporting frozen shrimp to about 30 countries of the world of which USA, JAPAN, BELGIUM, UK, THE NETHERLANDS AND GERMANY are the most leading buying countries. During the year1996-97 the country exported 56.75 million pounds of shrimps to the overseas countries.

Maintenance of appropriate quality of the products is considered vital for achieving desired success in the global trade of this product. Underscoring the need significant improvement has been brought about in the country s fishery sector as regard infrastructure, quality control and management of the processing plants along with quality of product to meet the growing demand of the overseas consumers. Government Fish inspecting and Quality Control (FIQC) Department have been well equipped with modern laboratory facilities. The Fish and Fishery Product Inspection and Quality Control rules pertaining to fish collection, storage and processing has been enforced by the Government thereby empowering Department of Fisheries (DOF) with legal authority to inspect firms dealing with fish business.

Bangladesh shrimp and fish is grown under natural environment maintaining the original taste and texture of the products. Scientifically processed and absolutely free from industrial pollution, Bangladesh offers a unique combination of natural resources and export friendly infrastructure, thereby making country's fisheries items genuinely popular all over the world.

LIST OF FROZEN FOOD INDUSTRIES IN BANGLADESH	
1-M/s. A-fish Limited, 5, Bangabandhu Avenue. Dhaka, Bangladesh Tel:252515 Fax : 880-2-883737 Tlx : 27239 AFISH BJ Khulna	**2. M/s. Ajmiriganj Fish** Industries Ltd., 28, Dilkusha C/A, Dhaka, Bangladesh Tel:250345,256469 Fax : 880-2-863957 Khulna
3. M/s. A.K. Khan & Co. Ltd., (Marine Division), Batali Hills, Chittagong, Bangladesh Tel:613953.613084	**4. M/s. Anraj Fish** Products Industries Ltd., 15, Reazuddin Road, Chittagong, Bangladesh

Fax : 880-31-610596 880-2-241 147	Tel:614264,613014 Fax : 880-31-610955
5. M/s. Angler's Limited, **64, New Satmasjid Road,** **Dhanmondi, Dhaka,** Bangladesh. Tel : 329951 Fax : 880-2-884530	**6. M/s. Amam Sea Food Industries Ltd.,** Dhaka Chamber Building,(6th Floor), 65-66 Motijheel C/A, Dhaka, Bangladesh. Tel:867411-5 Fax : 880-2-863826,833010
7. M/s. Amin Fish Farms & Industries Ltd., 6/7, BSCIC Industrial Estate, FIDC Road, Kalurghat, Chittagong, Bangladesh Tel 670889,670104 Fax : 880-31-670104 880-31-710243	**8. M/s. Amin Agencies (1947) Ltd.,** (Cold Storage Division), Guptakhal, Patenga, Chittagong. Bangladesh Tel:50414 (0),500275. Tlx : 66223 BSFIC BJ
9. M/s. Apex Foods Limited, Dhaka Chamber Building. 65-66, Motijheel C/A, Dhaka-1000, Bangladesh Tel:867411-5 Fax : 880-2-863826 Tlx : 632312 AFL BJ	**10. M/s. Aqua Foods Limited,** A/12, BSCIC Ind. Estate, Sagarika Road, P.O. Code 4219, Chittagong, Bangladesh. Tel : 51558, 51316 Pax : 880-31-710609
11. M/s. Aqua Resources Limited, 146/A, New Baily Road, Dhaka, Bangladesh. Tel : 831338 Fax : 880-2-833510 880-41-61203 Tlx : 675632 BIL BJ (Attn : AQUA)	**12. M/s. Asian Sea Food Limited,** 71, Motijheel C/A (1st Floor), Dhaka-1000, Bangladesh. Tel:234180,255976, 251081 Fax : 880-2-863407
13. M/s. Anwara Sea Food Limited, Mohananda Bhaban, 61, Khan Jahan Ali Road, Khulna, Bangladesh. Tel : 22561, 20442, Fax : 880-41-61245, 880-2-863519	**14. M/s. A.H.M. Fishing Ltd.,** 109/A, Kakrail C/A, Dhaka, Bangladesh. Tel : 401223, 607492
15. M/s. Baghkhali Fisheries Ltd., Kadir Chamber, 97, Agrabad C/A, Chittagong, Bangladesh. Tel : 502223, 505639 (0) Fax : 880-2-863470	**16. M/s. Bangladesh** Frozen Fish & Froglegs Ltd., Arag Chamber, 68, Agrabad C/A, Chittagong, Bangladesh. Tel : 031-503369,501882 Fax : 880-31-710934 Tlx : 66486 GLOBAL BJ
17. M/s. Bangladesh Fresh	**18. M/s. Barisal**

Frozen Sea Poods Ltd., Al Islam Chamber (1st Floor), 91, Agrabad C/A, Chittagong, Bangladesh. Tel :505631 Fax : 880-31-710165	Fishing Ltd., 109/A, Kakrail C/A, Dhaka, Bangladesh. Phone : 414782 Fax : 880-2-831755

FLOWERS EXPORT

Flowers symbolise beauty and serenity. Right from the garden of Eden down to the green grocers' basket, flowers have been regarded as an embodiment of human taste and aesthesis. Flowers inspired great songs to be composed, great souls to be unfolded and great feelings to be expressed. This unique and unparalleled nature of flowers has given rise to its commercial transaction all over the world and Bangladesh has ventured to enter this expanding export market.

The country has a favourable climatic condition and is capable of producing a wide array of cut-flowers and foliage of international standard. Improved method of transportation is also helping this perishable merchandise reach major market destinations within the shortest possible time in as fresh a condition as it is at the time of harvesting.

No one could think of exporting Bangladeshi flowers even a few years ago. But this a reality today and a prosperous bonanza for tomorrow. In view of the marketing prospect, a vast agricultural land has been turned into a flower growing area and the farmers are now in a position to make available any quantum of flowers for export, according to market requirements. This is encouraging both the exporters and the importers to strengthen their contacts and stimulate commercial operations of flowers.

The varieties of cut-flowers that Bangladesh can supply, with edge over others, include rose, tuberose, gladiola, anthorium, carnation, helliconia, gerbera, ginger lily and a host of orchids and foliage. The fact that these are wholly originated agricultural produces of Bangladesh enables the importers to enjoy preferential tariff treatment under the GSP. This has widened the scope of export development of our flowers. Developed countries like the EU, the USA and Japan find the shopping of flowers from Bangladesh highly attractive, since they can buy duty-free. They also find investment in flower cultivation in Bangladesh extremely profitable, as the environment is friendly and labour is inexpensive. The ethnic markets of the Middle East and the South East Asia also hold up high prospects for investment and export.

As a young nation, Bangladesh is striving hard for the future and the Government policy is one of inducement and facilitation for promotion of investment and export. In response to this policy, entrepreneurs have already started investing in commercial farming of flowers and exporters are getting increasingly involved in channelising the produce to all potential market destinations.

So next time, when you look for a dependable source of flower supply, give a positive consideration to Bangladesh. Hygienically processed, absolutely free from pollution and hundred percent natural, Bangladeshi fresh and lively flowers will meet your expectation in terms of both quality and price.

ASSOCIATIONS

1. BANGLADESH FLOWERS GROWERS & BABSHAYEE SAMITI
Contact Person : Mr. Sher Ali Sarder
Godkhali, Jhikhar Gachha, Jessore, Bangladesh.

2. BANGLADESH FLOWERS GROWERS & EXPORTERS ASSOCIATION
Contact Person : Mr. M. A. Samad
274/2, Jafrabad Rayer Bazar, Dhaka, Bangladesh.
Tel: 880-2-325355

3. DHAKA MAHANAGARI NURSERY MALIK SAMABAY SAMITI
Contact Person : Mr. Abdul Hossain
D.M.C. Market, Gulshan-2 Dhaka, Bangladesh.
Tel: 880-2-603605, 880-2-884990

4. M/S. ORCHID SOCIETY OF BANGLADESH
Contact Person : Mrs: Naseem Iqbal
House # NWK-8, Road # 50,Gulshan, Dhaka, Bangladesh.
Tel: 880-2-881144, 880-2-881203 Fax : 880-2-881035

MAJOR EXPOERTERS

1. MR. A.M.M. IQBAL & MRS. NASEEM IQBAL
House # NWK 8, Road # 50
Gulshan, Dhaka-1212
Bangladesh.
Tel : 880-2-881144, 880-2-881203 ,880-2-882550
Fax : 880-2-881035
E-mail : tiali@citecho.net

2. ALPHA AROMATIC LTD.
Contact Person : Mr. M. Ahsanullah
25/8, Tajmahal Road
2nd Floor, Dhaka-1207
Bangladesh.
Tel: 880-2-9128739
880-2-9126612 Ext. -117

3. ASIA POT & PLANT
Contact Person : Mr. Shahidul Alam
6/11, Humayun Road
Mohammadpur, Dhaka-1207
Bangladesh.
Tel: 880-2-9110169

4. BADHON ENTERPRISE
Contact Person : Mr. Shahidul Alam
6/11, Humayun Road, Block-B
1st Floor, Mohammadpur
Dhaka-1207, Bangladesh.
Tel: 880-2-9110169
Fax : 880-2-817957, 880-2-9110169

5. COMA CREATION
Contact Person : Mr. Md. Khairul Bashar
59, Kaji Nazrul Islam Avenue
3rd Floor, Tejgaon, Dhaka-1208
Bangladesh.
Fax : 880-2-863409, 880-2-863378

6. DEWAN INTERNATIONAL
Contact Person : Mr. Dewan Nasirul Haque
8, Bangabandhu Avenue
3rd Floor, Dhaka-1000
Bangladesh.
Tel: 880-2-251729

7. DHANMONDI NURSERY
Road No. 7, Dhanmondi R/A
Dhaka-1205, Bangladesh.
Tel: 880-2-508409

8. GREEN GARDEN AGRICULTURAL CO.
Contact Person : Mr. Raisul Islam
95/1, Elephant Road
Dhaka-1205, Bangladesh.
Tel : 880-2-500458
Fax : 880-2-866458

9. INTERNATIONAL TRADE ASSOCIATES
Chand Mansion (5th Floor)
66, Dilkusha C/A.
Dhaka-1000, Bangladesh.
Tel : 880-2-9564597
Fax : 880-2-9564710

10. M/S KARABI PUSHPALAYA
Contact Person : Mr. M. A. Mannan
Vashani Sarak, Shahbagh
Dhaka-1000, Bangladesh.
Tel: 880-2-869595

FRUITS AND VEGETABLES

A tropical location, lush greenery, moisture-rich loamy soil and production-friendly climate-all these make Bangladesh one of the notable growers of a vast range of fruits and vegetables of impeccable quality.

The quantum of export is not big, but sizeable enough to cater to the large ethnic population of the south Asian sub-continent residing in the UK and the Middle East. They have provided to be the biggest consumers of Bangladeshi produce. The present export of vegetables is over 10,000 MT per year. There has been an encouraging growth of export of fresh fruits and vegetables to other European countries also in recent years.

Bangladesh has an agro-based economy and her fertile alluvial plains are ideal for the cultivation and growth of export of fruits and vegetables Important of technology has led to manifold increase in production for export.

The changing seasons see Bangladesh producing a variety of fruits and vegetables. The winter brings ripe oranges and other citrus fruits, cauliflower, and cabbages; summer brings succulent mangoes, lychees, water melons, brinjals, yam and ladies fingers; monsoons brings sweet and juicy pineapples. A Variety of bananas are available all the year round.

Fruits and vegetables growers have taken various steps not only to augment production, but also to enhance the quality standard. The Government has created the infrastructure and is providing promotional support. Export village for fresh fruits and vegetables have been set up with backward linkage developed between the producer and the exporter, soft loans are being provided to the producers and facilities have been created for better processing and packages. Fruits and vegetables being easily perishable, storing facilities have been created at the airport to facilitate preshipment strong as well as strong for emergency.

With a countrywide road-rail network , an international airport and two sea-ports, Bangladesh is all set to serve the world in the increased supply of fresh fruits and vegetables

LIST OF FRESH FRUITS AND VEGETABLES EXPORTED FROM BANGLADESH

VEGETABLES

Local name	English name	Time of Production/Availability
1. Aamphul	Mango flower	December-February
2. Alu	Potato	November-March
3. Amra phul	Golden Apple flower	December-February
4. Bash Karul	Bamboo shoots	April-October
5. Begoon	Brinjal/Aubergine	All season
6. Bilati Dhania	Tong Ho	All season
7. Borboti	Cowpea	All season
8. Chal Kumra/Jali	Dhudi	All season
9. Chichinga	Snake ground/chichora/Parval	April-October
10. Data sak	Amaranthus	All season
11. Dhane pata	Coriander leaves	November-February
12. Dheki sak	Fiddlehead greens	All season
13. Dherosh	Okra/Ladies finger	All season
14. Dhundul	Bath sponge(green)	November-February

15. Jhinga	Ribbed ground/Turia	All season
16. Kacha Marich	Green Chili	All season
17. Kacha pepe	Green Papaya	All season
18. Kacha kala	Mattock/Plantain	All season
19. Kachu Lati	-	April-October
20. Kakrol	Kantola	July-September
21. Kala bogli	-	All season
22. Kala Thur	Banana Flower	All season
23. Kalmi sak	Kang Kong	April-October
24. Korolla	Bitter ground/Korela	All season
25. Lal sak	Red Amaranthus	All season
26. Lau	Squash	All season
27. Man-Kachu	Toro	All season
28. Misti Alu	Sweet patato	April-October
29. Misti Kumra	Sweet ground/Pumpkin	November-February
30. Moola	Radish	November-April
31. Mukhi Kachu	Eddoes	April-October
32. Ol-Kachu	Toro	All season
33. Palong sak	Spinach	All season
34. Pancha Mukhi Kachu	Colocass/Taro	April-October
35. Pani Kachu	Toro	All season
36. Pat sak	Jute Leaf	April-October
37. Potal	Palwal/Tindori	All season
38. Pui sak	Callaloo	All season
39. Sak Alu	Yam beam	April-October
40. Shajna	Sijin/Saragwo/Drumstick	All season
41. Shapla	Water lilly	All season
42. Shasha	Cucumber/Courgettes	All season

43. Sim	Flat bean	November-February
44. Peaz	Onion	
45. Chauna	Over matured Dhudi	
46. Shim Bichi	Flat bean seeds	

FRUITS

Local name	**English name**	**Time of Production/Availability**
1. Aam	Mango	May-September
2. Ada Lebu	Lemon	April-October
3. Amloki	Embica	July-October
4. Amra	Golden Apple	April-October
5. Ata	Cherimoya	March-May
6. Boroi	Berr/Jujubi	November-February
7. Chalta	-	April-October
8. Champa Kala	Apple Banana	All season
9. Gab	Sharonfruit	April-june
10. Golap Jam	Jam	May-June
11. Jalpai	Olive	November-February
12. Jambura/Batabilebu	Shaddoc/Pummelo	April-October
13. Jamrul	Rose Apple	April-October
14. Kaggji Lebu	Lime	All seasons
15. Kamranga	Carambola/Star fruit	April-October
16. Kathal	Jackfruits	April-October
17. Koronja	Konanda	April-October
18. Kul/Boroj	Plum/Jujubi	November-February
19. Latka	Longan	April-October
20. Lichu	Lychee/Litchee	June-July
21. Pani phal	Water chestnut	April-October

22. Peara	Gauva	All season
23. Safeda	Sapodila/ Sapota/Chico	April-October
24. Sharifa	Atemoya	August-December
25. Shatkora	Shatkora	April-October
26. Tal	Mangoesteen/Plam	April-October
27. Tetul	Tarmarind	All season
28. Kacha Aam	Green Mango	
29. Alachi Lebu	Lime	
30. Jhara Lebu	Lime	
31. Bel	Wood Apple	
32. Kad Bel	-	

Others

Local name	**English name**	**Time of Production/Availability**
1. Ada	Ginger	All season
2. Akh	Sugar Cane	All season
3. Holud	Termaric	All season
4. Lebupata	Limeleaf	All season
5. Mete Alu	Yams	All season
6. Pan (Bangla)	Betel leaf	All season
7. Pan (Khashia)	Betel leaf	

LIST OF EXPORTERS OF FRUITS AND VEGITABLES

1. **M/s. Afco Abedin Limited**
   188/1, Motijheel Circular Road, Dhaka, Bangladesh
   Tel: 417456
   Fax: 880-2-831993

2. **M/s. Akhi Rakhi Enterprise**
   25, Haji Abdul majid Lane, Dhaka, Bangladesh
   Tel: 259934, 250816

3. **M/s. Al-Amin Export Trading**
   47, Dilkusha C/A, Dhaka-1000, Bangladesh

4. M/s. Ali Enterprise
20/1, Nowab Katra, Dhaka, Bangladesh
Tel: 247603, 255308

5. M/s. Ahmed Traders
904/A, Shahid Bagh, Dhaka, Bangladesh
Tel: 844428, 414340, 408500

6. M/s. Aqua Food Co.
130, Fakirapool, Dhaka, Bangladesh
Tel : 419341, 834253

7. M/s. Anowar Traders
4, Malakartala Lane, Dhaka, Bangladesh
Tel: 241429

8. M/s. Azizur Rahman
Kazi Mansion, Zinda Bazar, Sylhet, Bangladesh
Tel: 0821-5242, 4983
Fax: 0821-5272

9. M/s. Bangladesh Food Store
86/2/Ka, Sheorapara, Mirpur, Dhaka, Bangladesh
Tel: 814554

10. M/s. Barkat Traders
59/1, K.B. Road, Faridabad, Dhaka, Bangladesh
Tel: 251320

11. M/s. B.D. Corporation
9, DIT Avenue, Dhaka, Bangladesh
Tel: 240929, 886260

12. M/s. Eva Enterprise
11/12, Pratap Das Lane, Dhaka, Bangladesh
Tel: 242821, 247041

13. M/s. E. H. Enterprise
58/1, Purana Paltan, Dhaka, Bangladesh
Tel: 235123

14. M/s. Elahi Enterprise
24, Mohini Mohon Das Lane, Dhaka, Bangladesh
Tel : 231275

15. M/s. Fortune Company
125/A, Motijheel C/A, Islam Chamber, Dhaka, Bangladesh
Tel: 258932, 233491
Fax: 880-2-863379, 863170

16. M/s. Friend Int'l. Traders
60/23/E, Dhalpur, Noth Jatrabari, Dhaka, Bangladesh
Tel: 282284
Fax: 880-2-863379, 863170

17. M/s. Fuad Impex
76, Dinanath Sen Road, Dhaka, Bangladesh
Tel:257132, 251114
Fax: 880-2-868466

18. M/s. Falcon International
20/A, Modan Mohan Shah Lane, Dhaka, Bangladesh
Tel: 256929, 242942

19. M/s. Gaffar Enterprise
27/6B, Jogi Nagar, Dhaka, Bangladesh
Tel: 245512

20. M/s. Green Trade House
21, Shantinagar, Dhaka, Bangladesh
Tel: 401651, 835280

21. M/s. G.S. Enterprise
29, B.B. Avenue, Dhaka, Bangladesh
Tel: 282875, 255167

22. M/s. Harun & Company
42, Dilkusha C/A, Dhaka, Bangladesh
Tel: 230996

23. M/s. Hazi Hafez Ahmed & Sons
81, Patla Khan Lane, Dhaka, Bangladesh
Tel:401610

24. M/s. H. M. Trading
79/1, Fakirapool, Dhaka, Bangladesh
Tel:418750, 407832

25. M/s. International Trading Company
101, Arambagh, Dhaka, Bangladesh
Tel: 318426
Fax: 880-2-863797

26. M/s. Islam Brothers
904/A, Shahid Bagh, Dhaka, Bangladesh
Tel:417713

27. M/s. Jahangir Overseas
130, Fakirapool, Dhaka, Bangladesh
Tel: 253371

28. M/s. Zaman Bhai
188, Circular Road , Motijheel, Dhaka, Bangladesh
Tel: 401165, 413717

29. M/s. Jamshar Enterprise
237, City Suoer Market (Khilgoan Taltola), Dhaka, Bangladesh
Tel: 41176, 403615
Fax: 880-2-833244, 868466

30. M/s. Kamaly Enterprise
237, Khilgoan, City Super Market, Dhaka, Bangladesh
Tel: 41176, 403615
Fax: 880-2-833244, 868466

31. M/s. Khaled Trade Syndicate
370/B, Mirja House, Khilgoan, Dhaka, Bangladesh
Tel: 405384

32. M/s. Jewel Enterprise Ltd.
206, Central Bashaboo, Dhaka, Bangladesh
Tel: 418151, 419325
Fax: 880-2-863379

33. M/s. Liberty Impex
176/6, Shantibagh, Dhaka, Bangladesh
Tlx: 256929, 241942, 256929

34. M/s. Meredian Enterprise International
27, New Eskaton, Ramna, Dhaka, Bangladesh
Tel: 832567
Fax: 880-2-863060

35. M/s. Muhit International
345/C, Malibagh, Dhaka, Bangladesh
Tel: 418418

36. M/s. Munshi Traders
195/8, Shantibagh, Dhaka, Bangladesh
Tel: 407836

37. M/s. Mun Mun Exports
33/34, Station Road, Dhaka, Bangladesh
Tel: 811817

38. M/s. Navila Trade Syndicate
17/B, Reazbagh, Dhaka, Bangladesh
Tel:403615

39. M/s. Nina Corporation
6/3-D, Chamipataly Lane, Dhaka, Bangladesh
Tel: 233841
Fax: 880-2-833244, 868466

40. M/s. Nizampur Trading
48/5, R.K. Mission Road, Dhaka, Bangladesh
Tel: 256104

41. M/s. Nargis Traders
702/A, Shahid Bagh, Dhaka, Bangladesh
Tel: 408500

42. M/s. Noor Mohammad & Co.
20, B.K. Das Road, Dhaka, Bangladesh
Tel: 239239

43. M/s. Prince International
237, Khilgoan, Taltola, City Super Market, Dhaka, Bangladesh
Tel: 411476

44. M/s. Rahim Brothers
6/1, Forashgonj, Dhaka, Bangladesh
Tel: 256408
Fax:880-2-833983

45. M/s. Shahid Brothers
447/B, Khilgoan, Dhaka, Bangladesh
Tel: 328791

46. M/s. Shayem Enterprise
60, Dilkusha C/A, Al Islam Overseas (1st Floor), Dhaka, Bangladesh
Tel: 507246

47. M/s.Shatadal Enterprise
8/1, B.K. Das Lane, Dhaka, Bangladesh
Tel: 865565

48. M/s. S. N. Trading Co.
11/12, Protab Das Lane, Dhaka, Bangladesh
Tel: 247041, 242821

49. M/s. Tushar Enterprise
Al-Helal Building, Arambagh, Dhaka, Bangladesh
Tel: 407123

50. M/s. Trade International
20, outer Circular Raod, Dhaka, Bangladesh
Tel: 250219, 317972

51. M/s. Narila Trade Syndicate
17/B, Riazbagh, Taltala, Khilgoan, Dhaka, Bangladesh
Tel: 403615, 411476
Fax:880-2- 833244, 868466

52. M/s. Shamoly Trading Overseas (Pvt) Ltd.
32/1, South Kamalapur, Motijheel C/A, Dhaka, Bangladesh
Tel: 245029, 835919
Fax:880-2- 863357, 864753

53. M/s. Greenway traders
6/D, Naya Paltan, Dhaka, Bangladesh
Tel: 403891, 415805

CONCERNED ASSOCIATION

Bangladesh Fruits, Vegetables and Allied Products Exporters Association
56/57 Motijheel C/A, Sharif Mansion (6th floor)
Dhaka-1000, Bangladesh
Tel: 868953
Fax:880-2- 868466, 880-2-833244
Tlx: 642895 SOYD BJ

GARMENTS

The Bangladesh Garment Manufacturers and Exporters Association (BGMEA) is the only recognized trade body that represents the export oriented garment manufacturers and exporters of the country.Struck by the 70s' political turmoil in Sri Lanka and price hike in other Asian countries, garment buyers in the international markets explored the potential of the newly born Bangladesh. Fortunately, with the timely policy support from the government, entrepreneurs talent and efforts as well as the labour of the work force, the ready-made garment (RMG) industry could impressively succeed and the buyers got confidence in it. Now its development rate is, on an average, 20% per annum. With a huge supply of cost-effective labour force, country's economic factors are in favour of development in this relatively low capital and high labour intensive industry.

Starting in late 70s as a small nontraditional sector of export. Ready-made Garment (RMG) emerged as a promising export earning sector of the country by the year 1983. Bangladesh at that time lacked a sectoral trade body, non-government in nature, free from traditional bureaucracy, to help the sector to boost up the country's foreign exchange earnings. Entrepreneurs and the government in the post independence years felt and emphasised the urgent need to develop non-traditional items of export for helping the struggling economy. As a result, 1977 marked the birth of Bangladesh Garment Manufacturers and Exporters' Association (BGMEA). Since its humble inception with only nineteen (19) garment manufacturers and exporters, BGMEA has grown into a strong and dynamic body. Today it proudly declares registered membership of more than 2700 garment manufacturers and exporters. Of the total 2700 units, about 1932 garment factories are located in Dhaka while about 1 55 and 415 factories are located in Naryanganj and Chittagong respectively.factories are located in Dhaka while about 1 55 and 415 factories are located in Naryanganj and Chittagong respectively.These 2700 garment factories having about 1.5 million workforce is earning 73% of the country's total foreign currency. About 1 5 million people are directly dependent on this sector.

The growth of Freight Transport, Bank, Insurance, hotel etc. in the country are the gift of the garment industry. In a nutshell, the garment industry has become the pivot of the country's economy.The fundamental objective of BGMEA, however, is to establish a healthy business environment for a close and mutually beneficial relationship between the manufacturers, exporters and importers in the process ensuring a steady growth in the foreign exchange earnings of the country. To this end, BGMEA has been playing a very strong role to lead the industry in concurrence with the government. The following are the regular activities of BGMEA for its members, owners, apparel buyers and other partners.

a. Organizing members to hold or to participate in apparel fairs at home and abroad; (For further information, any interested party can use BGMEA's web page at http://www.agn i.net/batexpo).
b. Establishing and promoting contacts with foreign buyers, business associations, chambersetc.
c. Providing the members, apparel buyers and other information users with various relateddata.
d. Monitoring international apparel trade and trade.fairs and disseminating the relevant information through its Computer-Network-System linked with various online data sources in the USA and the EU.
e. Encouraging co-operation between industries, companies, firms engaged in manufacturing of garments, allied industries and exporters of ready-made garments.
f. Organizing seminars and symposia on current trade issues to develop awareness and consensus amongthe members and other related parties.
g. Helping in Government's textile quota negotiation with USA and Canada. h. Helping to resolve trade disputes between the members and the buyers.
i. Maintaining computerized membership information and providing information on quota matters.
j. Monitoring implementation of MoU on child labour elimination from the export oriented garment sector of Bangladesh.
k. Educating the displaced workers belowthe age of 14 years and the children of the workers through setting up of school-cum-health centres in different zones of Dhaka, Narayangonj and Chittagong.
l. Publishing a monthly magazine styled "BGMEA Newsletter" that provides updated information about the garment sector.
m. Helping disposal of stock-lots of fabrics.
n. Recommending for correct utilization of fabrics/yarn/acrylic/wool.
o. Giving permission for Interbond sub-contract of bonded warehouse goods.
p. Issuing Utilization Declaration (U/D), Export Orders for clearance of raw materials imported by member-factories.
q. Ensuringadoption of Safety Measures in orderto avert fire accidents in factories.
r. Contributing financial aid for the victims in case of casualty in fire accidents in member-factories.
s. Having regular co-ordination with the labour organizations in the garments sector to resolve labour related issues and establish cordial employer-worker relationship.
t. Creating awareness of the member-units on labour matters by giving expert advice as and when required. u. Giving legal assistance to member-units through our Legal Adviser as and when required.
v. Co-sponsoring with GOB, ILO and UNDP for implementation of welfare measures for garment workers in broader areas of primary health care, transportation, social security & insurance coverage, housing and skill training.

BANGLADESH GARMENT MANUFACTURES & EXPORTS ASSCOSIATION
BTMC BHABAN, 7-9 KAWRAN BAZAR,DHAKA-1215,BANGLADESH
TEL : (02)815597, 815751, fax : 880-2-813951
Telex : 632430 BGMEA BJ E-mail : BGMEA@bgmea agni.com

HANDICRAFTS

The traditional crafts of Bangladesh have been a focal point of interest for visitors from abroad for centuries. The rural-based infrastructure has made it a potential ground for the development of numerous items crafted out of wood, jute, cane, bamboo, grass, straw, clay and other indigenous raw materials. The items produced by early craftsmen were not only singularly beautiful, but also representative of the culture, tradition and customs of the country. With the passage of time, however, new and modern styles and designs have been adapted and this has paved the way for a unique blend of the old and the new.

Bangladesh is now very much a part of the international scene and keeping in mind the discerning taste of the consumers, a vast range of crafts and novelties are now produced in the country under the technical supervision of qualified product development specialists,

With the resurgence of worldwide interest in cane, development of cane products has gained momentum. Bamboo, another tropical grass is often used as a base for support of cane furniture and handicrafts, Bamboo baskets of various shapes and sizes are in great demand in Europe and America. Popular items in vogue are bamboo mirror and picture frames. Split bamboo shoots can be used as wall lining to create the ultimate tropical decor. Bamboo and cane furniture as well as rattan, grass and cane handicrafts and cane screens are just a few of the products available in an amazing array. Leather goods of attractive design and finishing are being produced by skilled craftsmen, The items produced are handbags, wallets, belts, shoe uppers, travel bags, pen holders, card holders and many other utility items. Jute again is another fibre from which a variety of useful products can be fashioned-be it bags, belts, light shoes, wall hangings, draperies and of course jute carpets. Colour fast, fire-resistant, hazard-free jute carpets are unbelievably price advantageous. They are also popular for health and environmental reasons all over the world.

All said and done,Bangladesh offers a great opportunity to the discriminating shoppers for a wide variety of handicrafts which are doubly attractive because of good quality and reasonable price tag.

LIST OF EXPORTERS OF HANDICRAFT	
1. M/s. Alpha Beta Co. Ltd., 65, Dilkusha C/A (3rd Floor), Dhaka-1000, Bangladesh. Tel : 281869, 241333 Fax : 880-2-863263	**2. M/s. Alarmco International,** 47, Dilkusha C/A (4th Floor), Dhaka, Bangladesh. Tel:239914,817023 Fax : 880-2-816189
3. M/s. BRAC Aarong, 66, Mohakhali C/A, Dhaka, Bangladesh. Tel : 884184-87 (PABX), 811349,811273 Fax : 880-2-883614	**4. M/s. Bangladesh Export Limited,** Ellal Chamber (6th Floor), 11, Motijheel C/A, Dhaka-1000, Bangladesh. Tel : 862252, 242059,862211 Fax : 880-2-861133
5. M/s. Bangladesh Trade, House No. 8, Road No. 3, Section 6, Uttara Model Town, Dhaka, Bangladesh. Tel : 891356 Fax : 880-2-893078 (Attn : Bangladesh Trade)	**6. M/s. Conexpo** 36, DIT Extension Road, Naya Paltan (2nd Floor), Dhaka-1000, Bangladesh. Tel : 415846, 836606 Fax : 880-2-832826

7. M/s. Corr-The Jute Works, 30, Senpara Parbata, Mirpur, Dhaka-1216, Bangladesh. Tel : 802589, 801458,801470 Fax : 880-2-803536 Tlx : 642940 ADEB BJ	**8. M/s. Euro Bangla Ltd.,** 3/6 Asad Avenue (3rd Floor), Mohammadpur, Dhaka, Bangladesh. Tel : 816473,814729, 812349 (Res)
9. M/s. Island Trading Corporation, House No. 81/C, Road No. 6, Banani, Dhaka, Bangladesh. Tel:887260,415128,889123 Fax : 880-2-888564,880-2-870003 Tlx : 671040 RGL BJ.	**10. M/s. Jahanara Cottage Ind.,** 7, Aziz Co-operative Super Market, Shahbagh, Dhaka, Bangladesh. Tel : 327239 (Res) Fax : 880-2-862036 880-2-863958
11. M/s. Karika, 27, Paribagh Super Market, Mymensingh Road, Dhaka-1000, Bangladesh. Tel : 504362 Fax : 880-2-813095 (Attn. Karika) Tlx : 642940 ADAB BJ	**12. M/s. Kumudini Welfare** Trust of Bengal, 72, Serajuddowla Road, Narayangonj, Bangladesh. Tel : 0671-71010, 71020, 73028
13. M/s. Pallab, 86, New Circular Road, Dhaka-1217, Bangladesh. Tel : 408131, 409506 Fax : 880-2-831917 Tlx : 632364 JIL BJ	**14. M/s. Rafco International** 128/1, New Circular Road, Dhaka-1217, Bangladesh, Tel : 409302, 403655 (Res)

KNITTED ITEMS

The art of weaving is perhaps as old as human civilization. Bangladesh can proudly claim to have many branches of this ancient art, of which the best known and most popular is the specialty Jamdani, which is one of the varieties of the famous Dhaka Muslin or Mul-mul. For over ten centuries, the Dhaka area has been renowned for this fine fabric. So fine was its texture and quality that it was said to be woven with the "thread of the winds" and the Greek and the Roman texts mention the "Gangetic muslins" as one of the most coveted luxury items. Woven from superfine cotton or silk yarn, jamdani fabric is embroidered or inlaid on the loom with silk, gold and silver threads. Over the years, the weavers simplified the designs making them more stylized and geometric.

A new handloom product has been developed by Grameen Bank- a leading non-government rural-oriented financial institution with trade name "GRAMEEN CHECK" which is soft, colour fast and 100% cotton, The "Grameen Check" fabric and the apparels made out of it have already made a breakthrough in the European markets with potential of penetrating Other- parts of the world.

Another delicate and finely woven product is the glowing soft silk of Rajshahi in rainbow hues. Very ethnic are the striking, bold designs which is the trademark of the colourful, tough fabric woven by the weavers belonging to the various tribal races who inhabit the hilly areas like Cox's Bazar, Rangamati and Sylhet.

Apart from those that already have been mentioned, there are numerous other handloom materials which have made their particular district of origin famous. The most notable are sarees of Dhaka, Tangail and Pabna, Monipuri blankets of Sylhet and Khadi or Khaddar products of Comilla.

At present, the number of handlooms in Bangladesh is five hundred thousand and there are about one million weavers. Handloom products have shown decisive upward trend in the export market since 1972 and Bangladeshi handloom products with their distinctive design and superior quality have created a niche for themselves in overseas markets. We can now proudly claim to be equipped to meet the demand for the latest fashion. An international expert's study reveals that the technical skill of the weavers of Bangladesh is second to none in the handloom producing world.

The product range of handloom is simply amazing and include Muslin Jamdani Sarees, Bedcovers, Bedsheets, Tapestry, Upholstery, Place mats, Rugs or Blankets, Satranji or Durees, Crochet, Muslin, Tribal textiles, Silk fabrics, Sofa covers, Block Prints, Table cloth and Napkins, Towels, Dusters, Kitchen towels, Gents, Ladies and Baby Wear and Shirts, Panjabis, Bedsheets and other household linen in printed, plain or embroidered Khadi.

Bangladesh with its export friendly climate, competitive labour cost and enviable expertise is marching ahead in the handloom sector. Why don't you be a partner in this development either by investing in this sector or through import of handloom products?

LIST OF EXPORTERS OF HANDLOOMS	
1. M/s. Aarong, 9/B, Shamoli, Street No. 1, Dhaka, Bangladesh, Tel: 811273, 325851, 811349 Fax: 880-2-883614(Attn: Aarong)	**2. M/s. Bisudda Khaddar Bhander,** Monoharpur,Comilla Bangladesh. -10 Tel : 081/5470
3. M/s. Corr-The Jute Works, 30, Senpara Parbata, G.P.O. Box-2154, Mirpur,Dhaka-1216 Bangladesh Tel:802589,801458,801470 Fax : 880-2-803536 Tlx : 642940 ADEB BJ	**4. M/s. Gramin Bank,** Gramin Bank Bhaban, Mirpur-2 Dhaka-1216, Bangladesh Tel : 801431, 383081-5 Fax : 880-2-803559 880-2-801138
5. M/s. Heed Handicrafts, 19, Main Road, Block A, Section 11 Mirpur, Dhaka 1221, Bangladesh. Tel:802249,807154 Fax : 880-2-803582	**6. M/s. Karika,** 27, Paribagh Super Market,(1st Floor). Mymensingh Road, IP"1 Dhaka-1000, Bangladesh. Tel : 504362 Fax : 880-2-813095 (Attn.Karika) Tlx : 642940 ADAB BJ

	Attn : Karika
7. M/s. Kumudini Welfare Trust of Bengal, 72, Serajuddowla Road, NarayanganJ, Bangladesh. Tel : 0671/71010, 0671/71020, 0671/73028	**8. M/s. Nipun Ltd.** 38, Free School Street, Kathalbagan, Dhaka-1205, Bangladesh. Tel : 505416 Fax : 880-2-864184

JEWELRY

Bangladesh is known all over the world as an abode of artistic designs and craftsmanship. Jewellery is an area where manifestation of these artistic desingns and craftsmanship has found its way to excellence. The high degree of precision combined with the touch of human imagination has made jewellery produced in Bangladesh as one of the best in the world. The most attractive part of our jewellery is its workmanship and the special effect created out of it. This makes every piece of jewellery unique and gives it an exclusive look with finest details.

Because of the compartative advantage the country possesses and in the persuit of product diversification to broaden the export base, the Government of Bangladesh has adpoted a crash programme to develop a few non-traditional high potential items for export. Jewellery is one of them. A new Jewellery Export policy has already been formulated to simplify and streamline the export procedures and create an investment-friendly environment with a view to promoting export of this product. All these measures have generated a good deal of interest and enthusiasm among the business community and the export of jewellery has started picking up.

Interested importers of jewellery can now just place their order with the manufacture-exporters and get the customs-made product out of the materials either supplied by the importers or procured by the manufacturers from national or international sources. Quality is given the topmost consideration and the Bangladesh Jewellery Association or the Bangladesh Standard Testing Institute will be obliged to issue a pre-shipment quality inspection certificate, if so required by the customers. All types of jewellery are on the export list. The present range of production includes gold-made or gold cotated/plated ornaments; silver-made or silver-coated/plated ornaments, precious/semi-precious tone-studded gold /silver ornaments; and platinum, palladium, iridium, precious/semiprecious, artifical, synthetic stone-studded ornaments. Within these borad categories, the usual types of jewellery products that are found in demand encompass necklace, bracelets, earrings, fingerrings, chains, mantasas, bangles, wedding sets, bridal and other occasional souvenirs, decorative pieces etc.

Although a new entrant in the jewellery export market, Bangladesh thus offers a great opportunity to the discriminating importers represeting discerning tates of the consumers for a wide variety of jeweellery products. Our strength lies in quality and workmanship. Our advantage is reasonable price and prompt delivery. If you are an importer of jewellery, why don't you try ours?

LIST OF JEWELLERY EXPORTERS

1. INTERNATIONAL JEWELLERY MANUFACTURING COMPANY LTD Contact Person : Mr. Anwer Hossain Electronics Complex (2nd Floor) Sectior # 7, Avenue # 4 Main Road # 3, Mirpur Dhaka-1216, Bangladesh Tel: 880-2-807970 880-2-9345129	**2. AMIN JEWELLERS LTD.** Contact Person : Mr. Quazi Sirazul Islam 73, Baitul Mukarram Dhaka-1000, Bangladesh. Tel : 880-2-9555873-4 880-2-8130
3. GUNEA EXCHANGE JEWELLERS Contact Person : Mr. Aftab Ahmed Khan 27, B. B. Avenue, Dhaka-1000 Bangladesh. Tel :880-2-9557991 880-2-232644 Fax : 880-2-833489	**4. GENERAL JEWELLERS LTD.** Contact Person : Mr. Liaquat Hossain H-101, Mouchak Market (1st Floor) Dhaka-1217, Bangladesh. Tel : 880-2-841075, 880-2-407261 Fax : 880-2-9345129
5. KANAK BAHAR JEWELLERS Contact Person : Mr. Biplob Basak 1st Floor Biponi Bitan Chitagong, Bangladesh. Tel : 880-31-9563454 880-31-612993 Fax : 880-2-9555868	**6. L. RAHMAN JEWELLERS** Contact Person : Mr. Anisur Rahman 65, Baitul Mukarram, Dhaka-1000 Bangladesh. Tel : 880-2-9563454 880-2-8555868
7. NEW GOLDEING JEWLELLERS Contact Person : Mr. Enamul Hoque Bhuya 55, Baitul Mukarram, Dhaka-1000 Bangladesh. Tel : 880-2-9551905 880-2-9558189	**8. THE APON JEWELLERS** Contact Person : Mr. Guljar Ahmed 47 Baitul Mukarram (G. Floor) Dhaka-1000, Bangladesh. Tel : 880-2-9552904 880-2-851708

Association

1. **BANGLADESH JEWELLERS ASSOCIATION**
   3, Batiul Mukaram (2nd Floor), Dhaka-1000, Bangladesh.
   Tel : 880-2-9550642, 880-2-9550282, 880-2-9333109

2. **BANGLADESH JEWELLERY MANUFACTURERS & EXPORTERS ASSOCIATION**
   H-101, Mouchak Market (1st Floo), Dhaka-1217, Bangladesh.
   Tel : 880-2-841075, 880-2-4072-61 Fax : 880-2-884120

LEATHER

From time immemorial, the arts and crafts of Bangladesh are closely linked to our culture and heritage. Leather and leather products have always been a part of that heritage and after the emergence of an independent Bangladesh in 1971, the industry received a fresh impetus. Today the country earns a sizeable amount of foreign exchange every year through export of leather and leather products to a number of overrseas market. The Leather Industry of Bangladesh has been given particular attention for developing its infrastructure. By combining the latest in leather technology with abundant raw materials and inexpensive skilled labour, leather and leather products are now playing an important role in earning foreign exchange for the country. Export of leather and Leather goods (including Footwear) earned US$228 Million for Bangladesh in the fiscal year 1997-98.

Bangladesh is capable of producing 180 Million sft of Leather annually. The industry also produces the world's finest quality goatskin of a very fine and smooth grain pattern. Country's cowleateher has excellent natural compact fibre structure with a round feel and touch. More than eighty percent of the country's annual production is exported worldwide as semifinished/finished Leather, footwear and accessories.

Footwear and Leather accessories had indeed made great strides during the decade. There are 15 large scale modern shoe factories engaged in the production of high quality footwear with 2500 smaller footwear units spread all over the country. These units are producing for the domestic market. Over 50 manufacturers are producing various Leater items such as travel goods, suitcases, briefcases and fashion accessories, alongwith belts, wallets, hand bags, case holders etc. for overseas export. Bangladesh has also entered the field of Leather fashion garments with items of distinction and prestige.

MANUFACTURERS & EXPORTERS OF CRUST, FINISHED LEATHER	
01. M/s. Apex Tannery Ltd. Dhaka Chamber Building 65-66, Motijheel C/A (2nd Floor) Dhaka Fac. 127, Hazaribagh, Dhaka Tel : 88-02-9551203, 9560766 Fax : 88-02-9562386	**02. M/s Ayub Brothers Tannery Ltd.** 143/1, Hazaribagh, Dhaka Tel : 88-02-866518
03. M/s Amin Tannery Limited 60/1, Hazaribagh, Dhaka Tel : 88-02-860475, 506981	**04. M/s Anower Tannery (Pvt.) Ltd.** 104, Hazaribagh, Dhaka. Tel : 88-02-9664078, 506168
05. M/s Bangla Tan Leather Products 148/3, Hazaribagh, Dhaka. Tel : 88-02-503502, 500905 Fax : 88-02-813483	**06. M/s Bay Tanneries Limited** 21, Hazaribagh, Dhaka. Tel : 88-02-811445, 811466 Fax : 88-02-813581
07. M/s Bikrampur Tannery Limited 180/2, Hazaribagh, Dhaka. Tel : 88-02-502950	**08. M/s Bengal Peli Export Company** Hazaribagh, Dhaka. Tel : 88-02-9122452, 500197 Fax : 88-02-813213
09. M/s Brother Chemical Ltd. 9/1, Gaujmahal, Hazaribagh, Dhaka. Tel : 88-02-9551725, 501622 Fax : 88-02-9561895	**10. M/s Begal Leather Com. Ltd.** 147, Hazaribagh, Dhaka. Tel : 88-02-9660284, 864077
11. M/s Crescent Tannery Limited 143. Hazaribagh. Dhaka.	**12. M/s Dhaka Hide & Skins Ltd.** 147. Hazaribagh. Dhaka.

Tel : 8-02-504467, 9663659 Fax : 88-02-9120063	Tel : 88-02-861263, 9669849 Fax : 88-02-863515
13. M/s Dhaka Tanneries Limited 124, Hazaribagh, Dhaka. Tel : 88-02-865179, 863563	**14. M/s F.K. Leather Complex Ltd.** 95/3A, Hazaribagh, Dhaka. Tel : 88-02-502411, 506921 Fax : 88-02-868368
15. M/s Green Arrow Tannery 135, Hazaribagh, Dhaka. Tel : 88-02-503650, 864182 Fax : 88-02-864182	**16. M/s. H&H Leather Industries Ltd.** House # 69, Road # 8/A Dhanmondi R/A, Dhaka. Tel : 88-02-9113776, 9111209 Fax : 88-02-813348
17. M/s. Helal Tannery 74, Hazaribagh, Dhaka. Tel : 88-02-866305 88-02-9665981	**18. M/s. H.B. Tannery Ltd.** House # 69, Road # 8/A Dhanmondi R/A, Dhaka. Tel : 88-02-811526, 9111209 Fax : 88-02-813348
19. M/s. International Tannery Hazaribagh, Dhaka. Tel : 88-02-504401	**20. M/s. Haroon Leather Ltd.** 18, Kemal Ataturk Avenue Banani C/A (6th Floor) Dhaka-1213 Tel : 88-02-884976, 881024 Fax : 88-02-886114

MANUFACTURERS & EXPORTERS OF LEATHER GOODS, FOOTWEAR, LEATHER GARMENTS ETC.

01. M/s Apex Footwear Limited Dhaka Chamber Building 65-66, Motijheel C/A (2nd Floor) Dhaka Tel : 88-02-9560236, 9566181-3 Fax : 88-02-9562389	**02. M/s Apex Leathercraft Limited** Dhaka Chamber Building 65-66, Motijheel C/A (2nd Floor) Dhaka. Tel : 88-02-9560236, 9551117 Fax : 88-02-886414
03. M/S Alamin Brenton Leather goods Limited 70, Dilkusha C/A, Dhaka Tel : 88-02-9566025-6, 9564507 Fax : 88-02-9564512	**04. M/s Bata Shoe Co. Bangladesh Ltd.** Tongi I/A, Ghagipur, Dhaka Tel : 88-02-9800501-5, 9800513 Fax : 88-02-9800511
05. M/s Comfort Footwear Ltd. 86, Laboratory Road Dhaka-1205 Tel : 88-02-862415, 500516 Fax : 88-02-862415	**06. M/s Crystal Corporation Ltd.** Shilpo Plot 9, Block-C Tajmahal Road, Mohammadpur Dhaka Tel : 88-02-325449 Fax : 88-02-815548
07. M/s Crown Leather Products Ltd. 179, East Kafrul, Dhaka Tel : 88-02-9880799, 837259	**08. M/s Continental Footwear Ind. Ltd** 240, New Elephant Road, Dhaka Tel : 88-02-866239, 862408

Fax : 88-02-884170	Fax : 88-02-863695
09. M/s Dhaka Footwear Ltd. 147, Hazarihagh, Dhaka. Tel : 88-02-866239, 861263 Fax : 88-02-863515	**10. M/s Desma Shoe Industries Ltd.** 10, Kazi Nazrul Islam Avenue (2nd Floor) Karwan Bazar, Dhaka Tel : 88-02-814053, 810782-3 Fax : 88-02-814536
11. M/s Dhaka Leather Crafts 147, Hazarihagh, Dhaka. Tel : 88-02-9664705-07	**12. M/s H.N. Shoe Limited** House # 69, Road # 8/A Dhanmondi R/A, Dhaka Tel : 88-02-9111209
13. M/s. Inter Fashion Leather & Footwear Ind. Ltd. Dhaka Chamber Building 3rd Floor, Room 410 65-66, Motijheel C/A, Dhaka Tel : 88-02-9560591, 9567986 Fax : 88-02-9560866	**14. M/s Jennys Shoes Ltd.** 53, DIT Ext. Road Naya Paltan, Dhaka Tel : 88-02-886350, 884885 Fax : 88-02-883372
15. M/s manzur Industries Ltd. Dhaka Chamber Building 65-66, Motijheel C/A, Dhaka Fac. 127, Hazarihagh, Dhaka. Tel : 88-02-9551117, 9566182-3 Fax : 88-02-9562389	**16. M/s Riverside Leather & Footwear Ind. (Pvt.) Ltd.** 2/1 R.K Mission Road, Dhaka Tel : 88-02-9563162-5, 9560147-9 Fax : 88-02-9562405
17. M/s Spectra Leather Goods Ltd. Namazi Chamber (1st Floor) 16, Motijheel C/A, Dhaka Tel : 88-02-9565301, 9564543 Fax : 88-02-9551017	**18. M/s Uttama Leather Products Ltd.** 252, Elephant Road, Dhaka Tel : 88-02-863160 Fax : 88-02-866891

TOYS AND LUGGAGE

Bangladesh,since its emergence as a sovereign democratic country, has placed utmost priority on the development of industries, Among the new exportable items, toys and luggage have tremendous potential. These items have a define edge over others, since their production involves little capital and low technology with the added advantage of locally available cheap labour.

The fact that Bangladesh enjoys quota free status and preferential tariff treatment under the under the GSP has given a marked fillip to their growth and development. Developed countries like the USA, Australia and the EU find the purchase of toys and luggage from Bangladesh extremely attractive, since they can buy unlimited quantities duty-free.

All over the world, people now -a-days travel in vast number, either for business or for pleasure. Today's discerming travellers' foremost priority is the perfect choice of smart, good-looking luggage. Fierce competition, of course, has brought in infinite choices and variety. Today's child is exposed to a wide array of toys. Bangladesh is now in a position to cater to the needs of both these types of products. As a yoyng nation, the country is constantly looking towards the future and the Government's policy has been one of inducement for promotionof various industries.

As a result, a sizeable number of enterpreneurs have set up industries, producing a wonderful range of toys and electronically operated toys like trains, aeroplanes, cars and numberous other items to attract children of all ages. There is also a vast array of Luggage and travel kits, the materials of wich range from leather to synthetic like rexine.

EXPORTERS OF TOYS AND LUGGAGES

1. M/s. Ananta Toys
Ananta Plaza
136, Elephant Road, Dhaka, Bangladesh
Tel: 505668, 507169 Fax:880-2-865738

2. M/s. Best Toys Limited
28/A/2/A, Toyenbee Circular Road,
Motijheel C/A, Dhaka, Bangladesh
Tel:232840, 230573 Fax:880-2-868087

3. M/s. Eastern Toys Ltd.
Bidisha Bhaban(3rd Floor) Plot No. 2,
Gulshan North Circle, Dhaka, Bangladesh
Tel: 881977

. M/s. Friends Toy Co. Ltd.
7, HatKhola, Shahid Nazrul Islam Road
Dhaka, Bangladesh Fax: 880-2-813466

5. M/s. Lion Toys Limited
Lion Shopping Complex, 73
New Airport Road, Dhaka, Bangladesh
Tel: 324356, 816940, 249727
Fax: 880-2-816940
Tlx: 632352 ANIE BJ

6. M/s. Master Products Ltd.
3/B, Darus Salam Road
Mirpur-1, Dhaka, Bangladesh
Tel: 801438
Fax: 880-2-805156

5. M/s. Lion Toys Limited
Lion Shopping Complex, 73
New Airport Road, Dhaka, Bangladesh
Tel: 324356, 816940, 249727
Fax: 880-2-816940
Tlx: 632352 ANIE BJ

6. M/s. Master Products Ltd.
3/B, Darus Salam Road
Mirpur-1, Dhaka, Bangladesh
Tel: 801438
Fax: 880-2-805156

7. M/s. Nima Corporation Ltd.
146/1, Road No. 2A
Dhanmondi R/A, Dhaka, Bangladesh
Tel: 508737, 501595

8. M/s. Quality Toys Limited.
19, West Malibagh, Dhaka, Bangladesh
Tel: 834307, 831258(Res)
Fax: 880-2-835927
Tlx: 632277 RUPA BJ

9. M/s. Smanns Industry
3/3C, North South Road
Purana Paltan, Dhaka, Bangladesh
Tel: 861695, 802985 Fax: 880-2-863379, 863170

10. M/s. Sunjari Toys (Pvt.) Ltd.
Block-F, Road-8, House-61, Banani, Dhaka, Bangladesh
Tel: 610462
Fax: 880-2-832967 Tlx: 632381 ACE BJ

IMPLEMENTATION OF PRIVATIZATION PROGRAM

Privatization in Bangladesh has gone through various phases since its Independence. Just after the war of Independence in 16 December 1971, the Government had to step in to fill the vacuum in the economy as the then-owners, abandoned their properties and left the country. In addition, the nationalization policy of March, 1972 of major industries like Jute, Textile, Chemical and other basic industries, DFIs, Banks and Insurance etc. brought into fold nearly 90% of such enterprises under Government control. However these public sector enterprises right from inception could not run profitably and efficiently and many of them ran into severe financial difficulties and serious management problems. As stated earlier, by 1975, the Government began to reverse its policy of nationalization due to the heavy burdens created by the public sector enterprises on the national exchequer.

During the period 1976-1992 about 500 SOEs had been sold or returned to their former owners. Since the creation of Privatization Board as the special agency in March, 1993 by the Government to implement the programme of divestiture of SOEs, till to- date 33 SOEs got the final approval for sale from the GOB. It is worth mentioning that 17 (seventeen) SOEs have so far been handed over to the new buyers since March, 1993. LOI (Letter of Intent) have been issued for 9 (nine) SOEs to be handed over to the new buyers during the same period. Moreover, decission to off-load the shares of 9 (nine) public limited companies have been taken.

SECTORS FOR PRIVATIZATION

Jute Sector	**Textile Sector**	**Disposal of Govt. Shares**
Steel & Engg. & Miscellaneous Sector	**Sugar & Food Sector**	**Chemical Sector**
Power Sector	**Natural Gas & Oil Exploration**	**Tele Communication**
Transport Sector	**Port & Container Handling**	**Aviation & Tourism**
Banking & Insurance		

Power Sector : In view of the gradual widening of demand-supply gap, government has recently opened up investment in power generation, transmission and distribution to the private sector. Significant private foreign investment is envisaged for power generation. It may be mentioned here that power Development Board (PDB) has signed initial agreements for setting up Barge-Mounted Power Plants with the following international companies recently:

1) Smith Co-generation International - 100 MW	2) New England Power Company - 100 MW
3)Wartsila Power Development Ltd. - 100 MW	4)Westmont Offshore - 100 MW

Natural Gas and Oil Exploration : National Petroleum Policy which came into force from July 1993 has already attracted foreign investment in oil and gas exploration and development. Five international oil companies have signed production sharing contracts for exploration and development of hydrocarbon. The five companies are :

1) Occidental Exploration of Bangladesh Ltd.	2) Occidental of Bangladesh

3)Cairn Energy PLC and Holland Sea Search Bangladesh	4)Rexwood Oakland
5) United Merridian International Corporation (UMIC)	

Tele Communication : Telecom services used to be provided exclusively by Bangladesh. Telephone and Telegraph Board (BTTB)-a government functionary. The recent revolution in information technology has opened up a new area for private investment in the telecom sector. In the meantime, the following two private companies are operating in rural telecom sector-

1) Bangladesh Rural Tele Communication Authority 2) Sheba

For Cellular/Mobile telephone, the following private companies have been allowed to operate:

1)Pacific Bangladesh Telephone Ltd.	2)Grameen Telephone
3) Sheba	4) Telecom Malaysia International Ltd.

Transport Sector : Recent studies on sectoral reform had identified suitable privatization prospects in both the Road & Highways and in Inland Water Transport. Contracting out the existing operations and maintenance functions of these organizations is an immediate promising possibility. Besides private shipping liners and vessel services are in full operation in the country, having no restrictions whatsoever.

Port & Container Handling : There are quite bright prospects of private sector participation in improving port services in Mongla and Chittagong and in handling container services in the ports and other areas. Reforms are in the initial stages and may take sometime before such implementation take place.

Aviation & Tourism : Serious reforms have taken place in the civil aviation sectorby allowing operation of private sector airlines in the domestic services. Tourism sector is fully open for the private sector to operate.

Banking & Insurance : At the moment financial sector reform programmes are underway. Private banks and insurance companies with few exceptions are functioning creditably. Uttara, Pubali and Rupali Banks which were formally owned by the GOB were privatized. Shadaran Bima Corporation's (General Insurance) 49% shares are contemplated to be off loaded in the local stock markets soon.

LIST OF COMPANIES TO BE PRIVATIZED

JUTE SECTOR-21

(1) Rajshahi Jute Mills Ltd, Shyampur, Rajshahi;	(2) Jessore Jute Industries Ltd, Jessore;
(3) Aleem Jute Mills Ltd, Khulna;	(4) Latif Bawany Jute Mills Ltd, Dhaka;
(5) Star Jute Mills Ltd, Chandani Mahal, Khulna;	(6) R.R. Jute Mills Ltd, Chittagong;
(7) Eastern Jute Mills Ltd, Khulna;	(8) Gul Ahmed Jute Mills Ltd, Chittagong;
(9) Hafiz Jute Mills Ltd, Chittagong;	(10) Karnafuli Jute Mills Ltd, Chittagong;

(11) Nishat Jute Mills Ltd, Tongi, Gazipur;	(12) Daulatpur Jute Mills Ltd, Khulna;
(13) Crescent Jute Mills Ltd, Khulna;	(14) M.M. Jute Mills Ltd, Chittagong;
(15) Amin Jute Mills Ltd, Shola Shahar, Chittagong;	(16) Amin Old Field, Shola Shahar, Chittagong;
(17) Peoples Jute Mills Ltd, Khalishpur, Khulna;	(18) Quami Jute Mills Ltd, Sirajganj;
(19) UMC Jute Mills Ltd, Narsingdi;	(20) Plutinum Jute Mills Ltd, Khulna;
(21) Carpetting Jute Mills Ltd, Noapara, Jessore;	

TEXTILE SECTOR

(22) Tangail Cotton Mills Ltd, Gorai, Tangail;	(23) Kariline Silk Mills Ltd, Foujderhat, Chittagong;
(24) Engineering Industries Ltd, Tongi, Gazipur;	(25) Ahmed Bawany Textile Mills Ltd, Demra, Dhaka;
(26) Chittaranjan Cotton Mills Ltd, Godnayl, Narayanganj;	(27) Luxminarayan Cotton Mills Ltd, Godnayl, Narayanganj;
(28) RR Textile Mills Ltd, Chittagong;	(29) Amin Textile Mills Ltd, Shola Shahar, Chittagong;
(30) Darwani Textile Mills Ltd, Darwani, Nilphamari;	(31) Olympia Textile Mills, Tongi, Gazipur;
(32) Zeenath Textile Mills Ltd, Tongi, Gazipur;	(33) Monno Textile Mills, Tongi, Gazipur;
(34) Fine Cotton Mills, Tongi, Gazipuir;	(35) Satrang Textile Mills, Tongi, Gazipur;
(36) Kokil Textile Mills, Brammanbaria;	(37) Meghna Textile, Tongi, Gazipur;
(38) National Cotton Mills, Foujderhat, Chittagong;	(39) Kurigram Textile Mills, Kurigram;
(40) Magura Textile Mills, Magura;	

STEEL & ENGG. & MISCELLANEOUS SECTOR-21

(41) Chittagong Board Mills, Chittagong;	(42) Eastern Wood Works, Dhaka;
(43) Fidco Furniture Complex, Chittagong;	(44) Khulna Cabinet Manufacturing Unit, Khulna;
(45) Common Finishing Facilities, Dhaka;	(46) Amin Agencies, Chittagong;
(47) Bangladesh Machine Tools Factory, Dhaka;	(48) General Electric Manufacturing Co., Chittagong;
(49) Chittagong Dry Dock, Chittagong;	(50) Bangladesh Diesel Plant, Dhaka;
(51) Bangladesh Blade Factory, Dhaka;	(52) Eastern Tubes, Dhaka;

(53) Khulna Industrial and Trading Company, Khulna;	(54) Prince Iron, Dhaka;
(55) Gazi Wire Ltd, Chittagong;	(56) Chittagong Steel Mill, Chittagong;
(57) Dockyard & Engg Works Ltd, Narayanganj;	(58) Khulna Shipyard, Khulna;
(59) Pragoti Industries, Chittagong;	(60) Bangladesh Oil Mills, Khulna;
(61) Meher Industries, Dhaka;	

IV. SUGAR & FOOD SECTOR-10

(62) Panchagarh Sugar Mill, Panchagarh;	(63) Mobarakgonj Sugar Mills, Kaligonj, Jhenaidah;
(64) Faridpur Sugar Mills, Faridpur;	(65) Thakurgaon Sugar Mills, Thakurgaon;
(66) Rangpur Sugar Mills, Rangpur;	(67) Kushtia Sugar Mills, Kushtia;
(68) Setabgonj Sugar Mills, Dinajpur;	(69) Rajshahi Sugar Mills, Rajshahi;
(70) Carew & Co. Ltd., Chuadanga;	(71) Jaipurhat Sugar Mill, Jaipurhat;

V. CHEMICAL SECTOR-8

(72) Khulna Hardboard Mills, Khulna;	(73) Khulna Newsprint Mills, Khulna;
(74) Chittagong Chemical Complex, Chittagong;	(75) Chattak Cement Factory, Sunamganj;
(76) Karnaphuli Rayon & Chemicals Ltd, Rangamati;	(77) North Bengal Paper Mills, Rajshahi;
(78) Sylhet Pulp & Paper Mills, Sylhet;	(79) Bangladesh Insulator & Sanitaryware factory, Dhaka;

METHODS OF PRIVATIZATION

Sale by international tender	Local and foreign buyers may participate in all such tenders. Association of workers, employees and officers of the tendered enterprise may also offer bid for purchase of the enterprise.
Sale by public offer of shares	Government-Owned shares in different companies and shares of the SOEs converted into public limited companies may be sold to the general public either directly or through the stock exchange.

OPPORTUNITIES FOR THE FOREIGNERS

The Industrial Policy 1991 and its recently announced amendments, the associated reforms in trade policies and fiscal and taxation policies now augur well for investment by the foreign nationals and companies and also non-resident Bangladeshi nationals. No approval is required for any investment by the foreign investors in any sectors of the economy except for a few areas (strategic ones) which are still reserved for public investment only. The foreign investment (promotion & protection) Act, 1980 guarantees protection to foreign investment against

nationalization and also guarantees equitable treatment. Bangladesh is a signatory of Multilateral Investment Guarantee Agency (MIGA) of the World Bank group, Overseas Private Investment Corporation (OPIC) and International Center for Settlement of Investment Disputes (ISCID) and therefore, also gurantees investors protection against political and other risks. Following facilities are also available for foreigners and non-resident Bangladeshis:
Foreign investment with 100% foreign equity holding; Repatriation of all post tax dividends, capital, and capital gains is permitted fully; Employment of expatriate technical and professional personnel is allowed; Remittances of 50% of the salary of foreign nationals employed in local companies is allowed; Remittances of savings from earnings, retirement benifits, personal assets of individuals employed in recognized industries on retirement/termination of service is allowed; Foreigners employed in recognized industries are exempted from income taxes for first 3 years; Multiple entry visas are allowed; Relief is given from double taxation; Re-investment of reportable dividends is treated as new investment; Foreign investors have unhindered access to local banks and financial institutions for obtaining long term loans and working capital loans; Enterprises with foreign ownership may remain private limited companies. In the case of public limited companies, the public offering of shares is optional; Foreigners are allowed to invest in shares and securities through stock exchange etc.

Tender Procedures

Before inviting tender for sale of the identified SOEs, valuations of the assets and liabilities are made by Chartered Accountant (C.A) firms or by the consultants engaged by the Board. Valuation reports are examined and reviewed by the Privatization Board and a re-valuation can be made by another C.A. firm/valuer firm if considered necessary. Tenders are invited after the finalization of the valuation. Valuation and other relevent documents are made available to the prospective bidders before submission of the bids.

In the case of sale of enterprise, the prospective buyers will submit quotation according to the terms and conditions of the tender. Bidder shall have to accept all long-term loans against the fixed assets.

Value of stocks and stores will be adjusted with the short-term bank liabilities and the buyer will accept the bank loan equivalent to the value of stocks and stores. If the value of stocks and stores exceeds the bank loans, the excess will be payable to the Government by the buyer either in cash or within one year along with a simple interest of 10% per annum. Bank loans in excess of the value of stocks and stores will be taken over by the Government.
Value of current assets such as sundry debtors, advances etc. will be payable to the Government by the buyer either in cash or within one year along with a simple interest rate of 10 % per annum.

In the cases mentioned above the buyer will have to provide irrevocable bank guarantee without recourse in case the payment is not made in cash.

Short-term liabilities such as, sundry creditors, claims of employees and workers and income taxes etc. accrued before the transfer of the enterprise will be taken over by the Government.

As regards employees of the tendered enterprise (if it is a running one) the Corporation and the buyer will jointly determine the number of redundant employees in the light of technical and operational feasibility. Retained employees, however, will be offered new terms and conditions by the buyer.

Buyers will be liable to pursue all pending court cases.

Land under the enterprise will be used normally for establishment and expansion of industries. A substantial amount of unutilized but developed land can, however, be used for other productive activities.

In case of sale of Government-owned shares in different companies the prospective buyers will submit quotations for the total number of shares offered for sale. The company whose shares are offered for sale, will repay all quasi-equity loans of the Government and dues of the Corporations within a period of 10 years in 6-monthly installment carrying a simple interest of 10% per annum and will submit an irrevocable bank guarantee without recourse from a scheduled bank. In addition to the above, the buyer will also give a personal irrevocable bank guarantee without recourse for the above quasi-equity loans and dues or will keep the share certificates of all the shares bought by him, under the custody of the Government.

While implementing the policy of privatization, efforts will be made to make the ownership of the industrial enterprises as broad-based, as possible.

PAYMENT PROCEDURE

In case of sale of Government-owned shares in limited companies, the bidder will have to pay 20% of the bid amount as earnest money. The successful bidder will have to pay the balance 80% of the bid amount within 60 days of issue of Letter of Intent.

In case of sale of enterprise, the bidder will have to pay 2.5% of the bid amount as earnest money. The successful bidder will have to the pay in cash an additional amount of 22.5% of the bid amount as down payment within 30 days of the issue of Letter of Intent (i,e, 2.5%+22.5%=25%). The bidder will have to pay the balance 75% of the bid amount within 5 years at 6-monthly installment along with a compound interest rate of 9% annually and will also give irrevocable bank guarantee without recourse for the installment payment. A rebate of 15% will be allowed if the full payment is made within 30 days of issue of Letter of Intent.
In case of sale of enterprise to association of workers,employees and officers, all claims and liabilities with the enterprise may be adjusted with the bid amount.

The buyer will take over all long term loans and will have to negotiate repayment agreement with the lender institutions before transfer of the enterprise.

INSTITUTIONAL FRAME WORK

The Privatization Board which came into being in March, 1993 is entrusted with the overall responsibility of privatizing State-Owned Enterprises identified for privatization, whether small, large, profitable or non-profitable. The Board is now headed by a chairman with the rank and status of a State Minister to the Government. The Board consists of two full-time members and twelve part time members including six Members of Parliament. The Board has been placed under the administrative jurisdiction of the Cabinet Division which is headed by the Hon'ble Prime Minister. The Board reports directly to the Cabinet Committee on Economic Affairs which is chaired by the Hon'ble Minister of Finance. Ministries having SOEs under their control have either set up or in the process of setting up Privatization Cells for assisting the Privatization Board in identifying, preparing, processing, implementing and monitoring SOEs for privatization.

Project Profile

THE COMPANY	CHITTAGONG DRY DOCK LTD.
Company Description	Chittagong Dry Dock Ltd. was set-up 1985 at Potenga Chittagong. Total land area 43.27 acres. It has facilities of Dry Docking and repair of seagoing vessels upto 16,500 DWT, on board repair facilities for trawlers / coastal vessels etc.

	also for manufacturing of portable steel bridges, trucks, sluice gate, steel tower and other various heavy steel structures. It is provided with Plate Bending Roller, Welding machine, Lathe, Drilling M/S, Power Saw, Milling, Grinding, Press, Cutting, Soldering, Compressor, Fork lift and various Testing & Checking Equipments.
History of the Company	The project work has started in 1967. In 1971 the project work stopped due to liberation war. After independence the project work restarted after revival and revalidation of the agreement with Yougoslave Govt. and their firms M/S. PIM and Brodimeks. In 1978 a new dock was integrated for construction of seagoing vessels in place of a slipway with a plan to construct three vessels of 16,500 DWT in two years and carry out docking of 30 vessels and repair 50 vessels a year. Later on, due to financial constraint the project dock was not constructed. Though finnaly implemented in 1985 the plant actually started its operation in 1981 after the commissioning of the gracing dock.
Operational Structure	Chittagong Dry Dock Ltd. is a job type industry. Types of job done are ship repair with Dry Docking, Afloat repair, Heavy structure works & Misc. works. As per requirement ships are dry docked & necessary repair & maintenance works are done and after inspection jobs are decliered. During repair workshop facilities are used. Heavy steel fabrication & Misc. works are done in shops.

Human Resources	Officers	Technical	Non-Technical	Staff	Workers	Total
	-	45	29	169	209	452

Organisation	The limited company with authorised capital of TK. 100.00 core and paid up capital of TK. 71.05 core divided 7,104,520 no. of ordinary shares of TK. 100.00 each. The Company is run by a Board Of Directors appointed by Govt. under Company Act. Operation of Company is controlled by a Managing Director appointed by BSEC. (Bangladesh Steel & Engineering Corporation). He is also a Director of the Company Board.
Sector	Industrial Sector of the Country : Shipbuilding & Engineering Sector.
Regulatory Environment	Regulated under the industrial policy of the Govt. externally by fiscal and monitory policy of the Govt. and budgetary control. The company internally regulated by the Memorandum and Articles of Association of the Company.
Current Status	Running
Shareholders	Govt of Peoples Republic of Bangladesh. Percentage(%) 100 %

Income Statement (1996-97)

Income Statement (1996-97)	Taka in Core
Particulars	-
Sales (net of Taxes)	12.53
Less : Cost of Sales	10.75
Gross Profit :	1.78
Less Admn. & Selling Expenses	3.04
Financial Expenses	3.68
Net Profit/(Loss)	(4.94)

Balance Sheet (1996-97)

Particulars	Taka in Core
Assets	-

	Current Assets	20.00
	Fixed Assets	216.04
	Total Assets	236.04
	Liabilities of Capital	-
	Current Liabilities	5.47
	Long Term Liabilities	205.83
	Capital	24.74
	Total Liabilities & Capital	236.04
Key Balance Sheet Features	Current Ratio	3.66:1
	Quick Ratio	2.35:1
	Gross Profit to Sales	11.45%
Prequalification Conditions for Potential Bidders		Nill
Key Contacts	Privatization Board, 10 Dilkusha C/A, Jibon Bima Tower (14th Floor), Dhaka-1000, Bangladesh. Tel: 88-02-9551986 Fax: 88-02-9556433	

PROCESSING OF TENDER BIDS

Processing of Tender Bids	All tender bids received are examined by the Privatization Board as expeditiously as possible and its findings and recommendations are placed before the Cabinet Committee on Economic Affairs for decision.

INVESTMENT AND BUSINESS ENVIRONMENT

INDUSTRIAL POLICY REFORMS

- Liberalized Industrial Policy
- Export-oriented, private sector-led growth strategy
- No limitation pertaining to equity participation i.e. up to 100 per cent foreign private investment allowed
- Except five reserve sectors, all industries are open for private investment> Industries earmarked for public sector investment are included in the reserve sector namely: (I) arms, ammunition and other defence equipment and machinery (ii) production of nuclear energy (iii) forest plantation and mechanized extraction within the bounds of reserved forests (iv) security printing (currency notes) and minting, and (v) railways and air transportation (except certain domestic routes and air cargo)
- No permission of the Government required to set up new industries
- For obtaining institutional facilities like procurement of land, electricity, gas and sewerage connection, importation of capital machinery and raw materials, tax rebate, duty drawback facilities etc., industries need only to be registered with the Board of Investment (BOI) in a simple prescribed from

REFORM AND LIBERALIZATION OF POLICIES

- Creation of Law Reform Commission to update existing Laws

- Setting up Administrative Reform Commission to modernise the administrative system and to remove bureaucratic roadblocks
- Enactment of law allowing private sector to establish export processing zones
- Approval of policy parameters and incentives for private power generation
- Identification of road blocks on the way of implementation of projects and measures to remove them
- Updating of Companies Act and relevant laws

INVESTMENT GUARANTEE

Foreign Private Investment (Promotion and Protection) Act, 1980 ensures legal protection to foreign investment in Bangladesh against nationalization and expropriation. It also guarantees repatriation of capital and dividend and equitable treatment with local investors. Adequate protection is available for intellectual property rights, such as patents, designs and trade marks and copyrights. Bilateral Investment Guarantee Agreements have been signed with a number of countries. Bangladesh is signatory to MIGA, OPIC of USA, ICSID and member of WIPO Permanent Committee on development co-operation related to industrial property.

FACILITIES INCENTIVES

- tax holiday from 5-10 years depending on location of industries
- 15 year's tax holiday for private power generation companies
- facilities for repatriation of invested capital, profit and dividend
- exemption of tax on interest on foreign loan
- tax exemption on royalties, technical know-how and technical assistance fees
- avoidance of double taxation on the basis of bilateral agreement
- six months multiple entry visa for the investors
- TAKA, the nation's currency, is convertible for international payments in the current account
- Re-investment of repatriable dividend treated as new investment
- Working capital loan, as well as term loan, from local commercial banks allowed to the industries set up with foreign capital
- Citizenship by investing a minimum of US$ 5,00,000 or by transferring US$ 10,00,000 to any recognized financial institution (non repatriable)

INCORPORATION OF A COMPANY IN BANGLADESH

In Bangladesh, business may be carried on by a locally incorporated company and a foreign company incorporated outside but registered in Bangladesh.

POTENTIAL AREAS FOR INVESTMENT

Investments in areas of manufacturing and services are welcome. Investors are free to choose fields of investment. However, from the point of view of comparative advantage, the following are potential areas for investment.

Textile: export market of US$ 2 billion from the garments sector and a large domestic market.

Infrastructure: energy, telecommunication, oil and gas, ports, highways and bridges.

Agrobased Industry: dairy of poultry, processing of fruits and vegetables, shrimp, fish culture and processing, shrimp feed plants etc.

Labour-intensive Industries: electronics, data processing and software development, electrical goods and accessories, light engineering goods, toys, jewellery and others.

COMMUNICATION FACILITIES

Adequate sea, rail, road and air services to facilitate both domestic and international transportation.

TELECOMMUNICATIONS

Internet, telex, fax, international direct dialing services and e-mail facilities.

MAJOR EXPORTABLE ITEMS

Readymade garments, leather and leather products, frozen shrimp/prawn and fish, raw jute and jute goods, tea, newsprint, urea fertilizer, furnace oil, naphtha etc.

TOURISM

Bangladesh has a rich tradition, history and architecture. Incredible greenery, mighty rivers and attractive rever cruises, sunny beaches, colourful tribal life and attractive cultural functions offer great tourist attractions.

FACILITIES TO NON-RESIDENT BANGLADESHI

- Non-resident Bangladeshi investors enjoy facilities similar to foreign investors
- Allowed to buy newly issued shares/debentures of Bangladeshi companies
- Quota of 10% reserved for non-resident Bangladeshis in primary shares (IPO)
- Foreign currency deposits in the Non-resident Foreign Currency Deposit (NFCD) account

BANKING AND FINANCING

Bangladesh offers adequate banking facilities to the investors for establishment of industries and to facilitate their business transactions. 14 private and 13 foreign commercial banks, 10 financing institutions and 3 nationalized commercial banks having network of correspondents and branches operating all over the country and abroad.

EXPORT PROCESSING ZONES

Export Processing Zones in the port city Chittagong and capital city Dhaka with necessary fiscal and infrastructure facilities for export oriented enterprise. Another Export Processing Zone, near the capital city (at Gazipur) is under implementation.

COURTESY SERVICE

Board of Investment extends courtesy service such as airport reception, hotel and transport booking and fixing appointment with the Government and Chamber official is accordance with the needs of foreign entrepreneurs visiting Bangladesh. For availing courtesy service, entrepreneurs need to contract BOI in advance.

RELEVANT ORGANIZATIONS

BOARD OF INVESTMENT

Prime Minister's Office
91 Motijheel C.A. Dhaka

Bangladesh
Tel : 880-2-9563573, 9563570, 9567541, 9563782
Fax : 880-2-9562312

E-mail : ecboi@bdmail.net

BANGLADESH EXPORT PROCESSING ZONES AUTHORITY (BEPZA)

Tel: 880-2-832553, 835325
Fax : 880-2-834967

EXPORT PROMOTION BUREAU (EPB)

Chamber Building
122-124 Motijheel C.A.
Dhaka, Bangladesh
Tel : 880-2-9562245-49
Fax : 880-2-9568000
E-Mail : epb.tic@pradeshta.net

BANGLADESH PARJATAN CORPORATION

233 Airport Road, Tejgaon, Dhaka, Bangladesh
(National Tourism Organization)
Tel : 880-2-817855-59
Fax : 880-2-817235

THE FEDERATION OF BANGLADESH CHAMBER OF COMMERCE AND INDUSTRY

60 Motijheel C/A, Dhaka, Bangladesh
Tel : 880-2-9560102-3, 9560588-9
Fax : 880-2-9556503, 863213

FOREIGN INVESTORS CHAMBER OF COMMERCE AND INDUSTRY

35/1 Purana Paltan Lane (4th Floor)
Mahbub Castle (4th Fl), Inner Circular Road
GPO Box No. 4086, Dhaka
Tel : 880-2-839448
Fax : 880-2-839449

PRACTICAL INFORMATION FOR CONDUCTING BUSINESS IN BANGLADESH[1]

INVESTMENT CLIMATE

OPENNESS TO, AND RESTRICTIONS UPON, FOREIGN INVESTMENT

With six percent annual growth sustained over the past two decades, a large workforce, and vibrant private sector, Bangladesh, the world's seventh largest country by population, offers opportunities for investment, especially in the energy, power, pharmaceutical, information technology, telecommunications, and infrastructure sectors as well as in labor-intensive industries such as readymade garments, household textiles, and leather processing. There is also significant demand in major cities for U.S. consumer products and franchises. The Government of Bangladesh actively seeks foreign investment, particularly in energy, power, and infrastructure projects. It offers a range of investment incentives under its industrial policy and export-oriented growth strategy, with few formal distinctions between foreign and domestic private investors.

According to the 2013 World Investment Report, Bangladesh received $990 million in foreign direct investment (FDI) in FY13, down from $1.13 billion in the previous year. This is a nominal amount of investment compared to $38.9 billion in foreign investment that the entire South Asia region attracted, as India continues to dominate FDI inflows for the region. Bangladesh has made gradual progress in reducing some constraints on investment, but inadequate infrastructure, financial constraints, bureaucratic delays, and corruption continue to hinder foreign investment. The lack of effective alternative dispute resolution mechanisms and slow judicial processes impede the enforcement of contracts and the resolution of business disputes.

National elections in January 2014 were preceded by a year of unprecedented political violence and uncertainty, which adversely affected the business and investment climate. The political turbulence subsided after the election, and the return to stability has helped restore business confidence to some extent.

Energy and Infrastructure Development

The Government of Bangladesh has pursued ambitious plans for infrastructure development, particularly in the power sector, where it pledged to double generation capacity from 6,000 MW to 12,000 MW by 2015 and to 20,000 MW by 2021. In late-2013 the government announced it had an installed capacity of 10,000MW. In 2009, the government launched an initiative with modest funding for public private partnerships (PPP) and began to develop a legal and regulatory framework to implement this initiative. In 2010, due to critical power shortages and chronic delays in implementing power projects, the government amended procurement requirements to allow unsolicited bids and expedited the approval of power generation projects. It also aims to formulate a coal policy to encourage investment in developing coal resources and coal-based power projects. Administrative approval of the production plan of a foreign-owned, open-cast coal mine in northwest Bangladesh has remained pending since November 2005 due to local opposition and political pressure from civil society groups. The government has improved the efficiency of the main seaport in Chittagong and is constructing a four-lane highway to connect Chittagong with the capital city of Dhaka. Prolonged and contentious public procurement processes, however, continue to challenge government efforts to develop infrastructure projects. The landmark $3.1 billion donor financed Padma Multipurpose Bridge project, which would have

[1] US Departmetn of commerce materials

substantially improved interregional connectivity, was shelved by the government because of disputes with the World Bank on the way forward after the World Bank raised concerns about transparency in the procurement process. On January 23, 2014, the Prime Minister announced six fast-tracked large infrastructure projects to address transportation and energy bottlenecks, among them a new self-financed Padma Bridge project.

Legal Framework

Major laws affecting foreign investment include: the Foreign Private Investment (Promotion and Protection) Act of 1980; the Industrial Policy Act of 2005, the Bangladesh Export Processing Zones Authority Act of 1980; the Companies Act of 1994, and the Telecommunications Act of 2001. Legislation offers incentives for investors, including: 100 percent foreign ownership in most sectors, tax holidays and exemptions, reduced import duties on capital machinery and spare parts, and duty-free imports for 100 percent exporters of ready-made garments. The government extended a tax holiday scheme for start-up industries through June 30, 2015.

Beneficiary industries include agro-processing, steel production, jute industries, some textile units, and telecom infrastructure except for mobile phones. A tax rebate facility to non-resident Bangladeshi investors was also extended to induce investment from abroad. Import duties and supplemental taxes remain high and constitute an important source of government revenue. Customs bonded warehouses enable companies located in export processing zones (EPZs) to avoid duty payments on inputs for goods that will be exported. There are few performance requirements, and these do not generally

impede investment. Land registration has historically been prone to disputes over competing titles, and scarcity of land is a significant investment constraint.

While discrimination against foreign investors is not widespread, the government frequently promotes local industries and some discriminatory policies and regulations exist. For example, the government closely controls approvals for imported medicines that compete with domestically-manufactured pharmaceutical products and it has required majority local ownership of new shipping companies, albeit with exemptions for existing foreign-owned firms, following a prime ministerial directive.

Investment Promotion Agencies

The Board of Investment (BOI) and the Bangladesh Export Processing Zones Authority (BEPZA) are the primary investment promotion agencies in Bangladesh. Companies must register with the BOI to obtain benefits such as tax incentives or preferential duties for imported equipment. The BOI also administers the approval of some foreign loans and payments on behalf of the Bangladesh Bank. Though the BOI is frequently touted as a one-stop shop for all investors, authority for managing foreign investment remains fragmented. The BOI can register investors in industrial projects outside the EPZs and assist them with tax inquiries, land acquisition, utility hook-ups, and incorporation. The BEPZA performs the same functions for companies investing in the EPZs. Investors in infrastructure and natural resource sectors, including power, mineral resources and telecommunications must seek approval from the corresponding government ministries. Although the BOI is housed organizationally in the Prime Minister's Office, regulatory and administrative powers remain vested in the line ministries. Companies often complain that ministries require unnecessary licenses and permissions.

Currency Convertibility

Free repatriation of profits is allowed for registered companies and profits are almost fully convertible on the current account; however, companies report that the procedures for repatriation of foreign currency are lengthy and cumbersome. When rising fuel imports helped swing balance of payments from surplus to deficit in 2010-2011, scarcity of foreign exchange and currency depreciation temporarily increased convertibility risks. Since 2011, the balance of payments has swung back into surplus, foreign reserves reached an all-time high of over $20 billion, and convertibility risks have declined.

Privatization

The government privatized some state-owned enterprises (SOEs) during the past twenty years, but many SOEs retain an important role in the economy, particularly in the financial and energy sectors. The current government has taken steps to restructure several SOEs to improve their competitiveness. Biman Bangladesh Airline was converted into a public limited company that initiated a rebranding and fleet renewal program, including the purchase of 10 aircraft from Boeing, four of which were delivered by March, 2014. Three nationalized commercial banks (NCBs) -- Sonali, Janata and Agrani -- have been converted to public limited companies. Bangladesh allows private investment in power generation and natural gas exploration, but efforts to allow full foreign participation in petroleum marketing and gas distribution have stalled.

The telecommunications sector was liberalized during the last decade, leading to the development of a competitive cellular phone market. The government has been slow to allow greater competition for international connectivity and internet telephony. In 2007, the government revised the International Long Distance Telecommunication Services Policy (ILDTSP) to legalize voice over internet protocol (VoIP), but has not yet implemented this policy, and restrictions remain on international video conferencing and voice chat. IP Telephony Service has been licensed under IP Telephony Service Providers (IPTSP) but infrastructure constraints limit its use. Business process outsourcing companies (BPOs), particularly call centers, are limited by stringent policy that affects the cost of business. Although the present government has further liberalized licensing ILDTS Policy 2010, a VoIP gray market exists.

TABLE 1: The following chart summarizes several well-regarded indices and rankings.

Measure	Year	Rank or value	Website Address
TI Corruption Perceptions index	2013	(136 of 177)	http://cpi.transparency.org/cpi2013/results/
Heritage Foundation's Economic Freedom index	2014	(131 of 178)	http://www.heritage.org/index/ranking
World Bank's Doing Business Report "Ease of Doing Business"	2014	(130 of 189)	http//doingbusiness.org/rankings
Global Innovation Index	2013	(130 of 142)	http://www.globalinnovationindex.org/content.aspx?page=gii-full-report-2013#pdfopener
World Bank GNI per capita	2012	USD 840	http://data.worldbank.org/indicator/NY.GNP.PCAP.CD

CONVERSION AND TRANSFER POLICIES

Bangladesh Bank, the central bank of Bangladesh, does not fix the exchange rate against foreign currencies, but it regulates conversion. The Bangladesh taka is almost fully convertible for current account transactions, such as import trade and travel needs, but not for capital account transactions, such as investing, currency speculation, or e-commerce. The Foreign Investment Act guarantees the right of repatriation of invested capital, profits, capital gains, post-tax dividends, and approved royalties and fees for businesses. The central bank's exchange control regulations and the U.S.-Bangladesh Bilateral Investment Treaty (in force since 1989) provide similar investment transfer

guarantees. The BOI may need to approve repatriation of royalties and other fees. The Bangladesh taka depreciated more than 15 percent against the U.S. dollar in 2011, but strengthened at the end of 2012, and has remained relatively stable, supported by overseas remittances and foreign reserves reaching record highs.

EXPROPRIATION AND COMPENSATION

Since the Foreign Investment Act of 1980 banned nationalization or expropriation without adequate compensation, the Government of Bangladesh has not nationalized or expropriated property from foreign investors. In the years immediately following independence in 1971, widespread nationalization resulted in government ownership of over 90 percent of fixed assets in the modern manufacturing sector, including textile, jute and sugar industries as well as all banking and insurance interests, except those in foreign (but non-Pakistani) hands. The government has since taken steps to privatize many of these industries during the last twenty years and the private sector has developed into a main driver of the country's sustained economic growth of 5-6 percent per year during the past two decades.

DISPUTE SETTLEMENT

A fundamental impediment to investment in Bangladesh is a weak and slow legal system in which the enforceability of contracts is uncertain. The judicial system does not provide for interest to be charged in tort judgments, thus there is no penalty for delaying proceedings. In a significant milestone, the government in 2007 separated the country's judiciary from the executive, but the executive retains strong influence over the judiciary through control of judicial appointments. Other pillars of the justice system including the police, courts, and legal profession are also closely aligned with the executive branch. In lower courts, corruption is widely perceived as a serious problem. The High Court's previous reputation for impartiality has also been brought into question in recent years. Nonetheless, Bangladeshi law allows contracts to refer dispute settlement to third country forums for resolution. Bangladesh is a signatory to the International Convention for the Settlement of Disputes (ICSID) and it acceded (on May 6, 1992) to the United Nations Convention for the Recognition and Enforcement of Foreign Arbitral Awards. Bangladesh is also a party to the South Asia Association for Regional Cooperation (SAARC) Agreement for the Establishment of an Arbitration Council, signed November 13, 2005, which aims to establish a permanent alternative dispute resolution center in one of the SAARC member countries. A provision of the U.S.-Bangladesh Bilateral Investment Treaty permits submission of investment disputes to ICSID for third-party settlement.

The ability of the Bangladeshi judicial system to enforce its own awards is weak, and there is no reason to believe that enforcement of foreign judgments would be stronger. The Bangladesh Export Promotion Bureau is sometimes helpful in facilitating dispute settlement for export-related transactions. Major Bangladeshi trade and business associations can also help to resolve transaction disputes.

Many laws affecting investment in Bangladesh are old and outdated. Bankruptcy laws, which apply mainly to individual insolvency, are sometimes not used in business cases because of a web of falsified assets and uncollectible cross-indebtedness supporting

insolvent banks and companies. A Bankruptcy Act was enacted in 1997 but has been ineffective in addressing these issues. A new Companies Act is in process of enactment by the parliament. Some bankruptcy cases fall under the Money Loan Court Act, which has more stringent and timely procedures.

Dispute settlement is also hampered by shortcomings in accounting practices and in the registration of real property. With the exception of those conducted by a few internationally affiliated accounting firms, audits of balance sheets and profit and loss statements often follow clients' instructions and fail to conform to international standards. Documents affecting title to real property are often not registered, complicating transfer of ownership and collateral agreements.

PERFORMANCE REQUIREMENTS AND INCENTIVES

The government's industrial policies favor manufacturing and labor-intensive industries that use local inputs. A variety of subsidies and other incentives are available to different industrial ventures, primarily in export sectors and, to a certain extent, import substitution sectors. The Government also provides loans at concessionary rates through state banks and government-owned development banks for exports, cottage industries, and agriculture. These incentives are available to both domestic and foreign investors.

In order to simplify the tariff structure and generate more revenue through import duties, the government developed a four-tier duty structure with higher duties on finished products, but reduced duties on industrial inputs such as capital machinery, spare parts, basic raw materials, and intermediate raw materials.

The government also offers a variety of tax incentives to selected sectors of the economy, including:

-- A 50 percent rebate for taxable income generated from export earnings (according to section 44(1) and the paragraph 28 of 6th Schedule Part A of Income Tax Ordinance, 1984);

-- An income tax exemption on export earnings from handicrafts and cottage industries (according to S.R.O No. 339-L/86, dated the 13th August, 1986);

-- Tax holidays of five to seven years, depending on location, for new industrial enterprises in the textile, pharmaceuticals, plastic, ceramics, sanitary ware, iron, steel, fertilizer, insecticide, computer hardware, petrochemicals, pharmaceutical raw materials, agricultural equipment, and industrial machinery. (Note: This provision has been extended annually, with the current extension allowing business to begin claiming this incentive by June 2015);

-- Industries set up within EPZs are exempted from five to seven years depending on the location of the EPZ according to SRO No. 219 of 2012;

-- Accelerated depreciation for enterprises not eligible for a tax holiday is provided for in paragraph 7 of 3rd Schedule of Income Tax Ordinance, 1984;

-- Power projects are exempt from income taxes for up to 15 years according to the National Power Policy, S.R.O. 211-Law/Income Tax/2013 dated 1 July, 2013 amended by S.R.O. 354-Law/Income Tax/2013 dated 18 November, 2013 and S.R.O. 213-Law/Income Tax/2013 dated 1 July,2013.

RIGHT TO PRIVATE OWNERSHIP AND ESTABLISHMENT

Foreign and domestic private entities can establish and own, operate, and dispose of interests in most types of business enterprises. Four sectors, however, are reserved for government investment:

-- Arms and ammunition and other defense equipment and machinery;

-- Forest plantation and mechanized extraction within the bounds of reserved forests;

-- Production of nuclear energy;

-- Security printing.

PROTECTION OF PROPERTY RIGHTS

Although land, whether for purchase or lease, is often critical for investment and as security against loans, antiquated real property laws and poor record-keeping systems can complicate land and property transactions. Land registration records have been historically prone to competing claims. Instruments take effect from the date of execution, not the date of registration, so a bona fide purchaser can never be certain of title. Property owners can obtain mortgages, but parties avoid registering mortgages, liens, and encumbrances due to the high cost of stamp duties (i.e., transaction taxes based on property value) and other charges.

Bangladesh has slowly made progress bringing its legislative framework into compliance with the Agreement on Trade-Related Aspects of Intellectual Property Rights (TRIPS). The government enacted a Copyright Law in July 2000 (later amended in 2005) and a Trademarks Act in 2009, and it is preparing draft Patent and Design laws to modernize its current Patent and Design legislation dating from 1911. Once fully implemented, this legislation is intended to bring the country's intellectual property laws into full compliance with TRIPS requirements. Department of Patent, Designs and Trademarks (DPDT) drafted a new Patent Act, 2014 which has been prepared in compliance with the requirements of the TRIPS Agreement, and is under Ministry of Industries review. After Ministry of Industry review, it will be uploaded on DPDT's website for public comment.

The government has limited resources for intellectual property rights (IPR) protection. Enforcement actions against IPR violators are rare despite widespread availability of pirated goods, and industry estimates that 90 percent of business software is pirated. BSA, the Software Alliance, launched a Bangladesh office in early 2014 as a platform to improve IPR protection in Bangladesh. A number of American firms, including film studios, manufacturers of consumer goods, and software firms, have reported violations of their intellectual property rights. Bangladesh is a member of the World Intellectual Property Organization (WIPO); and acceded to the Paris Convention on Intellectual Property in 1991.

For additional information about treaty obligations and points of contact at local IP offices, please see WIPO's country profiles at http://www.wipo.int/directory/en/ .

Local attorneys list: http://dhaka.usembassy.gov/legal_resources.html

TRANSPARENCY OF REGULATORY SYSTEM

Starting from a position of extreme over-regulation, the government has gradually moved since 1989 to decrease regulatory obstruction of private business. Although some officials have shown genuine commitment to these reforms, in general, changes encountered broad-based resistance from many domestic groups in the economy, including influential members of the business community. The official chambers of commerce include manufacturers in protected industries and well-connected commission agents pursuing government contracts. Chamber members have called for a greater voice for the private sector in government decisions and for privatization, but at the same time many support protectionism and subsidies for their own industries.

Policy and regulations in Bangladesh are often not clear, consistent, or publicized. Generally, the civil service, businesses, professionals, trade unions, and political parties have vested interests in a system in which confidentiality is used as an excuse for lack of transparency and in which patron-client relationships are the norm. Registration and regulatory processes are often used as rent-seeking opportunities. Bangladesh has made incremental progress in using information technology to improve the transparency and efficiency of some government services and developing independent agencies to regulate the energy and telecommunication sectors.

In practice, government laws, regulations and their implementation often do not reduce distortions or impediments to investment, but create them. The government has historically limited opportunities for the private sector to comment on proposed regulations but several agencies, including the Commerce Ministry and telecommunications regulator have posted draft legislation and regulations online and solicited input from the business community.

EFFICIENT CAPITAL MARKETS AND PORTFOLIO INVESTMENT

While Bangladesh has made gradual progress in developing capital markets, the markets have relied primarily on domestic investors with limited participation from international portfolio investors. A 2010-2011 stock market bubble and correction underscored weaknesses in capital markets and deficiencies in regulatory oversight. The Dhaka Stock Exchange (DSE) market capitalization rose to a peak of $48 billion in December 2010 before declining to roughly $30 billion in January 2012. A sharp increase in retail investors combined with loose monetary policy and lax regulatory oversight fueled inflation of share prices in 2010. Since this episode, regulatory oversight has nonetheless improved.

As steady economic growth has fueled rising domestic investment, Bangladeshi firms have increasingly relied on capital markets to finance investment projects. The DSE has

attracted some foreign portfolio investors to the country's capital market; however the volume of foreign investment in Bangladesh has remained a small fraction of total market capitalization. As a result, foreign portfolio investment has had limited influence on market trends and Bangladesh's capital markets have been largely insulated from volatility of international financial markets.

Foreign investors have access to local credit markets, but many seek offshore financing at more competitive rates. If they finance locally, it is usually with a foreign bank branch. State-owned banks, known as nationalized commercial banks (NCBs), comprise roughly 25 percent of the total lending. Financial analysts estimate that a significant share of the country's total asset base is non-performing based on their long-outstanding debts to the NCBs. Following the January 2014 elections, the government agreed to allow financial institutions to reschedule non-performing loans until June 2014. An important part of the IMF's ongoing Extended Credit Facility (ECF) with Bangladesh is related to financial sector reforms.

The Securities and Exchange Commission (SEC) was formed in 1993 to regulate the Dhaka Stock Exchange (DSE) and Chittagong Stock Exchange (CSE) and protect investors. In 1997, the SEC imposed new restrictions on the involvement of foreign investors in the Bangladesh capital market. The guidelines stipulate that 10 percent of primary issues are reserved for non-resident Bangladeshis. Foreign investors have complained that this measure exacerbates a significant market drawback: the difficulty of buying or selling in volume over a reasonably short period. Nonetheless, Bangladesh is a rare case in South Asia which allows 100 percent company ownership by foreigners in most sectors. The SEC considers the 10 percent allowance for non-resident Bangladeshis to be an incentive for foreign investment.

COMPETITION FROM STATE OWNED ENTERPRISES

SOEs are active in banking, energy, transportation and agricultural sectors. SOEs usually report to line ministries, though the government has allowed some increased autonomy for certain SOEs such as national carrier Biman Bangladesh Airline. State-owned banks generally maintain a wider network of branches and depositors than private banks, but private banks have gradually increased their role. Private energy companies can invest in power generation through independent power purchase (IPP) agreements with the Bangladesh Power Development Board. Oil and gas firms can pursue exploration and production ventures through production sharing agreements with the state-owned oil and gas company, Petrobangla. SOEs maintain control of rail transportation, but private companies compete freely in air and road transportation.

CORPORATE SOCIAL RESPONSIBILITY

The business community is increasingly aware and engaged in corporate social responsibility (CSR) activities with multinational firms and local business conglomerates leading the way. U.S. companies present in Bangladesh maintain diverse CSR activities. Consumers are generally less aware of CSR and there is little pressure from consumers or shareholders for companies to engage in CSR activities. While many international firms are aware of OECD guidelines and international best practices in CSR, most local firms have limited familiarity with international standards.

POLITICAL VIOLENCE

Incidents of violence targeting foreign projects or installations have been isolated and criminal, rather than political, in nature. Extortion of money from businesses by thugs claiming political backing is common. Clashes between supporters of rival political parties and their student and youth wings and even factions within the same party are frequent occurrences, particularly in the run-up to elections. General strikes and blockades called by political parties mostly affect businesses by keeping workers away with the threat of violence and blocking transport, resulting in productivity losses. Vehicles and other property are at risk from vandalism or arson during such programs, and looting of shops has occurred.

Responding to public concern over law and order, the government in March 2004 created a special elite force, known as the Rapid Action Battalion (RAB) as part of its anti-crime initiative. The RAB is comprised of members of the armed forces, the police, and the Bangladesh Border Guard and Ansars, both paramilitary groups. The RAB became operational in June 2004 and has been credited by many Bangladeshis with improving domestic law and order. Soon after its formation, however, the local media began reporting on "cross-fires," a euphemism for extrajudicial killings, particularly by the RAB. Reports of cross-fire incidents continue.

In February 2005 the government banned two extremist groups: Jama'atul Mujahedin Bangladesh (JMB) and Jagroto Muslim Janata Bangladesh (JMJB). On August 17, 2005, JMB, with the assistance of JMJB, set off over 500 small, improvised explosive devices (IEDs) in a coordinated attack in 63 of the 64 districts of Bangladesh. The devices were accompanied by leaflets demanding the establishment of Islamic law in Bangladesh. From September to early December 2005, JMB conducted several suicide attacks targeting local judges, courts and district government facilities. The government responded vigorously, arresting several high-ranking leaders of JMB and recovering detonators, explosives and related materials used to construct IEDs. As of January 2014, there had been no attacks by extremist groups on foreign diplomatic, commercial or social interests in Bangladesh; the current Awami League government has demonstrated a strong commitment to combating terrorism.

CORRUPTION

Corruption, including bribery, raises the costs and risks of doing business. Corruption has a corrosive impact on both market opportunities overseas for U.S. companies and the broader business climate. It also deters international investment, stifles economic growth and development, distorts prices, and undermines the rule of law.

It is important for U.S. companies, irrespective of their size, to assess the business climate in the relevant market in which they will be operating or investing, and to have an effective compliance program or measures to prevent and detect corruption, including foreign bribery. U.S. individuals and firms operating or investing in foreign markets should take the time to become familiar with the relevant anticorruption laws of both the foreign country and the United States in order to properly comply with them, and where appropriate, they should seek the advice of legal counsel.

The U.S. Government seeks to level the global playing field for U.S. businesses by encouraging other countries to take steps to criminalize their own companies' acts of corruption, including bribery of foreign public officials, by requiring them to uphold their obligations under relevant international conventions. A U. S. firm that believes a competitor is seeking to use bribery of a foreign public official to secure a contract should bring this to the attention of appropriate U.S. agencies, as noted below.

U.S. Foreign Corrupt Practices Act: In 1977, the United States enacted the Foreign Corrupt Practices Act (FCPA), which makes it unlawful for a U.S. person, and certain foreign issuers of securities, to make a corrupt payment to foreign public officials for the purpose of obtaining or retaining business for or with, or directing business to, any person. The FCPA also applies to foreign firms and persons who take any act in furtherance of such a corrupt payment while in the United States. For more detailed information on the FCPA, see the FCPA Lay-Person's Guide at: http://www.justice.gov/criminal/fraud/

Other Instruments: It is U.S. Government policy to promote good governance, including host country implementation and enforcement of anti-corruption laws and policies pursuant to their obligations under international agreements. Since enactment of the FCPA, the United States has been instrumental to the expansion of the international framework to fight corruption. Several significant components of this framework are the OECD Convention on Combating Bribery of Foreign Public Officials in International Business Transactions (OECD Anti-bribery Convention), the United Nations Convention against Corruption (UN Convention), the Inter-American Convention against Corruption (OAS Convention), the Council of Europe Criminal and Civil Law

Conventions, and a growing list of U.S. free trade agreements. This country is party to [add instrument to which this country is party], but generally all countries prohibit the bribery and solicitation of their public officials.

OECD Anti-bribery Convention: The OECD Anti-bribery Convention entered into force in February 1999. As of March 2009, there are 38 parties to the Convention including the United States (see http://www.oecd.org/dataoecd/59/13/40272933.pdf). Major exporters China, India, and Russia are not parties, although the U.S. Government strongly endorses their eventual accession to the Convention. The Convention obligates the Parties to criminalize bribery of foreign public officials in the conduct of international business. The United States meets its international obligations under the OECD Anti-bribery Convention through the U.S. FCPA. [Insert information as to whether your country is a party to the OECD Convention.]

UN Convention: The UN Anticorruption Convention entered into force on December 14, 2005, and there are 158 parties to it as of November 2011 (see http://www.unodc.org/unodc/en/treaties/CAC/signatories.html). The UN Convention is the first global comprehensive international anticorruption agreement. The UN Convention requires countries to establish criminal and other offences to cover a wide range of acts of corruption. The UN Convention goes beyond previous anticorruption instruments, covering a broad range of issues ranging from basic forms of corruption such as bribery and solicitation, embezzlement, trading in influence to the concealment and laundering of the proceeds of corruption. The Convention contains transnational business bribery provisions that are functionally similar to those in the OECD Anti-bribery Convention and contains provisions on private sector auditing and books and records requirements. Other provisions address matters such as prevention,

international cooperation, and asset recovery. [Insert information as to whether your country is a party to the UN Convention.]

OAS Convention: In 1996, the Member States of the Organization of American States (OAS) adopted the first international anticorruption legal instrument, the Inter-American Convention against Corruption (OAS Convention), which entered into force in March 1997. The OAS Convention, among other things, establishes a set of preventive measures against corruption, provides for the criminalization of certain acts of corruption, including transnational bribery and illicit enrichment, and contains a series of provisions to strengthen the cooperation between its States Parties in areas such as mutual legal assistance and technical cooperation. As of December 2009, the OAS Convention has 34 parties (see http://www.oas.org/juridico/english/Sigs/b-58.html) [Insert information as to whether your country is a party to the OAS Convention.]

Council of Europe Criminal Law and Civil Law Conventions: Many European countries are parties to either the Council of Europe (CoE) Criminal Law Convention on Corruption, the Civil Law Convention, or both. The Criminal Law Convention requires criminalization of a wide range of national and transnational conduct, including bribery, money-laundering, and account offenses. It also incorporates provisions on liability of legal persons and witness protection. The Civil Law Convention includes provisions on compensation for damage relating to corrupt acts, whistleblower protection, and validity of contracts, inter alia. The Group of States against Corruption (GRECO) was established in 1999 by the CoE to monitor compliance with these and related anti-corruption standards. Currently, GRECO comprises 49 member States (48 European countries and the United States). As of December 2011, the Criminal Law Convention has 43 parties and the Civil Law Convention has 34 (see www.coe.int/greco.) [Insert information as to whether your country is a party to the Council of Europe Conventions.]

Free Trade Agreements: While it is U.S. Government policy to include anticorruption provisions in free trade agreements (FTAs) that it negotiates with its trading partners, the anticorruption provisions have evolved over time. The most recent FTAs negotiated now require trading partners to criminalize "active bribery" of public officials (offering bribes to any public official must be made a criminal offense, both domestically and trans-nationally) as well as domestic "passive bribery" (solicitation of a bribe by a domestic official). All U.S. FTAs may be found at the U.S. Trade Representative Website: http://www.ustr.gov/trade-agreements/free-trade-agreements . [Insert information as to whether your country has an FTA with the United States: Country [X] has a free trade agreement (FTA) in place with the United States, the [name of FTA], which came into force. Consult USTR Website for date: http://www.ustr.gov/trade-agreements/free-trade-agreements.]

Local Laws: U.S. firms should familiarize themselves with local anticorruption laws, and, where appropriate, seek legal counsel. While the U.S. Department of Commerce cannot provide legal advice on local laws, the Department's U.S. and Foreign Commercial Service can provide assistance with navigating the host country's legal system and obtaining a list of local legal counsel.

Assistance for U.S. Businesses: The U.S. Department of Commerce offers several services to aid U.S. businesses seeking to address business-related corruption issues. For example, the U.S. and Foreign Commercial Service can provide services that may assist U.S. companies in conducting their due diligence as part of the company's

overarching compliance program when choosing business partners or agents overseas. The U.S. Foreign and Commercial Service can be reached directly through its offices in every major U.S. and foreign city, or through its Website at www.trade.gov/cs .

The Departments of Commerce and State provide worldwide support for qualified U.S. companies bidding on foreign government contracts through the Commerce Department's Advocacy Center and State's Office of Commercial and Business Affairs. Problems, including alleged corruption by foreign governments or competitors, encountered by U.S. companies in seeking such foreign business opportunities can be brought to the attention of appropriate U.S. government officials, including local embassy personnel and through the Department of Commerce Trade Compliance Center "Report A Trade Barrier" Website at tcc.export.gov/Report_a_Barrier/index.asp .

Guidance on the U.S. FCPA: The Department of Justice's (DOJ) FCPA Opinion Procedure enables U.S. firms and individuals to request a statement of the Justice Department's present enforcement intentions under the anti-bribery provisions of the FCPA regarding any proposed business conduct. The details of the opinion procedure are available on DOJ's Fraud Section Website at www.justice.gov/criminal/fraud/fcpa . Although the Department of Commerce has no enforcement role with respect to the FCPA, it supplies general guidance to U.S. exporters who have questions about the FCPA and about international developments concerning the FCPA. For further information, see the Office of the Chief Counsel for International Counsel, U.S. Department of Commerce, Website, at http://www.ogc.doc.gov/trans_anti_bribery.html . More general information on the FCPA is available at the Websites listed below.

Exporters and investors should be aware that generally all countries prohibit the bribery of their public officials, and prohibit their officials from soliciting bribes under domestic laws. Most countries are required to criminalize such bribery and other acts of corruption by virtue of being parties to various international conventions discussed above.

Bangladesh has made some progress in reducing corruption during the last decade, but it remains a serious impediment to investment and economic growth in Bangladesh. While the Government has established legislation to combat bribery, embezzlement and other forms of corruption, enforcement is inconsistent. The Anti-Corruption Commission (ACC) is the main institutional anti-corruption watchdog. The current Awami League-led government has publicly underscored its commitment to anti-corruption efforts and reaffirmed the need for a strong ACC. However, efforts to ease public procurement rules and proposals to curb the independence of the ACC may undermine institutional safeguards against corruption. Bangladesh is a party to the UN Anticorruption Convention, but has still not joined the OECD Convention on Combating Bribery of Public Officials.

Corruption is common in public procurement, tax and customs collection, and regulatory authorities. Corruption, including bribery, raises the costs and risks of doing business. By some estimates, off-the-record payments by firms may result in an annual reduction of 2–3 percent of GDP. Corruption has a corrosive impact on the broader business climate market and opportunities for U.S. companies in Bangladesh. It also deters investment, stifles economic growth and development, distorts prices, and undermines the rule of law.

Anti-Corruption Resources

Some useful resources for individuals and companies regarding combating corruption in global markets include the following:

* Information about the U.S. Foreign Corrupt Practices Act (FCPA), including a "Lay-Person's Guide to the FCPA" is available at the U.S. Department of Justice's Website at: http://www.justice.gov/criminal/fraud/fcpa .

* Information about the OECD Anti-bribery Convention including links to national implementing legislation and country monitoring reports is available at: http://www.oecd.org/department/0,3355,en_2649_34859_1_1_1_1_1,00.html . See also new Anti-bribery Recommendation and Good Practice Guidance Annex for companies: http://www.oecd.org/dataoecd/11/40/44176910.pdf .

* General information about anticorruption initiatives, such as the OECD Convention and the FCPA, including translations of the statute into several languages, is available at the Department of Commerce Office of the Chief Counsel for International Commerce Website: http://www.ogc.doc.gov/trans_anti_bribery.html .

* Transparency International (TI) publishes an annual Corruption Perceptions Index (CPI). The CPI measures the perceived level of public-sector corruption in 180 countries and territories around the world. The CPI is available at: http://www.transparency.org/policy_research/surveys_indices/cpi/2009 . TI also publishes an annual *Global Corruption Report* which provides a systematic evaluation of the state of corruption around the world. It includes an in-depth analysis of a focal theme, a series of country reports that document major corruption related events and developments from all continents and an overview of the latest research findings on anti-corruption diagnostics and tools. See http://www.transparency.org/publications/gcr .

* The World Bank Institute publishes Worldwide Governance Indicators (WGI). These indicators assess six dimensions of governance in 213 countries, including Voice and Accountability, Political Stability and Absence of Violence, Government Effectiveness, Regulatory Quality, Rule of Law and Control of Corruption. See http://

info.worldbank.org/governance/wgi/index.asp . The World Bank Business Environment and Enterprise Performance Surveys may also be of interest and are available at: http://data.worldbank.org/data-catalog/BEEPS .

* The World Economic Forum publishes the *Global Enabling Trade Report*, which presents the rankings of the Enabling Trade Index, and includes an assessment of the transparency of border administration (focused on bribe payments and corruption) and a separate segment on corruption and the regulatory environment. See http://www.weforum.org/s?s=global+enabling+trade+report .

* Additional country information related to corruption can be found in the U.S. State Department's annual *Human Rights Report* available at http://www.state.gov/g/drl/rls/hrrpt/ .

* Global Integrity, a nonprofit organization, publishes its annual *Global Integrity Report*, which provides indicators for 106 countries with respect to governance and anti-corruption. The report highlights the strengths and weaknesses of national level anti-corruption systems. The report is available at: http://report.globalintegrity.org/ .

BILATERAL INVESTMENT AGREEMENTS

The U.S.-Bangladesh Bilateral Investment Treaty, signed on March 12, 1986, entered into force on July 23, 1989. Bangladesh has also signed investment treaties with a number of other countries. The Foreign Investment Act includes a guarantee of national treatment.

A bilateral treaty between the United States and Bangladesh for the avoidance of double taxation was signed on September 26, 2004 and ratified by the United States on March 31, 2006. The parties exchanged Instruments of ratification on August 7, 2006. The treaty has been effective for most taxpayers beginning in the 2007 tax year.

On June 27, 2013, President Obama announced his decision to suspend Bangladesh's trade benefits under the Generalized System of Preferences (GSP) in view of insufficient progress by the Government of Bangladesh in affording Bangladeshi workers internationally recognized worker rights. At the time of the announcement, the Administration provided the Government of Bangladesh with a 16-point action plan outlining next steps in a longstanding effort to address in a meaningful way worker safety problems in Bangladesh – the severity of which were exemplified in the tragedies of the November 2012 Tazreen Fashions factory fire and the April 2013 Rana Plaza building collapse – and, more broadly, the ability of Bangladeshi workers to exercise their full range of labor rights. If implemented, the plan would provide a basis for the President to consider reinstating GSP trade benefits; it would also drive transformation of the Bangladeshi apparel sector by bringing it to international standards in terms of fire safety, factory structural soundness, and respect for labor rights.

The United States also associated itself with the July 8, 2013 European Union (EU)-Bangladesh-International Labor Organization (ILO) *Sustainability Compact for continuous improvements in labor rights and factory safety in the ready-made garment and knitwear industry in Bangladesh* (Compact). The United States works as a full partner with the EU, Bangladesh, and the ILO to implement the goals of the Compact, many of which are broadly consistent with the GSP Action Plan.

On November 25, 2013, the U.S.-Bangladesh Trade and Investment Cooperation Forum Agreement (TICFA) was signed in Washington, D.C. The agreement provides a mechanism for both countries to meet regularly and identify obstacles to increasing bilateral trade and investment and how to overcome those obstacles. The successful inaugural TICFA Council meeting was held in Dhaka on April 28, 2014.

Bangladesh has successfully negotiated several regional trade and economic agreements, including the South Asian Free Trade Area (SAFTA), the Asia-Pacific Trade Agreement (APTA), and the Bay of Bengal Initiative for Multi-Sectoral, Technical and Economic Cooperation (BIMSTEC). Bangladesh has taken steps to strengthen bilateral economic relations with India by reducing trade barriers and improving connectivity. Bangladesh gained duty free access to India via regional not bilateral trade agreements.

The first is the South Asian Association for Regional Cooperation (SAARC) Preferential Trading Arrangement (SAPTA) which was signed in April 1993, operationalized in December 1995 that gives limited preferential market access to exports of member countries. The second is the South Asian Free Trade Area (SAFTA) which was signed in January 2004 in Islamabad and entered into force from January 2006. Tariff reduction under SAFTA started from July 2006. Under these two agreements, Bangladesh can export duty free to India except alcohol, tobacco, RMG and a limited number of other products from a 'sensitive list.' As a founding member of the World Trade Organization (WTO) and as a least-developed country (LDC), Bangladesh has been an active advocate for LDC interests in WTO negotiations.

OPIC AND OTHER INVESTMENT INSURANCE PROGRAMS

The U.S. Overseas Private Investment Corporation (OPIC) provides insurance coverage for some U.S. firms currently doing business in Bangladesh. OPIC and the Government of Bangladesh signed an updated bilateral agreement in May 1998. More information on OPIC services can be found on www.opic.gov . Bangladesh is a member of the Multilateral Investment Guarantee Agency.

The Export-Import Bank (EXIM) of the United States provides U.S. export-oriented risk protection and financing for some U.S. firms exporting to Bangladesh. In 2013, EXIM maintained $240,590,228 in exposure related to Bangladesh

LABOR

Bangladesh has a population of over 155 million people and a labor force of 57 million people, including 2.5 million union members, with over 60 percent working in the agricultural sector, roughly 10 percent in industry, and the remaining in the services sector. Low official unemployment statistics obscure a huge and growing under-employment problem in Bangladesh. Bangladesh's comparative advantage in cheap labor for manufacturing is partially offset by low productivity due to low skills, poor management, and inefficient infrastructure and machinery, as well as rising minimum wage rates, particularly in the garment sector.

Bangladesh has labor laws that specify employment conditions, working hours, minimum wage levels, leave policies, health and sanitary conditions, and compensation for injured workers. Freedom of association and the right to join unions are guaranteed in the constitution. In practice, compliance and enforcement of labor laws are inconsistent, and companies frequently discourage the formation of active labor unions. Historically, unions are heavily politicized, and labor-management relations are often contentious, particularly in the ready-made garment (RMG) sector which registered over 100 new unions in 2013.

In July 2004, the Bangladesh parliament enacted a law granting limited freedom of association in the export processing zones. Workers of the industrial units are allowed to form a welfare council to develop and grow into organizations, defending their welfare through collective bargaining, according to the law which was renewed and updated in 2010. These special labor provisions for export processing zones were due to expire in 2013, but remain in force. Employers are required to form worker welfare councils once the workers apply for such formation. However, some restrictions related to strikes

expired in 2013. For industries outside of EPZs the Labor Act, 2006 provides similar rights to form labor union by the workers. The implementation of worker welfare councils in the export processing zones is uneven with many larger factories ignoring the provision altogether. Labor disputes do not necessarily need to be heard before a court. Many companies have found it effective to resolve issues before a Labor Tribunal.

The ILO also launched in October 2013 a US$24.2 million, a three-and-a-half year program to support implementation of Bangladesh's National Tripartite Plan of action on fire safety an structural integrity in the ready-made garment (RMG) sector. Key elements are already being implemented, including building and fire safety assessments; labour inspection reforms; and occupational safety and health, rehabilitation and skills training. The ILO, in partnership with the International Finance Corporation (IFC), also initiated the largest ever Better Work program in Bangladesh in an effort to improve labor standards. Better Work will provide assessments of factory compliance with national law and core international labor standards, paired with transparent public reporting on findings. The program will also provide advisory services to factories, concentrating on building worker/management dialogue to improve working conditions and competitiveness, and engage with national partners to promote sectoral changes, including effective industrial relations.

CHILD LABOR

Bangladeshi law sets a minimum age of 14 for employment and 18 for hazardous work. Numerous laws prohibit child labor in certain sectors, ranging from transport workers to tea plantation labor, but these have not been consistently applied to informal sectors, such as agriculture and domestic work, where the majority of children are employed. As a result, child labor in Bangladesh has historically been a problem. On July 4, 1995, Bangladesh's garment exporters association signed a memorandum of understanding (MOU) with the United Nations Children's Fund (UNICEF) and the ILO under which child laborers were removed from EPZ textile factories and enrolled in education programs. ILO-assisted monitoring teams, which found child laborers in 43 percent of EPZ factories in 1996, found them in fewer than 5 percent in 2001. The MOU program has been phased out, and the U.S. Embassy considers the project a success, with most child labor now eradicated from the EPZs, and from the garment sector in general. Child labor laws are not effectively enforced outside of the EPZs, particularly in the informal sector that employs 80 percent of the workforce. Bangladesh, however, is working to improve compliance with ILO conventions on child labor.

FOREIGN-TRADE ZONES/FREE PORTS

Under the Bangladesh Export Processing Zones Authority Act of 1980, the government established an EPZ in Chittagong in 1983. Additional EPZs now operate in Dhaka (Savar), Mongla, Ishwardi, Comilla, Uttara, Karnaphuli (Chittagong) and Adamjee (Dhaka). Korean investors are developing a private EPZ in Chittagong. Investments that are wholly foreign-owned, joint ventures and wholly Bangladeshi-owned companies are all permitted to operate and enjoy equal treatment in the EPZs. Approximately a dozen U.S. firms -- mostly textile producers -- are currently operating in Bangladesh EPZs, and U.S. garment sector buyers source heavily from

EPZs. Investors are generally satisfied with the operation of Bangladesh's EPZs, which have played a significant role in the success of Bangladesh's RMG industry.

In 2010, Bangladesh enacted a Special Economic Zone Law that allows the creation of privately-owned special economic zones (SEZs) that can produce for export and domestic markets. The IFC is assisting the government to establish a SEZ authority, Bangladesh Economic Zones Authority (BEZA), modeled after BEPZA, to implement the new law and oversee the establishment of SEZs. The Bangladesh Economic Zones Act 2010 is still in place. On 18 April 18 2012 the BEZA Governing Board decided to establish five economic zones in the country:

1. Mongla, Bagerhat (http://www.beza.gov.bd/mongla_khulna.php)
2. Sirajganj, Rajshahi (http://www.beza.gov.bd/sirajganj_rajshahi.php)
3. Anowara, Chittagong (http://www.beza.gov.bd/anwara_chittagong.php)
4. Mirershorai, Chittagong (http://www.beza.gov.bd/mirershorai_chittagong.php)
5. Maulvibazar, Sylhet (http://www.beza.gov.bd/moulvibazar_sylhet.php)

FOREIGN DIRECT INVESTMENT STATISTICS

According to the United Nations Conference on Trade and Development (UNCTAD) World Investment Report 2013, FDI inflows to Bangladesh decreased by 13 percent to just under $1 billion. Nonetheless, Bangladesh remained the third largest recipient of FDI in the region, after India and the Islamic Republic of Iran. Outward FDI flows stood at $53 million, approximately 76 percent more than that of 2012. Major sources of investment include the United States, the United Kingdom, South Korea, Japan, Norway and India.

TABLE 2: Key Macroeconomic data, U.S. FDI in host country/economy

Economic Data	Year	Amount	Year	Amount	
Host Country Gross Domestic Product (GDP) (Millions U.S. Dollars)	2012	11,579	2012	11,640	http://www.worldbank.org/en/country
Foreign Direct Investment	Host Country Statistical source*	USG or international statistical source	USG or international Source of data: BEA; IMF; Eurostat; UNCTAD, Other		

U.S. FDI in partner country (Millions U.S. Dollars, stock positions)	2013	551.43	2012	368	* http://www.bea.gov * By Country only (all countries) (Millions of Dollars)

Host country's FDI in the United States (Millions U.S. Dollars, stock positions)	N/A	N/A	2012	5		* http://www.bea.gov * By Country only (all countries) (Millions of Dollars)
Total inbound stock of FDI as % host GDP (calculate)	2012	6.5	2012	6.5		* UNCTAD World Investment Report 2013

* http://www.mof.gov.bd/en/budget/13_14/ber/en/chapter-2_en.pdf
* www.bangladesh-bank.org
* http://www.mincom.gov.bd

TABLE 3: Sources and Destination of FDI (US Dollars, Millions)

From Top Five Sources/Destinations of FDI					
Inward Direct Investment	Outward Direct Investment				
Total Inward	8,063	100%	Total Outward	90	100%
United Kingdom	886	11%	United Kingdom	26	28%
Australia	877	11%	United Arab Emirates	21	23%
United States	702	9%	India	12	13%
Korea, Republic of	628	8%	Sri Lanka	9	10%
Netherlands	516	6%	Nepal	6	7%
"0" reflects amounts rounded to +/- USD 500,000.					

Source: http://cdis.imf.org/

Contact Point at Post
Etienne LeBailly
Economic & Commercial Officer
Embassy of the United States of America, Madani Avenue, Baridhara, Dhaka – 1212
Tel: +880 2 885 5500
Email: LeBaillyES@state.gov

STARTING BUSINESS BASICS

MARKET OVERVIEW

* Bangladesh, a densely-populated country of 155 million people in an area the size of Iowa, has registered steady annual GDP growth of 5-7 percent since 1990 driven by a booming garment industry and rising remittance flows.

* Thanks to a stable macroeconomic environment and dynamic private sector the IMF estimates that Bangladesh's GDP in 2013 rose to $141 billion.

* The IMF projects real GDP growth to increase to 6.25 percent in Fiscal Year (FY) 2015 (July 2014 – June 2015).

* Led by cotton, aircraft, soybeans, and gas turbines, U.S. exports to Bangladesh reached $712 million in 2013, up from $502 million in 2012. U.S. exports in the first quarter of 2014 reached $545 million.

* Nearly ten million Bangladeshis, concentrated mainly in Dhaka and Chittagong, have annual incomes well in excess of $10,000, offering a sizable market for a wide range of goods and services.

* Bangladesh's garment industry currently produces roughly 80 percent of the country's exports. Garment exports have expanded steadily since 1990 despite chronic energy shortages, infrastructure constraints, occasional labor unrest and periods of weakening global demand.

* With a workforce growing by roughly 2 million per year and one of the world's lowest wage rates, Bangladesh has an opportunity to replicate its success in ready-made garment production by developing other labor-intensive industries.

* The rapid growth of Bangladesh's garment industry and increasing investment in energy sector projects have created growing opportunities for U.S. exports of machinery and raw materials.

* Bangladesh is one of the top 10 remittance earning countries in the world and remittance growth remained buoyant through the world economic downturn, though remittances peaked in the FY 2013 (July 2012-June 2013) at $14.4 billion. Remittances in FY 2014 decreased to $10.4 billion.

MARKET CHALLENGES

* Despite a relatively good economic growth performance in the last decade, investment climate constraints, notably deficiencies in energy and transportation infrastructure, have prevented Bangladesh from achieving higher growth.

* Election year political unrest including frequent disruptive general strikes have heightened political uncertainty and dampened investment in 2013, but projections of continued 6% GDP growth show the resilience of Bangladesh's economy in weathering these short-term challenges.

* A series of garment industry accidents including the death of 1,127 workers in the collapse of Rana Plaza in April 2013 have highlighted the urgent need for Bangladesh to improve worker rights and develop durable mechanisms for ensuring workplace safety in order to preserve and expand its existing markets.

* Economic weaknesses include an undeveloped and undercapitalized financial sector, an inefficient and chronically loss-making public sector, and a decision-averse bureaucracy that often resists measures to improve the investment climate.

* While Bangladesh made some progress in reducing corruption during the last decade, corruption is still widely perceived to be endemic at all levels of society.

* Shortages of land, gas, and power are also major impediments to investment. Bangladesh's long-term energy security could benefit from domestic gas prices that more closely match international gas prices. Development of infrastructure to allow Bangladesh to access LNG imports would also support economic development.

MARKET OPPORTUNITIES

The leading commercial sectors for U.S. exports and investment include:

* Power Systems

* Textile Machinery/Equipment

* Oil, Gas and Mineral Exploration/Production Services

* Computers/Peripherals and Computer Software

* Architectural, Construction and Engineering Services

* Pharmaceutical Machinery/ Equipment

Leading agricultural sectors for U.S. exports include:

* Cotton

* Wheat

* Soybeans

* Animal Feed

* Dairy Products

MARKET ENTRY STRATEGY

* Personal relationships are important when selling products in Bangladesh. Many

companies identify distributors or local agents to sell their products on an exclusive or non-exclusive basis. U.S. companies can evaluate potential business partners based on technical capacity, market experience and other factors. (The U.S. Trade Center at the U.S. Embassy can offer services to help identify and assess Bangladesh companies as potential business partners.)

* Many firms service Bangladesh from their regional offices in India, Singapore and other offices in South or Southeast Asia.

* As companies become more established in the market, they may choose to open a branch or subsidiary office.

* Some consumer goods companies have established manufacturing facilities in Bangladesh.

* Some companies have begun granting franchise licenses in Bangladesh, including casual theme restaurants, clothing, health spas and specialty goods.

* Successful companies adapt their products to the demands of the local marketplace. This may include smaller packaging to reduce retail pricing and marketing strategies that appeal to local consumer preferences.

SELLING U.S. PRODUCTS AND SERVICES

USING AN AGENT OR DISTRIBUTOR

U.S. companies may appoint a Bangladeshi firm or individual as an exclusive or nonexclusive agent or distributor. The local agent should be reputable, imaginative, active, politically astute, well connected, and technically competent. A local agent may be authorized to service industrial consumers, to bid on government tenders, to place orders or book indent orders for his own account.

Given the level of corruption that pervades Bangladesh, exporters are cautioned to screen carefully any potential agents working on their behalf. The U.S. Embassy's experience suggests that a significant proportion of local agents do not adhere to U.S. standards of business ethics. Many local agents admit to having paid bribes and using undue influence to get a contract awarded in public procurement. Although local agents routinely sign documents agreeing to comply with the Foreign Corrupt Practices Act, many of them continue to conduct under-the-table deals without the U.S. companies' knowledge or approval. Companies need to exercise caution when hiring local agents and thoroughly educate the agent about acceptable business practices. Companies also should monitor local agents' activities as closely as possible. Personal interviews are useful in discussing a business proposal with a potential agent or distributor. Close political ties with the current government do not automatically guarantee success, as new governments have delayed or re-tendered deals from their predecessors.

American firms looking for agents or distributors in Bangladesh may wish to contact a district Department of Commerce office or the U.S. Trade Center in Dhaka (ustc-dhaka@state.gov) to discuss commercial services that can assist identifying and evaluating potential business partners. These services include: the International Partner

Search (IPS) service providing a list of pre-screened companies with experience in different fields; the International Company Profile (ICP) service providing background information on a specific company, including sales and after-sales capabilities, as well as bank and trade references; and the Gold Key Service (GKS) providing full-service support to U.S. companies including U.S. Embassy briefings, scheduling of meetings with local firms and logistical support to visiting U.S. companies. Details on these services are available at: dhaka.usembassy.gov/doing_business .

ESTABLISHING AN OFFICE

Any foreign firm with its corporate head office outside Bangladesh wishing to open a branch or liaison office must submit an application to the Board of Investment (BOI) where they can also confirm whether other Government approvals would be necessary depending on the nature of the investment. More details on registration forms, requirements and investment rules can be found on the BOI website: boi.gov.bd Under the provisions of the Companies Act of 1994, companies can fulfill registration requirements by filing a registration form with the Registrar of Joint Stock Companies and Firms (www.roc.gov.bd)

A business in Bangladesh may be organized as a sole proprietorship, a partnership, or as an incorporated or unincorporated association. Foreign investors normally form corporations in Bangladesh. Two broad categories of corporations exist: public and private. Companies of either type may be limited or unlimited. The liability of the shareholders of a limited company is restricted to the amount of share capital subscribed by them or held in their name. The liability of the shareholders of an unlimited company is not limited. A minimum of seven shareholders is required to establish a public limited company; there is no limit on the number of shareholders. A private company requires a minimum of two shareholders, and its total number of shareholders may not exceed fifty.

FRANCHISING

Although less common than agent or distributorship agreements, there are a growing number of franchised businesses in Bangladesh, including: Pizza Hut, Kentucky Fried Chicken, Gold's Gym, Movënpick, Baskin Robbins, Andersen's of Denmark, Nandos, Wimpy, A&W, and Pizza Inn. There are no regulations to restrict the establishment of franchises in Bangladesh.

DIRECT MARKETING

While there are no laws in Bangladesh regulating or prohibiting the direct marketing model of product distribution, the Embassy is not aware of any companies using direct marketing distribution in Bangladesh.

JOINT VENTURES/LICENSING

Bangladeshi businesses are eager to collaborate with foreign partners, and the government encourages joint ventures. Local businessmen are particularly receptive to joint ventures in which the foreign partner provides the foreign exchange capital, equipment, technology and expertise, while the local partner provides land, building(s), labor and knowledge of the local market. The Industrial Policy of 2010 available on the

Ministry of Industries website (www.moind.gov.bd) ensures equal treatment for local investment, joint ventures, and 100% foreign investment. According to the policy, no special permission of the government is required to set up a joint venture project, although normal commercial licensing requirements may apply.

SELLING TO THE GOVERNMENT

The government is the country's largest importer. Most government agencies, autonomous organizations, and public sector corporations import directly through public tenders, which are publicly announced or issued to registered suppliers. The principal government organizations issuing public tenders include:

Bangladesh Chemical Industries Corporation (BCIC)

Bangladesh Oil, Gas and Mineral Corporation (BOGMC or Petrobangla)

Bangladesh Power Development Board (BPDB)

Bangladesh Steel & Engineering Corporation (BSEC)

Bangladesh Sugar & Food Industries Corporation (BSFIC)

Bangladesh Telecommunications Regulatory Commission (BTRC)

Civil Aviation Authority of Bangladesh (CAAB)

Dhaka Electric Supply Company Limited (DESCO)

Directorate General of Defense Purchase (DGDP)

Rural Electrification Board (REB)

Trading Corporation of Bangladesh (TCB)

Water and Sewage Authority (WASA)

A large number of public tenders are published in the local media and posted on the Central Procurement Technical Unit (CPTU) website (www.cptu.gov.bd). The U.S. Embassy's Commercial Section monitors procurement notices and reports the significant opportunities as "Trade Leads" through the Department of Commerce. These trade leads can be found at www.export.gov/eac/trade_leads .

Notwithstanding efforts to increase transparency, the public procurement process is often highly contentious and widely perceived as subject to manipulation. Delays, reversals and retendering are quite common as competing firms often trade allegations of technical deficiencies and corruption in the tender process. While local agents can sometimes help to navigate the challenging procurement process, it is important for firms to be particularly proactive with local partners and vigilant to ensure compliance with the Foreign Corrupt Practices Act.

DISTRIBUTION AND SALES CHANNELS

The primary channels for distribution and sales of U.S. goods in Bangladesh are through resident agents, representatives and licensed distributors. A substantial share of Bangladesh's imports is purchased through tender or direct purchase by public sector corporations, autonomous bodies, and government-controlled corporations. These agencies often prefer to deal with local firms acting as exclusive agents or licensed distributors of foreign manufacturers and suppliers. In the private sector, too, businesses prefer to deal with agents to ensure after sales service and continuous supply of spare parts, and to resolve any future technical problems. Non-exclusive arrangements are common for commodities such as cotton, wheat, edible oil, chemicals, and metals,

where brand names are not as important.

SELLING FACTORS/TECHNIQUES

Consumer goods are marketed primarily through distributors based in Dhaka to a price-sensitive market with a gradually growing appetite for higher-priced branded goods. Suppliers of capital goods, agricultural products and raw materials for garment and other export industries frequently market their products through local agents experienced in working with government and industrial buyers. U.S. firms may also consider promoting their products/services through the annual U.S. Trade Show usually held in February in Dhaka and cosponsored by the U.S. Embassy and the American Chamber of Commerce in Bangladesh.

ELECTRONIC COMMERCE

Electronic commerce is very limited in Bangladesh due to the low rate of internet penetration, low per capita income levels and limited development of e-commerce services. Business-to-Business e-commerce is practiced on a limited scale in the export sector of Bangladesh and a few international and private banks offer online banking services. Due to low internet penetration and widespread availability of cell phones, government and private companies have developed diverse applications for cell phone payments. The government is developing legislation to authorize electronic payments and encourage greater e-commerce applications. In 2009, Bangladesh Central Bank introduced online payment systems facilitating fund transfers and online payment of utility bills by credit card.

According to Bangladesh Telecommunication Regulatory Commission , Bangladesh now has more than 100 registered Internet Service Providers (ISPs). Bangladesh is connected to the SEA-ME-WE4 submarine fiber cable. The Government owned Bangladesh Telecommunications Company Ltd. (BTCL) is in charge of the distribution of the undersea fiber capacity. Most ISPs rely on SEA-ME-WE4 bandwidth from the submarine cable but most keep a satellite backup in case of fiber outage. Bandwidth is expensive compared to rates in the region and in developed countries. Standard consumer "broadband" (an always-on WAN connection) speeds ranges from 128 kbps to 2 mbps or more for residential and corporate users at various price levels. ISP backbone bandwidth is generally inadequate for peak demand, which can result in degraded connection speeds. Under the Digital Bangladesh initiative, the government is working to expand internet connectivity, develop a network of shared internet access points and expand e-services by government agencies.

TRADE PROMOTION AND ADVERTISING

Bangladesh has a small but growing advertising and market research industry. Product and trade advertisements are the most commonly used sales promotion vehicle in Bangladesh, and are carried through the range of advertising media, including newspapers, magazines, radio, television, billboards, and exhibitions. Television is widely accessible in urban and rural areas, with print media and radio targeting a more limited audience.

Bangladesh has a large and vigorous newspaper and magazine sector, with over 200 English and Bengali newspapers and magazines, including over 100 dailies. The principal English-language dailies published in Dhaka include The Daily Star , The Dhaka Tribune , BDNews24 , The Financial Express , The Independent and New Age . The primary Bangla dailies are Jugantor , Ittefaq , Prothom Alo , Janakantha , Manabzamin , and Naya Diganta .

Bangladesh has several private satellite television stations: Channel i , ATN Bangla, NTV , RTV , Bangla Vision, Boishakhi, Channel I , Ekushey TV (ETV) and Islamic TV. The government-run Bangladesh Betar (Radio) offers commercial advertisements, generally in Bangla, while government-run Bangladesh Television (BTV) carries advertisements in English and Bangla. In the private sector, Bangladesh has four FM radio stations: Radio Furti, Radio Today, Ekushey Radio , and ABC Radio. Broadcast hours of public and private stations vary, with some offering 24 hour coverage.

Satellite television is increasingly popular in urban areas, with most programs beamed from Hong Kong (Star TV) and India. CNN, BBC, ESPN, Cartoon Network, Discovery, National Geography, MTV and other channels from the U.S. and Europe are also available though local or regional distributors and may carry local advertising. Local cable TV companies, which have sprung up in Dhaka and Chittagong during the last three years, offer a relatively wide selection of foreign programming. The Export Promotion Bureau is the local authority that arranges trade fairs both in country and outside of the country.

PRICING

Other than a few essential pharmaceutical products and petroleum products, the government does not impose price controls and market pricing prevails. Due to inefficiencies in the market, the price level for most products is often higher in Bangladesh than in more developed markets. VAT and excise taxes are imposed at various rates, depending on the class of goods, but are not uniformly collected from all sellers in the marketplace. Enforcement sometimes discriminates against foreign suppliers.

SALES SERVICE/CUSTOMER SUPPORT

Sales service and customer support are critical, particularly for private sector customers. Marketing consumer durables such as electric generators, capital machinery, and large air conditioning plants requires sound technical support for installation as well as maintenance needs. Agents of U.S. firms dealing with these products should maintain sufficient technical staff and spare parts stock to support their customers.

PROTECTING YOUR INTELLECTUAL PROPERTY

Bangladesh has been a member of the World Intellectual Property Organization (WIPO) in Geneva since 1985. Bangladesh is a signatory of the Uruguay Round agreements, including the WTO's Agreement on Trade-Related Aspects of Intellectual Property

Rights (TRIPS). As a least-developed country, Bangladesh has been given until July 1, 2013 to provide protection for trademarks, copyrights, patents and other intellectual property under the WTO agreement, following a decision by WTO members in December 2005 in Hong Kong. The government has made incremental progress in bringing its legislative framework for IPR protection into compliance with TRIPS. Notwithstanding these efforts, the Government of Bangladesh has limited institutional capacity for IPR enforcement and, as a result, IPR infringements are common.

Protecting Your Intellectual Property in Bangladesh:

Several general principles are important for effective management of intellectual property ("IP") rights in Bangladesh. First, it is important to have an overall strategy to protect your IP. Second, IP is protected differently in Bangladesh than in the U.S. Third, rights must be registered and enforced in Bangladesh, under local laws. Your U.S. trademark and patent registrations will not protect you in Bangladesh. There is no such thing as an "international copyright" that will automatically protect an author's writings throughout the entire world. Protection against unauthorized use in a particular country depends, basically, on the national laws of that country. However, most countries do offer copyright protection to foreign works under certain conditions, and these conditions have been greatly simplified by international copyright treaties and conventions.

Registration of patents and trademarks is on a first-in-time, first-in-right basis, so you should consider applying for trademark and patent protection even before selling your products or services in the Bangladesh market. It is vital that companies understand that intellectual property is primarily a private right and that the US government generally cannot enforce rights for private individuals in Bangladesh. It is the responsibility of the rights' holders to register, protect, and enforce their rights where relevant, retaining their own counsel and advisors. Companies may wish to seek advice from local attorneys or IP consultants who are experts in Bangladesh law. The U.S. Commercial Service can provide a list of local lawyers upon request.

While the U.S. Government stands ready to assist, there is little we can do if the rights holders have not taken these fundamental steps necessary to securing and enforcing their IP in a timely fashion. Moreover, in many countries, rights holders who delay enforcing their rights on a mistaken belief that the USG can provide a political resolution to a legal problem may find that their rights have been eroded or abrogated due to legal doctrines such as statutes of limitations, laches, estoppel, or unreasonable delay in prosecuting a law suit. In no instance should U.S. Government advice be seen as a substitute for the obligation of a rights holder to promptly pursue its case.

It is always advisable to conduct due diligence on potential partners. Negotiate from the position of your partner and give your partner clear incentives to honor the contract. A good partner is an important ally in protecting IP rights. Consider carefully, however, whether to permit your partner to register your IP rights on your behalf. Doing so may create a risk that your partner will list itself as the IP owner and fail to transfer the rights should the partnership end. Keep an eye on your cost structure and reduce the margins (and the incentive) of would-be bad actors. Projects and sales in Bangladesh require constant attention. Work with legal counsel familiar with Bangladesh laws to create a solid contract that includes non-compete clauses, and confidentiality/non-disclosure provisions.

It is also recommended that small and medium-size companies understand the importance of working together with trade associations and organizations to support efforts to protect IP and stop counterfeiting. There are a number of these organizations, both Bangladesh or U.S.-based. These include:

* The U.S. Chamber and local American Chambers of Commerce

* National Association of Manufacturers (NAM)

* International Intellectual Property Alliance (IIPA)

* International Trademark Association (INTA)

* The Coalition Against Counterfeiting and Piracy

* International Anti-Counterfeiting Coalition (IACC)

* Pharmaceutical Research and Manufacturers of America (PhRMA)

* Biotechnology Industry Organization (BIO)

* Intellectual Property Association of Bangladesh (IPAB)

IP Resources

A wealth of information on protecting IP is freely available to U.S. rights holders. Some excellent resources for companies regarding intellectual property include the following:

* For information about patent, trademark, or copyright issues -- including enforcement issues in the US and other countries -- call the STOP! Hotline: 1-866-999-HALT or register at www.StopFakes.gov .

* For more information about registering trademarks and patents (both in the U.S. as well as in foreign countries), contact the US Patent and Trademark Office (USPTO) at: 1-800-786-9199.

* For more information about registering for copyright protection in the US, contact the US Copyright Office at: 1-202-707-5959.

* For more information about how to evaluate, protect, and enforce intellectual property rights and how these rights may be important for businesses, a free online training program is available at www.stopfakes.gov .

* For US small and medium-size companies, the Department of Commerce offers a "SME IP Advisory Program" available through the American Bar Association that provides one hour of free IP legal advice for companies with concerns in Brazil, China, Egypt, India, and Russia. For details and to register, visit: http://www.abanet.org/intlaw/intlproj/iprprogram_consultation.html

* For information on obtaining and enforcing intellectual property rights and market-specific IP Toolkits visit: www.StopFakes.gov This site is linked to the USPTO website for registering trademarks and patents (both in the U.S. as well as in foreign countries), the U.S. Customs & Border Protection website to record registered trademarks and copyrighted works (to assist customs in blocking imports of IP-infringing products) and allows you to register for Webinars on protecting IP.

* The U.S. Commerce Department has positioned IP attachés in key markets around the world. You can get contact information for the IP attaché who covers Bangladesh at: kalpana.reddy@trade.gov

DUE DILIGENCE

Traditional commercial instruments, like letters of credit, may be used to protect buyers and sellers from basic transactional risks. When considering a more extensive commercial relationship, however, U.S. businesses are advised to exercise due diligence appropriate to the relationship. To check the bona fides of a bank, agent, or customer, U.S. firms can contact one of several Bangladeshi chambers of commerce or business associations. The U.S. Embassy's Commercial Section may also be able to provide some useful information. No fee is charged for primary information about firms. For a more detailed check, the U.S. Embassy offers the International Company Profile (ICP) service. An ICP is a confidential business report providing background information on individual Bangladeshi firms. Each report includes information on product lines, value and size of business, volume of operations, business reputation, and trade references.

U.S. firms may request an ICP by contacting the U.S. Department of Commerce or the nearest Export Assistance Center in the United States or by directly contacting us at US Trade Center - Dhaka.

The fee for an ICP ranges from U.S. $ 350 to $900 and it is prepared within 30 working days from the date of request. For more information on services, fees and modes of payment, please contact the US Trade Center - Dhaka .

LOCAL PROFESSIONAL SERVICES

We suggest the following web links for the principal professional associations and business chambers in Bangladesh:

American Chamber of Commerce in Bangladesh (AmCham) Association for Economic and Development Studies on Bangladesh Dhaka Chamber of Commerce and Industry (DCCI) Bangladesh Chamber of Industry (BCI) Federation of Bangladesh Chambers of Commerce and Industry (FBCCI) Foreign Investors' Chambers of Commerce & Industry (FICCI) Metropolitan Chamber of Commerce and Industry, Dhaka (MCCI) The Institute of Chartered Accountants of Bangladesh The Institute of Cost and Management Accountants of Bangladesh Bangladesh Association of International Recruiting Agencies (BAIRA) Chittagong Chamber of Commerce and Industry (CCCI)

International Business Forum of Bangladesh (IBFB)

Bangladesh Employers' Federation (BEF)

WEB RESOURCES

Business Chambers

American Chamber of Commerce in Bangladesh (AmCham) Bangladesh Chamber of Industry (BCI) Dhaka Chamber of Commerce and Industry (DCCI) http://www.amchambd.org/

Federation of Bangladesh Chambers of Commerce & Industry (FBCCI) Foreign Investors' Chambers of Commerce & Industry (FICCI) Metropolitan Chamber of Commerce & Industry (MCCI) http://www.ficci.org.bd/ficci-home.asp

Media – Electronic

ATN Bangla http://www.atnbangla.tv/
Bangladesh Betar
Bangladesh Television (BTV)
Channel i TV http://www.channel-i-tv.com/
Ekushey Radio
NTV Bangla http://www.ntvbd.com/
RTV

Media – Print
Daily Ittefaq http://www.ittefaq.com/
Daily Janakantha http://www.dailyjanakantha.com/
Daily Naya Diganta http://dev.dailynayadiganta.com/

Daily Prothom Alo http://www.prothom-alo.org/
Daily Star http://www.thedailystar.net/
Manabzamin http://www.manabzamin.net/
Financial Express
Independent http://www.theindependentbd.com/
Jugantor http://www.jugantor.com/
Daily New Age http://www.newagebd.com/

Associations
Association for Economic and Development Studies on Bangladesh http://www.aedsb.org/
Center for Policy Dialogue (CPD)
Development Design Consultants Ltd. (DDC) http://www.ddclbd.com/
Bangladesh Association of International Recruiting Agencies (BAIRA) http://www.hrexport-baira.org/history_background.htm
Bangladesh Garment Manufacturers and Exporters Association (BGMEA) http://www.bgmea.com.bd/
Bangladesh Knitwear Manufacturers and Exporters' Association (BKMEA) http://www.bkmea.com/
Survey Research Group of Bangladesh [SRGB] http://www.srgb.org/
The Institute of Chartered Accountant of Bangladesh http://www.icab.org.bd/
The Institute of Cost and Management Accountants of Bangladesh http://www.icmab.org.bd/

BANGLADESH GOVERNMENT

Bangladesh Bureau of Statistics Bangladesh Chemical Industries Corporation (BCIC) Bangladesh Oil, Gas and Mineral Corporation (BOGMC or Petrobangla) Bangladesh Power Development Board (BPDB) Bangladesh Steel & Engineering Corporation (BSEC) Bangladesh Sugar & Food Industries Corporation (BSFIC) Board of Investment -Bangladesh Export Promotion Bureau Industrial Policy of 2005 Registrar of Joint Stock Companies and Firms Rural Electrification Board (REB) Trading Corporation of Bangladesh (TCB) - http://www.bbs.gov.bd/

Bangladesh Bank (Central Bank) http://www.bangladesh-bank.org/
Ministry of Commerce http://www.mincom.gov.bd/
Ministry of Labor and Employment http://www.mole.gov.bd/

US Government

Department of Commerce Trade Leads http://www.commerce.gov/
U.S. Export Assistance Center www.sba.gov
U.S. Trade Center - Dhaka http://dhaka.usembassy.gov/trade.html

Additional Sites
Bangladesh Net Information Portal http://www.bangladesh.net/
Bangladesh Yellow pages http://www.bangladeshyellowpages.com/

LEADING SECTORS FOR U.S. EXPORT AND INVESTMENT

POWER SYSTEMS

With widespread consensus that energy shortages are Bangladesh's biggest economic constraint, the government regards efforts to expand energy supplies as a top priority. After nearly a decade of limited investment resulted in worsening power shortages by 2010, the government loosened public procurement rules for energy projects in order to expedite a wide range of short-term rental power projects and longer-term projects.

While the Government of Bangladesh has made progress in increasing generation capacity through rental power projects, supply has not kept pace with energy demand growing at 12% annually. Since 2010, the Bangladesh Power Development Board has approved 20 rental power projects to provide roughly 2,000 megawatts (MW) of additional capacity. Bangladesh currently possesses an installed capacity of roughly 10,000 megawatts (MW). With much of the installed generating base nearing the end of its useful life, frequent breakdowns reduce generation capacity by nearly 1,800 MW and gas shortages render an additional 1,500 MW idle. The Government is developing a gas pipeline to reduce gas shortages while pursuing ambitious plans to develop medium and long-term projects to develop gas-fired, dual fuel and coal power plants to double generation capacity by 2015. Financing constraints, fuel shortages and bureaucracy have historically slowed the development of energy projects and these challenges are likely to continue.

Several multilateral development banks are involved in supporting energy policy reforms and financing power plant construction. The Asia Development Bank and Islamic Development Bank have approved loans of $300 million and $200 million respectively for projects to upgrade several gas generation plants to more efficient turbines with higher output. Under the $290 million Rural Electrification and Renewable Energy Development Project, the World Bank and other donors are providing technical assistance to support the distribution of solar panels in substantial areas outside the electricity grid.

Though natural gas has long served as the dominant energy source in Bangladesh, gas transmission constraints have contributed to idle generation capacity and power shortages. As a result, the government is seeking to diversify energy resources through dual fuel, nuclear, coal-fired, and renewable energy projects. Bangladesh has estimated reserves of about 14-16 trillion cubic feet (tcf), but low domestic gas prices and legal disputes have limited new investment in gas exploration. While renewable energy technologies struggle to compete with gas-fired generation and other low-cost energy sources, the government is seeking to expand renewable energy, particularly through wind power and the use of off-grid solar panels in rural areas.

Bangladesh also plans to import coal in order to fire proposed coal-fired power plants, which will be developed in coordination with India and Japan. Bangladesh has substantial high-quality coal reserves, an estimated 2 billion tons, enough to power the country for 50 years, in two adjacent fields in northwestern Bangladesh. While a Chinese firm has conducted small-scale shaft mining in one coal field, public controversy

over environmental risks and displacement of people has delayed proposals to undertake open-pit mining. The government has acknowledged that open-pit mining is the most economically viable means of developing these coal deposits and it is currently crafting a new coal policy that will govern foreign involvement in the coal sector.

BEST PROSPECTS/SERVICES

Generators, turbines, substations, transmission cables and power plants

OPPORTUNITIES

By 2015, Bangladesh plans to generate 11,500 MW and 20,000 MW by 2021.

Web Resources

Bangladesh Power Development Board http://www.bpdb.gov.bd/bpdb/

Ministry of Power, Energy and Mineral Resources http://www.powerdivision.gov.bd/

TEXTILE MACHINERY AND EQUIPMENT

The steady growth of textile and garment industry is providing opportunities for exporters of machinery and supplies for the textile and garment industries. Bangladesh exported nearly $21.5 billion worth of ready-made garments in 2013, almost 80% of the total export of Bangladesh, including roughly $5 billion to the United States, the largest single export market. The European Union, Canada, Japan, and Australia are also important export markets. During the last decade, Bangladesh has increased the level of local content in its garment industry as producers have increased linkages with the textile industry and diversified into higher-value products. Most raw materials for knitwear products are now produced domestically, while a smaller but increasing share of woven materials are produced domestically.

Existing companies continue to invest in new machinery to improve efficiency and remain competitive in the market. The market for textile machinery and components is expected to grow steadily over the next several years, and U.S. suppliers of sophisticated weaving, spinning, finishing and dying machinery should find a ready market. New machinery from Japan, Korea, Britain, Switzerland, and Germany also competes in this market. There have been signs of increased interest in used and reconditioned equipment from the U.S., which often offers better value. Suppliers should take care to clarify expectations from Bangladeshi firms, as some buyers have complained about communication and responsiveness of U.S. suppliers of used and reconditioned equipment. Bangladeshi buyers typically prefer to see a demonstration of the machinery they intend to purchase.

Best Prospects/Services

Textile machinery and equipment

Opportunities

Bangladesh continues to increase production capacity to meet rapidly growing demand for knitwear and woven garment exports while expanding linkages to domestic yarn and fabric suppliers.

Web Resources

Bangladesh Garment Manufacturers and Exporters Association (BGMEA) http://www.bgmea.com.bd/

Bangladesh Knitwear Manufacturer & Exporters Association (BKMEA) http://www.bkmea.com/

Bangladesh Textile Mills association (BTMA) http://www.btmc.gov.bd/

OIL, GAS, AND MINERAL EXPLORATION/PRODUCTION SERVICES

While Bangladesh has substantial proven gas reserves (estimated at more than 15 trillion cubic feet), rising demand and inadequate gas transmission infrastructure have led to shortages, estimated in 2012 at roughly 500 million cubic feet per day or 20 percent of peak demand. Subsidiaries of the national petroleum company, Petrobangla and several International Oil Companies (IOCs) produce an average of 2,200 million cubic feet per day (mmcfd), supplying roughly 80% of Bangladesh's commercial energy consumption. Chevron has expanded its production over the past five years to become the largest gas producer responsible for roughly half of total gas supply. Chevron is expanding its Bibiyana gas field to increase production by 300 mmcfd in 2014.

Economic growth, as well as increases in the number of compressed natural gas vehicles has boosted demand for natural gas. With rising demand exceeding gas supply, Petrobangla plans to build an offshore Liquified Natural Gas (LNG) terminal to supplement domestic gas supply. After decades with very little exploration, several agreements for offshore exploration in 2012 and 2013. Artificially low regulated gas prices have long reduced incentives for further exploration and development of gas resources, as well as international oil company interest in exploration in Bangladesh.

In 2014, the government began to take steps to increase the domestic gas price and reduce energy subsidies. In order to address gas transmission constraints, the government has taken steps to build a new pipeline and develop new gas compression stations with donor and private sector support. Chevron built the Muchai compression project that increased transmission capacity and recoverable reserves. The Asian Development Bank (ADB) is financing the construction of two additional compression projects. Petrobangla and its subsidiaries regularly publish bid notices for pipeline and facilities construction. U.S. firms have won such contracts in the past.

BEST PROSPECTS/SERVICES

Oil and gas exploration services, equipment and transmission pipes

OPPORTUNITIES

Companies include Chevron, Conoco-Phillips, ONGC, and state-owned Petrobangla.

WEB RESOURCES

Bangladesh Oil, Gas and Mineral Corp (PetroBangla) South Asia Regional Initiative for Energy Cooperation and Development (SARI/Energy) http://www.petrobangla.org.bd/

COMPUTERS/PERIPHERALS AND COMPUTER SOFTWARE

Bangladesh has a steadily growing market for computer hardware, peripherals and software, particularly mobile computing and smartphone applications. Under the Digital Bangladesh initiative, the Government of Bangladesh is expanding internet connectivity through Bangladesh while increasing the use of information technology to improve access to information and government services. As part of this effort to encourage the use of information technology, the government removed tariffs on most information technology products.

Bangladesh ranks tenth in the world in terms of mobile phones in use at roughly 114 million. As prices reduce and 3G penetration expands, Bangladesh will become an increasingly significant market for smart phones and mobile computing equipment and applications. A large number of computer and phone assemblers import components from Taiwan, China, and South Korea. Most vendors target small offices and home users. A growing number of computer training schools, including one sponsored by Microsoft, will increase skilled computer personnel. Since the introduction of internet services in 1997, a growing number of businesses are using information technology. U.S. suppliers are well-placed to access this market, given widespread consumer preference for U.S.-made information technology.

BEST PROSPECTS/SERVICES

Computer hardware, software and peripherals

OPPORTUNITIES

Bangladesh's mobile phone market is the tenth largest in the world, and 3G penetration means that smart phones and mobile computing are significant opportunities.

WEB RESOURCES

Bangladesh Assoc. of Software & Info Services (BASIS) Bangladesh Computer Samity Bangladesh Computer Council (BCC) http://www.basis.org.bd/

ARCHITECTURAL, CONSTRUCTION AND ENGINEERING SERVICES

U.S. architectural, construction, and engineering services are competitive in Bangladesh. Most donor-funded infrastructure projects require consultant services. While Asian firms are usually more cost-competitive in construction work, the government seems to prefer U.S. or European consultants to do project design and supervision. With efforts to improve building and fire safety in the garment sector underway, additional opportunities exist for services in the sector. Government and private firms have also turned to U.S. consultants for specialized engineering and construction oversight for major infrastructure projects including an oil refinery and grain silo projects. With new road and bridge construction projects in the works, the demand for engineering consultants is likely to increase.

BEST PROSPECTS/SERVICES

Consulting services

OPPORTUNITIES

The Bangladesh construction industry is growing with funding from the government, World Bank and other different agencies.

WEB RESOURCES

Government of the People's Republic of Bangladesh
http://www.bangladesh.gov.bd/www.bangladesh.gov.bd/

World Bank Group http://www.worldbank.org/

AGRICULTURAL SECTORS

COTTON

Driven by steady growth of the textile and garment industry, Bangladesh has been consistently in the top three positions as a cotton importing country. USDA estimates of Bangladesh cotton import in FY 2013-14 is 4.1 million bales (895,000 tons) with a projected import volume expected to reach 4.3 million tons next year. The United States' share in the imported raw cotton market in Bangladesh declined from 20 percent in 2004 to less than ten percent in 2008, declining further to 4.5 percent and 5.5 percent in last two years. While Central Asian countries and India have emerged as major competitors, Bangladesh importers recognize the advantages of more consistent quality standards from U.S. suppliers.

Table: U. S. Cotton Export to Bangladesh

Years*	2009	2010	2011	2012	2013
Quantities (in Tons)	101,474	79,531	107,659	33, 645	47,896
Values (in thousand US$)	144,334	142,892	365,956	87,081	97,472

*Cotton Marketing Years (August-July)

Bangladesh is a growing market for ELS and superior quality cotton. Approximately 40% of cotton imports are destined for export oriented spinning mills. These mills regularly import U.S. Pima and Upland cottons. They appreciate U.S. quality, consistency and better ginning, and are willing to pay reasonably higher prices. However, high freight costs and longer delivery periods often lead Bangladeshi importers to source their cotton from non-American suppliers. In addition to price competitiveness, export credit programs and direct contacts between U.S. suppliers and Bangladeshi buyers, through exchange visits, training, and trade shows, could contribute to the further growth of U.S. raw cotton exports to Bangladesh.

In the early 1990s, export-oriented woven, hosiery, and knitwear garments were entirely dependent on imported fabrics and yarns. Export bonuses at a rate of 25% for locally manufactured garments played a key role in enhancing the private textile mills' ability to supply yarns and fabrics for export garments. Recently, however, the government reduced cash incentives for the export-oriented textile sector to 5 percent. The country produces around 725 million kilograms (kg) of yarn, and there is additional domestic demand for 300 million kilograms. While 40% of yarn requirements for garment exports are met from domestic production, the shortfall is typically met through bonded imports. Most of the bonded yarn is imported from India, which supports domestic producers by

ensuring low raw cotton prices for Bangladeshi mills.

Currently, Bangladesh has 392 spinning mills, 782 textile weaving mills, and 240 dyeing and finishing mills. The country's more than 4,000 ready-made garment factories employ nearly 3.6 million workers; of them 80 percent are women. This industrial base is capable of supplying around 90% of the knitwear fabrics and 40-45% of the woven fabrics for the country's export oriented ready-made garment sector. Despite a remarkable growth in backward linkage industries, the country's current demand-supply gap of fabric is about 50 percent in terms of cotton-based fabrics and around 25 percent in terms of non-cotton based fabrics for the garment sector.

WHEAT

Bangladesh meets 75 percent of its wheat consumption needs through imports as annual wheat production of more than 1 million tons falls well short of the 4.5 million tons of demand. The country traditionally sources lower quality wheat from India, Russia and Ukraine, and higher quality wheat from Canada, Australia and the United States. Bangladesh has a price sensitive market and typically prefers imports of lower cost wheat. While India's geographic proximity offers a clear competitive advantage, India's occasional restriction of wheat exports has compelled importers to seek alternative suppliers including the European Union, Argentina and Brazil. Bangladeshi buyers are usually willing to pay a premium of around $10-15 per metric ton for U.S. wheat. However, it is difficult to import sufficient volumes to offset the high freight costs.

While wheat production has increased in response to higher prices, limited land availability and significant competition from other remunerative crops like rice, corn, potato, and winter vegetables limits the expansion of wheat cultivation. The absence of suitable high-yielding varieties (HYVs) and strong competition from imports will further limit the growth of wheat production in Bangladesh. However, wheat cultivation remains a preferred option for non-irrigated land with low farm input-use (fertilizer, insecticides, and labor). Government wheat distribution has been scaled down in recent years, with focus on rural areas. However, wheat consumption by the medium to higher income urban population is growing steadily due to changes in food habits prompted by health consciousness and lifestyle changes. The organized bakery and biscuit industries as well as the emerging hotel, restaurant, and institutional sector are also contributing to the consumption of an additional 200,000 tons of higher quality wheat every year.

Wheat stocks have fluctuated as imports and production have diverged from consumption trends. Wheat stocks declined in 2011 as private stocks fell by 1 million tons and government stocks rose to 371,000 tons. This followed a rise in wheat stocks the previous year when imports and production exceeded market demands. There are some signs that private wheat imports are gaining momentum and predictions that wheat stocks may exceed 2 million tons by the end of 2012.

In FY 2013/14 Bangladesh wheat imports were estimated at 3 million tons (800,000 tons by the government and 2.2 million tons through private commercial sales) up by around 10 percent from the last marketing year's imports due to soft international price. Assuming the international price remains soft, Bangladesh wheat imports in FY 2014/15 are forecast to reach 3.3 million tons on anticipated growth in consumption demand.

Following the withdrawal of an export ban, India has emerged as the principal supplier accounting for 76 percent of the Bangladeshi imported wheat.

Wheat imports are currently duty free and face no quantitative restrictions. However, the public wheat tendering process does not encourage wide participation. Many government tenders are never finalized as bidders often quote high prices to cover various risk factors. The government has recently taken some steps to bring specifications more in line with international practices. These include reducing of the performance guarantee from 10 to 5 percent, increasing the maximum shipment period from 30 to 60 days, and increasing the minimum quantity offered from 25,000 to 30,000 tons. These changes have not increased participation, however, in part because unfavorable provisions remain in the tender specifications such as "weight and quality at final discharge."

VEGETABLE OIL

Vegetable oils are normally imported in crude form (primarily soybean oil and palm oil) and refined in the local refineries before they are marketed for local consumptions. Total edible oil imports in FY 2013 were estimated at 1.4 million tons. Following the increase in domestic oilseed production and in soybean imports for crushing, the current share of domestically produced oils in the total edible oil consumption is about 18 percent. The sustained price competitiveness versus soybean oil resulted in imports of an estimated 900,000 tons of palm oil, the rest being soybean oil. Bangladesh imports crude soybean oils mainly from Argentina and Brazil, and crude palm oils from Malaysia. Bangladesh also imports small quantities (around 25,000 tons per year) of refined edible oils.

A large majority of the refiners dilute soybean oil with palm oil to exploit overwhelming consumer preference for soybean oil and soybean oil blends, especially during the summer season. The blending proportions tilt towards palm oil when price difference between these two kinds of oils and their transportation costs widen. Under normal conditions, the consumption of edible oil in Bangladesh grows at 3-4 percent in a year. Though most edible oils are marketed without branded packaging, some refiners market their product in packaged condition with brand names.

In FY 2013 (Oct-Sept) Bangladesh imported $33.5 million worth of soybeans and $31.8 million worth of soybean meal from the United States up from only $0.3 million and $9.9 million respectively in the previous year.

Imports of soybean and palm oils enjoy zero tariffs, though other edible oils (sunflower, canola, groundnut etc.) are subject 10% or 25% tariff. Additional border charges include a 15% VAT (value added tax) and 3% AIT (advance income tax).

FRUITS

Bangladesh is a net importer of apples, grapes and pears. California grapes and Washington apples have a limited market in Bangladesh. Supplies of these fruits have to compete with those from India (the dominant and cheapest source due to its proximity), Bhutan, South Africa, Australia, and China. In FY 2011 Bangladesh's fruits import from

the U.S reached at a record $10.3 million, which was about 7.4 percent of the country's total outlays for fruit import. A growing number of middle-class consumers prefers U.S. fruits for their higher quality and are willing to pay a small price premium. Despite high tariffs, apple imports and consumption have been growing at about 2-3% a year. However, due to political turmoil during FY13 Bangladesh's fruit import fell significantly, also affecting imports from the United States.

Imports of Fresh Fruits into Bangladesh (in thousand US$)

Years*	Total Imports	Imports from the U. S
2009-2010	105,236	5,039
2010-2011	139,500	10,300
2011-2012	161,400	3,014
2012-2013	113,940	1,000

**Fiscal years from July 1 – June 30*

Current Tariffs for imports of citrus fruits, grapes, apples, and pears

Import Tariff and Border Charges	Canned Fruits (Up to 2.5 kg)	NES (Others)	Remarks
Custom Duty (CD)	25%	25%	On C&F Value
Supplementary Duty (SD)	20%	20%	On C&F Value
Regulatory Duty (RD)	5%	5%	On C&F Value
Value added tax (VAT)	15%	-	-
Advance Income Tax (AIT)	5%	5%	-
Advance Trade VAT (ATV)	4%	-	-
Total Tax Incidence (TTI)	92.3%	61%	On C&F Value

Source: National Board of Revenue, Bangladesh

DAIRY PRODUCTS

Despite being an agrarian country, Bangladesh has very poor cattle resources both in numbers and productivity. Bangladesh imported $213 million worth of dairy products in FY2013 (July – June). Major dairy products come from India, China, New Zealand, Australia and Denmark. Few foreign companies have established dairy processing and packaging industries targeting the growing demand from middle class population of the county. U.S. dairy product exports to Bangladesh were roughly $12.7 million in FY 2012 (Oct-Sept), but declined to $1.4 in FY 2013. However U.S. dairy exports to Bangladesh reached $1.75 million in the October –July period of FY 2014, which is 97 percent increase over the previous year. There is high potential for increased trade in U.S. dairy exports to Bangladesh. With 5% to 25% customs duties depending on the form of milk powder and types of packaging (from consumer pack to bulk for industrial use) total tariff

for imports of dairy products varies from 31.07% to 92.3%.

TRADE REGULATIONS, CUSTOMS AND STANDARDS

IMPORT TARIFFS

Although Bangladesh has reduced tariffs over the past twenty years, they remain high due in part to their importance as a source of government revenue. Bangladesh currently has no tariff quotas on imports. Customs duties are levied on all imports except capital machinery, raw materials of medicine, poultry medicine, feed & machinery, defense stores, chemicals of leather and leather goods, private power generation unit, textile raw materials and machinery, solar power equipment, relief supplies, and goods for disabled people. Bangladesh allows duty-free (bonded) imports of certain raw materials to be used for producing finished goods for export. Additional information on customs duties is available on the National Board of Revenue website.

Duty rates fall primarily within three tiers:

Certain machineries and basic raw materials	0.0% & 6%
Intermediate Products	6% & 13%

Finished products	25%

Bangladesh allows 1,491 and 1,861 products to enter into the local market through lower and mid level duty tiers while some 3,148 come in through the highest tier. The Customs Service also collects variety of additional border charges, including a 4% infrastructure development surcharge levied on almost all imports, excepting some commodities like rice and cotton. (Details are available online: National Board of revenue Tariff Database.) An advance income tax is levied on importers; the advance tax payments can be claimed as a tax credit at the end of the tax year. A trade neutral value added tax (VAT) of 15% is levied on all imports and domestically produced goods, with some exceptions, although uneven enforcement may favor domestically produced goods. The Government developed a new VAT law that, once implemented, aims to broaden coverage and increase VAT revenues. Supplementary duties of 20%, 35%, 65%, 100% and higher are levied on certain products with the highest duties on beer (250%) and alcohol & cigarettes (350%). Excise duties have been abolished on all items except bank accounts and airline tickets. Certain products are exempt from VAT. Other export-oriented industries and indirect exporters can claim a duty-drawback at stated rates.

TRADE BARRIERS

In addition to high tariff rates and supplementary duties, Bangladesh has registration procedures and other regulatory requirements that often impede market access. Bangladesh is a member of the Bay of Bengal Initiative for Multi-Sectoral Technical and Economic Co-operation (BIMSTEC) that was formed in 1997 with the key goal of a tariff free zone by 2017. The members of the cooperation are: Bangladesh, India, Myanmar, Sri Lanka, Thailand, Bhutan and Nepal. The BIMSTEC free trade agreement in goods took effect on July 1, 2006. Bangladesh is also a member of the South Asia Association for Regional Cooperation (SAARC) , along with Bhutan, India, Pakistan, the Maldives, Nepal, and Sri Lanka. SAARC members have agreed to pursue tariff reductions under the South Asia Free Trade Agreement (SAFTA) .

IMPORT REQUIREMENTS AND DOCUMENTATION

Unless otherwise specified, all imports must be made by opening an irrevocable letter of credit (L/C) which requires an approved Letter of Credit Authorization (LCA) form from Bangladesh Bank (the central bank). As a safety cushion against currency fluctuations, banks prefer to source foreign currency for letters of credit (L/Cs) over $500,000 from the central bank. Typically, 1-2 days are required to obtain registration from the central bank. Even in those cases where an L/C is not mandated, the Embassy strongly recommends U.S. exporters use them. Despite its name, the LCA is required whether or not the transaction involves a letter of credit. Import against an LCA may be made without opening an L/C in the following areas:

* Books, journals, magazines, and periodicals on sight draft of issuance bill basis

* Any permissible item for an amount not exceeding $25,000 in any one local fiscal year (July 1 - June 30) against remittances made from Bangladesh

* Commodity aid, grant or such other loan for which there are specified procurement procedures for import of goods without an L/C

* "International Chemical References" through bank drafts by recognized pharmaceutical (allopathic) firms on the approval of the Director, Drug Administration, for the purpose of quality control of their products

Importers must submit to their nominated banks the following documents with the LCA:

* L/C application form duly signed by the importer

* Indents for goods issued by indenter or a pro forma invoice obtained from the foreign supplier

* Insurance cover note

Foreign firms are allowed to import permissible commercial items with prior permission from the Chief Controller of Import and Export and need to provide the following documents:

* Photocopy of the valid Import Registration Certificate

* Photocopies of invoices, bill of lading, and import permit duly certified by the bank

* Original or copy of the General Index Register (GIR) certificate from the Income Tax Authority

* Certified copy of the last income tax assessment order

* Name and description of each item to be imported with quantity and approximate CIF value

Public sector importers also need to provide the following documentation:

* Attested photocopy of allocation letter issued by the allocating authority in favor of the concerned public sector agency specifying the source, amount, purpose, validity, and the terms and conditions

* Attested photocopy of sub-allocation letter, if any, issued in favor of the importing agency or unit

* Attested photocopy of sanction letter from the administrative ministry or authority, where applicable

* A declaration by the authorized officer of the importing agency indicating the amount of utilized/unutilized government funds and that imported raw materials will not be sold

Private sector importers need to furnish the following documents:

* Valid membership certificate from the registered local chamber of commerce and industry or any trade association, established on an all-Bangladesh basis, representing any special trade or business

* Proof of payment of renewal fees for the Import Registration Certificate (IRC) for the concerned fiscal year

* Copy of a "TIN Certificate" issued by the tax authority. The TIN (Tax Identification Number) Certificate is intended to ensure collection of income tax, VAT and other revenues from importers

* A declaration, in triplicate, that the importer has paid income tax or submitted an income tax return for the preceding year

* Any such documents as may be required by import policy order or public notice, or instruction issued by the Chief Controller of Imports and Exports

In the following case, neither an LCA nor the opening of an L/C will be necessary, but an import permit (IP) or clearance permit (CP) will have to be obtained by the importer:

* Books, magazines, journals, periodicals and scientific and laboratory equipment against surrender of UNESCO coupons

* Pay-as-you-earn scheme for a limited number of cars, fishing vessels, cargo or passenger vessels, and new machinery on the basis of clearance from the Bangladesh Bank

* Items by passengers coming from abroad in excess of the permissible limits as per permitted allowance

* Free samples, advertising materials, and gift items above prescribed ceilings

U.S. EXPORT CONTROLS

Exports of goods and services to Bangladesh are generally permitted, subject to U.S. laws and regulations governing export of certain goods generally. Information and guidance on the application of U.S. export controls to a company's products is available from US Export Controls and Licenses and the Bureau of Industry and Security .

TEMPORARY ENTRY

Agents and representatives of foreign manufacturers are allowed to import machinery and equipment from their principals for purposes of demonstration or exhibition, subject to the following conditions:

* The goods brought into Bangladesh will be re-exported within a period of one year

* The importer executes a bond and furnishes a bank guarantee or understanding or a legal instrument to the satisfaction of Customs at the time of clearance indicating that the goods will be re-exported in a timely manner

* If the goods include any banned or restricted items, prior permission is required from the Chief Controller of Imports and Exports

Equipment or machinery imported on a temporary basis can be exempt from duty if the importer obtains an import/export permit.

LABELING AND MARKING REQUIREMENTS

Imported goods (including their containers) must not bear any words or inscriptions of a religious connotation, the use or disposal of which may injure the religious beliefs of any class of the citizens of Bangladesh. In addition, imported goods should not bear any obscene pictures, writing, inscription, or visible representation. Milk and any products containing milk may be imported in cans and in bulk. The container must indicate the ingredients in Bangla as well as the manufacturing and expiration dates in Bangla or English. A measuring spoon must be supplied in all containers of dehydrated baby food. Non-fat dried milk is importable only in airtight containers with the date of manufacture and expiration noted in Bangla or English. Pesticide containers must be able to withstand "handling by sea," be labeled with the chemical contents, and meet other specifications.

PROHIBITED AND RESTRICTED IMPORTS

Bangladesh's places controls on imports of some items currently listed in the Import Policy Order 2012-2015 . Items banned on either religious, social, health, or economic policy grounds include illegal drugs, materials that would offend religious sensitivities, certain agricultural products and several types of reconditioned equipment. In addition, the import of goods from Israel and shipment of goods on vessels operating under the Israeli flag is prohibited. Additional items are restricted, but not banned, from import for religious, social, health, security or trade reasons. Of the restricted items, some may be imported with prior permission, while other items may be imported only by authorized industrial users, (e.g., pharmaceutical enterprises) or government agencies (e.g., arms and ammunition).

CUSTOMS REGULATIONS AND CONTACT INFORMATION

Bangladesh Customs operates under the National Board of Revenue (NBR), which is the lead tax collection agency in Bangladesh. The NBR is part of the Internal Resources Division (IRD) under the Ministry of Finance. The Customs wing of the NBR formulates policy concerning the levy and collection of customs duties and related taxes. For more information, please visit the National Board of Revenue .

The two main customs offices in Bangladesh are:
Dhaka Custom House
Kurmitola, Dhaka.
Phone: +880-2-8914890 - 5(PABX)
Fax : +880-2 - 8911132
Contact Person:
Commissioner Customs House (Dhaka) Phone: +880-2-8911101
Chittagong Custom House
Chittagong
Phone: +880-31 - 723101 - 7 (PABX)
Fax : +880-31 - 7139

INDUSTRIAL AND TRADE STANDARDS

The Bangladesh Standards and Testing Institution (BSTI) is responsible for monitoring product quality and acceptability. The institute inspects products for conformity with applicable product standards and safety regulations and issues product certifications.

STANDARDS ORGANIZATIONS

Quality standards are set and monitored by the Bangladesh Standards and Testing Institution (BSTI). Quality standards are set following international standards, such as those established by the International Standards Organization. Bangladesh also recognizes and accepts goods bearing certifications from standards institutions of other countries. The Department of Drugs Administration under the Ministry of Health and Family Welfare controls the standards for pharmaceuticals. The Bangladesh Atomic Energy Commission tests imported food items to ensure that the prescribed standard for radioactivity is maintained.

NIST Notify U.S. Service

Member countries of the World Trade Organization (WTO) are required under the Agreement on Technical Barriers to Trade (TBT Agreement) to report to the WTO all proposed technical regulations that could affect trade with other Member countries. Notify U.S. is a free, web-based e-mail subscription service that offers an opportunity to review and comment on proposed foreign technical regulations that can affect your access to international markets. Register online at Internet URL: http://www.nist.gov/notifyus/

CONFORMITY ASSESSMENT

Product conformity with applicable standards is monitored by the applicable standards organization, as described above.

PRODUCT CERTIFICATION

When required, products are certified by the standards organizations identified above. There are no mutual recognition agreements (MRAs) between the U.S. and Bangladesh. Bangladesh is developing MRAs with India.

ACCREDITATION

Accreditation, when required, is done through the applicable standards organization, as described above.

PUBLICATION OF TECHNICAL REGULATIONS

The Bangladesh Government Press, the government printing office, publishes the weekly "Bangladesh Gazette" every Thursday. The gazette provides official notice of government actions, including the issuance of government rules and regulations and the transfer and promotion of government employees.

LABELING AND MARKING

Imported goods (including their containers) must not bear any words or inscriptions of a religious connotation, the use or disposal of which may injure the religious feelings and beliefs of any class of the citizens of Bangladesh. In addition, imported goods should not bear any obscene pictures, writing, inscription, or visible representation. Milk and any products containing milk may be imported in cans and in bulk. The container must indicate the ingredients in Bangla as well as the manufacturing and expiration dates in Bangla or English. A measuring spoon must be supplied in all containers of dehydrated baby food. Non-fat dried milk is importable only in airtight containers with the date of manufacture and expiration noted in Bangla or English. Pesticide containers must be able to withstand "handling by sea," be labeled with the chemical contents, and meet other specifications.

Contacts The Bangladesh Standards and Testing Institution (BSTI) http://www.bsti.gov.bd/

TRADE AGREEMENTS

Bangladesh is a founding member of the World Trade Organization, where it has been active in promoting the interests of the least developed countries. Bangladesh is a member of the South Asia Preferential Trade Agreement (SAPTA) and the South Asia Free Trade Agreement (SAFTA), both under the umbrella of the South Asia Association for Regional Cooperation (SAARC). Bangladesh is also a signatory to the Bangkok agreement, which aims at trade liberalization between LDCs in Asia. Bangladesh is a member of BIMSTEC, an organization that seeks to promote economic cooperation among its members: Bangladesh, India, Burma, Sri Lanka, Thailand, Bhutan and Nepal.

WEB RESOURCES

South Asia Association for Regional Cooperation (SAARC) Bay of Bengal Initiative for Multi-Sectoral Technical and Economic Co-operation (BIMSTEC) http://www.saarc-sec.org/

South Asia Free Trade Agreement (SAFTA) SAARC Preferential Trading Arrangement (SAPTA) Bangladesh Standards and Testing Institution (BSTI) http://www.bsti.gov.bd/

Bangladesh University of Engineering & Technology (BUET) Bangladesh Board of Investment http://www.buet.ac.bd/

TRADE AND PROJECT FINANCING

METHODS OF PAYMENT

Unless the importer is a multinational company operating in Bangladesh or a reliable, long-standing Bangladeshi customer, the Embassy strongly recommends all U.S. exporters require their local buyers to present irrevocable, confirmed letters of credit to secure payment, preferably from a U.S. bank. This is true whether the importer is a private firm or part of the government and whether or not the importer is being financed by a multilateral institution or bilateral donor agency or government. U.S. exporters should also be aware that it is a normal business practice for government procurement agencies to require exporters to post performance bonds. Performance bonds can be arranged with a bank operating in Bangladesh, including several international banks.

BANKING SYSTEM

The banking sector in Bangladesh started with six nationalized commercialized banks, two State-owned specialized banks, and three foreign banks. Throughout the 1980s a number of private banks entered the sector private banks. Bangladesh has two primarily types of banks:

* Scheduled Banks: The banks which are licensed to operate under Bank Company Act, 1991 (Amended in 2003) are termed as Scheduled Banks.

* Non-Scheduled Banks: The banks which are established for special and definite objectives and operate under the acts that are enacted for meeting up those objectives, are termed as Non-Scheduled Banks. These banks cannot perform all the functions of scheduled banks.

There are 56 scheduled banks in Bangladesh who operate under full control and supervision of Bangladesh Bank, the Central Bank, which is empowered to do so through Bangladesh Bank Order, 1972 and Bank Company Act, 1991. Scheduled Banks are classified into following types:

* State Owned Commercial Banks (SOCBs): There are four SOCBs which are fully or majority-owned by the Government of Bangladesh.

* Specialized Banks (SDBs): Four specialized banks were established for specific objectives including agricultural or industrial development. These banks are also fully or majority-owned by the Government of Bangladesh.

* Private Commercial Banks (PCBs): There are 39 private commercial banks which are majority-owned by the private entities. PCBs can be categorized into two groups:

o Conventional PCBs: 31 conventional PCBs perform conventional banking operations involving interest.

o Islamic Shariah based PCBs: There are eight Islamic Shariah based PCBs in Bangladesh, and they execute banking activities according to Islamic Shariah-based principles, i.e. Profit-Loss Sharing (PLS) mode.

* Foreign Commercial Banks (FCBs): Nine FCBs operate in Bangladesh as the branches of the banks which are incorporated abroad.

There are now four non-scheduled banks in Bangladesh which are:

* Ansar VDP Unnayan Bank,

* Karmashangosthan Bank,

* Probashi Kollyan Bank,

* Jubilee Bank

Currently, there are 31 Non-Bank Financial Institutions (NBFIs), which are regulated under Financial Institution Act, 1993 and controlled by Bangladesh Bank. Out of the total, two are fully government-owned, one is the subsidiary of an SOCB, 13 were initiated by private domestic initiatives, and 15 were initiated by joint venture initiatives.

Government-owned or controlled banks tend to have weak financial soundness due to historic patterns of directed lending to money-losing state-owned enterprises and to unsecured private borrowers without sufficient due diligence, resulting in high percentages of non-performing loans..

Bangladesh Bank regulates all banking institutions with influence from the Ministry of Finance. The Bangladesh Bank Governor and other senior officials are appointed by the Prime Minister and coordinate monetary policy and banking regulations with the Finance Ministry and other

Executive Branch Ministries. The central bank has taken several steps to improve bank oversight, including expanded use of core-risk analysis in its bank audits and establishment of an anti-money laundering unit.

FOREIGN-EXCHANGE CONTROLS

The Bangladesh Bank maintains an approval process for foreign currency transfers, including transfers relating to trade and investment transactions. While the approval process can be cumbersome, currency convertibility has historically not been a major impediment to trade and investment. In 2011, balance of payments deficits contributed to temporary foreign currency shortages that delayed some import transactions, but strong remittances helped restore a balance of payments surplus in 2012, and balance

of payments was not an issue in 2013.

U.S. BANKS AND LOCAL CORRESPONDENT BANKS

All scheduled banks have arrangements with U.S. correspondent banks for their U.S. dollar clearing requirements. Additional information is available from the U.S. Embassy's Trade Center: phone: 880-2-885-5500; email: ustc-dhaka@state.gov.

PROJECT FINANCING

The government procurement market encompasses a wide range of projects that are usually financed by donors, although from time to time the government may finance its own projects or ask bidders to propose financing. The U.S. Agency for International Development (USAID), the Japanese government's development aid program (JICA), the World Bank, and the Asian Development Bank (ADB) are important sources of development project financing in Bangladesh.

The U.S. Foreign Commercial Services maintains liaison offices at the World Bank and the ADB to assist U.S. suppliers and consultants in competing for projects and activities funded by these organizations. The commercial liaison office works closely with ADB's U.S. Executive Director who represents the U.S. on the bank's board of directors.

WEB RESOURCES

Export-Import Bank of the United States: http://www.exim.gov
Country Limitation Schedule: http://www.exim.gov/tools/country/country_limits.html
OPIC: http://www.opic.gov
Trade and Development Agency: http://www.tda.gov/
SBA's Office of International Trade: http://www.sba.gov/oit/
USDA Commodity Credit Corporation: http://www.fsa.usda.gov/ccc/default.htm
U.S. Agency for International Development: http://www.usaid.gov
Bangladesh Government Web Portal: www.bangladeshgov.org/
Asian Development Bank: www.adb.org

BUSINESS TRAVEL

BUSINESS CUSTOMS

Personal contact is an important element in building business relationships in Bangladesh. Bangladeshi business executives are usually very courteous, and try to make their foreign guests feel at ease. Business visitors should be aware that in Bangladesh, men and women do not usually shake hands with each other, and may avoid doing so with a visitor of the opposite sex. Foreign visitors often find that hosting meals for their Bangladeshi agents or business contacts helps to smooth business negotiations. Visitors may also be invited to share meals as guests of their Bangladeshi hosts. Attire for social functions is often "informal," meaning business attire as opposed to formal wear. Women should dress conservatively but are not expected to cover their heads. While meetings generally start on time, conferences and social functions often start significantly later than their announced time.

TRAVEL ADVISORY

Updated travel advisory information on Bangladesh is available from the State Department's Bureau of Consular Affairs in several formats. For recorded information, call (202) 647-5225. For information by fax, call (202) 647-3000. Travel advisory information for Bangladesh can also be found on the U.S. Embassy website: http://dhaka.usembassy.gov/acs_tips_travelers.html

http://dhaka.usembassy.gov/msg-for-us-citizens.html

For further details on entry requirements for Bangladesh, travelers can contact:

Bangladesh Embassy in Washington: http://www.bdembassyusa.org/ 3510 International Drive Washington, D.C. 20008 Telephone: (202) 244-0183, fax: (202) 244-5366

Consulate General of the People's Republic of Bangladesh, New York 211 East 43rd St., Suite 502 New York, NY 10017 Telephone: (212) 599-6767/599-6850, fax (212)682-9211

Consulate General of the People's Republic of Bangladesh, Los Angeles

10850 Wilshire Blvd., Suite 1250 Los Angeles, CA, 90024 Telephone: (310) 441-9399, (310) 441-5983, fax: (310) 441-4458.

Foreign nationals staying on regular or temporary visits longer than 90 days are required to show a Submission of Income Tax Clearance Certificate or Income Tax Exemption Certificate when departing Bangladesh. For additional information on these forms, travelers may contact:

National Board of Revenue (NBR): www.nbr-bd.org

Rajasha Bhaban, Segunbagicha Dhaka Telephone: +880-2 933-3444.

The International Certificate of Vaccination is no longer required for travel to Bangladesh, but typhoid and hepatitis immunizations are required. Malaria suppressants are recommended for those traveling outside Dhaka.

VISA REQUIREMENTS

Travelers are encouraged to contact the Bangladesh Embassy in Washington or the nearest Bangladesh consulate to obtain a visa before traveling to Bangladesh. Travelers can also apply for visas upon arrival, but the rules and fees governing visas on arrival are subject to change. For visa extensions, travelers may contact the Department of Immigration and Passport Office, Agargaon, Sher-e-Bangla Nagar, Dhaka, telephone (880-2) 911-3318, fax: (880-2) 912-3399. Generally, extensions are granted for 3-6 months (short-term) with a single entry. A one year or more (long-term) extension for an expatriate working on a government project may require a letter from the relevant ministry and a security clearance from the Home Ministry through the related ministry, along with the prescribed visa extension application form. This process can be long and complicated. Travelers expecting to visit Bangladesh for extended periods are recommended to apply for a long-term multiple entry visa from a Bangladeshi embassy or consulate in the U.S.

U.S. Companies that require travel of foreign businesspersons to the United States should be advised that security evaluations are handled via an interagency process. Visa applicants should go to the following links.

State Department Visa Website: http://travel.state.gov/visa/
United States Visas.gov: http://www.unitedstatesvisas.gov/
Embassy Dhaka's Consular Section: http://dhaka.usembassy.gov/visa_services.html

TELECOMMUNICATIONS

Bangladesh has made steady progress in developing telecommunications services, particularly mobile telephone and internet services. While the government-run telephone service has been slow to expand land lines, six mobile phone operators have rapidly expanded mobile phone networks to cover nearly 100 percent of Bangladesh territory. At the same time, mobile phone providers expanded their subscriber base from less than 1 million subscribers in 2001 to more than 110 million subscribers by the end of 2013, with a growth rate of 17.1%. In FY 2012-13 the contribution of telecom industry to

country's GDP was over 3.1% compared to 0.8% in India, Pakistan and Indonesia; 1% Sri Lanka and 1.8 % in Malaysia and Thailand.

The expansion of mobile networks has also contributed to the increase in internet connectivity in Bangladesh. As a growing number of internet service providers have offered broadband internet connections through DSL, fiber optic and WIMAX connections, mobile phone operators offer more limited connectivity through over a wider area through mobile phone networks. Bangladesh relies on the SEA-ME-WE-4 submarine fiber-optic cable system for international connectivity and the Government is seeking to expand broadband connectivity through additional connections.

TRANSPORTATION

Bangladesh's main international airport, Shahjalal International Airport, is located at Kurmitola, about 12 kilometers north of Dhaka city. The national air carrier, Biman Airlines, is the major domestic carrier. Private airlines GMG, Regent and United Airways have flights from Dhaka to Chittagong, Cox's Bazaar, Jessore, and Sylhet. GMG and United have also offered international routes to Kolkata, New Delhi, Bangkok, Kathmandu, Kuala Lumpur, Singapore, Dubai and London. Public transportation is limited in Dhaka but business travelers can use rental car services and hotel transportation in Dhaka and other metropolitan areas.

LANGUAGE

Although Bangla (Bengali) is the official language of Bangladesh, English is widely spoken and used in official and business circles. U.S. business people may greet their Bangladeshi counterparts with normal English salutations. The usual greeting among Bangladeshis is the Arabic phrase "as-salaam-alaikum" (meaning "peace be with you"). The cordial response is "walaikum salaam" ("peace to you as well"). A polite parting phrase is "Khoda haafez" ("God preserve").

HEALTH

Visitors should exercise care in what they eat and drink since water-borne intestinal illnesses are common in Bangladesh. Travelers are advised to drink bottled/boiled water and eat only fruits and vegetables that have been cooked or peeled. Undercooked meat should be avoided. Travelers should also avoid eating uncooked dairy products and food sold on the streets. There are periodic outbreaks of dengue fever, which is transmitted by a day-biting mosquito. Travelers may bring insect repellent as a precautionary measure. Visitors who take medication on a regular basis should bring enough for the duration of their visit. It is not always possible to find equivalents for American prescriptions on the local market. In general, local medical facilities are substandard, except for a few outpatient clinics. Some modern hospital facilities Apollo Hospital , Square Hospital and United Hospital opened since 2005. Travelers are strongly encouraged to obtain medical insurance including medevac insurance before traveling to Bangladesh.

LOCAL TIME, BUSINESS HOURS, AND HOLIDAYS

Bangladesh observes a Sunday-Thursday workweek. Business hours are 9:00 am –

5:00 pm. The Embassy observes a two-day weekend (Friday and Saturday). Muslim religious holidays vary with the appearance of the moon.

Local & American holidays will be observed by the U.S. Embassy in 2014 are as follows:

HOLIDAYS DATES MISSION CLOSED

New Year's Day American January 1 Wednesday
Martin Luther King's Birthday American January 19 Sunday+
President's Day American February 16 Sunday+
Independence Day (Bangladesh) Bangladeshi March 26 Wednesday
Bengali New Year Bangladeshi April 14 Monday
May Day Bangladeshi May 1 Thursday
Buddha Purnima# Bangladeshi May 13 Tuesday#
Memorial Day American May 25 Sunday+
Independence Day (U.S.) American July 3 Thursday
Eid~ul~Fitr* Bangladeshi July 29 & 30 Tuesday & Wednesday*
Janmashtami# Bangladeshi August 17 Sunday#
Labor Day American August 31 Sunday+
Eid~ul~Azha* Bangladeshi October 5 & 6 Sunday & Monday*
Columbus Day American October 12 Sunday+
Veterans Day American November 11 Tuesday
Thanksgiving Day American November 27 Thursday
Victory Day Bangladeshi December 16 Tuesday
Christmas Day American December 25 Thursday+

There are additional local holidays that are not observed by the Embassy.

TEMPORARY ENTRY OF MATERIALS AND PERSONAL BELONGINGS

Agents and representatives of foreign manufacturers are allowed to import machinery and equipment from their principals for purposes of demonstration or exhibition, subject to the following conditions:

* The goods brought into Bangladesh will be re-exported within a period of one year

* The importer shall execute a bond and furnish a bank guarantee or understanding or a legal instrument to the satisfaction of Customs at the time of clearance indicating that the goods will be re-exported in a timely manner

* If the goods include any banned or restricted items, prior permission is required from the Chief Controller of Imports and Exports Equipment or machinery imported on a temporary basis is exempt from duty if the importer obtains an import/export permit.

CONTACTS

BUSINESS CHAMBERS

American Chamber of Commerce in Bangladesh (AmCham) http://www.amchambd.org/

Dhaka Chamber of Commerce & Industry http://www.dhakachamber.com/

Bangladesh Chamber of Industry (BCI) http://www.bangladeshchamber.org/

Foreign Investors' Chambers of Commerce & Industry (FICCI)

Federation of Bangladesh Chamber of Commerce & Industry (FBCCI) http://www.fbcci-bd.org/fbcci/

Metropolitan Chamber of Commerce and Industry (MCCI) http://www.mccibd.org/

BANGLADESH GOVERNMENT OFFICES

Bangladesh Government Portal http://www.bangladesh.gov.bd/www.bangladesh.gov.bd

Bangladesh Export Processing Zones Authority (BEPZA) http://www.epzbangladesh.org.bd/

Board of Investment http://www.boi.gov.bd/

Bangladesh Bank (the Central Bank) http://www.bangladesh-bank.org/

Export Promotion Bureau http://www.epb.gov.bd/

National Board of Revenue http://www.nbr-bd.org/

Securities & Exchange Commission http://www.sec.gov.bd/

U.S. TRADE CENTER AT THE U.S. EMBASSY IN DHAKA:

U.S. Embassy Phone Number: +880-2-885-5500 ext. 2712
U.S. Embassy Fax Number: +880-2-882-3744, 988-7826
U.S. Embassy Website: US Embassy - Bangladesh
U.S. Trade Center Email Address: US Trade Center - Dhaka

EXPORT POLICY AND REGULATION

Acceleration of production and expansion of trade result in growth of national wealth. Increased production in export sectors may become the prime mover in the development cycle in a densely populate of Bangladesh like our as this will generate employment opportunities which in turn will generate savings and investment on consequent flow of capital. The prime national objective of poverty alleviation will thus be materialised. As a first step towards reaching this goal we need to look at the country's production infrastructure.

Our export trade is featured by the dominance of a few commodities in a narrow market. Such dependence on at limited number of export items targeted a limited market is not desirable for economic development. We must, therefore, aim both at product and market diversification or else our export trade will become stagnant in the near future.

Our export trade must keep pace with the projected GDP growth @ 7% and make due contribution through increased export earning. In this exercise it is imperative to identify new thrust sectors, increased export of higher value added items, diversify product wise , ensure products quality, improve packaging, attain efficient productivity. We should aim at marketing quality products at competitive price at the correct time.

The Export Policy 1997-2002 has been designed to operate in the imperatives and opportunities of the market economy with a view to maximizing export growth and narrowing down the gap between import payment and export earning.

OBJCTIVES

The principal objectives of this policy are :

To achieve optimum national growth through increase of export in regional and international market;

To narrow down the gap between the country's export earning and import payment through achievement of the export targets ;

To undertake timely steps for production of exportable goods at a competitive price with a view to exporting and strengthening existing export markets and making dent in new markets;

To take the highest advantage of entering into the post Uruguay liberalized and globalized international market;

To make our exportable items more attractive to the market through product diversification and quality improvement;

To establish backward linkage industries and services with a view to using more indigenous raw materials, expand the product base and identify and export higher value added products ;

To simplify export procedures and to rationalize and solidify export incentives;

To develop and expand infrastructure ;

To develop trained human resources in the export sector;

To raise the quality and grading of export products to internationallyrecognized levels.

STRATEGIES

The following strategies shall be undertaken to attain the objectives of the export policy 1997 - 2001 :

Simplifying export procedures, and helping the private sector achieve efficiency. The Govt.. desires more and more involvement of the private sector while the govt. will continue to play its facilitating role;

Enhancing technological strength and productivity and facilitating reduce cost and attain internationally accepted standard of quality of exportable products and thereby consolidate their competitiveness ;

Ensuring maximum use of local raw materials in the production of export goods and encouraging establishment of backward linkage industries;

Participation in the international trade fairs, specialized fairs, single country exhibitions abroad and also sending out trade missions, with a view to consolidating our position in the existing market and creating new markets;

Encouraging export of new category high value added readymade garments and also encouraging the concerned trade associations for establishment of a Fashion Institute ;

For promotion of high value added leather and leather goods export: providing various facilities including bonded warehouse facilities for import of materials such as raw hides, pickled, wet blue, crushed and finished leather, components and chemicals etc. to 100% export oriented leather industries;

For promotion of export of shrimp: Extension and modernization of traditional/semi-intensive method of shrimp cultivation and ensuring quality as per buyers requirements ;

For promotion of export of jute and jute goods: Undertaking extensive publicity of jute and jute goods as environment-friendly natural fibre and diversification of the uses of jute products;

For promotion of export of tea undertaking programmes for establishing brand name and developing linkage with established blending and distributing agents;

For promotion of export of agrobased products: undertaking programmes for raising quality standard and expansion of market;

For the promotion of export of electrical and electronic goods (including computer software and data entry) : Building and ensuring conducive infrastructure;

For the promotion of export of engineering consultancy and other services and sub-contracting involving, in a bigger way, Bangladesh missions abroad obtaining contracts;

Organizing regularly international trade fairs and product-specific fairs with the country;

Making appropriate development and expansion of infrastructure conducive to export;

Making arrangements for necessary technical and practical training for development of skilled manpower in the export sector;

Ensuring maximum utilization of financial and other assistance extended by the World Trade Organization to the Least Developed Countries;

Ensuring maintenance of ecological balance and pollution-free environment in the production of exportable goods;

Extending technical and marketing assistance for development of new products and for finding appropriate marketing strategies;

Taking necessary steps to assist procurement of raw materials by the export oriented industries at world price ;

SCOPE AND GENERAL PROVISIONS

This policy shall apply to the customs areas (excluding Export Processing Zones) of Bangladesh.

This policy shall take effect from 01.07.1998 and remain in force till 30.06.2002. However, the policy shall be considered valid until the next Export Policy is announced.

If any provision of this policy is found inconsistent with any provisions of the Imports and Exports (Control) Act, 1950, or of the Import Policy Order, the Ministry of Commerce shall be entitled to amend, alter or modify such provision.

The Ministry of Commerce may, as and when necessary, amend, alter or modify any provision of the Export Policy including the export negative/restricted items.

Different aspects of the Export Policy shall be reviewed annually.

TARGET

For the policy period Export targets have been set at US dollar 5020 million for the fiscal year (F.Y.) 1997-98, US dollar 5,630 million for the F.Y.1998-99, US dollar 6,340 million for the F.Y. 1999-2000, US dollar 7,175 million for the F.Y. 2000-2001 and US dollar 8,100 million for the F.Y. 2001-2002. Details of the export targets have been shown at annexure 'A'.

EXPORT PROMOTION COUNCILS/COMMITTEES

A National committee on export has been formed. The highest level committee on export promotion, is headed by the Honourable Prime Minister and consists of the Honourable Ministers for Foreign Affairs, Finance, Commerce and Industries, Planning, Jute and Textile as well as senior government officials and representatives of important trade associations. The committee reviews the export situation, provides necessary directions and readily resolves problems.

For immediate attention and action on export related problem a task force has been formed under the chairmanship of the Honourable Minister forCommerce.

With a view to exchanging ideas with Chambers of Commerce and Industries, Exporters' Associations and private sector organizations in formulating export policy and strategies, and up lamenting policy decisions an export council has been formed.

A task force shall also be formed to recommend practical measures for export increase and monitoring the implementation of incentives and facilities of thrust sector and crash programme items.

Commodity Councils

Commodity Councils shall be formed for jute, tea, shrimp, readymade garments and leather & leather products.

THRUST SECTOR

Leather and leather goods industries, high and high value added readymade garments, computer software and agro-processing sectors have been identified as thrust' sectors in this export policy. Although the leather and leather goods sector has enormous export potential the sector has not been able, till date, to achieve desired results. On the other hand, the readymade garments sector is expected to stage a breakthrough in the export of high-priced, high value added garments of newer categories after having survived successfully the initial phase of exporting low-end garments. Like wise computer software and agro-processing sectors could not record the desired level of export through the sectors offer bright prospects for earning foreign exchange. These -four sectors have been declared, 'Thrust Sectors', in this policy to ensure priority with the following lines of actions :

LEATHER & LEATHER GOODS

Leather manufacturing units shall be modernized in order to enable them to produce increased quality of finished leather out of raw hides.

With a view to reducing cost of production, steps shall be taken to establish accessories industries for producing necessary chemicals and other inputs within the country.

The existing Leather Technology Institute shall be modernized for use as a 'Common Facilities Centre' for the suscountry leather units.

Necessary credit facilities shall be extended for setting up of leather goods industries and efforts for marketing the produces shall be strengthened.

Cluster industries comprising small units of leather goods factories shall be set up with a view to generating employment.

A 'Leather Council' shall be formed.

Industrial units having no bonded warehouse at the same time not interested to avail of duty draw back facilities shall be entitled to cash benefit in lieu of duty drawback.

Import of raw hides including wet blue and pickled leather, shall continue with the prevailing customs duty (2.5%) and import licence fee (2.5%) leviable on the importation of raw leather for three years.

Uniform policy on bank loan as regards criteria and rate of interest shall be followed for credit to leather sector.

The total credit excluded to the leather sector shall be brought under a single bank and export will also be effected through that designated bank.

After careful revision of the overall situation prevailing in the leather industries, the time-limit for export of crust leather has been extended upto the year 2000. Facilities for BMRE and other transformation process shall be made available to all tanning units to enable them to switcher by 2000, to processing crust/finished leather from wet blue leather.

READYMADE GARMENTS:

All out efforts would be made and steps taken for production and export of high priced readymade garments in the light of the prevailing market demand.

Immediate steps shall be taken to establish a Fashion Institute pending establishment of the Fashion Institute measures will be taken, under special arrangements, to extend expert services to match the actual demand.

Liberal credit may be considered for capacity building and hiring technology for producer of high quality garments.

COMPUTER SOFTWARE

For the development of human resources in the software information of computer science, courses in all universities including B.I.T. and Polytechnic Institute and selected colleges shall be considered similarly for having a pool of skilled and trained instructors basic computer scheme at graduation level may be introduced.

An Information Technology Village making multifacet facilities shall be established as part of infrastructure development for promotion of export in this sector.

As a fillip to effective software marketing appropriate provisions on protection of intellectual imports shall be incorporated in the existing copyright Act.

AERO PROCESSING

For the development of the agro-processing industries 'Hortex Foundation' has already been established. Development activities of this sector under the Foundations programmes will go on.

EXPORT INCENTIVES

In the light of the objectives and strategies of the Export Policy 1997-2002, several new incentives and facilities have been made available to the exporters. Besides, some existing incentives have been modified and improved to make them more workable. The rest of the existing facilities and incentives will remain unchanged. The incentives as offered are enumerated below:

FISCAL INCENTIVES

Restructuring of the Export Credit Guarantee Scheme (ECGS): At present, there are four schemes, namely, the Export Credit Guarantee (Pre-shipment), Export Credit Guarantee (Post-shipment), Export Payment Risk Policy (Comprehensive Guarantee) and Whole Turnover Pre-shipment Finance Guarantee, available under the Export Credit Guarantee Scheme (ECGS) covering risks on export credit as well as probable commercial and political risks occurring abroad. These schemes, however , are becoming effective to the desired extent due to existence of various complicacies in realizing their benefits. To strengthen the role of the Export Credit Guarantee the schemes shall be restructured.

CONVERTIBILITY OF TAKA

Taka has been made convertible in the current account in lieu with the policy of export-led growth in the liberalized world market. As a result, earning from the trading account shall be freely convertible into foreign exchange for import of goods (barring a few banned items). Under this arrangement, exporters shall be allowed to retain their foreign exchange earnings in their respective foreign exchange accounts gradually at higher proportion.

UTILIZATION OF FOREIGN EXCHANGE BY EXPORTERS

So long exporters were allowed to retain 20% of their FOB earnings in their respective foreign currency accounts in US dollar or Pound Sterling. From now on they will be entitled to retain either 40% of such earning or at a rate fixed by the government from time to time on proper review. However, in cases of export products where the import contents used in the manufacture of such items are relatively high (such as, naptha, furnace oil, bitumen and other petroleum products, readymade garments and electronic goods) and in the case of export of services (legal advice, consultancy and similar professional services), the exporters concerned will be entitled to retain only 7.5% of their FOB export earnings. Immediately on realization of export proceeds, the concerned banks will credit the exporters' foreign currency account in proportion to their respective entitlements.

Exporters may utilize this foreign exchange for bonafide business purposes, namely, undertaking business trips abroad, participating in export fairs and seminars, importing raw materials, machineries and spares and even setting up overseas business offices. Foreign exchange may also be kept in the renewable fixed deposit account which will bear interest.

EXPORT PROMOTION FUND (EPF)

The following assistance and support would be provided out of the Export Promotion Fund to producers/exporters of new and non-traditional items including those under the crash programme for product development and product and market diversification:

(a) Venture capital on easy terms and low interest rates ;
(b) Assistance in obtaining foreign technology and consultancy for product development and diversification;
(c) Assistance in fielding marketing missions abroad and participating in international fairs for market compatibility of products;
(d) Assistance in Establishing Sales and Display Centres abroad and extending warehousing facilities ; (e) Assistance for participation in overseas training programmes on product development and marketing help develop technical skill and marketing expertise ;
(f) Assistance in any other activity related to product and market development.

EXTENSION OF TIME-LIMIT FOR ADJUSTMENT OF EXPORT CREDIT FROM 180 DAYS TO 270 DAYS.

At present export credit is allowed at consessional rate of interest for a maximum period of 180 days. A section of exporters however cannot enjoy the benefit of such concessionary credit facility due to structural characteristics of certain commodities. Under such circumstances, the time-limit for repayment of export credit has been extended from 180 days to 270 days in case of export of frozen food, tea and leather by way of relaxing the condition of submission of firm contract/L.C. and considering working capital as export credit. The time limit for export credit under the Export Promotion Fund in certain cases shall be extended upto 270 days.

EXPORT FINANCING

(a) Introduction of Credit Card : In view of the risks involved in carrying of cash foreign exchange/travellers
cheque while undertaking business trip abroad, the practice of issuing credit cards to exporters against their respective foreign exchange entitlements will continue.
(b) Limit of Export Credit : Exporters may obtain export credit from commercial banks upto 90% of the value of their irrevocable letter of credit/confirmed contract.
(c) Credit to first time applicant : With a view to encouraging the new comers to enter into export trade the commercial banks will consider their credit proposals on a priority basis.
(d) Monitoring the Over-all flow of export credit :
Bangladesh Bank will take necessary steps to ensure that normal flow of export credit is maintained. The C.C. limit of the exporters will be determined only on the basis of their export performance in the preceding year. Tthis will not be subject to any general credit squeeze measure. Such credit facilities will also be available to new contracts.
(e) Overdue interest : No overdue interest will be charged by the commercial banks in cases of export against irrevocable letter of credit on sight payment basis. In such cases, however, exporters will be required to submit necessary export documents within the specified time.
(f) Export credit cell : As special export cell to supervise and monitor the export financing has been functioning in Bangladesh Bank. Besides, in every commercial bank a special unit has been created for processing exclusive export credit proposals.
(g) Export monitoring : A high-powered committee has been functioning to assess the export credit requirement and to review and monitor the flow of export credit to ensure that adequate and timely credit are made available to the exporters.
(h) Inland back-to-back letter of credit : Authorised dealers may establish inland back-to-back letter of credit in favour of local suppliers of raw materials, against the corresponding master letter of credit.

REBATE ON INSURANCE PREMIUM

Special rebates are allowed on premium covering fire and marine insurance to export-oriented industries (non-traditional items). Such rebates will be available also to the exporters of these items on shipment of goods.

Incentives for export of non-traditional industrial products :
Incentives will be provided for export of non-traditional/new industrial products, especially where value addition is 50% or more.

Similarly, export firms having exceeded the proportionate export target set for that product-sector will be considered for incentives facilities.

FISCAL INCENTIVES

IMPORT FACILITIES OF RAW MATERIALS FOR EXPORT-ORIENTED LEATHER INDUSTRIES

To encourage increase in production export at competitive price of finished leather customs duty and import license fee leviable on import of wet blue and pickled leather by export-oriented leather industries will be exempted.

INCOME TAX REBATE ON EXPORT EARNINGS

Previously, 50% rebate on taxable income generated from export earning was admissible under the Finance Act every year. From now on 50% of the income tax on any income on export will be exempted through incorporation of a new provision in the Income Tax Ordinance itself rather than as a temporary relief hitherto granted under the Finance Acts on a yearly basis.

LOWERING THE RATE OF AIT AT SOURCE

Tax at source on all export earnings shall be deducted at the rate of 0.25%

PAYMENT OF DUTY DRAWBACK THROUGH COMMERCIAL BANKS

For quick disbursement of duty drawback with a view to giving a competitive edge to our export in the international market, payments will be made by the commercial banks immediately on receipt of foreign exchange against all exports except the deemed exports, determined on the basis of the principles laid down by the National Board of Revenue.

BONDING FACILITIES FOR EXPORT-ORIENTED INDUSTRIES

Bonded warehouse facilities have generated special enthusiasm among the import-led export-oriented industries. To sustain such interest the procedures for providing bonded warehouse facilities to such industries will be further simplified, and will be extended to all industries recognised as 100% export-oriented industries.

DUTY-FREE IMPORT OF CAPITAL MACHINERY BY EXPORT-ORIENTED INDUSTRIES

Presently, items produced in the Export Processing Zones (EPZ) are entirely exported. Likewise 100% export-oriented industries located elsewhere in the country are also required to export their produces entirely from this point of view as the objectives and functions of the industries of both locations are identical. Duty free import facility of capital machinery has also been extended to the 100% export oriented industies out side the EPZ.

ALTERNATIVE FACILITIES IN LIEU OF CUSTOMS BOND OR DUTY DRAWBACK FOR EXPORT-ORIENTED DOMESTIC TEXTILE SECTOR AND GARMENTS INDUSTRIES

During fiscal year 1995-96, the government, in an attempt to give incentive to the domestic textile and garments sector, allowed 25% compensatory assistance to the industries of this sector. In future also, these sectors will continue to receive reasonable facilities. Such compensatory assistance will also be admissible to a composite unit producing both fabric and garments or to the manufacturer only in case the exporter is not the producer of the local fabric provided no bonded warehouse or duty drawback facilities were availed of for such importation. If, however, the exporter is an intermediary buyer, the facility will go to the original producer of goods.

TAX HOLIDAY

To encourage a rapid growth and attract entrepreneurs to export oriented industries tax holiday incentive will continue till the year 2000 in consonance with the Industrial Policy. The industrial enterprises enjoying the benefit of tax holiday shall be exempted from deduction of tax at source. After 2000, decision on tax holiday will be taken in the light of the government policy of that period.

DUTY DRAWBACK SCHEME

(a) Exporters of manufactured products are entitled to draw back after the export is effected. The amount of duties and taxes paid on importation of raw materials under any of the three systems, namely, actual drawback, notional drawback and flat rate drawback. However, as a simpler mechanism of getting drawback, the flat rate method shall continue to receive greater weightage.
(b) The rate of duty drawback payable on export of all traditional and non-traditional items will be renewed at
regular intervals and more and more, new products will be brought under the duty drawback system.

VALUE ADDED TAX (VAT) ON PACKAGING MATERIALS

Should jute clothes and bags be used in the packing of export goods VAT paid on such products will be refunded.

SIMPLIFICATION OF THE PROCEDURE FOR REFUND OF VAT PAID ON EXPORT SUPPORT SERVICES

To maintain competitiveness of export prices, VAT paid on export support services, namely, C & F service, telephone, telex,fax, electricity, insurance premium, shipping agent's commission/bill will be refunded under a simplified procedure.

PERMISSION FOR SALE OF GOODS REJECTED FOR EXPORTATION

20% of the rejected goods of the 100% export-oriented industries including leather goods and readymade garments will be admissible for sale in the local market subject to payment of usual duties and taxes.

GENERAL INCENTIVES

DECLARING 80% EXPORT ORIENTED LEATHER INDUSTRIES AS 100% EXPORT-ORIENTED INDUSTRIES

Most of the leather industries are able to export at least 80% of their products; rarely they are in a position to export 100 of their product. In order to bringing about dynamism in the leather sector 80% export oriented leather producing units have been declared 100% export-oriented industries.

OTHER 80% EXPORT-ORIENTED INDUSTRIES TO GET IDENTICAL INCENTIVES AVAILABLE TO 100% EXPORT-ORIENTED INDUSTRIES

Other 80% export oriented industries (other than leather industries) will be given following incentives with a view to encouraging their export operations:
(a) Financial incentives including bank loan as available to 100% export-oriented industries. However, the benefits allowed to the 100% export-oriented industries by the National Board of

Revenue in respect of duties and taxes will not be applicable to them.
(b) Sale permission upto 20% of their production in the local market on payment of usual duties and taxes.

REDUCED AIRFREIGHT FOR EXPORT OF ALL CRASH PROGRAMME ITEMS INCLUDING FRUITS AND VEGETABLE

(a) Airfreight at lower rate will be changed for export of all crash programme items including fruits and vegetables.
(b) Withdrawal of royalty from foreign airlines extending cargo services :
In order to ensure export of goods by cargo services of foreign airlines and sell export goods at competitive price, the royalty being presently imposed by Biman Bangladesh Airlines may, if necessary, be further reduced or may be withdrawn altogether.

SETTLEMENT OF TRADE DISPUTES

With the expansion of exports trade disputes are also increasing. In many cases Bangladesh's image as an exporting country is being tarnished because of such disputes. On the other hand, Bangladeshi exporters are also incurring financial losses. To remove such difficulties, the Export Promotion Bureau will initiate steps for settlement of trade disputes through conciliation. For this, necessary amendment will be made in the Charter of Export Promotion Bureau to enable them to perform this responsibility effectively.

RECOGNIZING SMALL AND MEDIUM SIZE AGRICULTURAL FARMS AS INDUSTRY

To encourage production of fruits, vegetables, fresh flowers, orchid etc. for export, agricultural farms of a minimum size of 5 acres have been recognized as 'Industry' and become eligible for all facilities of export-oriented industries.

RESEARCH AND DEVELOPMENT

Marketing of products in the international market is becoming increasingly competitive due to globalization and liberalization of trade.To sustain in the face of such stiff competition, continuous quality improvement and market adaptability have become necessary. For this purpose, industrial enterprises should be equipped with their own Research and Development (R & D) facilities . For this duties and taxes on machinery and equipments imported by export units will be gradually lowered. Research institutions on the recommendation by the Export Promotion Bureau will also be entitled to such benefit.

EXPORT ON THE BASIS OF SUB-CONTRACTING

The sub-contracting service sector has immense potential for export. All out efforts will be made to exploit the opportunities in this sector especially in the automobile industry in Japan and the printing industries in the western countries.

ASSISTANCE TO CONTRACT SERVICES ABROAD LIKE ENGINEERING CONSULTING SERVICES CONTRACT AND CIVIL CONSTRUCTION CONTRACT ETC.

Contract Services like engineering, consulting and civil construction contract abroad have been identified as potential export sector. The following facilities are being extended to assist this sector :

(a) Issuance of bid bond and performance bond, at 1% margin by commercial banks for submission of tender and on receipt of work order respectively;
(b) Allocation of fifty thousand dollars annually to eachorganization to meet the expenditure like maintaining communication, sending representatives, making overseas trips, purchasing tender documents etc. before receipt of actual work order ;
(c) Permission for setting up overseas office and appointment of staff;
(d) Permission for Sadharan Bima's Individual professional guarantee/insurance in favour of project specialists ;
(e) Involving Bangladesh missions abroad to provide information and assistance.

ANNUAL CEILING FOR DESPATCH OF EXPORT SAMPLES

At present, the annual ceiling for despatch of samples to international trade fairs is fixed at US $ 2000 (two thousand). The ceiling for sending samples for purposes other than international fairs was however considered inadequate. It has been raised in phases from Tk.1000 per annum to US $ 1500 (approximately Taka 65,000) per annum. The maximum limit for sending out samples by parcel post will be raised from its present limit of Taka 2,000.00 to Taka 5,000.00

COMMODITIES UNDER THE CRASH PROGRAM

(a) At present toys, luggage and fashion items, electronics, leather goods, diamond cutting and polishing, jewelry, silk fabric, stationery goods, cut and artificial flowers and orchid, gift items, vegetables and engineering consultancy and services have been included under the crash program. In order to boost production and export, promote goods/services under the crash program, soft term credit will be provided for product development, market adaptation, and marketing. Import of raw materials, facilities will be provided for export on consignment basis and into duty drawback/bonded warehouse facilities. In addition assistance will be provided for market exploration obtaining joint venture. Fresh flower, fruits and bamboo, cane and wooden furniture shall be included in list of crash programming items apart form the items listed above.
(b) In order to increase the export of agro-based products, necessary assistance will be provided to the high value added agricultural products.

INCREASED IMPORT FACILITIES OF SAMPLES FOR PRODUCT DEVELOPMENT

For product development and market promotion any exporter except of RMG sector is entitled to import duty free:
Samples upto a maximum of US $ 1000 (One thousand) annually on obtaining clearance from the Export Promotion Bureau. For import of samples exceeding US $ 1000 (One thousand), clearance shall have to be obtained from the Chief Controller of Imports & Exports which will approve the import on the recommendation of the Export Promotion Bureau issued on the basis of export earnings.

MULTIPLE ENTRY VISA TO IMPORTERS AND FOREIGN INVESTORS

Multiple entry visas are being issued to foreign investors and importers to make their entry into and stay in Bangladesh easy and trouble free.

PARTICIPATION IN INTERNATIONAL TRADE FAIRS, ORGANIZING SINGLE COUNTRY EXHIBITIONS AND UNDERTAKING MARKET DEVELOPMENT PROGRAM ABROAD

As part of export promotion Bangladesh regularly takes part in international trade fairs, organizes single country exhibitions and undertakes market development programmes in different countries of the world Private enterprises and organizations are encouraged to take part in such export-oriented events and are accorded various incentives. Besides, programmes to organize single country exhibitions in different countries through combined public and private initiaves will continue.

STRENGTHENING TRAINING ON EXPORT-RELATED MATTERS

Knowledge about the facilities and incentives available in the export trade leads to intensified export activities in the country. To apprise the country's exporters of the various facilities/incentives available, training sessions, seminars and workshops in different parts of the country under the National Export Training Programme of the Export Promotion Bureau will continue to be organized.

ESTABLISHMENT OF WORLD TRADE CENTER

The government has decided to establish a World Trade Centre in Dhaka in a bid to strengthen infrastructural facilities for the development and expansion of export. An area of 6.12 acres near Hotel Sonargaon has been earmarked for this purpose.

International Trade Centre

Simultaneously with the establishment of a World Trade Centre in Dhaka, it has been decided to set up, in Chittagong, an International Trade Centre at private initiative. Necessary land for this purpose has already been allotted.

C.I.P. (Export)

Every year commercially important persons (CIPS) are selected from the highest export performers item- wise in recognition of their contribution to export.

National Export Trophy

As mark of national accolade, 45 National Trophies are awarded every year to the most outstanding exporters in 15 product sectors. The trophy winning exporters are given C.I. P. facilities at the airport.

Deemed Export Facilities

Local raw materials used as direct import for export production for products supplied to local projects procurement in foreign exchange against international tender are regarded as 'deemed export' and qualify for all export incentives and **benefits including duty drawback that extended to direct exporters.**

Organizing Local Fairs of International Standard

Organizing trade fairs of international standard plays a very important role in the promotion of exports. Trade fairs, help product familiarization on the one hand and establishment of closer contacts between foreign buyers and local sellers on the other hand. Considering this aspect general as well as specialized trade fairs of international standard will be organized within the country apart from participating in general and specialized International Trade Fairs abroad.
8.23. Import of samples by Export Promotion Bureau and TCB :

The Export Promotion Bureau and the Trading Corporation of Bangladesh will be entitled to import duty free samples upto a maximum annual limit of taka 30,000.00 (Taka Thirty thousand).

IMPORT OF BANNED ITEMS

Export-oriented industries may be entitled to import raw materials put under the banned/restricted list of import against specific export orders subject to permission from the Ministry of Commerce.

WIDENING THE SCOPE OF DEEMED EXPORT

The coverage of "deemed export" has been widened to include supply of goods to the Export Processing Zones and export of turn-key projects like engineering services contract, consulting services contract and various other construction contracts. The net foreign exchange earnings generated by such project exports will be considered as actual export and become eligible for all export incentives and facilities.

WAIVER ON SHIPMENT OF GOODS

To avoid unnecessary delay in shipment of export cargo the Ministry of Shipping will grant waiver for shipment of export goods except those which are covered within 24 (twenty four) hours of receipt of application in the transportation of export goods. Besides, should an exporter decide to charter an aircraft for quick transportation of his export consignment, the government will consider for according necessary permission in this regard.

RE-EXPORT (ENTRE-POT)

The existing system of taking permission from the Ministry of Commerce on case-to-case basis for re-export of imported cargo (entre-pot) trade will not be necessary henceforth. The rate of value addition required for entre-pot trade has been lowered to 5% from the previous rate of 10%. However, each package under the re-export consignment must bear the mark 'entre-pot' or 'temporary importation' and must not claim Bangladeh as country of origin.

EXPORT WITHOUT L/C

With a view to further simplifying export procedures, from now on, export may be effected without L.C. on the basis of purchase contract, agreement, purchase order or advance payment. In such cases, the exporter will be required to submit only the EXP Form and the Shipping Bill. In addition, export of all commodities including vegetables and electronic goods shall be allowed without L.C. and on the basis of advance encashment or on consignment basis. In order that such exports can be effected smoothly, genuine exporters will be allowed, for a minimum period of one year, to export their goods on the basis of contract, purchase order or advance payment, besides export L.C.

IMPORT WITHOUT L.C

Import without L/C is permissible in cases of import of capital machinery essential raw materials for export-oriented industries, and perishable goods for eventual re-exportation, irrespective of value ceiling.

Relaxation of provisions for import of raw materials for export- oriented industries

For import of raw materials through back-to-back L.C. by 100% export-oriented industries, restrictions of the import policy order or the requirement of this rules of origin shall be relaxed.

Provision for Direct Air Booking

Direct air booking facility from Rajshahi and Syedpur airports up to the destinations shall continue for export of fresh vegetables and other perishable items produced in the northern regions of the country to ensure quick transport and preservation of quality.

Inter-Agency, Inter-Sector Project for product diversification

An Inter-Agency, inter-sector project shall be taken up with the aim of product diversification. The existing bonding system, duty drawback, cash incentive etc. shall be reviewed under the proposed project, with a view to keeping the export prices competitive. The project will encompass issues like product development, market expansion, trade cooperation, identification and removal of infrastructural impediments of the export trade. Appropriate project, aided by the World Bank or other sources, shall also be taken up for technology transfer in order to bringing about quick transformation of the export trade.

Encouraging increased use of local raw materials

Composite knit/hosiery and garments manufacturing units operating under the bonded warehouse system have been increasingly using local raw materials. These units are presently enjoying bonded warehouse facilities for 50% - 70% of their imports. This rate of bonded warehouse facilities shall be gradually lowered in an attempt to ensure increased use of local raw materials.

Establishment of M.I.S. at the Ministry of Commerce

With the financial assistance of the UNDP, an M.I.S. shall be established at the Ministry of Commerce under the Uruguay Round Study Project. Internet connection shall be available to the proposed M.I.S. allowing easy access to all information concerning world trade including imports and exports.

PRODUCT-SPECIFIC DECISIONS

READYMADE GARMENTS

Provisions have been made for the exporters of readymade garments to retain in their respective foreign currency accounts the portion of their export earnings required for meeting the expenses on importing fabrics and other accessories through back-to-back letter of credit. The exporters that way shall be saved from incurring losses by first converting their export earnings to Taka and then re-converting the same to foreign exchange for payment of import bills on raw materials.

For making hand-woven sweaters of natural and synthetic wool imported under customs and permission would be accorded to take up such wool outside the bonded area, provided the concerned firm furnishes a bank guarantee for equivalent amount of customs duty leviable on such raw materials.

Import of samples for each category of garments :
At present, facility exists for duty free import of 20 pieces of samples for each category of

garments subject to a maximum of 100 pieces. Imported samples are, however, subject to mutilation at the customs paid.

Rationalizing the rate of value addition:
(a) It has been found that keeping the rate of value addition flexible is congenial for the growth of the country's export trade. Therefore a Standing Committee will be formed for rationalizing the existing rates of value addition for all commodities including readymade garments.
(b) When a garment export unit relies exclusively on locally procured cotton and accessories through back to back L/c the maximum amount of back to back L/C in case of knitwear unit would be equal to the value of the master L/C.

IMPORT OF GREY CLOTHES

With a view to expanding the base of backward linkage industries, permission is being accorded for import of grey clothes, through usual procedure for use in the export industries or for direct export against specific export orders. So long this facility used to be given only to the dyeing, printing and finishing factories. Since value addition in the readymade garments sector did not take place up to its potentialities inspite of this facility the government has allowed the exporters of readymade garments to import grey clothes.

Establishment of Fashion Institute :
To sustain in the global competition , a Fashion Institute will be established in the private sector in cooperation with the Export Promotion Bureau for the improvement of quality and design of readymade garments (including leather garments).

FROZEN FISH

Emphasis has been laid on scientific cultivation of shrimps for increased production and export of shrimp. With this end in view, various programmes including setting up of a Shrimp Development Board, declaring shrimp hatchery as an 'industry',setting up of a Credit Assurance Fund for extending loan facilities to the shrimp cultivators and lowering of customs duty on import of equipments used in the cultivation of shrimps, will be taken up.

Exporters having fish processing plant will be considered for allotment of one hundred acres of 'Khas' land for cultivation of shrimps applying modem techniques.

Bank loan on easy terms will be made available on priority basis to the frozen food processing plants for the implementation of the HACCP system.
In an effort to strengthen the quality control system of frozen food, arrangements will be made for import of essential quality control equipments free of customs duty.

CULTIVATION OF BAMBOO, CANE AND COCONUT

Sac Inspestance has been given to plan cultivation of bamboo, cane and coconut keeping in view the need to increase supply of local raw materials to the handicrafts sector.

A Design Centre will be set up to improve the quality of handicrafts.

TEA INDUSTRY

The government is contemplating declaring the country's tea industry as export oriented industry.

Land under most of the tea estates at present do not enjoy long term lease which is a limiting factor for development activities of tea estates. To remove such impediment, land under the tea estates will be leased out on long term basis.

Tea estates will be provided with soft term bank loans for modernizing the plants to achieve high yield and improve quality of products to strengthen sustain ability in the international market. Development credit will also be considered for sick tea estates.

To encourage export of package tea duty drawback at that rates on FOB value will be provided on import of packing materials.

General waiver for shipment of goods will be granted in an effort to increase the export of tea.

Import of multiwall paper sacks on concessional customs duty for packing of tea will be allowed.

To establish reputation and brand name of Bangladeshi tea in overseas markets publicity measures will be strengthened.Liaison shall be maintained, for this purpose, with reputed blending and distributing agencies.

JUTE INDUSTRY

Reform programmes will continue for the development of the jute sector.

For developing the export of jute and jute goods, wide publicity will be undertaken abroad highlighting the comparative advantage as a natural fibre. Steps will also be taken to demonstrate the diversified uses of jute goods.

As an incentive to export jute yam and twine, marketing assistance at the rate of 10% ofF.O.B. value is being extended to the exporters of this sector for a period of three years commencing from 1997.

OTHER SECTORS

Six V-SAT lines have already been established to facilitate increase of the export of software. Steps will be taken to install more lines/connections to further increase export from this sector.

Realizing the importance of software as a potential export sector a committee was formed to recommend on the potentialities and technical aspects of the sector. In the light of the recommendations of the committee, the sorts is considering to offer some more facilities to this sector.

A jewelry export policy incorporating various facilities has already been formulated to provide necessary impetus to the jewelry and diamond cutting industry. Formulation of a diamond cutting policy is in its final stage.

MISCELLANEOUS

QUALITY CONTROL OF EXPORT PRODUCTS

Measures will be taken to create quality awareness among the exporters especially about the internationally recognized standards of export products. Quality control institutions will also be modernized. Quality standard compliance of health regulations and phytosanitary certification will be ensured before shipment of export cargo. Besides, exporters will be given training on and motivated for obtaining ISO 9000 for quality standard and ISO 14000 for environmental regulations. Activities of the concerned organizations will also be intensified.

INTRODUCTION OF HARMONIZED CODE FOR EXPORT PRODUCTS

Codes incorporating full description of export goods will be introduced intervation with the harmonized code followed by the world body in all import and export L.C. forms.

Increase of production and quality improvement of agricultural products:
With a view to increasing the export of agricultural produces, especially fresh vegetable, fruits and fresh flowers, emphasis will be laid on increasing production, improvement of quality and development of the packaging system.

The fiscal and financial incentives offered by the Export Policy will be reviewed at regular intervals and necessary measures will be taken accordingly.

Appropriate measures will be taken to simplify the export procedures and procedural difficulty, if any, will be referred to the Task Force for immediate solution.

Establishment of an Export-Import Bank shall be examined.

For development of infrastructure in export trade, the following actions would be undertaken :-
(a) Establishment of an Information Centre with network facilities at home and abroad;
(b) Establishment of a Foreign Trade and Investment Training Institute for human resource development in commercial fields ;
(c) Seek technical assistance for R & D by setting up research cells in the Export Promotion Bureau and Chambers of Commerce and Industry;
(d) Seek technical assistance from the World Bank for establishment of a Design and Fashion Institute.

Export trade has witnessed structural changes due to globalization and liberalization of trade which demand changes in the nature and pattern of the export services . In the light of such changed demands restructuring of the Export Promotion Bureau shall be considered.

NEGATIVE LIST OF EXPORT

The negative list of goods banned for export has been curtailed against the backdrop of the liberal trade policy pursued by the government. This list shall be reviewed/reconsidered as and when found necessary. Goods banned and restricted for export under the Export Policy for 1997-2002 are enumerated below :

LIST OF GOODS PROHIBITED FOR EXPORT :

Petroleum and petroleum products except naptha, furnace oil, lubricant oil and bitumen. However, this prohibition shall not be applicable to the export of petroleum and LNG by foreign firms operating in Bangladesh under production sharing contracts to the extent of their share as agreed upon.

Oil seeds and edible oil except Kapok seeds. However, edible oil processed/refined in the country out of oil seeds and crude oil imported for export purpose may be exported subject to permission of the Ministry of Commerce.

- Jute seeds and sun-hemp seeds.
- Wheat.
- Molasses and Khandseri sugar.

Live animals, all sorts and skins of animals and wild life covered in the Bangladesh Wild Life (Preservation) Ordinance, 1973(President's Ordinance No. XXIII of 1973, as amended in 1974) except the speciacs listed in the first shedule of the ordinance.

- Firearms, ammunitions, explosives and ingredients thereof.
- Fissionable materials.
- Rare archaeological items.
- Human skeleton, blood plasma or any other material produced out of human blood.
- Pulses, all sorts.
- Prawns and shrimps, except frozen and processed (S.R.O. No.60-L/76, dated, 14.2.76).
- Omon (S.R.O. No. 250-L/77 dated, 13.8.77).
- Saline water shrimps of 71/90 counts or below except 'harina'and 'chaka' variety and fresh water shrimps of 61/70 couunts or below (S.R.O. No. 345-L/83, dated 20.10.83).
- Rice bran (except deoiled rice bran).
- Bamboo and cane in whole form and wood log.
- Frogs of all species (live or dead) and froglegs.
- Chemicals included in schedule 1 of the Chemical Weapons Convention of the United Nations signed in Paris on 13 -15 January 1993.
- Raw Hides and wet blue leather.

LIST OF GOODS RESTRICTED FOR EXPORT (EXPORT ALLOWED UNDER SPECIAL PERMISSION OF THE MINISTRY OF COMMERCE)

Molasses: Permissible on case-to-ease basis.

Deoiled rice bran :

Permissible on case-to-case basis only in case the Ministry/Directorates of Fisheries and Livestock fail to purchase the available stock within a reasonable time and price.

Wheat bran:
Permissible on case-to case basis only in case the Ministry/Directorates of Fisheries and Livestock fail to purchase the available stock within a reasonable time and price.

Urea fertilizer:
Export of Urea fertilizer produced in the factories of the B.C.I.C. (except KAFCO) is permissible only on the recommendation of the Ministry of Industries on case-to-case basis.
11.2.5. Cow and Buffalo Permissible on case-to-case basis. horns and hooves:

Date-gur:
Half of the quantity produced in a year shall be exportable on case-to-case basis.

EXPORT TARGETS (COMMODITY-WISE) FOR FINANCIAL YEARS 1997-98 THROUGH 2001-2002 (In Million US dollar)

Commodity	1997-98	1998-99	1999-2000	2000-2001	2001-2002
Readymade Garments	2500	2756	3010	3280	3590
Jute goods	307	312	314	317	319
Leather	205	225	240	280	330
Frozen food	320	350	380	400	420
Knitwear	983	1178	1412	1687	2010
Raw Jute	125	132	140	150	160
Tea	40	42	48	50	55
Chemicals	94	98	100	102	102
Petroleum products	10	10	10	10	10
Engineering products	18	21	23	25	28
Agricultural products	32	35	37	40	42
Handicrafts	8	9	9	10	10
Others	378	462	617	824	1024
Total:	5020	5630	6340	7175	8100
* Rate of Exchange : US $ 1.00 = Taka 45.00					

IMPORT POLICY, REGULATIONS AND PROCEDURES

The Ministry of Commerce is responsible for formulating, implementing and monitoring trade policies. The National Board of Revenue (NBR) under the Ministry of Finance is in charge of tax policies, including customs and other matters relating to customs through the office of Bangladesh Customs .

Import and export activities are regulated by the Customs Act 1969 and every five years Customs issues a detailed import–export policy to guide import activities for that period. The scope of application of the Import Policy Order 1997–2002 was extended and remained in effect until the Cabinet Committee on Economic Affairs approved the new Import Policy 2004–2006 on 19 October 2003.

Importers are classified as private sector or public sector importers. The private sector importers include industrial consumers who register with the Bangladesh Export Processing Zones Authority (BEPZA), the Bangladesh Small and Cottage Industries Corporation (BSCIC) or the Board of Investment (BOI) and commercial importers who import goods for sale without further processing.

The public sector importers include government organizations, statutory bodies, corporations, universities, research institutions and industrial enterprises.

The Import Policy classifies imports as follows:

• Imports on a joint basis, made by groups of importers formed under the condition that industrial importers group with other industrial importers and commercial importers with commercial importers.

• Imports by an actual user, made by individuals or institutions not registered as importers to import permissible items. If the items are valued up to US$ 5,000 no permission from the Import Control Authority is required. Imports of value above US$ 5,000 require permission from the chief controller or regional import control authority.

• Imports of professional and scientific equipment made by Bangladeshi professionals abroad and paid from their earning abroad are allowed without permission from the Import Control Authority. There is no ceiling value for such imports.

• Imports of samples, advertising materials and gifts are allowed duty free under a limited quantity or value per year.

• Temporary importation with condition for re-export within a period of 1 year is allowed.

• Import–export activities from the export processing zone (EPZ) remain outside the purview of the Import Policy Order 1997–2002.

IMPORT APPROVAL

All private sector importers, except enterprises located in EPZs, are required to register with the Office of the Chief Controller of Imports and Exports (CCI&E) under the Ministry of Commerce. After registration, importers receive an import registration certificate (IRC), which specifies the value ceiling for each product an industrial user is allowed to import each year including items on the restricted list for imports.

Commercial importers are allowed to import non-restricted items without a quantity limit. The registration fee for an IRC is between Tk 500 and Tk 5,000 depending on the value of annual imports. Goods that require approval or a licence for import are listed in the section below.

LICENSING, QUOTAS AND PROHIBITIONS

Generally, no import licences are required for any imports. The following items require prior approval or permission:

Products	Concerned ministry/government agency
Explosives	Approval from the Chief Inspector of Explosives of the Ministry of Energy and Mineral Resources
Armaments	Importable only by the Government or by dealers approved by the Government
Narcotics	Foreign exchange-earning hotels with permission from the Director General, Narcotics Control Department or others with permission from the Director General, Narcotics Control Department and Ministry of Commerce

An import permit or a clearance permit is required for the import of the following items, although neither a letter of credit authorization (LCA) form nor a letter of credit is required:

• Imports of books, magazines, journals, periodicals, and scientific and laboratory equipment against surrender of UNESCO coupons;

• Imports under pay-as-you-earn (PAYE) schemes in the following cases need only clearance from Bangladesh Bank:

– Plant and machinery of permissible specifications, new or not exceeding 12 years old,

– Motor cars, new or not exceeding 5 years old,

– Cargo or passenger vessels of steel or wooden body,

– Plant or machinery for export-oriented industries,

– Trawlers and other fishing vessels;

• Imports of free samples, advertising materials and gift items;

• Imports of drugs and medicines (allopathic);

• Imports of capital machinery as share of capital of the foreign shareholder.

See annex I for the list of goods banned for imports and annex II for the list of goods restricted for imports.

Additionally, sources of procurement are restricted as follows:

• Goods from Israel or goods originating from that country shall not be importable. Goods from the flag vessels of that country are also not importable;

• All import from and export to Serbia and Montenegro shall be banned.

IMPORT REQUIREMENTS

Most import activities require an LCA authorizing the opening of an irrevocable letter of credit, unless otherwise specified. There are cases where imports against an LCA without opening a letter of credit are permissible:

• Import of books, journals, magazines and periodicals on a sight draft or issuance of bill basis;

• Import of any permissible items not exceeding US$ 25,000 in value only during each financial year against remittance made from Bangladesh;

• Import under commodity aid, grants or other such loans with specific import procedures;

• Import of "international chemical references" through bank drafts by recognized pharmaceutical industry companies on the approval of the Director, Drug Administration for the purpose of quality control of their products.

A letter of credit is not required for imports of perishable goods for eventual re-exportation valued at between US$ 5,000 and US$ 7,500 per consignment, or for import of machinery and raw materials by export-oriented industries.

To avoid demurrage charge, goods must be cleared within seven days of entry into the port. Customs duties must be paid within two months of entry or the goods will be subject to confiscation.

Machinery and equipment can be imported temporarily for re-export under the conditions that (a) such goods are imported for use in demonstrations or exhibitions, (b) the goods will be re-exported within one year and (c) the importers secure a bond, bank guarantee or other documents. If the importer obtains an import/export permit, such temporary imports are exempted from customs duties.

PACKING AND LABELLING REQUIREMENTS

1. Labelling

Imported goods including their containers must not bear any words or inscription of a religious connotation, the use or disposal of which may injure the religious feelings and beliefs of any class of the citizens of Bangladesh. Imported goods and their containers must not bear any obscene pictures, writing or inscription or visible representation.

Labels detailing the date of manufacture, expiry date and a statement of fitness for human consumption printed in Bangla or English are acceptable. However, ingredients for baby food and milk products must be printed in Bangla. The phrase "There is no alternative for breast feeding" must be clearly printed in Bangla on each tin container of baby food containing cream. Packets of cigarettes must bear the statement "Smoking is injurious to health" in Bangla.

Containers of approved pesticides and insecticides must be able to withstand handling and carrying by sea. Containers of such products must indicate technical/chemical names of the products, net weight, name and address of manufacturer, date of manufacture, date of test, normal storage stability and time limit, active ingredients and their percentage, and warning statements such as "Keep out of reach of children", "Dangerous", etc. Details on labels must be accurate.

Piece goods made partly or wholly of cotton or wool must be labelled with the yardage and country of origin, unless they are less than 4 yards long.

2. Marking

To facilitate the arrival of the shipment, the name of consignee, destination, weight of the shipment, quantity of goods and country of origin have to be marked in large capital letters or printed on all packages, crates and boxes.

3. Packing

All goods should be packed to withstand heat, moisture and rough handling. Import Policy 2004–2006 requires that permission be obtained from the Bangladesh Standards and Testing Institution (BSTI) and the Bangladesh Council for Science and Information Research for all imported food items. Packages of imported items must bear the name, address and tax identification number (TIN) of the importer.

INSPECTIONS

In 2000, the pre-shipment inspection became mandatory and was contracted to three pre-shipment inspections agencies: M/S Inspectorate Griffin Limited, M/S Intertek Testing Service International and M/S BIVAC International Bureau Veritas Group. Pre-shipment involves both the physical inspection and price comparison of goods.

The following goods are exempted from pre-shipment inspection:

• Duty-free goods and goods imported by government, semi-government, sector corporation or autonomous organizations;,

• Certain specified capital machinery;

• Goods imported by export-oriented industries under bonded warehouse facilities,

• Books, periodicals, newspapers; and

• Commercial samples.

TARIFF SCHEDULE – CUSTOMS

The NBR is in charge of formulating and implementing customs and tariffs policies. NBR operates under the Internal Resources Division of the Ministry of Finance.

CLASSIFICATION

Since 2000, Bangladesh uses the Harmonized Commodity Description and Coding System, generally referred to as the Harmonized System, or HS, at an eight-digit level. As a WTO member, Bangladesh offers most favoured nation (MFN) treatment to imports from all trading partners, including non-WTO members.

CUSTOMS DUTIES

Customs duties are classified into three categories: statutory, general exemption and concessionary rates. Statutory rates or operative rates are applicable to all imports unless an exemption is specified, while concessionary rates are applicable to items intended for exclusive agricultural use, goods for education, relief goods and raw materials and packaging for the pharmaceutical industry.

Customs tariffs are calculated ad valorem on c.i.f. values of imports, except for three tariff lines involving gold in different forms, which is subject to a duty rate of Tk 300 per tola (11.644 grams). Bangladesh has reduced the number of tariffs bands, which now range from zero to 37.5 per cent. As for bound MFN tariffs, 92 per cent of agricultural tariff lines are bound at 200 per cent and the remaining lines are bound at 50 per cent. The 50 industrial tariff lines are bound at 50 per cent.

Bangladesh has 20 categories of concessionary tariffs ranging from zero to 15 per cent. These concessionary tariffs are classified into three types: (1) those on imports of capital machinery and parts by the registered industrial consumers, including export-oriented industries; (2) those targeting exporters; and (3) those provided for a specific use or users (end use). For 100 per cent export-oriented industries, no import duty is payable.

The following products are exempted from import duties: raw cotton, textile machinery, certain irrigation and agricultural machinery, certain animal feeds, certain drugs and medical equipment, goods imported by the Government for use in the defence services and capital machinery imported by export-oriented industries.

Additionally, Bangladesh grants preferential tariffs under the following agreements:

Agreement	Participant	Coverage by Bangladesh	Preferential rates
Bangkok Agreement	Bangladesh, China, India, Republic of Korea, Sri Lanka	129 lines	10 to 60 per cent of MFN
SAARC Preferential Trading arrangement (SAPTA)	Bangladesh, Bhutan, India, Maldives, Nepal, Pakistan, Sri Lanka	237 lines and 13 additional lines for least-developed countries	10 to 15 per cent of MFN
GSTP	48 countries		
Bhutan	Bangladesh, Bhutan	58 lines	50 per cent of MFN

Source: WTO, *Trade Policy Review: Bangladesh,* WT/TPR/S/68 (Geneva, WTO, July 2000) page 46 Detailed Bangladesh customs tariff schedules are available at the Bangladesh Customs web site < http://www.nbr-bd.org/nbrweb/CustomsFiles/cusTariffindex.asp >.

TAXES AND SURCHARGES

A 2.5 per cent LCA or import permit fee is levied on the value of all imports above Tk 100,000 unless exempted by the import policy order (see annex III). Importers shall pay fees of between Tk 500 and Tk 5,000 for initial registration and annual renewal.

All importers are subject to an advanced income tax at 3 per cent of the c.i.f. value of imports. This is not an additional tax on imports as it will be credited to corporate tax of the importers. A value added tax (VAT) is imposed on all imports and domestically produced goods at a rate of 15 per cent.

Supplementary duties ranging from 5 to 270 per cent are levied on luxury goods including liquor, tobacco products, petroleum products, make-up materials, perfume, ceramic tiles, air-conditioners, refrigerators, televisions and motor vehicles.

FOREIGN EXCHANGE REGIME

The exchange rate policy of Bangladesh Bank aims at maintaining the competitiveness of Bangladesh products in the international markets, encouraging the inflow of wage earners' remittances as well as maintaining internal price stability and a viable external account position. Bangladesh Bank valued the taka on the basis of a real effective exchange rate with consideration of the nominal exchange rates and inflation rates of major trading partners. Since 31 May 2003, the taka is officially free of any band allowing individual banks to set their own buying and selling rates.

CURRENCY CONVERTIBILITY

The Bangladesh currency, taka, is fully convertible on the current account to facilitate international trading activities. However, the taka is not convertible in the capital account.

FOREIGN EXCHANGE ALLOCATION

Only authorized dealers, i.e. commercial banks and specialized financial institutions, licensed by Bangladesh Bank are allowed to engage in foreign exchange.

MONEY AND FINANCE MEASURES

Foreign exchange for imports is provided by authorized dealers when payment is due. Approval from Bangladesh Bank is required for advance payment of specialized or capital goods imports. Authorized dealers may issue letters of credit on an f.o.b. basis without approval of Bangladesh Bank when:

(a) The cost of goods, cost of freight and insurance are accommodated within the amount mentioned in the importer's LCA;

(b) The cost of freight is paid in local currency within the amount recorded in the LCA.

BANKING

The banking system is regulated by Bangladesh Bank , the central bank of Bangladesh. The banking system consists of 4 nationalized commercial banks, 5 State-owned specialized banks, 30 domestic private banks, 22 non-bank financial institutions including the Dhaka Stock Exchange (DSE) and the Chittagong Stock Exchange (CSE) and 12 foreign banks: Al Faisal Islamic Bank, American Express Bank, Citibank, Credit Agricole Indosuez, Habib Bank, Hanvit Bank, Hong Kong Shanghai Bank, Muslim Commercial Bank, National Bank of Pakistan, Scotia Bank, Standard Chartered Grindlays Bank and State Bank of India.

EXPORT-IMPORT DOCUMENTS

ALL SHIPMENTS

All importers, both private and public, shall submit to their nominated banks the LCA form accompanied by the following documents:

• Letter of credit application form signed by the importer;

• Invoice;

• Insurance cover note

In addition to the above documents, private sector importers also need to submit:

• Membership certificate from the registered chamber of commerce and industry or any trade association;

• Proof of IRC renewal payment;

• Declaration of income tax payment in three copies;

• Tax identification number, except in the case of imports for personal use;

• Any other documents required by the import policy order or other public notice.

Public sector importers need to submit an attested copy of the allocation letter issued by the administrative ministry, division or authority.

A valid and legally renewed IRC is essential for private sector importers to have their LCA forms accepted or letter of credit opened. However, as mentioned earlier, a letter of credit for imports of machinery and equipment to set up a new industrial unit may be opened without an IRC and without an exemption certificate from the Chief Controller.

Details on letters of credit and remittances against imports are provided in the *Bangladesh Bank Guidelines for Foreign Exchange Transaction*, Volume I, Chapter 15 .

IMPORT DOCUMENTS

Document	No. of copies	Body concerned	Cost	Time frame
Bill of entry	7	Customs		
Bill of lading/Air waybill	1	Shipping company Airline company		
Certificate of origin	1	Supplier Chamber of Commerce and Industry		
General index register (GIR) certificate	1	Income tax authority		
Health/sanitary certificate	1	Bangladesh Atomic Energy Commission Drug Administration		
Import permit or clearance permit	1	CCI&E		
IRC	1	CCI&E	Tk 500 – Tk 5,000	

Indent/proforma invoice	1	Indenter or supplier		
Inspection certificate	1	Recognized international surveyor		
Insurance document	1	Insurance companies		
Letter of credit	1	Commercial bank		
Letter of credit over US$ 5,000,000	1	Central bank		1-2 days
LCA	1	Commercial bank		
Prior permission for permissible import for foreign firms	1	CCI&E		
TIN	1	Income Tax Department		
Membership certificate	1	Chamber of commerce and industry/trade association		

SPECIAL REQUIREMENTS

1. Radioactivity test certificate

A test of radioactivity levels is mandatory for food imports for human consumption such as milk, milk products, edible oil and other food items produced in any country. The radioactivity test report from the authority of the exporting countries must indicate the level of CS 137 in each kilogram of food items shipped. Another certificate is required to state that such items are fit for human consumption. Food samples will be tested by the Bangladesh Atomic Energy Commission upon the arrival of such foods at a Bangladesh port.

A test of radioactivity levels is not required for food imported by hotels of international standard and diplomatic bonded warehouses. However, in such cases, a certificate from any internationally recognized testing agency or from the authority of the country where the food was produced is required and must be submitted together with the bill of lading.

A test of radioactivity levels is not required for palm olein and RBD palm stearin produced in Malaysia or to be imported from Malaysia or Singapore. However, a test of purity of such imported items, carried out by the Bangladesh Council of Scientific and Industrial Research, is obligatory.

A radioactivity test is not necessary for imports of cigarettes, cigarette paper, pipe tobacco, whisky, beer and other alcoholic beverages, concentrated essence, spices and medicines.

The radioactivity test procedure can be relaxed in cases of imported rice and foodstuff from SAARC and South East Asian countries provided that such imports are accompanied by a certificate of origin as well as by a certificate stating that such foodstuff or rice is fit for human consumption. Perishable foodstuff imported from SAARC countries requires a radioactivity certificate from the authority of the exporting countries.

The import of poultry feed and animal feed also requires radioactivity test reports, at CS 137 per kilogram, and a certificate stating that such items are fit for consumption by poultry or animals.

2. Sanitary and phytosanitary certificate

A sanitary certificate is required for all livestock and plants and most plant products, certifying that these items are free of insects, pests and diseases. An additional certificate is required for leaf tobacco attesting that the tobacco is free from *Ephestia elutella* or that this pest does not exist in the country of origin.

3. Other certificates

Imports of iron and steel must be accompanied by a certificate specifying that the products meet the requirements of one of the following organizations: the American Society for Testing Materials, Society of Automotive Engineers, American Iron and Steel Institute, American Society of Mechanical Engineers, Lloyds Register of Shipping, American Bureau of Shipping, American Petroleum Institute, American Association of Railroads and American Engineering Association. An additional producing mill (testing) certificate and the producer's packing list are required for each shipment.

A fumigation certificate is mandatory for imports of used clothing. Straw and hay used in packing must be certified to be free from insects and diseases. A certificate of cleanliness is required by law for the import of textiles and a special certificate is required for the import of drugs and pharmaceutical products.

MARKETING AND DISTRIBUTION REGUKLATIONS

MARKET REGULATIONS

Wholesale and retail channels are common in the Bangladesh market. Exclusive agents or distributors of foreign manufacturers and suppliers are preferred because they may ensure after-sales services, such as technical service, and a continuous supply of spare parts. Non-exclusive arrangements are common for commodities such as cotton, wheat, edible oil, chemicals and metals. Franchising is not common in Bangladesh although there are no regulations banning this type of business arrangement.

Another form of business arrangement is a joint venture. The Industrial Policy of 1991, updated in 1999, guarantees equal treatment for local investments, joint venture, and 100 per cent foreign investments. No permission from the Government is needed to set up a joint venture. However, the joint venture needs to be registered with the BOI.

PRODUCT STANDARDS

Bangladesh is a member of ISO. BSTI is the agency in charge of developing and maintaining the standards of products. However, the Ministry of Health and Welfare controls the standards for foods and pharmaceutical products. Bangladesh also recognizes and accepts goods certified by standards institutions of other countries.

All food items have to be tested for radioactivity levels. Milk food with fat content and baby food can only be imported in tin containers. All baby food (milk food with fat content up to 19 per cent) containers must include a measuring spoon. Non-fat dried milk can be imported in bags or tins.

PORT FACILITIES AND TRADING ROUTE

1. Port facilities

Over 90 per cent of Bangladesh international trade is transported by sea. Bangladesh is a member of the following conferences: the India-Pakistan-Bangladesh-Ceylon Conference, the Bay of Bengal-Japan Conference and the West Asia Gulf Conference. Bangladesh has also signed bilateral shipping agreements with 12 countries, mostly on a 50:50 or 40:40:20 sharing basis.

There are two major seaports providing services to international cargo: Chittagong port, which handles more than 80 per cent of the cargo (about 1,200 international ships annually), and Mongla port, which handles about 400 ships annually.

2. Air transport

The Zia International Airport is located in Dhaka. Biman Bangladesh Airlines, the national flag carrier, provides services to 8 domestic destinations and 25 international destinations.

The Government has recently opened the airline service sector to private investment. Six private companies have been allowed to operate domestically to destinations such as Chittagong, Cox's Bazar, Barisal, Jessore, Rajshahi and Sylhet.

GOVERNMENT PROCUREMENT AND STATE TRADING ORGANIZATIONS

The Government of Bangladesh is the largest importer in the country. Individual ministries or organizations are allowed to purchase directly from suppliers through public tender. The Department of Supply and Inspection, under the Ministry of Commerce, is the designated purchaser for the Government. Standardized legislation governing the procurement is currently under development.

Government procurement is carried out through public tenders, limited tenders for registered suppliers, selected tenders and single tenders. Major or bulk purchases to be made by public tender are published in the local media.

Some major government direct importers include: the Directorate of Defence Purchase; the Bangladesh Chemical Industries Corporation; the Bangladesh Textile Mills Corporation; the Bangladesh Steel and Engineering Corporation; the Bangladesh Sugar and Food Industries Corporation; the Trading Corporation of Bangladesh (TCB); the Bangladesh Oil, Gas and Minerals Corporation; and the Power Development Board.

In March 1993, the Government established the Privatization Commission as the overseeing body of the privatization process. Privatization is carried out through sale by international tender or by public offering of shares on the stock exchange. The Commission has listed 98 State-owned enterprises (SOEs) for privatisation, including 25 enterprises in the jute sector, 27 in the steel engineering sector, 22 in the textile sector, 14 in the sugar and food sectors, and 10 in the chemical sector. A list of SOEs to be privatized is available at < http://www.bangladeshonline.com/pb/re10.htm >.

PRINCIPAL IMPORT ITEMS

As mentioned earlier, Bangladesh depends on imported food. Imports of textile materials and equipment, as well as transportation equipment, chemicals and other semi-processed goods are gradually increasing (see table 2). India is the largest source of imports supplying around 12 per cent of total imports (see table 3). The United States is also a major supplier to Bangladesh. Imports of raw cotton from the United States account for about 19 per cent of total imports of cotton into the country. In 2002, Bangladesh imported textile machinery worth US$ 10 million from the United States.

Table 2. Composition of imports classified by HS code

(Millions of Taka, fiscal year ending 30 June)

Imports	1996	1997	1998	1999	2000	2001
Animals and animal products	2,509	2,961	2,889	3,603	4,012	4,778
Vegetable products	27,371	12,221	22,299	52,113	27,269	29,800
Animal or vegetable fats	7,374	9,298	9,915	13,982	13,094	11,955
Prepared foodstuffs	2,455	5,653	5,338	6,035	6,872	10,940
Mineral products	22,854	27,302	24,892	23,547	36,573	40,003
Chemical products	15,220	20,984	20,452	22,369	25,939	31,942
Plastics and rubber	7,593	7,753	9,290	9,171	11,594	14,105
Hides and skins	245	174	127	82	107	186
Wood and wood products	669	689	1,119	1,014	1,258	1,548
Wood pulp products	4,549	5,371	5,554	5,608	7,148	9,551
Textiles and textile articles	64,010	73,967	83,893	79,949	89,197	108,599
Footwear, headgear	377	392	364	363	215	238
Articles of stone, plaster, cement, asbestos	1,189	1,558	1,722	1,786	1,765	2,304
Pearls, precious or semi-precious stones, metals	21	31	131	16	17	54
Base metals and articles thereof	13,154	18,640	17,769	16,598	19,767	25,019
Machinery and mechanical appliances and electrical equipment	25,381	27,453	25,827	29,504	34,981	53,587
Transportation equipment	14,256	13,470	17,072	13,928	17,990	22,880
Instruments - measuring, musical	1,688	1,737	1,669	1,936	2,472	2,983
Arms and ammunition	295	384	412	380	1,035	332
Miscellaneous manufactured articles	1,362	1,450	1,457	2,074	2,583	2,944
Works of art	170	166	397	671	1,586	1,649

Source: Based on data from ADB

Direction of imports

(Millions of United States dollars)

	1996	1997	1998	1999	2000	2001
India	1,018	796	1,179	1,024	945	1,186
China	641	622	547	534	667	882
Singapore	313	251	430	659	761	901
Japan	673	472	456	559	850	581
Hong Kong, China	392	431	452	441	470	493

Republic of Korea	368	379	331	291	348	625
United States	250	285	242	446	214	297
United Kingdom	170	208	314	280	239	173
Australia	122	126	197	213	175	194
Indonesia	84	154	185	159	193	201
Total, world	6,935	6,863	7,370	8,352	8,993	9,959

Source: Based on data from ADB

BUYING FROM BANGLADESH IMPORTANT INFORMATION

EXPORT POLICY, REGULATIONS AND PROCEDURES

Bangladesh aims at product and market diversification. It focuses on maximizing export growth and narrowing the gap between import payment and export earning. The policy identifies "priority sectors" and "promising sectors". "Priority sectors" are software and information and communication technology products, agro-processing products, light engineering, leather goods and high value ready-made garments. The "promising sectors" cover several areas, including pharmaceuticals, cosmetics and toiletries, electronics, cards and calendars, silk fabrics, melamine, and stationary and handicraft products.

B. Export approval

Generally, no approval is required to export from Bangladesh, except for exports of goods classified under banned goods or restricted goods. Exporters need to obtain an export registration certificate (ERC), with the exception of those located in EPZs. The procedure to obtain an ERC is similar to that of an IRC described in part two and the fee is Tk 1,000.

Exports have to be made on the basis of a letter of credit issued by a commercial bank. However, exports without a letter of credit are allowed on the basis of a purchase contract, agreement, purchase order or advanced payment and therefore exporters are required to submit only the export form and the shipping bill. The export of commodities including vegetables and electronic goods is allowed without a letter of credit on the basis of consignment or advance encashment.

SHIPMENT

Permission from the Ministry of Shipping is normally required for each shipment of exports. However, a waiver for the shipment of certain cargo may be granted within 24 hours of receipt of application.

Under the Bangladesh Flag Vessel (Protection) Ordinance 1982, all foreign flag vessels have to obtain a waiver certificate for loading and unloading goods at ports in Bangladesh. Foreign ships cannot load cargo on the routes in which Bangladesh flag carriers are operating. In June 2003, the Ordinance was amended in order to exempt foreign feeder operators from obtaining waiver certificates before loading and unloading cargo at ports in Bangladesh.

LICENSING, QUOTAS AND PROHIBITIONS

See annex IV for the list of goods prohibited for export and annex V for the list of goods restricted for export.

OTHER REQUIREMENTS

Quality control licences are required from the BSTI for certain industrial export products, such as food items, beverage and construction materials (total 142 items).

Exports of cement from Bangladesh to India previously required a certification from the Bureau of Indian Standards (BIS). However, India has recently agreed to relax the testing requirements for Bangladesh cement and to accept the BSTI certification conforming to BIS.

Additional certificates are required for exports of certain products, as detailed below.

Product	Certificate or permit	Issuing ministry or agency
Any product as required by the importing country	Certificate of origin	Export Promotion Bureau or Chamber of Commerce and Industry
Frozen fish	Health-cum-quality certificate	Department of Fisheries
Goods of plant origin	Quarantine certificate	Ministry of Agriculture
Tea	Export authorization	Tea Board
Pharmaceutical products	No objection certificate (NOC)	Drug Administration
Goods for international fairs or exhibitions	NOC	Export Promotion Bureau
Jute	Export price certificate	Bangladesh Bank
Goods for repair	Export permit NOC	CCI&E Bangladesh Bank
Ready-made garments	GSP certificate	Export Promotion Bureau
Live wild animals	Export permit NOC	CCI&E Chief Conservator of Forests

Source: WTO, *Trade Policy Review: Bangladesh,* WT/TPR/S/68 (Geneva, WTO, July 2000) page 58

DOCUMENTARY EVIDENCE UNDER TRADE AGREEMENTS AND PREFERENTIAL SCHEMES

1. Bangkok Agreement

Bangladesh products enjoy tariff concessions or duty-free and quota-free access with the five other members of the Bangkok Agreement. Details of products and tariff concessions are available at < http://www.unescap.org/itid/mtg/concession.htm >. Bangladesh manufacturers need to obtain a certificate of origin issued by the Export Promotion Bureau in order to export their products under the Bangkok Agreement.

2. Bhutan

In May 2003, Bangladesh and Bhutan signed a revised five-year trade agreement offering tariff concessions to each other's market. Bangladesh major exports to Bhutan include ready-made garments, melamine products and dry foods. Exports of products from Bangladesh to Bhutan enjoy duty-free status.

3. Canada

On 31 December 2002, the Government of Bangladesh and the Government of Canada signed a Memorandum of Understanding under the Least Developed Countries Market Access Initiative . This initiative grants duty-free and quota-free privileges to products provided that (a) they have been manufactured or formed from inputs from any of the 48 eligible least developed countries, or (b) they have been formed from inputs from general preferential tariff beneficiary countries and the value added in the least developed exporting country is at least 25 per cent.

Rules of origin regulations under this scheme are available in the Canada Gazette 1 January 2003 . Exporters need to obtain the certificate of origin issued by the Bangladesh Export Promotion Bureau

4. European Union

The EU is Bangladesh's most important trading partner. Textile products account for 75 per cent of Bangladesh exports to the EU. Bangladesh's exports to the EU market benefit from preferential market access, i.e. duty-free and quota-free access through the generalized system of preferences (GSP) scheme, as well as access under the everything but arms (EBA) initiative.

Under the EU GSP for the period 2002-2004, textiles manufactured in Bangladesh need the following documents to enter the European markets under this scheme:

• GSP Form A issued by the Textile Cell under the Export Promotion Bureau;

• An export visa is required when the ready-made garments are obtained from woven fabrics or yarn originating either from an ASEAN member country (except Myanmar) or a SAARC member country or a Lomé Certificate of Origin Convention country, which were imported into Bangladesh for further manufacturing and then re-exported.[1] The Export Promotion Bureau issues the export visa;

• Export Licence issued by the Ministry of Commerce for products subject to export licence;

• Certificate of origin for textile products issued by the Export Promotion Bureau.

5. Global system of trade preferences among developing countries

As mentioned earlier, Bangladesh and 43 other member countries offer tariff concessions on a reciprocal basis. To export to the GSTP countries, Bangladeshi exporters need to have the certificate of origin issued by the Export Promotion Bureau.

6. Japan

In December 2002, Japan revised its GSP scheme by expanding its coverage, especially duty-free and quota-free treatment. To receive preferential tariff treatment under Japan's GSP scheme, goods must be accompanied by a GSP Form A which is issued by the Bangladesh Export Promotion Bureau.

The GSP Form A is not required for consignments of customs value not exceeding 200,000 Yen (about US$ 1,860) or of goods whose origins are evident. The latter are included in the list available from the Japan Ministry of Foreign Affairs .

Japan's GSP scheme also applies certain origin criteria, rules for transportation (direct consignment) and rules of cumulative origin for certain processed products. Details are available from the Japan Ministry of Foreign Affairs .

7. United States

Exports of textile products from Bangladesh to the United States are regulated by a quota system under The United States–Bangladesh Bilateral Textile and Apparel Agreement 1994 . Textile manufacturers need to provide the following documents prior to any shipment to the United States:

• Export visa: Under the Visa and Exempt Certification Arrangement between the Government of the People's Republic of Bangladesh and the Government of the United States of America concerning Textiles and Textile Articles , the "visa" issued by the Government of Bangladesh includes the description of the shipment (quantity, category), visa number, date of issuance and signature of the issuing official;

• An "ELVIS transmission" is a message, sent electronically to the United States Customs Service, by the Government of Bangladesh or by its representative, which details the shipment (quantity and category), manufacturer's ID number and visa number assigned to the shipment.

Under the visa and exempt certification arrangement, the following products from Bangladesh are exempted from quota restrictions, visa and ELVIS requirements:

• Certain floor coverings: HTS (harmonized tariff schedule) items 5701.10.1600, 5701.10.4000, 5702.51.2000, 5702.91.3000, 5702.92.0010 and 5702.99.1010;

• Hand-loomed fabrics, handmade and folklore products:

– Hand-loomed fabrics of the cottage industry;

– Handmade textile products made in the cottage industry from hand-loomed fabrics;

– Particular traditional folklore handicraft products: embroidered kaftan, Panjabi, bell-sleeve evening blouse, salwar, kameez, dopatta, lungi, borka, kurta, batwa, nakshi kantha and batik wall hangings.

Details on quotas are available from the Textile Status Report for Absolute Quotas by the United States Bureau of Customs and Border Protection.

According to the Export Policy 1997–2002, a tax at source on all export earnings was deducted at the rate of 0.25 per cent.

SETTLEMENT OF BILLS, LETTERS OF CREDIT

A. Export finance

There are three types of export financing in Bangladesh: (1) pre-shipment financing in local currency by commercial banks; (2) pre-shipment financing in foreign currency by commercial banks through the export development fund; and (3) back-to-back letter of credit facilities.

The export development fund, under the supervision of Bangladesh Bank, provides financing for imports of raw materials, spare parts and packing materials for exporters of non-traditional products. According to the DSE , non-traditional products include garments, frozen shrimps, other fish products, newsprint, paper, naphtha, furnace oil, urea, etc.

Interest rates of local currency at commercial banks are determined by Bangladesh Bank. Since 1994/1995, the interest rates for exports are set within the range of 8-10 per cent. Exporters can borrow up to 90 per cent of the value of their irrevocable letter of credit or sales agreement up to 180 days with payment extended up to 270 days.

Exporters of ready-made garments, specialized textiles, household linen, hosiery, toys, luggage and fashion goods, electronic items and leather goods may open back-to-back letters of credit for the import of raw materials against their export letters of credit.

B. Export insurance and guarantees

There are four guarantee schemes administered by the State-owned insurance company, Sadharan Bima Corporation:

(1) The export credit guarantee (ECG) pre-shipment, extended to banks, insuring banks against 75 per cent of losses on advances made to exporters. It can be converted to post-shipment cover of up to 95 per cent.

(2) ECG post-shipment, extended to banks.

(3) The export payment risk policy, extended to banks, offering comprehensive guarantee. This scheme is intended to protect exporters against overseas commercial and political risks, covering 85 per cent of commercial risk losses and 95 per cent of political risk losses.

(4) The whole turnover pre-shipment finance guarantee, extended directly to exporters.

DOCUMENTS, INCLUDING INSURANCE

Document	No. of copies	Body concerned	Cost
Bill of exchange	1	Exporter bank	
Bill of lading/air waybill	1	Shipping company/airline company	
Bond for re-exporting within one year	1	Bank	
Certificate of origin	1	Export Promotion Bureau/ Chamber of Commerce and Industry	
Commercial invoice	1	Exporter	
EXP Form	1	Bank	
ERC	1	CCI&E	Tk1,000
GIR certificate	1	Income Tax Authority	
GSP Form A	1	Export Promotion Bureau	
Income tax declaration (importer)	3	Bank/Bangladesh Bank	
Inspection certificate	1	Recognized international surveyor	
Insurance declaration	1	Insurance/bank	

Membership certificate	1	Chamber of Commerce and Industry/ Trade association	
Quality control licence	1	BSTI	
Shipping permit or waiver	1	Ministry of Shipping/ Director General of Shipping	
TIN	1	Income Tax Authority	

EXPORT INCENTIVE SCHEMES

An export-oriented industry is any industry exporting at least 80 per cent of its manufactured goods or any industry contributing at least 80 per cent of its products as an input to finished exportable goods. Similarly, any business exporting at least 80 per cent of services including information technology related products is also considered an export-oriented industry.

• Exporters are allowed to retain 40 per cent of their f.o.b. earnings in foreign currency. In the case of export items consisting of relatively high import components (such as naphtha, furnace oil, bitumen and other petroleum products, ready-made garments and electronic goods) or export items being services (such as legal advice, consultancy and similar professional services), exporters can retain only 7.5 per cent of their f.o.b. earnings in foreign currency.

• The time period for export credit to enjoy a concessional rate of interest has been extended up to 270 days (previously 180 days) for the frozen food, tea and leather sectors. Exporters may obtain export credit from commercial banks up to 90 per cent of the value of their irrevocable letter of credit or confirmed contracts. Moreover, no overdue interest is charged in the case of export against an irrevocable letter of credit on sight payment basis.

• VAT paid on jute cloth and bags, which are used in the packing of export goods, is refunded. VAT on export support services such as clearing and forwarding services, telephone, telex, fax, electricity bills, insurance premium, shipping agent's commission/bill can also be refunded.

• Export industries are entitled to a 50 per cent rebate on taxable income generated from export earnings. The total export earnings of handicraft and cottage industries are exempted from income tax (part four, chapter III). Export-oriented industries are also eligible for a tax holiday of five to seven years and they are exempted from tax deduction at source (0.25 per cent of export earnings). The 100 per cent export-oriented enterprises located outside the EPZs are entitled to duty-free imports of capital machinery.

• Permitted for sale in the local market, subject to payment of usual duties and taxes, are 20 per cent of the rejected goods from the 100 per cent export-oriented industries, including leather goods and ready-made garments.

• Exporters are entitled to a duty drawback scheme under three systems: actual drawback, national drawback and flat rate drawback. They are also entitled to use the special bonded warehouses, which allow 100 per cent exporters and "deemed" exporters (local firms supplying inputs to 100 per cent exporters) to import and stock inputs duty free.

• Non-traditional industrial products are entitled to incentives if their value addition is 50 per cent or more.

• To ensure backward linkages, incentives are extended to the "deemed" exporters supplying indigenous raw materials to export-oriented industries, including export-oriented ready-made garment industries. Local products supplied to local industries or projects against foreign exchange, letter of credit are treated as indirect exports and entitled to all export facilities.

• Export-oriented industries are allowed to import duty free capital machinery and spare parts up to 10 per cent of the value of such capital machinery.

• Additional foreign exchange is made available on a case-by-case basis, for publicity campaigns, opening overseas offices and participating in international trade fairs.

• Agricultural farms of a minimum size of 5 acres are recognized as potential export industries and thus are eligible for all facilities of export-oriented industries. Other contract services, such as engineering, consulting and civil construction contracts abroad, are also identified as potential export sectors.

• Export-oriented industries are allowed to send export samples to international trade fairs for up to US$ 2,000 annually. Samples sent for purposes other than international trade fairs can reach the value of US$ 1,500 annually and the maximum limit to send samples by parcel post is Tk 5,000.

SECTOR-SPECIFIC INCENTIVES

1. Textiles and garments

Cash assistance of 25 per cent f.o.b. export value is granted to 100 per cent export-oriented domestic textiles and garments industries if they use 100 per cent locally made raw materials or duty-paid raw materials.

Manufacturers of indigenous fabrics (woven, knit, hosiery, grey, printed, dyed, grameen check,[2] handloom, silk and other specialized fabrics) supplying their products to 100 per cent export-oriented garment industries are also entitled to cash assistance of 25 per cent of the value of the supply.

Exporters of ready-made garments are allowed to import grey clothes. They are also entitled to import duty free 20 pieces of samples for each category of garment but not exceeding 100 pieces in total.

2. Leather and leather goods

Export-oriented enterprises are exempted from customs duty (2.5 per cent) and import licence fee (2.5 per cent) for the import of raw hides, including wet blue and pickled leather.

The Export Policy 1997–2002 stipulates that 80 per cent export-oriented leather industries are considered as 100 per cent export-oriented industries, and thus are entitled to the same incentives available to the 100 per cent for export-oriented enterprises.

3. Frozen fish

Particular attention is given to shrimps and prawns. Shrimp hatchery is declared an "industry" and is eligible for reduced customs duty on import of equipment. Frozen fish exporters with fish processing plants are considered for the allotment of land up to 100 acres of "Khas" or land for shrimp cultivation.

4. Tea

Land under the tea estates will be leased out on a long-term basis (99 years). Duty drawback at a flat rate on f.o.b. value is available for imports of packing materials, and multi-wall paper sacks used in tea packaging which are allowed to be imported at concessional customs duty. A general waiver is granted for the use of ships in tea transport and export.

[2] Derived from Grameen Bank, a non-governmental organization and one of the main sources of microcredit in Bangladesh.

PRINCIPAL EXPORT ITEMS

Bangladesh exports depend heavily on the larger markets of Europe and North America, mainly through different textiles agreements. In 2002, about 47.2 per cent of Bangladesh total exports were sent to EU countries, while 39 per cent were destined for the North American market.

Over the past two decades, the structure of Bangladesh exports has changed from resource-based to process-based exports. In the early 1980s, primary commodities represented 29 per cent of total exports. This share was reduced to 17.8 per cent in the early 1990s and to 8.2 per cent in 1999/2000. The main primary products for exports in the 1980s, jute and jute products, have been gradually replaced by garments. Currently, textiles and clothing dominate Bangladesh exports, accounting for 83.5 per cent of total exports in 1998, up from 70.4 per cent in 1992.

Table 4. Composition of exports classified by HS code

(Millions of taka, fiscal year ending 30 June)

Exports	1995	1996	1997	1998	1999	2000	2001
Animals and animal products	13,859	13,551	14,435	15,288	15,000	18,300	20,704
Vegetable products	1,947	1,622	2,066	2,575	2,058	1,492	1,783
Animal or vegetable fats	27	17	12	8	19	29	18
Prepared foodstuffs	55	88	288	370	210	227	364
Mineral products	501	496	410	456	220	591	567
Chemical products	3,315	444	203	741	856	313	466
Plastics and rubber	10	25	98	289	372	639	642
Hides and skins	8,607	8,624	8,766	7,601	7,023	7,069	12,960
Wood and wood products	146	144	140	174	176	284	220
Wood pulp products	41	36	92	102	77	181	83
Textile and textile articles	91,911	98,797	119,496	147,403	149,054	178,937	232,458
Footwear, headgear	1,943	2,601	2,624	3,205	2,883	3,156	4,149
Articles of stone, plaster, cement, asbestos	353	463	670	697	699	799	1,127
Pearls, precious or semi-precious stones, metals	0	0	11	28	0	0	3
Base metals and articles thereof	72	66	148	74	94	186	154

Machinery and mechanical appliances and electrical equipment	203	88	184	118	376	179	393
Transportation equipment	23	17	52	65	47	23	198
Instruments - measuring, musical	3	13	41	11	14	15	14
Arms and ammunition	0	0	0	0	0	0	0
Miscellaneous manufactured articles	20	30	24	130	169	145	157
Works of art	44	99	82	90	56	72	65

***Source*: Based on data from ADB.**

DIRECTION OF EXPORTS

(Millions of United States dollars)

	1996	1997	1998	1999	2000	2001
United States	1,019	1,290	1,368	1,411	1,779	1,754
Germany	325	357	404	450	608	624
United Kingdom	379	368	347	364	440	500
France	227	262	254	263	289	301
Italy	160	197	232	200	228	263
Netherlands	173	178	189	187	234	253
Belgium	...	...	147	146	175	182
Canada	66	71	79	77	97	100
Hong Kong, China	101	91	70	62	87	98
Japan	104	87	64	71	67	64
Total, world	3,297	3,628	3,822	4,520	5,590	5,908

Source: Based on data from ADB

INVESTING IN BANGLADESH: STRATEGIC AND PRACTICAL INFORMATION

FOREIGN INVESTMENT POLICY AND REGULATIONS

The policy framework for foreign investment in Bangladesh is based on the Foreign Private Investment (Promotion and Protection) Act, 1980 , which ensures legal protection to foreign investment in the country against nationalization and expropriation. It also guarantees non-discriminatory treatment between foreign and local investment and repatriation of proceeds from sales of shares and profit.

Other major laws affecting foreign investment are the Bangladesh Export Processing Zones Authority Act (1984), the Companies Act (1994) and the Industrial Policy (1999) . In addition, foreign investors are also required to follow the regulations of Bangladesh Bank and NBR for taxation and customs matters.

The Government's role is that of a facilitator to help create an enabling environment for expanding private investment, both domestic and foreign. The BOI was established by the Government to accelerate private investment and provide institutional support services to investors.

Bangladesh does not request prior approval requirements for foreign investment. There are no limits for equity participation or restrictions on the repatriation of foreign profits and income. There are no restrictions to the acquisition of local enterprises by foreign investors who may also buy those enterprises earmarked for privatization.

Investment is welcome in all sectors, with the exception of (a) manufacturing of arms and ammunition or other defence equipment, (b) forest plantation and mechanized extraction of reserved forests, (c) the production of nuclear energy, and (d) security printing (currency notes) and minting. Additionally, foreign investment is discouraged in the following areas: ready-made garments, banks, insurance companies and other financial institutions.

The Government of Bangladesh particularly encourages foreign investment in the following areas:

• Export-oriented industries;

• Industries in the EPZ;

• High technology products which are either import substitutes or export oriented;

• Undertakings in which more diversified use of indigenous natural resources are possible;

• Basic industries depending mainly on local raw materials;

• Investment towards improvements in quality and marketing of goods manufactured and the increase of production capacities of existing industries;

• Labour intensive/technology intensive/capital intensive industries.

National treatment is provided in bilateral investment treaties for the promotion and protection of foreign investment. Bangladesh has concluded bilateral investment treaties with the following 22 countries:

BILATERAL INVESTMENT TREATIES

Belgium
Canada
China
Democratic People's Republic of Korea
France
Germany
Indonesia
Iran (Islamic Republic of)
Italy
Japan
Malaysia
Netherlands
Pakistan
Philippines
Poland
Republic of Korea
Romania
Switzerland
Thailand
Turkey
United Kingdom
United States

Separate bilateral agreements for avoidance of double taxation have been signed with the following 20 countries.

Belgium
Canada
China
Denmark
France
Germany
India
Italy
Japan
Malaysia
Netherlands
Pakistan
Poland
Republic of Korea
Romania
Singapore
Sri Lanka
Sweden
Thailand
United Kingdom

Bangladesh is a signatory to MIGA, Overseas Private Investment Corporation (OPIC) of the United States, International Centre for Settlement of Investment Disputes (ICSID) and a member of the WIPO Permanent Committee for Development Cooperation Related to Industrial Property.

Areas where Bangladesh offers investment opportunities are natural gas, fisheries and low-cost labour. The upgrading of the infrastructure sector also offers opportunities for foreign investment, especially power, telecommunications, ports, roads and railways.

The main flows of FDI into Bangladesh originate from India, the Republic of Korea, Malaysia, the United Kingdom and the United States. The power and gas sectors account for the bulk of FDI.

Institutions facilitating and promoting foreign investment in the country are the BSCIC for small industries, the BEPZA for industries located in these areas and the Privatization Commission and BOI . Two other government companies have been set up to facilitate investments in private sector infrastructure, namely, the Infrastructure Investment Facilitation Center (IIFC) and the Infrastructure Development Company Limited (IDCL).

Bangladesh has a considerable number of business associations, which play an important role in the economy. The Federation of Bangladesh Chambers of Commerce and Industry (FBCCI) is the apex body of the country's trade bodies. Influential associations are the Dhaka Chamber of Commerce and Industry (DCCI) , the Metropolitan Chamber of Commerce and Industry (MCCI), the Foreign Investors' Chamber of Commerce and Industry (FICCI) and the International Chamber of Commerce-Bangladesh (ICCB).

For further details on business and investment promotional agencies in Bangladesh, please refer to < http://www.betelco.com/bd/bdsbus/promo.html >.

INVESTMENT PROCEDURES

A foreign investor has the following choices when investing in Bangladesh:

• Establish a joint venture manufacturing company with a Bangladeshi counterpart;

• Establish 100 per cent foreign-owned manufacturing company;

• Set up the company's place of business by registering the company with the Registrar of Joint Stock Companies and Firms.

A. INCORPORATION

Business in Bangladesh may be undertaken by a company formed and incorporated locally or by a company incorporated abroad but registered in Bangladesh. The incorporation or registration is done by the Registrar of Joint Stock Companies and Firms under the provisions of the Company's Act 1994, once clearance has been obtained from the Securities and Exchange Commission (SEC) in respect of capital issue. The necessary forms for incorporation and registration are available with the Office of the Registrar of Joint Stock Companies and Firms. Nominal fees are charged for registering the memorandum and articles of association.

B. REGISTRATION

Registration allows for three types of company: (1) companies limited by shares (private and public limited companies), (2) companies limited by guarantees and (3) unlimited companies.

No prior approval or a no objection certificate (NOC) is required for the setting up of a joint venture or a 100 per cent FDI. However, pre-registration clearance is required for investment in the following areas: ready-made garments, banks, insurance companies and other financial institutions.

A company incorporated outside Bangladesh that would like to be registered in Bangladesh must furnish the following documents:

• Certified copies of the charter statutes or memorandum and articles of the company defining the constitution of the company;

• Full address of the registered or principal office;

• List of directors and mangers;

• Name(s) and address(es) of person(s) resident in Bangladesh authorized to operate on behalf of the company;

• Full address of the company office in Bangladesh.

The above documents require that they be duly attested by the Bangladesh Mission abroad in the respective country where the company is incorporated.

In addition, in order to benefit from the facilities and institutional support services provided by the Government of Bangladesh, entrepreneurs and investors are requested to apply for registration with the BOI in the prescribed Investment Application Form . To register with BOI, the following documents are required:

– TIN certificate;

– A trade licence from the local authority;

– A membership certificate of a relevant trade association or chamber of commerce and industry;

– A certificate from the nominated bank regarding opening of account;

– Incorporation certificate, in the case of limited companies.

BOI is also responsible for the allocation of industrial plots, issuance of import entitlements, approval of the payment of royalties, technical know-how or technical assistance fees, and the appointment and repayment of remuneration to foreign personnel.

Under the Environment Conservation Act 1995 , all industrial projects must obtain environmental clearance from the Department of Environment. The main criteria for obtaining clearance are set out in the Environment Conservation Rules 1997 which were established under this Act. Different levels of assessment are required depending on the particular industry concerned. The process takes 15 days for projects with low levels of potentially adverse environmental impact and 30 days for those with significant impact.

C. OBTAINING INDUSTRIAL PLOT

Entrepreneurs requiring an industrial plot for the setting up of an industry in any industrial areas or estates outside BEPZA and BSCIC may approach BOI mentioning the size of plot required along with copies of the sanction/registration letter and the industrial layout plan to justify the requirement. After receiving the application, BOI will assist in obtaining the industrial plot.

To obtain utility connection, entrepreneurs may apply either directly to the concerned authority for obtaining utility services or approach BOI for assistance together with a copy of the sanction/registration letter. The Utility Service Cell is responsible within BOI to assist investors in obtaining the necessary utility services.

INVESTMENT INCENTIVES

The Government of Bangladesh has liberalized the industrial and investment policies in recent years by reducing bureaucratic control over private investment. Currently, major incentives for private investment are as follows.

A. TAX HOLIDAY

Tax holiday facilities are available for five or seven years depending on the location of the industrial enterprise.

• Dhaka and Chittagong Divisions 5 years

(excluding three hill tract districts of Chittagong Division namely Rangamati, Khagrachhari and Bandarban designated as under-developed areas)

• Barisal, Khulna, Rajshahi and Sylhet Divisions 7 years

and the three Chittagong Hill Tracts

The period of tax holiday is calculated from the month of commencement of commercial production. A tax holiday certificate is issued by the NBR for the total period within 90 days of submission of application. This incentive applies to industries set up before 30 June 2005.

Industries specified by the NBR for the purposes of exemption under the tax-holiday scheme are: chemicals; drugs and pharmaceuticals (basic manufactures); insecticides and pesticides (basic manufactures); petrochemicals; wires and cables; agricultural machinery; boilers and compressors; tractors; machine tools and other capital equipment; the manufacture of trucks, cars, scooters, auto rickshaws and bicycles; shipping and repair; and diesel engines and internal combustion engines. Tax exemptions also apply to the exploration and extraction of mineral resources and the processing of agricultural products.

B. ACCELERATED DEPRECIATION

Industrial undertakings not eligible for a tax holiday can enjoy an accelerated depreciation allowance. Such an allowance is available at the rate of 100 per cent of the cost of machinery or plant if the industry is set up in the areas falling within the cities of Dhaka, Chittagong, Khulna and Narayangonj as well as in areas within a radius of 10 miles from the municipal limits of those cities. If industries are established somewhere else in the country, accelerated depreciation is allowed at the rate of 80 per cent in the first year and 20 per cent in the second year.

C. IMPORT DUTY CONCESSIONS

Export-oriented industries and industries enjoy a further concession of the import duty in the following manner:

• For 100 per cent export-oriented industries in underdeveloped areas, no import duty is charged in the case of capital machinery and spares. However, import duty of 5 per cent is secured in the form of a bank guarantee or an indemnity bond will be returned after installation of the machinery. VAT is not payable for imported capital machinery and spares.

• For export-oriented industries in developed areas, an effective rate of 5 per cent import duty is charged. Industries exporting a minimum of 70 per cent of the total annual production may submit a bank guarantee to the customs authority for 33.33 per cent of the total import duty payable at the rate of 7.5 per cent ad valorem. This bank guarantee will be returned after installation of the machinery and fulfilling the conditions of export. In this case the effective rate of import duty payable is 5 per cent ad valorem.

• For other industries in developed areas, an effective rate of 7.5 per cent import duty is charged.

• There is an effective rate of 2.5 per cent import duty for export-oriented industries outside developed areas. Other industries outside developed areas must pay an effective rate of 5 per cent import duty.

D. INCENTIVES TO FOREIGN INVESTMENT

In Bangladesh, foreign entrepreneurs are entitled to the same facilities as domestic entrepreneurs in respect of a tax holiday, payment of royalty, technical know-how, fees, etc. As mentioned earlier, there is no limitation pertaining to foreign equity participation for FDI, i.e. 100 per cent foreign equity is allowed. Additionally, foreign investors are also entitled to the following:

• Obtain full working loans from local commercial banks. The terms of such loans will be determined on the basis of the bank-client relationship;

• Make portfolio investments in stock exchanges in Bangladesh;

• Tax exemption on capital gains from the transfer of shares by the investing company;

• No restriction in issuing work permits to foreign nationals in Bangladesh. A multiple entry visa" will be issued to prospective foreign investors for three years. In the case of experts, a "multiple entry visa" will be issued for the whole tenure of their assignments;

• Provision for transfer of shares held by foreign shareholders to the local shareholders/investor with the permission of the BOI and Exchange Control Department of Bangladesh Bank;

• Foreigners employed in Bangladesh are entitled to remit up to 50 per cent of their salary and will enjoy facilities for full repatriation of their savings and retirement benefits. A foreign technician employed by a foreign company will not be subjected to personal tax for up to three years, and beyond that period the technician's personal income tax payment will be governed by the existence or non-existence of an agreement on avoidance of double taxation with the country of citizenship;

• Six-month multiple entry visa for prospective new investors;

• Re-investment of repatriable dividend treated as new investment;

• Citizenship by investing a minimum of US$ 500,000 or by transferring US$ 1,000,000 to any recognized financial institution (non-repatriable);

• Permanent residentship by investing a minimum of US$ 75,000 (non-repatriable).

Remittance of profits of branches of foreign firms, dividends/capital gains, salaries and savings by expatriates, royalty and technical fees, training and consultancy fees, receivables collected by shipping companies and lines towards freight and passage can be effected through authorized dealers without prior approval of the Bangladesh Bank.

E. INCENTIVES TO NON-RESIDENT BANGLADESHIS

Investments of non-resident Bangladeshis are considered part of FDI. Special incentives are provided to encourage non-resident Bangladeshis to invest in the country and enjoy benefits similar to those of foreign investors. They can buy newly issued shares/debentures of Bangladesh companies. A quota of 10 per cent has been fixed for non-resident Bangladeshis in primary public shares. They can maintain foreign currency deposits in the non-resident foreign currency deposit (NFCD) account.

F. INCENTIVES TO EXPORT-ORIENTED INDUSTRIES

Special facilities and venture capital support are provided to export-oriented industries operating in any of the following 16 "thrust sectors":

- **Agro-based industries**
- **Artificial flower making**
- **Computer software and information technology**
- **Electronics**
- **Frozen foods**
- **Floriculture**
- **Gift items**
- **Infrastructure**
- **Jute goods**
- **Jewellery and diamond cutting and polishing**
- **Leather**
- **Oil and gas**
- **Sericulture and silk industry**
- **Stuffed toys**
- **Textiles**
- **Tourism**

G. INCENTIVES FOR SMALL AND COTTAGE INDUSTRIES

An investor can set up a small or medium-sized enterprise in the industrial estates maintained by the BSCIC if the investment does not exceed Tk 100 million (US$ 2 million). These estates, intended to promote decentralized industrialization, offer land and utility services to investors in almost all district headquarters.

For the development and expansion of small and cottage industries, BSCIC will be responsible for the registration, determination of import entitlement of raw materials and packing materials, issue of import passbook recommendation for local raw materials, allotment of land in its own industrial zones and also for providing assistance in all other matters.

Small and cottage industry units registered with BSCIC are exempted from payment of advance income tax on the import of their raw materials.

H. PRIVATIZATION OF STATE-OWNED ENTERPRISES

Investment opportunities have emerged from the Government's decision to privatize most of the SOEs. The updated list of SOEs ready for immediate privatization as well as the list of enterprises ready for share transfer are available at < http://www.boibd.org/privatization.html >.

TAXATION

A. INCOME TAX

Income tax is administrated by the Income Tax Ordinance, 1984 and by the Income Tax Rules 1984. The Income Tax Department of the NBR is the apex body for matters relating to income tax.

The submission of an income tax return is due by 31 December for companies and 30 September for entities other than companies. The income tax rates are:

Personal Income	Tax (Percentage)
On first Tk 75,000 of total income	Nil
On next Tk 150,000 of total income	10
On next Tk 150,000 of total income	15
On next Tk 250,000 of total income	20
On the balance of total income	25

Source: NBR. *Note: The minimum tax payable will be Tk. 1,200.*

Form A of return of income tax under the Income Tax Ordinance, 1984 is available on the NBR web site. When applicable, the following documents must be submitted together with the form:

- Auditor's certificate/audited accounts in the case of a company;

- Statement of income and expenditure account/manufacturing, trading, profit and loss account and balance sheet in the case of other assesses;

- Depreciation chart claiming depreciation as per Income Tax Law;

- Computation of income according to Income Tax Law;

– Statement of assets, liabilities and expenses.

The Taxpayer Identification Number form , the Wealth Statement Form (IT-10B) and the Form Regarding the Standard of Living are also available on the NBR web site.

B. CORPORATE TAX

The corporate tax rate for industrial companies whose shares are publicly traded is 35 per cent. Companies whose shares are not publicly traded are subject to a corporate tax rate of 40 per cent. The tax rate on the income of all other companies, including banks, financial institutions, insurance companies and local authorities, is 40 per cent.

Companies enjoying a tax holiday are required to invest 30 per cent of their exempted income within two years from the end of the tax exemption period in the undertaking or in a new industrial undertaking or in stocks and shares of a public company or in government bonds or securities.

Return fields by public limited companies shall be accepted if accompanied by audited accounts and certified by a chartered accountant as to the correctness of total income of the assesses.

The expenditure incurred by an employer in respect of the remuneration of a foreign technician is fully exempted from income tax subject to the stipulated conditions.

Capital gains from the transfer of shares of public limited companies listed with a stock exchange are tax-exempt. In computing capital gain, deductions are made from the full value or sales proceeds or the fair market price, whichever is higher, of the capital assets. Dividend income in respect of shareholders other than companies is tax-exempt. This benefit, however, is not available to shareholders of private limited companies. Royalties and technical know-how fees received by any foreign collaborator, firm, company or expert are also tax-exempt.

C. OTHER TAXES

Bangladesh has mostly replaced the former sales and excise taxes with the VAT, imposed at a flat rate of 15 per cent. VAT is not payable for imported capital machinery and spares.

Excise duties still exist on items such as home-made biris (cigarettes), domestic textiles and bank services. A turnover tax is imposed on some small-scale activities which remain outside the purview of VAT.

FOREIGN EXCHANGE

The Foreign Exchange Regulation Act, 1947 established the general framework to regulate certain payments, dealings in foreign exchange and the import and export of currency to the country. Additionally, the Guidelines for Foreign Exchange Transactions, 1996 of Bangladesh Bank compile instructions to be followed by Bangladesh authorized dealers and their constituents in transactions relating to foreign exchange. In 1994, Bangladesh's domestic currency, the taka, was declared convertible for current external transactions.

Bangladesh has two stock exchanges, the Dhaka Stock Exchange , established in 1954 and the Chittagong Stock Exchange , established in 1995. Both stock exchanges are conducted by a computerized automated trading system.

The inter-bank foreign exchange market sets the exchange rates for customer and inter-bank transactions based on demand-supply interplay. Meanwhile, the exchange rates for Bangladesh Bank's spot purchase and sale transactions of United States dollars with authorized dealers are decided on a case by case basis. Bangladesh Bank does not undertake any forward transactions with authorized dealers, who are free to quote their own spot and forward exchange rates for inter-bank transactions and for transactions with non-bank customers.

Remittances have become an important source of foreign exchange in recent years and currently exceed aid provided in the form of concessional loans and grants. Therefore, Bangladesh Bank has introduced a series of measures to facilitate the flow of both remittances of non-residents into the country as well as remittances originating from commercial activities of foreign-related businesses operating in Bangladesh or with a local counterpart.

As part of these measures, the requirement of prior permission from the Bangladesh Bank has been waived for the following remittance-related operations:

1. Commercial remittances

Opening back-to-back import letters of credit on account of manufacture-exporters for their input imports as per prescribed input-output coefficients;

Issuing bank guarantee/performance bond on account of the merchandise exporters of Bangladesh in favour of foreign buyers;

Remittance on account of short weight, quality claim, partial shipment, etc., up to 10 per cent of realized export proceeds;

Payment of a discount not exceeding 10 per cent of the invoice value at the request of the exporter where foreign importers refuse to clear goods due to discrepant documents, etc.;

Remittance of premia on foreign currency policies taken by Bangladeshi nationals while residing abroad;

Remittance of premia on account of reinsurance;

Remittance of "general average" collected from consignees in Bangladesh;

Remittance of pre-shipment inspection fees;

Remittance of bona fide expenses incurred by Bangladesh Biman and Bangladesh Shipping Corporation in foreign ports or stations;

Remittance on account of charter hire of foreign ships;

Remittance of purchase price of ships acquired by private firms or companies;

Remittance of royalty/honoraria/fees to non-residents including foreign news agencies for features, articles, etc., subscribed by local newspapers/magazines;

Advertising of Bangladesh commodities in mass media abroad.

2. Remittance by shipping lines, airlines, courier service companies

Foreign shipping lines, airlines and courier service companies may send abroad, through authorized dealers, funds collected in Bangladesh towards freight and passage, after adjustment of local costs and taxes, if any.

LABOUR AND WORK FORCE REGULATIONS

There are about 47 labour-related laws which regulate: (a) wages and employment, (b) trade union and industrial disputes, (c) working environment and (d) labour administration and related matters. The main labour laws are:

• Employment of Labor (Standing Orders) Act, 1965

• Factories Act, 1965

• Industrial Relations Ordinance, 1969

• Maternity Benefit Act, 1936

• Payment of Wages Act, 1936

• Shops and Establishments Act, 1965

• Workmen's Compensation Act, 1923

The minimum age for workers in Bangladesh is 16 years of age in factories and establishments.

WORK PERMIT AND FOREIGN EMPLOYMENT

A work permit for expatriate personnel is a pre-requisite for employment in Bangladesh. Private sector industrial enterprises, which are employing foreign nationals, are required to apply in advance to the BOI .

The employment of expatriate personnel is allowed only in companies registered by the appropriate authority. This type of employment is allowed when local experts/technicians are not available in the country; persons below 18 years of age are not eligible. The decision of the Board of Directors of the concerned company for new employment or an extension is required.

The number of foreign employees should not exceed 5 per cent of the total number of employees including top management personnel. Initially, employment of any expatriate personnel is considered for a term of two years, which may be extended on the basis of performance. Necessary security clearance has to be obtained from the Ministry of Home Affairs.

WAGES, HOURS, HOLIDAYS AND OVERTIME

The following indicates average monthly basic wages and fringe benefits in United states dollars per worker in private sector organizations.

Wage	Unskilled	Semi-skilled	Skilled
Basic wages	30	38	45
Fringe benefits	20	20	25
Total US dollars	50	58	70

Source: BOI

Working hours in the public or private sector are eight and a half hours per day, including half an hour for a meal or rest, amounting to 48 working hours per week. Work in excess of these hours, is paid as overtime. The rate of overtime is two hours pay for one hour of work. Friday is a non-work day. Worker and employee leave and holidays are regulated by the Factories Act, 1965 and the Shops Establishment Act 1965.

SOCIAL SECURITY

Workmen Compensation, Maternity Benefit (Tea Estate) Act 1950, Maternity Benefit Act 1939, Employment of Labour (standing orders) Act 1965 are concerned with workers' provident funds and gratuities.

LABOUR UNIONS AND SETTLEMENT OF LABOUR DISPUTES

Freedom of association and the right to join unions are guaranteed in the Bangladesh Constitution. There are over 6,300 registered trade unions in Bangladesh with over 1.9 million union members.

Industrial Relations Ordinance, 1969 deals with trade unions in Bangladesh, and stipulates that any workers or employers have the right to form a union or association without previous authorization. Such a union or association cannot function as a trade union if it is not registered under the law. The Director of Labour of the Government acts as the Registrar of Trade Unions in Bangladesh.

Strikes are prohibited in the essential services, such as (a) electricity, gas, oil and water supply; (b) hospital and ambulance services; (c) fire brigades; (d) railways and airlines; and (e) ports.

Hartals are political strikes intended to disrupt the normal functioning of the society, typically for a day. A hartal usually bans most motorized transport on the day it is in effect. This mode of protest against the Government has a long history in South Asia and was used often in Bangladesh in the 1990s.

BUSINESS IMMIGRATION PROCEDURE

The following categories of business visas and extensions are allowed:

- Single entry for three months;
- Multiple entry for three months;
- Multiple entry for six months;
- Multiple entry for one year.

Foreign investors are identified on the basis of certification from the BOI/BEPZA/Ministry of Industries. Foreign business persons who are directly associated with the import of Bangladesh products are identified on the basis of the certificate by the relevant associations of the export-oriented commercial/industrial organizations or the FBCCI or the Bangladesh Garment Manufacturers and Exporters association (BGMEA). The certificate shall include the tax identification number of the respective local commercial or industrial organizations.

In April 2002, the Government issued a circular updating the provisions of the landing permit (LP)/visa on arrival (VOA) for travellers without a valid visa. In this case, foreign investors and business persons can request an LP/VOA from ZIA International Airport for at best 30 days under the following conditions:

- In no circumstances shall the period of validity of the LP/VOA be extended;
- The LP/VOA applicant shall have an endorsement of US$ 500 in the passport or cash in hand;
- The LP/VOA fee will be determined on the reciprocity policy with respective countries;
- The applicant shall have a return air ticket;
- The applicant shall utilize the same port for entry and departure.

DISPUTE SETTLEMENT

Dispute settlement in Bangladesh is governed by the Arbitration Act, 1940. Three types of arbitration are contemplated, namely: (1) arbitration in the course of a suit, (2) arbitration with the intervention of the court and (3) arbitration otherwise than in the course of a suit and without the intervention of the court.

Under the Arbitration Act of 1940, an arbitration agreement must be in writing, though it needs not be registered. The agreement might make a reference about present or future differences. The arbitrator may be named in the agreement or left to be designated later, either by consent of the parties or in some other manner specified in the agreement. In working on an arbitration agreement, the parties are free to lay down provisions regarding various matters of the procedure. However, in the absence of an agreement, the rules contained in the First Schedule to the Arbitration Act, 1940, apply.

One way companies have dealt with legal issues regarding dispute settlement has been by including a clause in arbitration agreements that allows for one of the parties to bring a dispute before another nation's court. This practice is allowed under Bangladesh law.

Bangladesh is a signatory to the Convention for the Settlement of Investment Disputes between States and Nationals of Other States and it acceded on 6 May 1992 to the United Nations Convention on the Recognition and Enforcement of Foreign Arbitral Awards. The Bangladesh Export Promotion Bureau assists in dispute settlements of export-related transactions.

CAPITAL MARKET

Bangladesh Bank , the central bank of the country, was established as a body corporate by the Bangladesh Bank Order, 1972 (P.O. No. 127 of 1972). Bangladesh Bank regulates all banking institutions and reports to the Ministry of Finance. The Bank has the legal authority to supervise and regulate all banks. It performs the traditional central banking roles of note issuance and banker to the Government and banks.

The Investment Corporation of Bangladesh (ICB) was established in 1976 with the objective of encouraging and broadening the base of industrial investment. ICB underwrites issues of securities, provides substantial bridge financing programmes, maintains investment accounts, floats and manages closed-end and open-end mutual funds and closed-end unit funds to ensure the supply of securities as well as generate a demand for securities. ICB also operates as a dealer in the Dhaka and Chittagong Stock Exchanges.

The Industrial Promotion and Development Corporation (IPDC) of Bangladesh and the ICB provide equity support to public limited companies in the private sector.

The Bangladesh banking sector is formed by 4 nationalized commercial banks, 5 government-owned specialized banks, 30 domestic private banks, 22 non-bank financial institutions, including the DSE and the CSE , and 12 foreign banks (see list on page 14).

To supervise the smooth functioning of securities and capital, SEC was established in 1993. It has the responsibility to ensure proper issuance of securities as well as the protection of the interest of investors in the capital market.

The domestic private banks share of deposits and lending is relatively small compared to that of the government banks. There are other specialized financial institutions like the House Building Finance Corporation, the Grameen (Rural) Bank and several cooperative banks.

In May 2003, the Money Loan Act 2003 replaced the Money Loan Court Act, 1990 requiring a mandatory repayment of 10 per cent of the total loan in the first year, 15 per cent in the second year and 25 per cent in the third year.

PROTECTION OF PROPERTY RIGHTS

A. INTELLECTUAL PROPERTY RIGHTS

Patents, trademarks and copyrights are governed by the following legislative framework:

• Patents and Designs Act, 1911 and the Patents and Designs Rules, 1933;

• Trade Marks Act, 1940 and the Trade Marks Rules, 1963;

• Copyright Ordinance, 1962, as amended by the Copyright (Amendment) Act, 1974 and the Copyright (Amendment) Ordinance, 1978.

As a least developed country, Bangladesh has a 10-year transitional period, i.e. up to the end of 2005, to meet its obligations under the Agreement on Trade-related Aspects of Intellectual Property Rights (TRIPS Agreement). The Government is in the process of amending the country's trademark, patent and copyright legislation. The current terms of intellectual property rights protection in Bangladesh are available in annex VI.

Bangladesh is a State party to the Universal Copyright Convention (since 1975) for the protection of literary, scientific and artistic works, the Paris Convention for the Protection of Industrial

Property (since 1991), and the Bern Convention for the Protection of Literary and Artistic Works (since 1999). Bangladesh has also been a member of the WIPO since 1985.

1. Patents

Applications for the granting of a patent or for the registration of an industrial design must be made to the Patent Office under the Ministry of Industries. According to the authorities, the time required for granting a patent or industrial design is 21 months and 9 months, respectively. The protection of industrial designs is provided for designs that are not previously published in the country and that are either new or original or both.

Patents are granted for new processes for the manufacture of chemical compounds, pharmaceutical compositions and micro-organisms, but product patents are granted for chemical compounds only if they are produced by new processes. Chemical products without specific reference to the process of manufacture, mathematical theory, nuclear fission, inventions that are considered to be against national law or morality and micro-organisms as products only are not protected by patent. Currently, the patentability of pharmaceutical and agricultural chemical products and of plant varieties is not covered.

There is a provision for compulsory licensing in the Patents and Designs Act, 1911, but such licence has never been issued in Bangladesh. Expected amendments of the Patents and Designs Act, 1911 include: broadening the definition of invention to include all fields of technology, provision of protection to plant varieties, extension of the term of patent protection to 20 years and incorporation of the provisions on layout or designs of integrated circuits.

2. Trademarks

The registration of trademarks is provided only in respect of goods and not services. The draft trademark legislation proposes to include provisions for the registration of service marks, as well as collective marks.

Applications for registration must be filed with the Trade Mark Registry, under the Ministry of Industries, and after examination they are advertised in the Trade Marks Journal. If they are uncontested, registration certificates are issued within a period of four months. The registration grants an exclusive right to the proprietor to use the registered marks for 7 years which may be renewed for further periods of 15 years. Parallel imports are not permitted.

Most of the provisions in the existing Trade Mark Act, 1940 are in conformity with the TRIPS Agreement. Remaining provisions are to be incorporated or amended in a new Trade Mark Act which is now under consideration by the Government. The proposed act also includes provisions for the protection of geographical indication which is not provided for under the 1940 Act.

3. Copyrights and related rights

Copyright registration is optional. Those who wish to register can file an application with the Copyright Office under the Ministry of Cultural Affairs. The registration certificate is granted within 30 days from the date of application.

The term for copyright protection in published literary, dramatic, musical and artistic works is the life of the author plus 50 years. In the case of films, records, government works, works of international organizations and photographs, the term of 50 years is from the date of publication. In the case of broadcasts, the term of 25 years starts after the first fixation.

Copyright legislation is in the process of being amended. The new draft law includes the extension of copyright protection to computer programs, the recognition of rental rights for computer programs, sound recordings and films, and the recognition of rights of performers, in addition to rights of phonogram producers and broadcasting organizations. Provisions concerning licensing are to be included and the role of performing rights societies, which will be replaced by copyright societies, is expected to be enhanced. Additionally, new provisions on compulsory licensing of unpublished works will also be included.

B. Enforcement

Infringement of intellectual property rights can be brought to domestic judicial courts. Producers or inventors, including foreign rights holders, can file a suit in a domestic court. An appeal against the lower court decision can be brought to the Appellate Court. Provisions on penalties for infringement of intellectual property rights are as follows:

(a) Patents and designs - Penalties for infringement of registered patents and industrial design range from Tk 500 to Tk 1,000. New amendments propose an increase from Tk 5,000 to Tk 10,000.

(b) Trademarks - Penalties for infringement of trademarks can be up to six-month imprisonment or a maximum fine of Tk 500, or both. The draft Trademarks Act proposes an increase of penalties to a maximum of two years' imprisonment and/or a fine. For a second conviction of infringement, imprisonment could be extended to three years, with or without a fine.

(c) Copyright - The proposed copyright law intends to increase penalties from a fine of Tk 5,000 and/or a maximum two years' imprisonment to "rigorous imprisonment, which may extend to three or four years with a fine".

The customs authority, upon complaint by the affected person, can inspect, seize and detain shipments of any counterfeit or pirated materials.

EXPORT PROCESSING ZONES IN BANGLADESH

BEPZA was created in 1980 and is the official body to promote, attract and facilitate foreign investment in EPZs. Two EPZs are now operational in Bangladesh, Chittagong EPZ (established in 1983) and Dhaka EPZ , in Savar near Dhaka (established in 1993). Three other EPZs are at the implementation stage, namely Comilla, Khulna and Ishurdi.

The primary objective of EPZs is to provide special areas where potential investors can find a conducive investment climate. The legal framework governing EPZs in Bangladesh and the operation of firms established in EPZs includes the Bangladesh Export Processing Zones Authority Act, 1980 and the Customs (Export Processing Zones) Rules, 1984 . Bangladesh Bank has issued several circulars concerning the operation of EPZs, the establishment of companies in EPZs, credit facilities available and conditions to access credit.

Bangladesh offers "one window same day service" to investors in EPZs. The service with its simplified procedure sanctions projects generally within one week, issues required import and export permits and required work permits for foreign nationals working in EPZ enterprises and provides required infrastructural facilities in EPZs.

Approximately a dozen of United States firms, mostly textile producers, are currently operating in Bangladesh EPZs. The Republic of Korea is the largest foreign investor in the two EPZs Japan;

Hong Kong, China; Singapore; the United Kingdom; Sweden; Thailand; India; Malaysia; Germany; Taiwan, Province of China; China; the United Arab Emirates; France; Italy; Denmark; Panama and Pakistan are other foreign investors in EPZs. The remaining EPZ industries are Bangladeshi. The United States is the top destination of exports from EPZs. Industries range from garments and textiles to electronics, sporting goods, steel chains and services (including equipment leasing, container repairs and handling).

I. SETTING-UP FIRMS IN EPZs

Bangladesh allows foreign investment in EPZs in convertible foreign currencies with the option of establishing public or private limited companies, or sole proprietorship or partnership undertakings. Industries allowed to be established in EPZs are classified as follows:

(a) Type A: 100 per cent foreign-owned firms, including investment by Bangladeshi nationals ordinarily resident abroad.

(b) Type B: Joint venture projects between foreign and Bangladeshi entrepreneurs resident in Bangladesh.

(c) Type C: 100 per cent Bangladeshi entrepreneurs resident in Bangladesh.

According to this classification, general conditions applicable to the establishment of firms in EPZs are as follows:

(a) General conditions applicable to Type A industries

1. Total investment cost of the project, including the cost of construction, must be financed by the entrepreneurs' own foreign exchange resources.

2. The raw materials and the entire working capital requirement must be financed out of remittances received in convertible foreign currencies or export proceeds of the enterprise, including payment of rental, rates and taxes, wages and salaries, transportation and local materials, and repairs and maintenance.

3. The entire products of the enterprise must be exported outside Bangladesh. However, the Government allows, under exceptional circumstances, sales in Bangladesh of any product manufactured in the zone. Such sales are payable in foreign exchange and subject to observance of other formalities, including payment of duties and taxes, if any, as applicable to imports.

4. The industries must declare to Bangladesh Bank the f.o.b. value of the goods exported out of Bangladesh immediately after the actual shipment of the goods has been effected; the export proceeds, when realized, are allowed to be retained on convertible foreign currency accounts.

5. No import duty, sales tax, octroi or other tax is levied on the import of capital machinery, instruments and equipment including replacements thereof, spare parts, raw materials, packaging materials, construction equipment and materials for use in EPZs.

6. Bangladesh goods or raw materials sold against foreign exchange for use or processing in EPZs are treated as exports from Bangladesh and are subject to the usual export formalities including payment of export duty, if any such exports are eligible for export incentives as specified

at that time.

7. There is no excise duty on goods produced in EPZs and no export duty is levied on the export of such goods.

8. The income, profits and gains of any industrial undertaking set up in a zone must be exempted from income tax payable under the Income Tax Act for a period of 10 years beginning with the month in which the commercial production of the undertaking is commenced without any condition of reinvestment. A rebate of 50 per cent of the income tax attributable to export sales of the undertaking is allowed after the expiry of 10 years.

9. The undertaking company's office must be registered as a foreign company under the Companies Act.

10. A foreign technician employed in a zone who is neither a citizen of taxable territories nor a resident in taxable territories in any of the four years immediately preceding the year of arrivel in taxable territories, is exempted from the payment of income tax on salaries for a period not exceeding three years from the date of arrival in the taxable territories provided that such salary is exempted from income tax in the country of domicile of the technician.

11. The enterprise must submit its audited and certified annual statement of accounts to Bangladesh Bank and the registrar of joint stock companies.

***Source:* BEPZA.**

(b) General conditions applicable to Type B industries

1. The cost of capital machinery and spare parts imported from abroad must be paid by foreign partners from their own resources.

2. The entire raw materials used for manufacturing or processing, either imported from abroad or locally procured, must be provided by foreign partners from funds from abroad.

3. The local currency cost of the investment, including working capital not provided by foreign partners except those mentioned in 1 and 2 above, may be contributed by the local partners.

5. In case the extent of investment to be made by the foreign partner as agreed upon and approved by the Authority does not cover the import of raw materials, the local partner is allowed by Bangladesh Bank to open a letter of credit for imported raw materials, on a case-by-case basis.

6. While dividends payable to foreign partners must be remittable in foreign exchange, the payment of dividends to local partners must be made in local currency.

7. The undertaking must be registered in Bangladesh as a Bangladesh company under the Companies Act.

***Source*: BEPZA**

(c) General conditions applicable to Type C industries

1. The machinery, spare parts, raw materials and other imported capital goods must be financed under non-repatriable foreign exchange, supplier's credit, PAYE or other approved arrangements allowed by the Government. Salaries and emoluments of foreign experts, if employed, must be financed under any of these arrangements.

2. The first consignment of raw materials may be imported by procuring foreign currency from the secondary exchange market subject to the approval of Bangladesh Bank. Such industries are eligible for cash foreign exchange for the subsequent import of raw materials and spares, etc., to the extent of the net foreign exchange earned and surrendered to Bangladesh Bank.

3. The cost of any construction and working capital and goods not covered in 1 and 2 above may be financed out of the local resources of the entrepreneurs.

4. The entire export proceeds must be surrendered to Bangladesh Bank.

5. These enterprises will be subject to the usual foreign exchange regulations of the country.

Source: **Bangladesh EPZ Authority**

II. GUIDELINES TO PREPARE INVESTMENT PROPOSALS FOR EPZ

Applicants wishing to invest in the Dhaka and Chittagong EPZs are advised to fill in a Project Proposal Form available from BEPZA. The information must be typed and provided in three sets of forms. Unless otherwise requested, all prices should be expressed in thousands and/or millions. If there is any particular aspect of the project not covered in the form, all relevant information must be submitted on separate sheets, which must accompany the form.

Incomplete proposals will not be considered for registration until they are complete and fully documented. The information must be submitted in tabular form wherever so desired in the project proposal form and any annexes attached. Wherever descriptive information is required, it should be provided succinctly stressing the relevant points. All the annexes and every page of the application should be initialized. The following documents must accompany the project proposal form:

1. Bank solvency certificates of the sponsors/directors;

2. Project feasibility report, if any;

3. Marketing agreement, if any;

4. Copy of memorandum and articles of association of the company if the same is already incorporated, or of the parent company if the company's office is to be registered in Bangladesh. In cases where the memorandum and articles of association of the foreign company are in a language other than English, an English translation of the same is required to be furnished with the project proposal;

5. Pro-forma invoice of the machineries to be imported, one set from the manufacturer or three sets from reputed suppliers;

6. Copy of joint venture agreement (if a joint venture project).

An indicative list of sectors currently operating in Bangladesh EPZs as offered by BEPZA is available at < http://www.bangladesh-epz.com/ind_list.htm >.

III. INCENTIVES OFFERED IN EPZ

Industries located in EPZs enjoy the following incentives and facilities:

Fiscal incentives

- Tax holiday for 10 years;
- Exemption of income tax on interest on borrowed capital;
- Relief from double taxation subject to bilateral agreements;
- Complete exemption from dividend tax for three years subject to certain conditions;
- Exemption of income tax on salaries of foreign technicians for three years subject to certain conditions;
- Duty-free import of machinery, equipment and raw materials;
- Duty-free import of three motor vehicles under certain conditions;
- Duty-free import of materials for constructing factory buildings; and
- Duty-free export of goods produced in the zones.

Non-fiscal incentives

- Project expansion and product diversification without permission;
- Off-shore, local and international banking facilities;
- Freedom from national import policy restrictions;
- Expeditious import of raw materials on a documentary acceptance basis;
- Back-to-back letter of credit for the import of raw materials in certain industries;
- Import of goods from the domestic tariff area (DTA);
- Option to sell 10 per cent of output to DTA under certain conditions;
- Option to relocate existing industries from abroad;
- Option to relocate from one zone to another;
- Option to subcontract within the zone;

• Inter-zone export and intra-zone export;

• Customs formalities carried out at enterprise site;

• Liberal allowance of expatriate employment (technicians/experts);

• No unions or strikes are allowed;

• Equal rights with Bangladeshi nationals for foreign employees.

Facilities

• Secured and protected industrial area;

• Land and factory buildings for rent;

• Electricity, telecommunication, gas and water facilities;

• Export and import permits issued in one day;

• Work permits for foreign nationals;

• Recreational facilities for foreign nationals;

• Only one authority (BEPZA) to deal with for all operational purposes.

IV. CUSTOMS REGULATIONS FOR EPZ

The customs procedure relating to export from or import into EPZs to or from any country outside Bangladesh is regulated by Bangladesh Bank and NBR . All movements of goods between EPZs and any other area in Bangladesh outside the zones are conducted in accordance with existing import and export control regulations.

BEPZA prepares a list of items (on the basis of a no objection certificate from NBR) required to be purchased from the Bangladesh customs area for use in the EPZ areas and seeks approval from the Ministry of Commerce. Any correction in, or amendment to, the list may be made in accordance with the same procedure.

BEPZA issues a passbook in the name of industrial units situated in the EPZ areas indicating, therein, the amount in taka up to which goods can be procured locally on a yearly, half yearly or quarterly basis. When the value ceiling mentioned in the passbook is exhausted, BEPZA may endorse a fresh value ceiling in the passbook or issue a new passbook.

BEPZA also issues the necessary "in-pass" and "out-pass" for the machinery and equipment which need to be brought out of the EPZ areas for repair. Wastes of commercial value originating as by-products of the industries situated in the EPZ areas are allowed to be imported into Bangladesh with the prior permission of the Ministry of Commerce, CCI&E and on payment of customs duties and other dues.

The list of items allowed to be purchased from the Bangladesh tariff area in local currency for use in EPZs includes:

1. All kinds of office stationery and printing materials;

2. All kinds of food and beverages;

3. POL: petrol, diesel, lubricants, kerosene, grease, mobile oil, tarpin oil, coconut oil, gas cylinders;

4. All kinds of construction materials: bricks, sand, cement, MS rods, nails, paints and varnishes;

5. Packing materials: poly bags, cartons, straps, manila boards, sweet cones, thread, hessian cloth, packing wood, iron belts, tapes, strap bends, clips, paper boards, tissue papers, belt hooks, foam/cork sheets;

6. Dyes and chemicals: thinner, bleaching power, soda ash, potassium permanganate, sodium sulphate, sulphuric acid, caustic flux, silicate and mica aiben;

7. Medicines for use in EPZs;

8. Accessories: woven labels, buttons, thread, elastics, zippers, pins, tapes, bends and clips;

9. Spare parts: needle plates, sewing machine parts, loppers, motor belts, generator parts, boiler parts, nut bolts, grinders, gate valves, welding electrodes, drills, hose pipes, steel sheets, angles, flat bars, bushes and bearings;

10. Electrical goods: induction motors, circuit breakers, switches, insulation tapes, bulbs of various kinds, heater coils, tube lights and dry starters.

***Source*: SAARC Business Information Network (Saarcnet) web site < http://www.saarcnet.org >.**

As stated earlier, all goods exported from and imported to EPZs are exempted from all customs duties, import duty, sales tax, supplementary duties and VAT. Specific regulations and exemptions apply for:

- **Exemption of customs duties and sales tax on import of machineries, equipment and raw materials (1981)**

- **Rules relating to supply of construction materials from domestic tariff area to export processing zones (1994)**

- **Exemption of customs duty and sales tax on imported motor vehicle for executives in industrial units in EPZs (1989)**

- **Exemption of value added tax on imported motor vehicle for industrial units in EPZs (1994)**

• Exemption of value added tax on imported car and micro-bus for industrial units in EPZs (1992)

V. EXPORTS FROM EPZ

Sales of Bangladesh goods or raw materials to enterprises in EPZs against payment in foreign currency are treated as exports from Bangladesh. Normal exchange control regulations concerning the declaration of the exports on EXP forms and repatriation of proceeds within four months are applicable.

Concerning the repatriation of export procedures, exports made from EPZs must be declared to Customs using export forms in six copies as in the case of ordinary exports from Bangladesh. For the purpose of indemnifications, these export forms must be rubber-stamped or over printed with the words "Export from EPZ" in bold letters to distinguish these exports from ordinary exports.

For export consignments of Type A enterprises operating in EPZs, bills of lading, air waybills and other title documents drawn to the order of authorized dealers are not compulsory. Documents drawn to the order of the letter of credit opening bank/consignee, as per conditions of export letter of credit/export agreement will be treated as valid documents. In such cases, authorized dealers shall certify the exporter of the consignments as an EPZs Type A industry. Endorsement in favour of the consignee or bank endorsement by authorized dealers as per conditions of the letter of credit/export agreement for bill of lading, air waybill and other title documents of export consignments, if drawn to the order of authorized dealers, will also be treated as valid.

Goods produced in EPZs can be exported to DTA subject to observance of the conditions related to the removal and restrictions on the removal of goods from the zones.[3] The concerned customs authority must accord permission to Bangladeshi importers to import goods to DTA produced in the EPZs through opening a letter of credit subject to fulfilment of the following conditions:

(a) Goods specified in annex VII shall only be permitted for import.

(b) The quantity of goods to be imported annually shall not exceed 10 per cent of the goods exported by the concerned enterprise during the previous financial year.

(c) The approval or permission of BEPZA shall have to be obtained for the import.

(d) Other terms of the Customs (Export Processing Zones) Rules, 1984 shall be applicable in this respect.

[3] As specified in Clauses 6 and 10 of the Customs (Export Processing Zone) Rules, 1984.

VI. IMPORTS TO EPZ

In order to buy products, EPZ enterprises must submit six copies of an import declaration form addressed to the Collector of Customs along with six copies of the invoices. The declaration will be received at a specific counter in the Customs Office in the zone.

The import declaration will be registered in the customs station and an entry number given with a date. After endorsing the necessary order on the declaration form, five copies of the declaration will be handed over to the importer or authorized agent. The original copy of the declaration will be retained. A requisition for escort may also be requested by the importer simultaneously at the time of filling the declaration.

The import declaration will be endorsed as "Passed out of Customs Control" by an authorized officer and the marks and number of the packages will be verified by the Customs Department. The goods will be escorted from the port to the EPZ enterprises without examination.

In case of doubt on the bona fide of the declaration made by the importer, Customs may physically examine the goods within the port area, before the goods are allowed to pass out of the jetty, and the duplicate copy of the declaration will be retained at the gate. This copy will be kept with the original copy in the main file as confirmation that the goods have been delivered to the importer. The remaining four copies of the declaration form for imports will be distributed for necessary action by the recipient as follows:

(a) The third copy will be retained by the enterprise;

(b) The fourth copy will be retained by the Exchange Control Department, Bangladesh Bank;

(c) The fifth copy may be forwarded to the Marketing Department of BEPZA;

(d) The sixth copy will be retained in the Gate Office at EPZ.

Each enterprise in the EPZs is assigned a registration number from Customs and all imports realized by each enterprise and their value will be briefly recorded in the register. Inventory and physical examination of the imported goods will be made within EPZs and, if possible, within the factory premises of the enterprise in presence of customs and EPZ officers. The importer shall remain accountable to BEPZA and Customs for proper use of the imported goods for manufacture of approved goods for export.

The list of items produced by firms established in EPZs is available at < http://www.saarcnet.org/newsaarcnet/govtpolicies/bangladesh/CHAPTER4/6.html >.

VII. LABOUR ISSUES IN EPZ

BEPZA is vested with the responsibility to administer labour matters for all enterprises located in EPZs. Minimum wages in EPZs are set as follows:

Minimum wages (monthly)

Apprentice/trainee US$ 22.00 Unskilled US$ 38.00 Semi-skilled US$ 45.00 Skilled US$ 63.00

Source: BEPZA.

Other benefits include conveyance allowance, house rent, medical allowance and festival bonus.

The normal working hours are 48 hours a week in a factory and 39 hours a week in an office, six working days a week. Employee leave is established 10 days casual leave and 17 days annual leave.

Technician[4] salaries are exempted from income tax for a period of three years from the date of arrival in Bangladesh, provided that such salaries are not subject to income tax outside Bangladesh.

References for part five: export processing zones in Bangladesh

– < http://www.epzbangladesh.org.bd >.

[4] **A technician is** defined as neither a citizen nor a resident of Bangladesh in any of the four years immediately preceding the year of arrival in Bangladesh, and who is employed in any industry set up in any export processing zone. The word “technician” signifies a person who possesses specialized knowledge in industrial arts and sciences and has experience in industrial practice and whose employment in Bangladesh, irrespective of his or her designation, is in a capacity in which such specialized knowledge and experience are both utilized.

SELECTED INVESTMENT AND BUSINESS OPPORTUNITIES

SELECTES ASIAN DEVELOPMENT BANK PROJECTS

ADB offers many opportunities for contractors, consultants, investors, and job applicants. This section contains information about proposed projects and contract awards. You can also find guidelines on the hiring of consultants and on procurement.

ADB funds development projects and programs in the Asian and Pacific Regions. Such funding generates opportunities for the business communities of its member countries.

Business Opportunities provides information on the requirements for goods, works, and services of projects under consideration by ADB.

A project is listed here once ADB is satisfied that it is suitable for financing. This is not an assurance that financing will be provided. New and proposed projects are listed until they have been approved for financing. Projects that have not proceeded will be removed.

Participation in bidding for contracts and offering services for projects financed by ADB is limited to nationals of ADB's **Member Countries**.

Guidelines For Procurement Under ADB Loans and **Guidelines on the Use of Consultants by ADB and Its Borrowers** are available upopn request

Consultants may submit expressions of interest (EOIs) online for any project listed under New, Removed or Proposed Projects. Select the project from the list by country and click the "EOI" button on the right. Enter the data into the EOI form, add any project details that are not in your firm's **DACON** registration and click the "Submit" button.

Alternatively, firms can send hard copies of their EOIs to the Director, Consulting Services Division (plus a copy to the project officer whose name is posted in the project details, if they wish).

Consultants are also required to send a copy of their EOI to the executing agency mentioned in the project summary (when applicable).

Representations and complaints concerning recruitment of consultants as well as prequalification, bidding and bid-evaluation process for procurement of goods and works should be referred to

Principal Director
Central Operations Services Office
Asian Development Bank
P.O. Box 789 0980 Manila, Philippines

BANGLADESH'S WEST ZONE POWER DEVELOPMENT PROJECT

NAME OF PROJECT: BANGLADESH'S WEST ZONE POWER DEVELOPMENT PROJECT

LOAN NO. 1885(SF)

DEADLINE: 5 July 2003

The People's Republic of Bangladesh has received a loan from the Asian Development Bank (ADB) towards the cost of the West Zone Power Development Project, and it is intended that part of the proceeds of this loan will be applied to eligible payments under the contract for which this Invitation for Bids is issued.

The Power Grid Company of Bangladesh Ltd. (PGCB) now invites sealed bids from eligible bidders from member countries of ADB for the design-build and turnkey contract for the following works:

Design, supply, delivery, installation, testing & commissioning on turnkey basis of 230kV Ashuganj-Serajganj double circuit transmission line (approx. 142km) which include 230kV double circuit overhead line from existing Ashuganj 230kV Substation to Serajganj 230kV Switching Station via Jamuna Multipurpose Bridge

(Details and specifications are provided in the Bidding Document)

International competitive bidding will be conducted in accordance with ADB's Two-Stage: Two-Envelope bidding procedure and is open to all bidders from eligible source countries of the ADB.

Interested eligible bidders may obtain further information from and inspect the bidding document at the office address given below.

The bidding document, in the English language, may be purchased by interested eligible bidders on the submission of a written application to the address below and upon payment of a nonrefundable fee of Tk. 20,000/= or US$400. The method of payment will be in the form of a demand draft or pay order in favor of PGCB.

Bids must be delivered to the address below on 5 July 2003. All bids must be accompanied by a bid security of US$600,000.00 or an equivalent amount in a freely convertible currency. Late Bids shall be rejected. Bids will be opened immediately thereafter in the presence of the bidders' representatives who choose to attend.

PGCB will not be held responsible for any costs or expenses incurred by bidders in connection with preparation or delivery of bids, including costs and expenses related to visits to the sites of installation of the works.

In the comparison of bids, ADB's Domestic Preference Scheme will be applied in accordance with the provisions stipulated in the Instructions to Bidders.

CONTACT: Power Grid Company of Bangladesh Ltd.

Red Crescent Concord Tower (6th Flr)

17, Mohakhali C/A, Dhaka-1212

Tel: 880-2-9888589; 880-2-9888970

Fax: 880-2-9888501

Attention: Company Secretary, PGCB

For more information or assistance on this project, please contact the Office of the U.S. Commercial Liaison to the ADB, Attention: Stewart Ballard, Senior Commercial Officer, Tel.: (63-2) 887-1345; Fax: (63-2) 887-1164; E-mail:manila.adb.office.boxmail.doc.gov.

ASSISTANCE TO PRIVATIZATION COMMISSION PROJECT

The ADB selects a consultant for a TA grant based on its prior Expression of Interest (EOI). An EOI can be transmitted on-line through the ADB's website (www.adb.org); afterward it will be acknowledged automatically. Firms may opt to send a hardcopy follow-up EOI addressed to Mr. S. Thuraisingham, Director, Consulting Services Division, with a copy to the ADB Project Officer. The EOI should relate a firm's experience and expertise to the ADB project. It is important for a U.S. firm to emphasize its similar project experience in the country or in a similar geographic area rather than presenting a general profile of its consulting activities. A separate EOI should be submitted for each project. The project name indicated in the EOI should exactly match that listed in the ADB Business Opportunities publication to avoid confusion.

To be considered for employment, consultants must register on the ADB's DACON (Data on Consulting Firms) and DICON (Data on Individual Consultants) Systems, otherwise, their EOIs will not be accepted. DACON and DICON registration can now be done on-line at www.adb.org/consulting.

Firms may also send a notification copy of their EOIs to the U.S. mailing address for the U.S. Commercial Liaison Office for the ADB, Attention: Stewart Ballard, Senior Commercial Officer, PSC 500 Box 33, FPO AP 96515-1000, or to the same office at its international mailing address:

25th Floor Ayala Life-FGU Center, 6811 Ayala Avenue, Makati City, Metro Manila, Philippines 1226; Phone: (63-2) 887-1345; Fax: (63-2) 887-1164; E-mail: manila.adb.office.box@mail.doc.gov. This office works closely with the Office of the U.S. Executive Director to the ADB to increase American awareness of, and participation in, the ADB's activities.

The project listed in this report is now being actively processed by the ADB. For more information on this project, the name of the ADB project officer is indicated in the project brief. The U.S Commercial Liaison Office is ready to provide assistance to U.S. firms upon request. (Please see paragraph 4.)

The following TA project will be listed for the first time in the APRIL 2003 issue of the Asian Development Bank's (ADB) Business Opportunities (ADBBO). (Note: The ADBBO is also available on the ADB's website .
NAME OF PROJECT: ASSISTANCE TO PRIVATIZATION COMMISSION
Project No.: BAN36307-01
Executing Agency: To be determined.
TA Amount: US$ 150.0 Thousand
Sector/Subsector: Finance Sector/Privatization
Objectives and Scope:

The TA will aim at providing assistance to Privatization Commission (PC) to "learn by doing" or executing privatization transactions for a selected group of pilot state-owned enterprises (SOEs) to illustrate the appropriate way to carry out privatization processes. It is envisaged that PC will gain better understanding of privatization processes and apply this "on-the-job" learning experiences to the subsequent divestment of other SOEs. The appropriate valuation method and divestment technique will enable the Government to maximize sales proceeds, which could be used for other priority sectors. The support of the Government in carrying out the privatization transactions will demonstrate its commitment to privatization and create a momentum for future privatization. Divestment of shares through public offering and listing on the stock exchanges that may result from the TA will enhance the supply of quality stocks on the exchanges and contribute to the development of the Bangladesh capital market. The consultants under the TA will provide hands-on assistance to PC to carry out the entire privatization processes, starting from conduct of due diligence to closing of the transaction for at least one SOE. The scope of consulting services will include (i) reviewing the current status of divestment of candidates for pilot cases including any draft valuation reports; (ii) conducting financial, operational and legal due diligence of the selected SOEs for pilot privatization; (iii) preparing a comprehensive Independent Business Review which will report on findings from the due diligence, assessment of business prospects, application of valuation model, and recommendation on appropriate divestment method; (iv) preparing a sales plan and necessary documentation for privatization.

Consulting Services: The TA will engage the services of (i) an international privatization expert who has experience in executing privatization transactions, (ii) a domestic consulting team comprising a financial adviser/privatization expert, an accountant, and a lawyer to provide the required consulting services totaling 13 person-months: 2 international, and 11 domestic. The international consultant will be recruited on an individual basis in accordance with ADB's Guidelines on the Use of Consultants. The domestic consulting team will be engaged in accordance with procedures satisfactory to ADB.

Recruitment of Consultants: Recruitment of Consultants is expected to take place in July 2003.

Project Processing Stage:
Fact-Finding Mission Completed: 6 Mar 2003
Project Officer: Saitien Thongplengsri;
Tel:(632) 632-6268
Governance, Finance, and Trade Division, SARD

In-country Commercial Officer: Dennis Winstead, Economic/Commercial Officer, American Embassy, Dhaka;

E-mail: WinsteadDA@state.gov

ADP POWER PROJECT

This report from the Commercial Service Liaison Office for the Asian Development Bank (CS/ADB) in Manila is one of a series of regular monthly reports which give U.S. exporters advance notice of Asian government tenders. Here, the focus is on a Bangladesh tender to be issued in March 2002 as part of an energy sector project financed by the ADB. Later in March, CS/ADB expects to report on public tenders in China, India, Indonesia, Fiji, Nepal, Tajikistan, and Uzbekistan, in a variety of sectors. END SUMMARY.

Begin Foreign Government Tender:

1. 565/03/T738

2. 031402
3. STEWART BALLARD
565
5. NAME OF PROJECT: WEST ZONE POWER SYSTEM DEVELOPMENT
- PROJECT
6. CONTACT: Director of Procurement, Rural
- Electrification Board (see complete contact
- information below)
LOAN NO.: 1884 (SF)/1885
DEADLINE: on or before 15 May 2002
204
10. Unknown
11. The People's Republic of Bangladesh has received a loan from the Asian Development Bank (ADB) towards the cost of West Zone Power System Development Project, and it is intended that part of the proceeds of this loan will be applied to eligible payment under the contract for which this Invitation for Bids is issued.

The Rural Electrification Board (REB) now invites sealed bids from eligible bidders from member countries of the ADB for the supply and delivery of the following:

Bid Package No. 03 (18 PBS-II)

IFB ADB W-23: Hardware
IFB ADB W-24: Insulator
IFB ADB W-25: Conductor
IFB ADB W-26: Conductor
IFB ADB W-27: Conductor
IFB ADB W-28: Conductor and Guy Accessories
IFB ADB W-29: Distribution Transformer
IFB ADB W-30: Distribution Transformer

(Details and specifications are provided in the Bidding Documents)

International competitive bidding will be conducted in accordance with ADB's Single-Stage: One-Envelope bidding procedure and is open to all Bidders from eligible source countries.

Interested eligible Bidders may obtain further information on the bid from and inspect the bidding documents at the following address:

Director of Procurement
Rural Electrification Board
Nikunza-2, Khilkhet
7th Floor (Head Office), Room No. 808
Dhaka-1229, Bangladesh
Tel. No. 880-2-891 64 20
Fax No. 880-2-891 6420

The Bidding Document, in the English language may be purchased by interested Bidders on the submission of a written application to the address above and upon payment of a non-refundable fee of US$50.00 or Tk. 3,000.00 in the form of Pay Order/Demand Draft in favour of REB.

Bids must be delivered to the address above in accordance with the Instructions to Bidders on or before 15 May 2002. All Bids must be accompanied by a Bid Security of not less than two percent (2%) of the total bid price. Late bids shall be rejected. Bids will be opened immediately thereafter

(REB's Auditorium, 1st Floor) in the presence of Bidders' representatives who choose to attend.

REB will not be responsible for any costs or expenses incurred by Bidders in connection with the preparation or delivery of Bids.

AGRIBUSINESS DEVELOPMENT

Project Name Agribusiness Development

Executing Agency Ministry of Agriculture

Tel. No. : 861-5367
Address : Building No. 4, Room 433
Bangladesh Secretariat
Dhaka

TA Amount (US$ '000)
650.00

Sector/Subsector
Agriculture and Natural Resources /Industrial Crops and Agro-industry

Date of First Listing
24 March 2003

Objectives and Scope

The purpose of the TA is to help the Government design an agribusiness development project to address the fundamental problems in the sector. The TA output is a feasibility study that includes (i) a detailed evaluation of the constraints and impediments to the development of the agribusiness sector; (ii) proposed strategies for addressing and overcoming the more significant constraints including meeting WTO and other international trade requirements; (iii) identification of the limiting factors in acquisition of technology and the mechanism to accomplish this; and (iv) formulation of a project for further development of the agribusiness sector.

Consulting Services

A total of 46.5 person-months (pm) of consulting services, comprising 19.5 pm of international and 27 pm of domestic inputs are required. A consulting firm or consortium of firms will be selected in accordance with ADB' Guidelines on the Use of Consultants using the quality-and cost-based selection method and other arrangements satisfactory to ADB for engaging the domestic consultants.

Environmental Assessment

Required

Project Processing Stage

Fact-Finding Mission Completed : 6 March 2003

Recruitment of Consultants

Recruitment of consultants expected to take place in Jun 2003.

Project Officer

Loh Ai Tee (632-6978)
Agriculture, Environment, & Natural Resources Division, SARD
atloh@adb.org

GAS SECTOR DEVELOPMENT PROJECT

Project Name
Gas Sector Development Project

Executing Agency
Ministry of Energy and Mineral Resources

Contact : Mr. Khairuzzaman Chowdhury, Secretary Energy
Address: Bhaban 6, Room 113, Bangladesh Secretary
Dhaka

Loan Amount (US$ million)
120.00

Sector/Subsector
Energy /Natural Gas

Date of First Listing
1 April 1998

Objectives and Scope
The proposed Sector Development Program loan consists of (i) Program component linked to the implementation of sector reforms; and (ii) Project component for construction of a major east-west pipeline.

Procurement
Goods
Procurement of pipes, city gate station.
Services
To be determined.

Environmental Category: B

Project Processing Stage
MRM Completed : 2 August 2000

Project Officer
S. Chander (632-6449)
Infrastructure Division, SARD
schander@adb.org

CHITTAGONG PORT TRADE FACILITATION PROJECT

Project Name
Chittagong Port Trade Facilitation Project

Executing Agency
Chittagong Port Authority

Contact: Commodore (Retd) Zulfriqar Ali, Chairman

TA Amount (US$ '000)
400.00

Sector/Subsector
Transport and Communications /Ports and Shipping

Date of First Listing
24 February 2003

Objectives and Scope

This TA will have three components. The first component will focus on improving the management practices of CPA and Customs at Chittagong Port for ship berthing and container clearance by improving processess, procedures and documentation simplification as well as better interfacing between Customs and CPA in the ship berthing and container clearance process. It will also prepare a master plan for the introduction of EDI at Chittagong Port. The second component will involve physical improvements necessary within Chittagong Port Authority area to complement the improved management practices in improving the container clearance process in Chittagong Port. This will include recommendations for improvement to the physical layout of the container yards and container freight stations, better vehicle traffic flow within the port operations area as well as preliminary engineering of structures, buildings and internal circulation roads needed within the port area to efficiently link with the proposed port access road. The third component will focus on environmental management. It will build upon the recommendations of TA 3357 BAN: Oil Spill Impact and Response Management Program as well as the environmental issues identified by CPA such as controlling pollution from shore-based sources and handling of hazardous material.

Consulting Services

The TA will require about 10 person-months of international consultants and 25 person-months of domestic consultants. Selection of consultants will be in accordance with the Bank's Guidelines on the Use of Consultants and other arrangements satisfactory to ADB for the engagement of domestic consultants.

Environmental Assessment

To Be Determined

Project Processing Stage

Fact-Finding Mission Completed: 10 February 2003

Recruitment of Consultants

Recruitment of consultants is expected to take place in end July 2003.

Project Officer

Prodyut Dutt (632-6852)
pdutt@adb.org

INSTITUTIONAL SUPPORT TO PRIMARY EDUCATION FOR QUALITY CONTROL

Project Name
Institutional Support to Primary Education for Quality Control

Executing Agency
Primary and Mass Education Division

Contact : Kazi Farid Ahammed, Joint Secretary
Fax. No.: 880-2-8618871
E-mail : pmed.gob@bd com.com
Address : Dhaka, Bangladesh

TA Amount (US$ '000)
1,000.00

Sector/Subsector
Social Infrastructure /Education

Date of First Listing
1 April 2003

Objectives and Scope
To support the Directorate of Primary Education in coordination and institutional and organizational development required under the Second Primary Education Development Program.

Consulting Services
To be determined

Project Processing Stage
Fact-Finding Mission Completed : 28 February 2003

Recruitment of Consultants
To be determined

Project Officer
Jouko Sarvi (632-6831)
Social Sectors Division, SARD
jsarvi@adb.org

SOCIAL PROTECTION FOR DISADVANTAGED WOMEN AND CHILDREN

Project Name
Social Protection for Disadvantaged Women and Children

Executing Agency
Ministry of Women and Children Affairs

Contact : Mr. Mahfuzul Islam, Secretary
Fax. No. : 880 2 8612892
Tel. No. : 880 2 8611012
Address : Bangladesh Secretariat
Dhaka

TA Amount (US$ '000)
500.00

Sector/Subsector
Multisector

Date of First Listing
15 November 2002

Objectives and Scope
The objective of the PPTA is to assist the Government in the preparation of the Project. It will have the task to explore the possible project interventions, involving all relevant Government partners on Central and District level, communities, target groups and stakeholders. Specifically, the TA will: (i) conduct a situation analysis including all ongoing projects and activities, especially those financed by other donors and those supported by the Government; (ii) identify best practices in the sector in Bangladesh and

those confirmed through international experience; (iii) define the scope of the sustainable interventions to improve the situation of the target groups; (iv) identify possible partners; (v) assess the need to strengthen the institutional capacity of local governments, communities and NGOs to manage planned initiatives; (vi) establish the qualitative framework and estimate costs of the Project; (vii) define key program components including management and financing requirements; (viii) identify possible investment components of the project; (ix) identify the geographical scope in which especially the service delivery component would be implemented; (x) identify suitable executing and implementing agencies for the project; and (xi) identify the need for TA and human resources.

Consulting Services

The TA will be carried out over six months, beginning latest mid-2003. There will be a total input of 35 person months of experts, 25 of those will be domestic and 10 international. The consulting team will include an institutional development specialist (3 pm), a strategic planning specialist (3 pm), an integrated service delivery specialist (team leader, 4 pm) as international consultants. Domestic consultants will include: a management specialist (co-team leader, 5 pm) a legal systems reform specialist (3 pm), a gender specialist (3 pm), a social protection specialist with focus on women's issues (3 pm), a child protection specialist (3 pm), a health and nutrition specialist (2 pm), a poverty assessment specialist (2 pm), a community development specialist (2 pm), and an economic and financial specialist (2 pm).

Environmental Assessment

To Be Determined

Project Processing Stage

Approved by the Bank: 11 February 2003

Recruitment of Consultants

All consultants will be recruited through a firm using a simplified technical proposal, in accordance with ADB's guidelines for the recruitment of consultants. Shortlisting of consultants has been completed. Expressions of interest are no longer accepted. Shortlisting of consultants have been completed. Queries regarding consultants should be sent directly to the Director of Consulting Services Division.

Project Officer

Axel Weber (632-6724)
Social Sectors Division, SARD
aweber@adb.org

ASSISTANCE TO PRIVATIZATION COMMISSION

Executing Agency
To be determined.

TA Amount (US$ '000)
150.00

Sector/Subsector
Finance Sector /Privatization

Date of First Listing
13 March 2003

Objectives and Scope

The TA will aim at providing assistance to Privatization Commission (PC) to "learn by doing" or executing privatization transactions for a selected group of pilot state-owned enterprises (SOEs) to illustrate the appropriate way to carry out privatization processes. It is envisaged that PC will gain better understanding of privatization processes and apply this "on-the-job" learning experiences to the subsequent divestment of other SOEs. The appropriate valuation method and divestment technique will enable the Government to maximize sales proceeds, which could be used for other priority sectors. The support of the Government in carrying out the privatization transactions will demonstrate its commitment to privatization and create a momentum for future privatization. Divestment of shares through public offering and listing on the stock exchanges that may result from the TA will enhance the supply of quality stocks on the exchanges and contribute to the development of the Bangladesh capital market. The consultants under the TA will provide hands-on assistance to PC to carry out the entire privatization processes, starting from conduct of due diligence to closing of the transaction for at least one SOE. The scope of consulting services will include (i) reviewing the current status of divestment of candidates for pilot cases including any draft valuation reports; (ii) conducting financial, operational and legal due diligence of the selected SOEs for pilot privatization; (iii) preparing a comprehensive Independent Business Review which will report on findings from the due diligence, assessment of business prospects, application of valuation model, and recommendation on appropriate divestment method; (iv) preparing a sales plan and necessary documentation for privatization.

Consulting Services

The TA will engage the services of (i) an international privatization expert who has experience in executing privatization transactions, (ii) a domestic consulting team comprising a financial adviser/privatization expert, an accountant, and a lawyer to provide the required consulting services totaling 13 person-months: 2 international, and 11 domestic. The international consultant will be recruited on an individual basis in accordance with ADB's Guidelines on the Use of Consultants. The domestic consulting team will be engaged in accordance with procedures satisfactory to ADB.

Project Processing Stage

Fact-Finding Mission Completed : 6 March 2003

Recruitment of Consultants

Recruitment of Consultants is expected to take place in July 2003.

Project Officer

Saitien Thongplengsri (632-6268)
Governance, Finance, and Trade Division, SARD
sthongplengsri@adb.org

CAPITAL MARKET DEVELOPMENT PROGRAM II

Project Name

Capital Market Development Program II

Executing Agency

To be determined.

TA Amount (US$ '000)

470.00

Sector/Subsector

Finance Sector /Capital Market Development

Date of First Listing

24 March 2003

Objectives and Scope

Capital Market Development Program II seeks to develop the domestic financial markets through policy, legal, regulatory, and institutional reforms. The Program will address the constraints on financial resource mobilization and the chanelling of funds for productive investments.

Consulting Services

To be determined.

Environmental Assessment

To Be Determined

Project Processing Stage

Beginning of Fact-finding Mission: Jul 2003.

Recruitment of Consultants

To be determined.

Project Officer

Virgilio T. Velasco (632-6386)
Governance, Finance, and Trade Division, SARD
vtvelasco@adb.org

SUPPORT TO ANTI CORRUPTION INITIATIVES

Project Name

Support to Anti Corruption Initiatives

Executing Agency

Ministry of Finance

Contact	:	Mr. Zakir Ahmed Khan, Secretary, Finance Division
Tel. No.	:	(8802)8610406 / (8802)8111159
Address	:	Bangladesh Secretariat
		Mr. Kamai Uddin Siddiqui, Prin.Secretary
		to the Prime Minister
		Old Sangsad Bhaban, Dhaka

TA Amount (US$ '000)

700.00

Sector/Subsector

Multisector

Date of First Listing

Objectives and Scope

There are two major objectives of the TA. Under Component A (Private Credit Markets Anti Corruption-Secured Financing Governance), the TA supports private credit markets anti-corruption through a triangle of sectoral governance initiatives for secured financing focused on (i) the development of an enabling legal and registry framework for use of movable property for enhanced access to credit; (ii) development of institutional governance based on governance audit indicators for secured financing institutions which use movable property collateral for providing credit under secured transactions; and (iii) regulatory governance for a new secured transactions registry based on governance audit indicators developed with the assistance of Bangladesh Bank. This triangle of governance initiatives will be underpinned through training and capacity building for the operation and use of the new enabling framework and to assist secured financing institutions to meet governance audit criteria. Under Component B (Public Sector Anti Corruption), the TA aims to bolster public sector anti corruption through a triangle of cross sectoral anti corruption initiatives focused on (i) enabling national framework for corruption prevention through establishment of the Independent Anti Corruption Commission (IACC) and a National Committee on Corruption Prevention; (ii) development of institutional corruption prevention in government line ministries thorugh governance audits resulting in rules, regulations, legal amendments and mechanisms; and (iii) operationalization of the national framework for corruption prevention and line ministry corruption prevention through training and capacity building.

Consulting Services

ADB will engage a firm of international consultants to provide consulting services for a total of 16 person months. Consultants' input will comprise 8 person months by international consultants and 8 person months by domestic consultants. The team comprises (i) Team Leader/Governance Audit Expert, (international, 4 person months); (ii) Deputy Team Leader/Forensic Accounting Expert (international, 4 person months); (iii) Administrative Review & Legal Expert (domestic, 2 person months); (iv) Accounting Expert (domestic, 2 person months); and (v) Training Expert (domestic, 4 person months). In addition, given the need for lead time and specialist skills involved for enabling framework support for Part A and Part B of the TA, ADB will engage the services of individual consultants for a total of 12 person months, consisting of: (i) a Secured Transactions Legal Expert (international, 4 person months) for Part A of the TA; (ii) Secured Transactions Registry Systems Expert (international, 4 person months)for Part A of the TA; and (iii) an Anti Corruption Legal Expert (international, 4 person months) for Part B of the TA. Such individual consultants will be expected to work as part of a team with consultants from the firm of international consultants led by the Team Leader. The Team of consultants will be selected and engaged according to ADB's Guidelines on the Use of Consultants, and other arrangements satisfactory to ADB on the engagement of domestic consultants. In this TA, the simplified technical proposal (STP) procedure will be used in selecting consultants.

Project Processing Stage

Fact-Finding Mission Completed : 18 March 2003

Recruitment of Consultants

Recruitment of Consultants is expected to take place in August 2003.

Project Officer

Arjun Goswami (632-6355)
Governance, Finance, and Trade Division, SARD
agoswami@adb.org

SELECTED LAWS AND REGULATIONS AFFECTING BUSINESS

THE COMPANIES (BANGLADESH) ACT, 1994[2]

CONTENTS

PART-II CONSTITUTION AND INCORPORATION

4. Prohibition of partnership exceeding certain number:

(1) Nor company, association or partnership consisting of more than ten persons shall be formed or a the purpose of carrying on the business of banking unless it is registered as a company under this Act or is formed by or under any other Act of Parliament.

(2) No company association or partnership consisting of more than twenty persons shall be formed for the purpose of carrying on any other business that has for its objects the acquisition of gain by the company, association or partnership, or by the individual members thereof unless it is registered as a company under this Act or is formed by or under any other Act of Parliament.

(3) This section shall not apply to joint family carrying on joint family business or trade.

[2] Selected articles

Provided that for the purposes of this section, in computing the number of persons of a partnership, association or company comprising two or more joint families, minor members of such families shall be excluded.

(4) Every member of a company, association or partnership carrying on business in contravention of this section shall be personally liable for all liabilities incurred in such business.

(5) Any person who is a member of a company, association or partnership formed in contravention of this section shall be punishable with fine not exceeding five thousand taka.

Memorandum of Association

5. Mode of forming incorporated company.

Any seven or more persons or, where the company to be formed will be a private company, any two or more persons associated for any lawful purpose may, be subscribing their names to a memorandum of association and otherwise with the requirements of this Act in respect or registration form an incorporated company, with or without limited liability, that is to say, either--

(a) a company limited by shares, that is to say, a company having the liability of its member limited by the memorandum to the amount, if any, unpaid on the shares respectively held by them; or

(b) a company limited by guarantee, that is to say, a company having the liability of its members limited by the memorandum to such amount as the members may respectively thereby undertake to contribute to the assets of the assets of the company on the event of its being wound up; or

(c) an unlimited company, that is to say, a company having no limit on the liability of its members.

6. Memorandum of company limited by sharees.

In the case of a company limited by shares.-

(a) the memorandum shall state.--

(i) the name of the company, with "limited" as the last word in its name;

(ii) The address of the registered office;

(iii) the objects of the company, and, except in the case of trading companies, the territories to which they extend;

(iv) that the liability of the members is limited;

(v) the amount of share capital with which the company proposes to be registered, and the divisions thereof into shares of a fixed amount;

(b) each subscriber of the memorandum shall take at least one share;

(c) each subscriber shall write opposite to his name the number of shares he takes.

7. Memorandum of company limited by guarantee.

In the case of a company limited by guarantee--

(a) the memorandum shall state--

(i) the name of the company, with "limited" as the last word in its name.

(ii) the address of the registered office;

(iii) the objects of the company, and, except in the case of trading companies, the territories to which they extend;

(iv) that the liability of the members is limited;

(v) that each member undertakes to contribute to the assets of the company in the event of its being wound up while he is a member or within one year afterwards, for payment of the debts and liabilities of the company contracted before he ceases to be a member, ad of the charges and expenses of winding up, and for adjustment of the right of the contributories among themselves, such amount as may be required, not exceeding a specified amount;

(b) if the company has a share capital--

(i) the memorandum shall also state the amount of share capital with which the company proposes to be registered and the division thereof into shares of a fixed amount;

(ii) each subscriber of the memorandum shall take at least one share;

(iii) each subscriber shall write opposite to his name the number of shares he takes.

8. Memorandum of unlimited company.

In the case of an unlimited company

(a) the memorandum shall state-

(i) the name of the company;

(ii) the address of the registered office of the company;

(iii) the objects of the company and, except in the case of trading companies, the territories to which they extend.

(b) if the company has a share capital-

(i) each subscriber of the memorandum shall take at least one share;

(ii) each subscriber shall write opposite to his name the number of shares he takes.

9. Printing and signature of memorandum.

The memorandum of every company shall--

(a) be printed;

(b) be divided into paragraphs numbered consecutively; and

(c) be signed by each subscriber, who shall add his address and description in the presence of at least two witnesses who shall attest the signature.

10. Restriction on alteration of memorandum.

(1) A company shall not alter the conditions on continued in its memorandum except provisions is made in the Act.

(2) Only those provisions which by any other specific provision contained in this Act, are required to be stated in the memorandum of the company concerned shall be deemed to be the conditions contained in its memorandum.

(3) Other provisions contained in the memorandum, including those relating to the appointment of director, managing agent or manager may be altered in the same manner as the articles of the company, but if there is any express provision in this Act permitting the alteration of such provisions in any other manner, they may also be altered in such other manner.

(4) All reference to the articles of a company in this Act shall be construed as including references to the other provisions contained in its memorandum as referred to in sub-section (3).

11. Name of company and change of name.

(1) A company shall not be registered by a name identical with that by which a company in existence is already registered, or so nearly resembling the name that there is likelihood of using the name to deceive, except where the company in existence is in the course of being dissolved and signifies its written consent in such manner as the Registrar requires.

(2) If a company, through inadvertence or otherwise, is, without the consent referred to in sub-section (1), registered by a name identical with that by which a company in existence is previously is registered, or so nearly resembling the name that there is likelihood of using the name to deceive, the first mentioned company shall, on he direction of the Registrar, change its name within a period of one hundred and twenty days.

(3) If a company makes a default in complying with the direction made under sub-section (2), the company shall be punishable with fine of five hundred take for every day during which the default continues and every officer who is in default shall be punishable with fine of one hundred taka for every day during which the default continues.

(4) Except with the previous consent in writing of the Government, no company shall be registered by a name which is declared by the Government by notification in the official Gazette, as undesirable:

Provided that nothing in this sub-section shall apply to companies registered before the commencement of this Act.

(5) No company shall be registered by a name containing in any form the name or any abbreviation of the name of the United Nations or of any subsidiary body set up by the United Nations or of the World Health Organisation unless the company has obtained the previous authorisation in writing of the Secretary General in the case of the United Nations or the subsidiary body as aforesaid or of the Director General of the World Health Organisation in the case of that Organisation.

(6) Any company may, by special resolution and subject to the approval of the Registrar signified in writing, change it name.

(7) Were a company changes its name, the Registrar shall enter the new name on the register in place of the former name, and shall issued a certificate of incorporation in its new name to meet the circumstances of the case and on the issue of such a certificate, the change of name shall be complete.

(8) The change of name shall not change any rights or obligations of the company, or render defective any legal proceedings by or against the company; and any legal proceedings that might have been continued or commenced against it by its former name may be continued or commenced against it by its new name.

(9) A company may, on payment of such fee as may be prescribed, apply to the Registrar for information whether any company is registered or proposed to be registered by a name specified in the application and the Registrar shall furnish the required information within a period of thirty days from the date of receipt of the application.

12. Alternation of memorandum.

(1) Subject to the provisions of this Act, a company may, by special resolution, alter the provisions of its memorandum with respect to the objects of the company, so far as may be required to enable it--

(a) to carry on its business more economically or more efficiently; or

(b) to attain its main purpose by new or improved means; or

(c) to enlarge or change the local area of its operations; or

(d) to carry on some business which, under the existing circumstances. may conveniently or advantageously be combined with the business of the company; or

(e) to restrict or abandon any of the objects specified in the memorandum; or

(f) to sell or dispose of the whole or any part of the undertaking of the company; or

(g) to amalgamate with any other company or body of persons.

(2) The alteration shall not take effect until and except in so far it is confirmed by the Court on petition.

(3) Before confirming the alteration, the Court must be satisfied--

(a) that sufficient notice has been given to every holder of debentures of the company, and to any person or class of person whose interest will, in the option of the Court, be affected by the alteration; and

(b) that, with respect to every creditor who in the opinion of the Court is entitled to object, and who signifies his objections in manner directed by the Court, either his consent to the alteration has been obtained or his debt or claim has been discharged or has been determined, or has been secured to the satisfaction of the Court;

Provided that the Court may, in the cases of any person or class, for special reasons, dispense with the notice required by this section.

13. Power of Court when confirming alteration.

The Court may make an order confirming the alteration either wholly or in part, and on such terms and conditions as it thinks fit, and may make such order as to costs as it thinks proper.

14. Exercises of discretion by Court.

The Court shall, in exercising its discretion under sections 12 and 13, have regard to the class of them, as well as to the rights and interests of the creditors, and may if it thinks fit, adjourn the proceedings in order that an arrangement may be made to the satisfaction of the Court for the purchase of the interests of dissenting members; and may give such directions and make such orders as it may think expedient for facilitating or carrying into effect any such arrangement;

Provided that no part of the share capital of the company may be expended in any such purchase.

15. Procedure on confirmation of the alternation.

A certified copy of the order confirming the alternation, together with a printed copy of the memorandum as altered, shall be filed by the company with the Registrar within ninety days from the date of the order or within such time as may be extended by the court, and he Registrar shall register the same. and shall certify the registration under his hand, and the certificate shall be conclusive evidence that all the requirements of this Act, with respect to the alteration and the confirmation thereof, have been complied with, and hence forth the memorandum so altered shall be the memorandum of the company.

16. Effect of failure to register within extended time.--No such alteration shall have any operation until registration thereof has been duly effected in accordance with the provisions of section 15, and if such registration is not effected within the period specified in that section such alteration and the order of the Court confirming the alteration, and all proceedings connected there with shall, at the expiration of the period specified under that section become absolutely null and void :

Provided that the Court may, on sufficient cause shown, revive the order on application made within a further period of thirty days after the said period.

Articles of Association,

17. Registration of articles.

(1) A company limited by guarantee and an unlimited company shall, and a company limited by shares may. have an articles of association herein provision shall be made for regulating the affairs of the company; and the article shall be signed by the subscribers of the memorandum and be registered together with the memorandum.

(2) Articles of association may adopt all or any of the regulations contained in Schedule I, and shall in any event be deemed to contain regulations identical with or to the same effect as regulation 56, 66, 71, 78, 79, 80, 81, 82, 95, 97, 105, 108, 112, 113, 114, 115, and 116 contained in that Schedule :

Provided that regulations 78, 79, 82, 81, and 82 shall not be deemed to be included in the articles of any private company except a private company which is the subsidiary company of a public company :

Provided further that regulation, 108 shall be deemed to require that a statement of the reasons why of the whole amount of any item of expenditure which may in fairness be distributed over several years, only a portion thereof is charged against the income of the year, shall be shown in the profit and, loss account, unless the company in general meeting shall determine otherwise.

(3) In the case of an unlimited company or a company limited by guarantee, the articles, if the company has a share capital, shall state the amount of share capital with which the company proposes to be registered.

(4) In the case of an unlimited company or a company limited by guarantee, if the company has not a share capital, the articles shall state the number of members with which the company proposes to the registered; and on the basis of such number the Registrar shall determine the fees payable on registration.

18. Application of Schedule I.

In the case of a company limited by shares and registered after the commencement of this Act, if articles not registered, or, if articles are registered, in so far as the articles do not exclude or modify the regulations in Schedule I, those regulations shall, so far as applicable be the regulations of the company in the same manner and to the same extent as if they were contained in the duly registered articles.

19. Form and signature of articles.

Articles shall

(a) be printed;

(b) be divided into paragraphs numbered consecutively;

(c) be signed by each subscriber of the memorandum, who shall add his address and description in the presence of at least two witness who shall attest the signature.

20. Alteration of articles by special resolution.

Subject to the provisions of this Act and to the conditions contained in its memorandum, a company may by special resolution alter, exclude from or add to its articles: and any alteration, exclusion or addition so made shall be as valid as if originally contained in the articles, and be subject in like manner to alteration, exclusion or addition by special resolution.

21. Effect of alteration in memorandum or articles.

Notwithstanding any thing in the memorandum or articles of a company,, no member of the company shall be bound by an alteration made in the memorandum or articles after the due on which he becomes, member, if and so far as the alteration requires him to take or subscribe for more shares than the number held by him at the date on which the alteration is made, or in any way increases his liability is at that date to contribute to the share capital of, or otherwise to pay money to the company.

General Provisions

22. Effect of memorandum and articles.

(1) The memorandum and articles shall when registered bind the company and the members hereof to the same extent as if they respectively had been signed by each member and contained a convenient on the part of each member his heirs and leal representatives to observe all the provisions of the memorandum and of the articles subject to the provisions of this Act.

(2) All money payable by any member to the company under the memorandum or articles shall be a debt one from him to the company.

23. Registration of memorandum and articles.

(1) The memorandum and articles if any shall be field with the Registrar who if satisfied that the requirements of this Act have been complied with shall retain and register them within thirty days from the date of their receipt and in the event of refusal he shall communicate the grounds within ten days after that period to the company.

(2) An person on being aggrieved by a refusal of the Registrar under sub-section (1) may make an appeal to the Government within thirty days of the receipt of the refusal order.

(3) The petition of appeal shall be accompanied by a treasury challan showing of a fee of two hundred fifty taka to be credited under the head of account specified in this behalf.

(4) The decision of the Government in an appeal under this section shall be final.

24. Effect of registration.

(1) On the registration of the memorandum of a company the Registrar shall certify under his hand that the company is incorporated and in the case of a limited company that the company is limited.

(2) From the date of incorporation mentioned in the certificate of incorporation the subscribers of the memorandum together with such other persons as may from time to time become members of the company shall be a body corporate by the name contained in the memorandum capable forthwith of exercising all the functions of an incorporated company and having perpetual succession and a common seal but with such liability on the part of the members to contribute to the assets of the company in the event of its being wound up as is mentioned in this Act.

25. Conclusiveness of certificate of incorporation.

(1) A certificate of incorporation given by the Registrar in respect of any association shall be conclusive evidence that all the requirements of this Act in respect of registration and of matters precedent and incidental thereto have been complied with and that the association is a company authorised to the registered and duly registered under this Act.

(2) A declaration by an advocate entitled to appear before the High Court Division who is engaged in the formation of a company or by a person named in the articles as a director manager or secretary of the company of compliance with all or any of the said requirements shall be filed with the Registrar and the Registrar may accept such a declaration as sufficient evidence of compliance.

26. Copies of memorandam and articles to be given to members.

(1) Every member of a company may request for a copy of the memorandum, and also for a copy of the articles, if any, and if such request is made in writing alongwith a fee of taka fifty or such less fee as may fixed by the company, the company shall, within fourteen days from the date of such request, send the copy to that member.

(2) If a company makes default in complying with the requirements of this section, it shall be liable for each offence to a fine not exceeding two hundred taka and every officer of the company who is knowingly and willfully in default shall be liable to like penalty.

27. Alteration of memorandum of articles to be noted in every copy.

(1) Where an alteration is made in the memorandum or articles of a company, every copy of the memorandum or articles issued after the date of the date of the alteration shall be in accordance with the alteration.

(2) If, where any such alteration has been made the company at any time after the date of the alteration, issues any copies of the memorandum or article which are not in accordance with the alteration, it shall be liable to a fine not exceeding one hundred taka for each copy so issued, and every officer of the company who is knowingly and willfully in default shall also bearable to a like penalty.

Association not for profit

28. Power to dispense with Limited In name of charitable and other companies.

(1) Where it is proved to the satisfaction of the Government that an association capable of being formed as a limited company has been or in about to be formed for promoting commerce, art, science, religion, charity, or any other useful object, and appllies or intends to apply its profits, if any or other income in promoting its objects and to prohibit the payment of any dividence to its membners the Government may, by licence with approval of one of its Secretaries, direct that the association be registered as a company with limited liability, without the addition of the word "Limited" to its name, and the association may be registered accordingly.

(2) A licence by the Government under this section may be granted on such conditions and subject to such restrictions as the Government thinks fit and those conditions and restrictions

shall be binding on the association and shallif the Government so directs be inserted in the memorandum and articles or in one of those documents.

(3) The association shall on registration enjoy all the privuleges of limited companies and be subject to all their obligations except those of using the word "Limited" as any part of its name and of publishing its name or of sending lists of members to the Registrar.

(4) A licence under this section may at any time be cancelled by the Government and upon cancellation the Registrar shall enter the word "Limited" at the end of the name of the association upon the register and the association shall cease to enjoy the exemptions and privileges granted by this section:

Provided that before a licence is sop cancelled the Government shall give to the association a notice in writing of its intention and the grounds their of and shall afford the association an opportunity of submitting a representation in opposition to the cancellation.

Companies Limited by Guarantee

29. Provision as to companies limited by guarantee.

(1) In the case of company limited by guarantee and not having a share capital and registered after the commencement of this Act every provision in the memorandum or articles or in any resolution of the company purporting to give any person a right to participate in the divisible profits of the company otherwise than as a member shall be void.

(2) For the purpose of this section and the other provisions of this Act. relating to the memorandum of a company limited by guarantee every provision in the memorandum or articles, or in any resolution, of any company limited by guarantee and registered after the commencement of this Act. purporting to divide the undertaking of thecompany into shares or interests shall be treated as a provision for as share capital notwithstanding that the nominal amount or number of the shares or interests is not specified thereby.

PART III SHARE CAPITAL, REGISTRATION OF UNLIMITED COMPANY AS LIMITED AND UNLIMITED LIABILITY OF DIRECTORS

Distribution of Share Capital

30. Nature of shares.

(1) The shares or other interests of any member a company shall be deemed to be movable property and shall be transferable in manner provided by the articles of the company.

(2) Each share in a company having a share capital shall be distinguished by the appropriate number.

31. Certificate of shares or stock.

A certificate under the common seal of the company specifying any shares or stock held by any member shall be prima facie evidence of the title of the member to the shares or stock therein specified.

32. Definition of Member.

(1) Every subscriber of the memorandum of company shall be deemed to have agreed to become a member of the company and on its registration shall be entered as a member in its register of members.

(2) Every other person who agrees to become a member of a company, and whose name is entered in its register of members shall be a member of the company.

33. Membership of holding company

(1) Except in the cases mentioned in this section a body corporate cannot be a member of a company which is its holding company and any allotment or transfer or shares in a company to its subsidiary shall be void.

(2) Nothing in this section shall apply; namely--

(a) Where the subsidiary is the legal representative of a deceased member of the holding company; or

(b) Where the subsidiary is concerned as trustee unless the holding company or a subsidiary thereof is beneficially interested under the trust and is not so interested only by way of security for the purposes of a transaction entered into by it in the ordinary course of business which includes the lending of money.

(3) This section shall not prevent a subsidiary from continuing to be a member of its holding company if it was a member thereof either at the commencement of this Act or before becoming a subsidiary of the holding company; but except in the cases referred to in sub-section (2), the subsidiary shall have no right to vote at meetings of the holding company or of any class of members thereof.

(4) Subject of sub-section (2) sub-sections (1) and (3) shall apply in relation to a nominee for a body corporate which is a subsidiary as if reference in the said sub-sections (1) and (3) to such a body corporate and a subsidiary included reference to a nominee for it.

(5) In relation to a holding company which is either a company limited by guarantee or an unlimited company the reference in this section to shares shall, whether or not the company has a share capital be construed as including a reference to the interest of its members as such whatever be the form of that interest.

34. Register of member

(1) Every company shall keep in one on or more books of register of its members, and enter therein the following particulars:--

(i) the name and addresses, and the occupations, if any of the members;

(ii) in the case of a company having a share capital, a statement of the shares held by each member, distinguishing each share by its number, and of the amount paid or agreed to be considered as paid on the shares of each member;

(iii) the date at which each person was entered in the register as a member;

(iv) the date at which any person ceased to be a member.

(2) If a company makes default in complying with the requirements of this section. It shall be liable to as fine not exceeding one hundred taka for everyday during which the default continues and every officer of the company who knowingly and willfully authorise or permits the default shall also be liable to a like penalty.

35. Index of members of company

(1) Every company having more than fifty member shall, unless the register of members is in such a form as to constitute in itself an index, keep an index of the names of the members of the company and shall within fourteen days after the date on which any alteration is made in the register members make any necessary alteration in the index.

(2) The index which may be in the form of a card index shall in respect of each member contain a sufficient indication to enable the account of that member to be readily found.

(3) If default is made in complying with the section the company shall be liable to a fine not exceeding five hundred taka and every officer of the company who is knowingly and willfully in default shall be liable to a like penalty.

36. Annual list of members and summary

(1) Every company having a share capital shall within eighteen months from its incorporation and thereafter once at least in every year make a list of all persons who on the day of the first or only ordinary general meeting in the year are members of the company, and of all persons who have ceased to be members since the date of the last return or in the case of the first return of the incorporation of the company.

(2) The following shall be stated in the list namely:--

(a) the names, addresses, nationality and occupation of all past and [present members;

(b) the number of shares held by each of the existing members at the date of return specifying the shares transferred since the date of last return or, in the case of first return, since the date of incorporation, by persons who are still members and by persons who have ceased to be members respectively and also the dates of registration of such transfer; and

(c) a summary distinguishing between shares issued for cash and shares issued as fully or partly paid up otherwise than in cash and specifying the following:-

(1) the amount of the share capital of the company, and the number of the shares into which it is divided;

(2) the number of shares taken from the commencement of the company up to the date of the return;

(3) the amount called up on each share;

(4) the total amount of calls received;

(5) the total amount of calls unpaid;

(6) the total amount of the sums, if any, paid by way of commission in respect of any share or debentures, or allowed by way of discount, in respect of any shares or debentures, since the date of the last return or so much thereof as has not been written of at the date of the return.

(7) the total number of shares forfeited;

(8) the total amount of shares or stock for which share warrants are outstanding at the date of the last return;

(9) the total amount of share-warrants issued and surrendered respectively since the date of the last return;

(10) the latest date on which the general meeting should have been held and whether it was actually so held;

(11) the number of shares or amount of stock comprised in each sharewarrant;

(12) the names and addresses of the persons who at the date of terurn are the directors of the company and of the persons, if any, who at the said date are the managers managing agents or auditors of the company, and the changes in the personnel of the directors, managers managing agents since the last return together with the dates on which the took place; and

(13) the total amount of debt due from the company in respect of all mortgages and charges which are required to be registered with the Registrar under this Act.

(3) The above list and summary shall be contained in a separate part of the register of members, and shall be completed within twenty-one days after the day of the first or only ordinary general meeting in the year; and the company shall, within that period file with the Registrar a copy signed by two directors, including the managing director, or where there is no managing director, by a director, and manging agent or manager or secretary of the company together with a certificate from such persons that the list and summary state the facts as they stood on the day aforesaid.

(4) A private company shall send with the annual return required by subsection (1) a certificate signed by a director or other officer of the company that the company has not, since the date of the last return or in the case of a first return since the date of the incorporation of the company, issued any invitation to the public to subscribe for any shares or debentures of the company, and where the annual return discloses the fact that the number of members of the company exceeds fifty, also a certificate so signed that the excess consists wholly of persons who under sub-clause (ii) of clause (g) of sub-section (1) of section 2 are not be included in reckoning the number o fifty.

(5) If a company makes default in complying with the requirements of this section, it shall be liable to a fine not exceeding two hundred taka for every day during which the default continues, and every officer of the company who knowingly and willfully authorises or permits the default shall be liable to the like penalty.

37. Trust not to be entered on register

No notice of any trust, expressed, implied or constructive, shall be entered on the register, or be receivable by the Registrar.

38. Transfer of shares

(1) An application for the registration of the transfer of shares in a company may be made either by the transferer or the transfere, provided where such application is made by the transferer no registration shall in case of party paid shares be effected unless the company gives motive of the application to the transferee and subject to the provisions of sub-section (7) the company shall, unless objection is made by the transferee two weeks from the date of receipt of the notice, enter in its register of members the name of the transferee in the same manner and subject to the same conditions as if the application for registration was made by the transferee.

(2) For the purpose of sub-section (1), notice to the transferee shall be deemed to have been duly given if despatched by prepaid post to the transferee at the address given in the instrument of transfer and shall be deemed to ave been delivered in the ordinary course of post.

(3) It shall not be lawful for the company to register a transfer of share in or debentures of the company unless the proper instrument of transfer duly stamped and executed by the transferor and the transferee has been delivered to the company along with script:

Provided that, where it is proved to the satisfaction of the directors of the company that an instrument of transfer signed by the transferor and transferee has been lost, the company may, if the directors think fit, on an application in writing made by the transferee and bearing the stamp required by an instrument of transferor register the transfer on such terms as to indemnity as the directors may think fit.

(4) If a company refuses to register the transfer of any shares or debentures the company, shall, within one month from the date on which the instrument of transfer was lodged with the company, send to the transferee and the transferor notice of the refusal.

(5) If default is made in complying with sub-section (4) of this section, the company shall be liable to a fine not exceeding one hundred taka for everyday during which the default continues and every director, manager secretary other officer who is knowing by a party to the default shall, be liable to a like penalty.

(6) Nothing in sub-section (3) shall prejudice any power of the company to register as shareholder or debenture holder any person to whom the right to any shares in or debentures of the company has been transmitted by operation of law.

(7) Nothing in this section shall prejudice any power of the company under its articles to refuse to register the transfer of any shares.

39. Certification of transfer.

(1) The certification by a company of any instrument of transfer of shares in, or debentures of, the company, shall be taken as a representation by the company to any person acting on the faith of the certification that there have been produced to the company such documents as on the face of them show a prime facie title to the shares or debentures in the transfer named in the instrument of transfer, but not as a representation that transferor has complete title to the shares or debentures.

(2) Where any person acts on the faith of an erroneous certification made by a company negligently, the company shall be under the same liability to him as if the certification has been made fraudulently.

(3) For the purposes of this section-

(a) an instrument of transfer shall be deemed to have certificated if it bears the words 'certificate lodged" or words to the like effect;

(b) the certification of an instrument of transfer shall be deemed to be made by a company, if-

(i) the person issuing the certificated instrument is a person authorise to issue such instruments of transfer on the company's behalf; and

(ii) the certification is signed by any officer or servant of the company or any other person authorised to certificate transfers on the company's behalf, or if a body corporate has been so authorised by any officer or servant of that body corporate;

(c) a certification shall be deemed to be signed by any person if it purports to be authenticated by his signature, unless it is shown that the signature was placed there neither by himself nor by any person authorised to use the signature for the purpose of certificating transfers on the company's behalf.

40. Transfer by legal representative.

A transfer of the share or other interest of a decease member of a company made by his legal representative shall, although the legal representative is not himself a member, be as valid, as if he had been a member at the time of the execution of the instrument of transfer.

41. Inspection of register of members.

(1) The register of members commencing from the date of the registration of the company and where section 35 applies also the index of members shall be kept at the registered office of the company, and such register and index shall, except when closed under the provisions of this Act shall during business hours subject to such reasonable restrictions as the company in general meeting impose, so that not less than two hours in each day be allowed for inspection, be kept open to the inspection of any member free of cost and to the inspection of any other person on payment of one hundred taka or such less sum as the company may prescribe for each inspection, and any such member or other person may make extract thereform.

(2) Any member or other person may require a copy of the register or of any part therof or of the list and summary required by this Act or any part thereof, on payment of five taka for every hundred words or fractional part thereof required to be copied and the company shall cause any

copy so required by any person to be sent to that person within a period of ten days commencing on the day next after the day on which the requirement is received by the company.

Explanation :

For the purpose of this sub-section in reckoning the ten working days, the non-working days and days on which the transfer books of the company remain closed shall be excluded.

(3) If any inspection required under this section is refused or if any copy required under this section is not sent within the proper period the company and every officer of the company who is in default shall be liable in respect of each offence to a fine not exceeding one hundred taka and to a further fine not exceeding one hundred taka for everyday during which the refusal or default continues, and the Court may by an order compel an immediate inspection of the register and index or direct that copies required shall be sent to the persons requiring them.

42. Power to close register.

A company may on giving seven day's previous notice by advertisement in some newspaper circulating in the district in which the registered office of the company is situated close the register of members for any time or times not exceeding in the whole forty-five days in each year but bot exceeding thirty days at a time.

43. Power of Court to rectify register

(1) If

> (a) the name of any person is without sufficient cause entered in or omitted from the register of members of a company; or
>
> (b) default is made or unnecessary delay takes place in entering on the register the fact of any person having become, or ceased to be, a member,

the person aggrieved, or any member of the company, or the company, may apply to the Court for rectification of the register.

(2) The Court may either refuse the application, or may order rectification of the register and payment by the company of any damages sustained by any party aggrieved and may also make such order as costs as it may consider proper.

(3) On any application under this section the Court may decide any question relating to the title of any person who is a party to the application to have his name entered in or omitted from the register whether the question arises between members or alleged members or between members or alleged members on the one hand and the company on the other hand and generally may decide any question necessary or expedient to be decided for rectification of the register and may also decide any issue involving any question of law.

44. Notice to Registerar for rectification of register.

In the case of a company required by this Act to file a list of its members with the Register, the Court when making an order for rectification of the register shall by its order direct notice of the rectification to be filed with the Registrar within from the date of completion of the order.

45. Register to be evidence.

The register of members shall be primafacie evidence of any matter by this Act directed authorised to be inserted therein.

46. Issue of share warrants to bearer

(1) A company limited by shares if so authorised by its articles may with respect to any fully paid-up shares or to stock issue under its common seal a warrant stating that the bearer of the warrant is entitled to the shares on stock therein specified and may provide by coupons or otherwise for the payment of the future dividends on the shares or stock included in the warrant in this Act termed as share-warrant.

(2) Nothing in this section shall apply to a private company.

47. Effect of sharewarrant.

A share warrant shall entitle the bearer thereof to the shares or stock therein specified and the shares or stock may be transferred by delivery of the warrant.

48. Registration of name of bearer of share warrant.

The bearer of a sharewarrant shall subject to the articles of the company, be entitled, on surrendering it for cancellation, to have his name entered as a member in the register of members; and the company shall be responsible for any loss incurre by any person by reason of the company entering in its register the name of a bearer of a share- warrant in respect of the share of stock therin specified without the warrant being surrendered and cancelled.

49. Position of bearer of Share-warrant.

The bearer of a share warrant may, if the articles of the company so provide be deemed to be a member of the company within the meaning of this Act either to the full extent or for any purpose defined in the articles except that he shall not be qualified in respect of the shares or stock specified in the warrant for being a director or manager of the company in cases where such a qualification is required by the articles.

50. Entries in register when share-warrant issued.

(1) On the issue of share-warrant, the company shall strike out of its register of members the name of the member then entered therein as holding the shares or stock specified in the warrant, as if he had ceased to be a member and shall enter in the Register the following particulars namely:-

(i) the fact of the issue of the warrant;

(ii) a statement of the shares or stock included in the warrant, distinguishing each share by its number; and

(iii) the date of issue of the warrant.

(2) If a company makes default in complying with the requirements of this section it shall be liable to a fine not exceeding two hundred taka for every day during which the default continues and every officer of the company who knowingly and willfully continues or permits the default shall also be liable to a like penalty.

51. Surrender of Share warrant.

Until the warrant is surrendered, the above particulars shall be deemed to be the particulars required by this Act to be entered in the register of members; and on the surrender the date of the surrender shall be entered as if it were the date at which a person ceased to be a member.

52. Power of company to arrange for different amounts being paid on shares

A company, if so authorised by its articles may do any one or more of the following things, namely--

(i) make arrangements on the issue of shares for a difference between he shareholders in the amounts and times of payment of calls on their shares;

(ii) accept from any member who assents thereto the whole or a part of the amount remaining unpaid on any shares held by him although no part of that amount has been called up;

(iii) pay dividend in proportion to the amount paid-up on each share where a larger amount is paid-up on some shares than on others.

53. Power of company limited by shares to alter its share capital.

(1) A company limited by shares if so authorised by its articles may alter the conditions of its memorandum, as follows that is to say it may--

(a) increase its share capital by the issue of new shares of such amount as it thinks expedient;

(b) consolidate and divide all or any of its share capital into shares of larger amount than its existing shares;

(c) convert all or any of its paid-up shares into stock and reconvert that stock into paid-up shares of any denomination.

(d) sub-divided ist shares, or any of them, into shares of smaller amount than is fixed by the memorandum, so that in the sub-division the proportion between he amount paid and the amount, if any, unpaid on each reduced share shall be the same as it was in the case of the share from which the reduced share is derived;

(e) cancel shares which, at the date of the passing of the resolution in that behalf, have not been taken or agreed to be taken by any person, and diminish the amount of its share capital by the amount of the share so cancelled.

(2) the powers conferred by this section can only be exercised by the company in its general meeting.

(3) A cancellation of shares in pursuance of this section shall not be deemed to be a reduction of share capital within the meaning of the other provisions of the Act.

(4) The company shall file with the Registrar notice of the exercise of any power referred to tin clause (d) or clause (e) of sub-section (1) within fifteen days from the exercise thereof.

54. Notice to Registrar for consolidation of share a capital, conversion of shares into stock etc.

(1) Where a company having a share capital has consolidated and divided its share capital into shares of larger amount than its existing shares or converted any of the shares into stock or re-converted stock into shares, it shall within fifteen days of the consolidation and division, conversion or re-conversion, file notice with the Registrar of the same, specifying the share consolidated and divided, or converted or the stock re-coverted.

(2) If a company makes default in complying with the requirements of this section, it shall be liable to a fine not exceeding two hundred taka for everyday during which the default continues, and every officer of the company who knowingly and willful authorises or permits the default shall also be liable to the like penalty.

55. Effect of conversion of shares into stock.

Where a company having a share capital has converted any of its shares into stock and filed notice of the conversion with the Register all the provisions of this Act which are applicable to shares only shall cease as to so much of the share capital as is converted into stock; and the register of members of the company, and the list of members to be filed with the Registrar shall show the amount of stock held by each member instead of the amount of shares and the particulars relating to shares hereinbefore required by this Act.

56. Notice of increase of share capital or of members.

(1) Where a company having a share capital, whether its shares have or have not been converted into stock, has increased its share capital, beyond the registered capital, and where a company not having a share capital has increased the number of its members beyond the registered number, it shall file with the Registrar, in the case of an increase of share capital, within fifteen days after the passing of the resolution authorising the increase and in the case of an increase of members within fifteen days after the increase was resolved on or took place, notice of the increase of capital or members, and the Registrar shall record the increase.

(2) The notice under sub section (1) shall include particulars of the classes of shares, affected and the conditions, if any, subject to which the new shares are to be issued.

(3) If a company makes a default in complying with the requirements of this section, it shall be liable to a fine not exceeding two hundred taka for every day during which the default continues, and every officer of the company who knowingly and willfully authorises or permits the default shall be liable to a like penalty.

57. Application of premiums received on issue of shares.

(1) Where a company issues shares at a premium, whether for cash or otherwise, a sum equal to the aggregate amount or value of the premiums on those shares, shall be transferred to an

account, to be called "the share premium account" and the provisions of this Act relating to the reduction of the share capital of a company shall, except as provided in this section, apply as if the share premium account were paid-up share capital of the company.

(2) The share premium account may be applied by the company--

(a) in paying up unissued shares of the company to be issued to member of the company as fully paid bonus shares;

(b) in writing of the preliminary expenses of the company,

(c) in writing off the expenses of, or the commission paid or discount allowed, on any issue of shares or debentures of the company; or

(d) in providing for the premium payable on the redemption of any redeemable preference shares or of any debentures of the company.

(3) Where is company has, before the commincement of this Act issued any shares at a premium this section shall apply as if the shares had been issued after the commencement of this Act:

Provided that any part of the premium which has been so applied that it does not at the commencement of this Act form an identificable part of the company's reserves within the meaning of Schedule XI shall be disregarded in determining the sum to be included in the share premium account.

Reduction of Share Capital

58. Restriction on purchase by company or loans by Company for purchase of its own shares

(1) No company limited by shares shall have power to buy its own shares or the shares of a public company of which it is a subsidiary company, unless the consequent reduction of capital is effected and sanctioned in the manner provided by sections 59 to 70.

(2) No company limited by shares other than private company or a subsidiary company of a public company, shall give whether directly or indirectly, and whether by means of a loan guarantee the provision of security or otherwise any financial assistance for the purpose of or in connection with a purchase made or to be made by any person of any shares in the company:

Provided that nothing in this section shall, where the lending of money is part of the ordinary business of a company, be taken to prohibit the lending of money by the company in the ordinary course of its business.

(3) If a company acts in contravention of this section, the company, are every officer of the company who is knowingly and willfully in default shall be liable to a fine not exceeding five thousand taka.

(4) Nothing in this section shall affect the right of a company to redeem any shares issued under section 154.

59. Reduction of share capital.

(1) Subject to confirmation by the Court, a company limited by shares, if so authorised by its articles, may by special resolution reduce its share capital in any way, and in particular the company may, as part of this general power--

(a) extinguish or reduce the liability on any of its shares in respect of share capital not paid-up;

(b) either with or without extinguishing or reducing liability on any of its shares, cancel any paid-up share capital which is lost or presented by available assets;

(c) either with or without extinguishing or reducing liability on any of its shares, pay off any paid-up share capital which is in excess of the wants of the company;

(d) so far as is necessary, alter its memorandum by reducing the amount of its share capital and of its shares accordingly.

(2) A special resolution under this section is in this Act called a resolution or reducing share capital.

60. Application to Court for confirming order

Where a company has passed a resolution for reducing share capital it shall apply by petition to the Court for an order confirming the reduction.

61. Addition to name of company of "and reduced"

On and from the passing by a company of a resolution for reducing share capital, or where the reduction does not involve either the diminution of any liability in respect of un-paid share capital or the payment to any share holder of any paid-up share capital, then on and from the making of the order by the Court confirming by the reduction the company shall add to its name, until such date as the Court may fix, the words "and reduced" as the last words in its name and those words shall until that date be deemed to be part of the name of the company:

Provided that where the reduction does not involve either the diminutior of any liability in respect of unpaid share capital or the payment to any shareholder of any paid-up share capital, the Court may, if it thinks expedient dispense altogether with the addition of words "and reduced".

62. Objections by creditors and settlement of list of objecting creditors:

(1) Where the proposed reduction of share capital involves either diminution of liability in respect of unpaid share capital or the payment to any shareholder of any paid-up share capital, without permission of the Court and in any other case if the Court so permits every creditor of the company, who at the date fixed by the Court is entitled to any debt or claim which if that date were the commencement of the winding up of the company would be admissible in proof against the company shall be entitled to object to the reduction.

(2)The Court shall settle a list of creditors so entitle to object, and for that purpose shall ascertain as far as possible without requiring an application from any creditor the names those creditors and the nature and amount of their debts or claims and may issue notices fixing a day or days within which creditors not entered on the list are to claim to be so entered on to be excluded from the right of objecting to the reduction; and after consideration such claims the Court shall finalise the list.

63. Power to dispense with consent of creditor on security being given for his debt

Where a creditor entered on the list of creditors whose debt or claim is not discharged or determined does not consent to the reduction, the Court may, if it thinks fit dispense with the consent of the creditor on the company securing payment of his debt or claim by appropriating as the Court may direct the following amount that is to say--

(i) if the company admits the full amount of his debt or claim or though not admitting it is willing to provide for it then the full amount of the debt or claim;

(ii) if the company does not admit or is not willing to provide for the full amount of the debt or claim, or if the amount is contingent or not ascertained, then an amount fixed by the Court after the like inquiry and adjudication as if the company were being wound up by the Court.

64. Order confirming reduction

The Court if satisfied with respect to every creditor of the company who under this Act is entitled to object to the reduction, that either consent tot he reduction has been obtained or his debt or claim has been discharged or has been determined or has been secured may make an order confirming the reduction on such terms and conditions as it thinks fit.

65. Registration of order minutes of reduction

(1) The Registrar shall, on production to him, register the following documents, namely:--

(a) the certified copy of the order of the Court confirming the reduction of the share capital of a company.

(b) a copy of the minutes approved by the Court, showing the following :

(i) the amount of the reduced share capital;

(ii) the number of shares into which it is to be divided;

(iii) the nominal value of each such share;.

(iv) the amount, if any, at the date of registration, deemed to be paid up on each such share.

(2) On the registration under sub-section (1) and not before, the resolution for reducing share capital as confirmed by the order so registered shall take effect.

(3) Notice of the registration shall be published in such manner as the Court may direct.

(4) The Registrar shall certify under his hand the registration of the order and minutes, and his certificate shall be conclusive evidence that all the requirements of this Act with respect to

reduction of share capital have been complied with, and that the share capital of the company is such as is stated in the minute.

66. Minutes to form part of memorandum

(1) The minutes when registered shall be deemed to be substituted for the corresponding part of the memorandum of the company, and shall be valid and alterable as if it had been originally contained therein, and it shall be embodied in every copy of the memorandum issued after its registration.

(2) If a company makes default in complying with the requirements of this section, it shall be liable to a fine not exceeding one hundred taka for each copy in respect of which default is made, and every officer of the company who knowingly and willfully authorises or permits the default shall be liable to a like penalty.

67. Liability of members in respect of reduced shares

(1) member of the company, past or present, shall not be liable in respect of any share to any call or contribution exceeding in amount the difference, if any, between the amount paid, or, as the case may be, the reduced amount, if any, which is to be deemed to have been paid, on the share and the amount of the share as fixed by the minutes:

Provided that, if any creditor, entitled in respect of any debt or claim to object to the reduction of share capital, is by reasons of his ignorance of the proceedings for reduction or of their nature and effect with respect to his claim, not entered on the list of creditors, and, after the reduction, the company is unable, within the meaning of the provisions of this Act or with respect to winding up by the Court, to pay the amount of his debt or claim, then--

(i) every person who was a member of the company at the date of the registration of the order for reduction and minute, shall be liable to contribute for the payment of that debt or claim an amount not exceeding the amount which he would have been liable to contribute if the company had commenced to be wound up on the day before that registration; and

(ii) if the company is wound up, the Court on the application of any such creditor and proof of his ignorance as aforesaid, may, if it thinks fit, settle accordingly a list of persons so liable to contribute, and make and enforce calls and orders on the contributors settle on the list as if they were ordinary contributories in a winding up.

(2) Nothing in this section shall after the rights of the contributories amount themselves.

68. Penalty on concealment of name of creditor:

If any officer of the company willfully conceals the name of any creditor entitled to object to the reduction or willfully misrepresents the nature or amount of the debt or claim of any creditor, or if any officer of the company abets, any such concealment or misrepresentation as aforesaid every such officer shall have punishable with imprisonment which may extend to two years, or with fine, or with both.

69. Publication of reasons for reduction:

In any case of reduction of share capital, the Court may require the company to publish, as the Court directs, the reasons for reduction or such other information in regard thereto as the Court may think expedient with a view to giving proper information to the public, and, if the Court think fit, also causes which led to the reduction.

70. Increase and reduction of share capital of a company limited by guarantee:

A Company limited by guarantee and registered after the commencement of this Act may, if it has a share capital and is so authorised by its articles, increase or reduce its share capital in the same manner and subject to the same conditions in and subject to which a company limited by shares may increase or reduce its share capital under the provisions of this Act.

Variation of Shareholder's Rights

71. Rights of holders of special classes of shares:

(1) If in the case of a company, the share capital of which is divided into different classes of shares, provision is made by the memorandum or articles authorising the variation of the rights attached to any class of shares in the company, subject to the consent of any specified proportion of the holders of the issued shares of that class or the sanction of are solution passed at a separate meeting of the holders of those shares, and in pursuance of the said provision the rights attached to any class of shares are at any time varied, the holders of the less in the aggregate than ten per cent of the issued shares of that class, being persons who did not consent to or vote in favour of the resolution for the variation, may apply to the Court to have the variation cancelled, and where any such application is made, the variation shall not have effect unless and until it is confirmed by the Court.

(2) An application under sub-section (1) must be made within fourteen days after the date on which the consent was given or the resolution was passed, as the case may be, under that sub-section and may be made on behalf of the shareholders entitled to make the application by such one or more of their numbers as they may appoint in writing for the purpose.

(3) On any such application, the Court, after hearing the applicant and any other persons who apply to the Court to be heard and appear to the Court to be interested in the application, may if it is satisfied having regard to all the circumstances of the case that the variation would unfairly prejudice the shareholders of the class represented by the applicant, disallow the variation and shall, if not so satisfied, confirm the variation.

(4) The decision of he Court on any such application shall be final.

(5) The company shall, within fifteen days after the service on the company of any order made on any such application, forward a copy of the order to the Registrar, and if default is made in complying with this provision, the company shall be liable to a fine not exceeding two hundred taka and every officer of the company who is knowingly and willfully in default shall be liable to a like penalty.

(6) The expression "variation" in this section includes "abrogation" and the expression "varied" shall be construed accordingly.

Registration of Unlimited Company as Limited

72. Registration of unlimited company as limited:

(1) Subject to the provisions of this section, any company registered as unlimited may register under this Act as limited and any company registered before the commencement of this Act as a limited company may re-register under this Act, but the registration of an unlimited company as a limited company shall not affect any debts, liabilities, obligations or contracts incurred or entered into by, to, with or on behalf of, the company before the registration, and those debts, liabilities, obligations and contracts may be enforced in manner provided by part VIII of this Act in the case of a company registered in pursuance of that Part.

(2) On registration in pursuance of this section, the Registrar shall close the former registration of the company, and may dispense with the delivery to him of companies of any documents with copies of which he was furnished on the occasion of the original registration of the company; but, save as aforesaid, the registration shall take place in the same manner and shall have effect as if it were the first registration of the company under this Act.

73. Power of unlimited company to provide for reserve share capital on registration

(1) An unlimited company having a she capital may, by its resolution for registration as a limited company in pursuance of this Act, do either or both of the following things, namely:--

(a) increase the nominal amount of its share capital by increasing the nominal amount of each of its shares, but subject to the condition that no part of the amount by which its capital is so increased shall be capable of being called up except in the event and for the purpose of the company being wound up;

(b) provide that a specified portion of its uncalled share capital shall not be capable of being called up except in the event and for the purpose of the company being wound up.

(2) the portion of the share capital increased or specified under sub- section (1) shall be called the reserved share capital.

Reserve Capital of Limited Company

74. Reserve Capital of Limited company:

A limited company may by special resolution, determine that any portion of its share capital which has not been already called up shall not be capable of being called up, except in the event and for the purposes of the company being wound up, and thereupon that portion of its share capital shall not be capable of being called up except in the event and for the purposes aforesaid; and such portion shall be called reserved share capital.

Unlimited Liability of Directors

75. Limited company may have directors with unlimited liability

(1) In a limited company the liability of the directors or of any director may, if so provided by the memorandum, be unlimited.

(2) In a limited company in which the liability of any director is unlimited, the directors of the company, if any, and the member, who proposes a person for election or appointment to the

office of director, shall add to that proposal a statement that the liability of the person holding that office will be unlimited and the promoter and officers of the company or one of them shall, before the person accepts the office or acts therein, give him notice in writing that his liability will be unlimited.

(3) If any director or proposer makes default in adding a statement as required by sub-section (1), or if any promoter or officer of the company makes default in giving a notice as required by that sub- section, the shall be liable to a fine not exceeding five thousand taka and shall also be liable for any damage which the person so elected or appointed may sustain from the default, but the liability of the person elected or appointed shall not be affected by the default.

76. Special resolution of limited company making liability of directors unlimited.

(1) A limited company if so authorised by its articles may, by special resolution, alter its memorandum so as to render unlimited the liability of its directors or of any director. (2) Upon the passing of any special resolution under sub-section (1), the provisions thereof shall be valid as if they had been originally contained in the memorandum.

PART X FOREIGN COMBINES' REGISTRATION, ETC.

378. application of sections 376 to 387 to foreign companies.--Sections 379 to 387 shall apply to all foreign Combines, that is to say, campiness falling under the following two classes, namely:--

(a) Combines incorporated outside Bangladesh which, after commencement of this Act establish a place of business within Bangladesh; and

(b) combines incorporate outside Bangladesh which have before the commencement of this Act, established a place of business within Bangladesh and continued to have an established place of business with Bangladesh, at the commencement of this Act.

379. Documents, etc. to be delivered to Registrar by foreign Combines carrying on business in Bangladesh--(1) Foreign Combines, which after the commencement of this Act, establish a place of business with Bangladesh shall, within one month of the establishment of the place of business,, deliver to the Registrar for registration--

(a) a certified copy of the charter or statues or memorandum and articles of the company or other instrument constitution or defining the constitution of the company; and if the instrument is not written in Beguile or English Language, a certified Penally or English translation thereof;

(b) the full address of the registered or principal office of the company;

(c) a list of the directors and secretary, if any, of the company;

(d) the name and address or the names and addresses of one or more persons resident in Bangladesh, authorized to accept on behalf of the company service of p[process and any notice or other document required to be served on the company;

(e) the full address of the office of the company in Ballades which to be deemed its principal place of business in Bangladesh.

(2) foreign Combines other than those mentioned in sub-section(1), shall if they have not delivered to the Registrar before the commencement of this Act the Documents and particulars specified in the sub-section (1) and section continue to be subject to the obligation to deliver those documents and particulars in accordance with this Act.

(3) If any alteration is made or coccus in--

(a) the charter, studies , or memorandum and articles of foraging company or other instrument constituting or defining the constitution of a foreign company, or

(b) the registered or principal office of a foreign company or

(d) the names and addresses of the persons authorized to accept service on behalf of a foreign company, or

(e) the principal place of business of a foreign company in Bangladesh, the Company sh , within the prescribed time, file with the Registrar a return containing the prescribed particulars of the alteration.

380 Accounts of foreign company.--(1) Every foreign company shall, in every calendar year.--

(a) make out a balance sheet and profit and loss account or in the case of a company not trading for profit, and income and expenditure account it the company is handling company, group accounts in such form and consigning such particulars and including such documents, and under the provision of this Act it would, if it had been accompany within the meaning of this Act, have been required to make out and lay before the company in general meeting; and

(d) deliver three copies of those documents to the Registrar:

Provided that the Government may by notification in the official Gazette direct that in the he case of a foraging company or class of foreign Combines the requirements of clause (a)) shall not apply, or shall apply subject to such exceptions and modification as many be specified in the notification.

(2) If any such document as is mentioned in sub-section (1) is not written in Penal or English language, there shall be annexed to it a certified translating thereof.

(a) in veery prospectus inviting subscription in Bangladesh for its shares or debentures, state the country in which the company is incinerated;

(b) conspicuously exhibit on the outside of every office or place where it carries on business in Bangladesh, the name of the company and the country in which it is incinerated, in the letters easily legible in Beguile or English character,

(c) cause the name of the company and of the country in which the company is incur outdated, to be stated in legible Penally or English characters in all bill heads and letter paper, and in all notices and other official publications of the company; and.

(d) if the liability of the members of the company is limited, cause a notice of that fact--

(i) to be stated in every Suva prospectus as aforesaid and in all bill heads, letter paper, notices, advertisements and other official publications of the company, in legible Penholders, in legible Penally or English characters.

382. Service on foreign company.-- Any process notice, or other document required OT be served on a foreign company shall be deemed to be sufficiently served, if addressed to any person mentioned in section 37991) (d) and left at, or sent by post to the address which has ben so delivered under that section to the Registration.

Provided that--

(a) where any such company make default in delivering to the Registrar in pursuance of that section the name and address of a person, or

(b) if at any time all the persons whose names and address have been delivered to the Registrar are dead, or ceased or have ceased so to reside at those addresses, or refused to accept on behalf of the company any process, notice or other document, or, those cannot be served or sent for any other reason, such document may be served on the company by leaving it at, or sending it by post to, any place of business established by the company in Bangladesh.

383. Notice of ceasing place of business of a company.-- If any foreign company ceases to have a place of business in Bangladesh, it shall forthwith give notice of the fact to the Registrar, and as from the date on which notice is so given, the obligation of the company to deliver any document to the Registrar shall cease, provided it has no other place of business in Bangladesh.

384. Penalties.-- If any foreign company fails to comply with any of the foregoing provisions of this Part, the company shall be punishable with fine which may extend to one thousand taka, or, in the case of a continuing offence, with an additional fine of five hundred taka for every day after the first day during which the default continues; and every officer or agent of the company who is knowingly willfully, makes such default, shall be punishable with the same fine.

385. Company's failure to cmoply with this Part not to affect its liability under contracts.-- Any failure by a foreign company to comply with any of the foregoing provisions of this Part shall not affect the validity of any contract dealing or transaction entered into by the company or its liability to be sued in respect thereof; but the company shall not be entitled to bring any suit, claim any set off, make any counter claim or institute any legal proceeding in respect of any such contract, dealing or transaction until it has complied with the provisions of this Part.

386. Fees for registration of documents under this Part.-- There shall be paid to the Registrar for registering any document required by the foregoing provisions of this Part such fees as specified in Schedule II.

387. Interpretation.-- For the purposes of the foregoing provisions of this Part--

(a) the expression "director" includes any person occupying the position of director by whatever name called.

(b) the expression "prospectus" has the same meaning as when used in relation to a company incorporated under this Act;

(c) the expression "place of business" includes a share transfer or share registration office;

(d) the expression "secretary" includes any person occupying the position of secretary, by whatever name called and

(e) the expression "certified" means certified in the prescribed manner to be a true copy or a correct translation.

388. Restriction on sale and offer for sale of shares.--(1) It shall not be lawful for any person--

(a) to issue, circulate or distribute in Bangladesh any prospectus offering to the public for subscription to shares in or debentures of a company incorporated or to be incorporated outside Bangladesh whether the company has or has not established, or when formed will or will not establish, a place of business in Bangladesh, unless--

(i) before the issue, circulation or distribution of the prospectus in Bangladesh a copy thereof, certified by the chairman and two other directors of the company as having been approved by resolution of the managing body, has been delivered for registration to the Registrar;

(ii) the prospectus state on the face of it that the copy has been so delivered;

(iii) the prospectus is dated; and

(iv) the prospectus other wise complies with this Part; or

(b) to tissue to any person in Bangladesh a form of application for shares in or debentures of such a company of intended company as aforesaid unless the form is issued with a prospectus which complies the requirements of this Part :

Provided that this clause shall not apply if it is shown that the form of application was issued in connection with a bonafide invitation to a person to enter into an underwriting agreement with respect to the shares of debentures.

(2) This section shall not apply to the issue to existing members or debentures holders of a company of a prospectus or form of application relating to shares in or debentures of the company, whether an applicant for shares or debentures will not have the right to renounce in favour of other persons, but, subject as aforesaid, this section shall apply to a prospectus or form of application whether issued or with reference to the formation of a company or subsequently.

(3) Where any document by which any shares in or debentures of a company incorporated outside Bangladesh are offered for sale to the public would, if the company concerned had been a company within the meaning of this Act, have been deemed by virtue of section 142 to be a prospectus issued by the company, that document shall be deemed to be, for the purposes of this section, a prospectus issued by the company.

(4) An offer of share or debentures for subscription or sale to any person whose ordinary business or part of whose ordinary business is to by or sell shares or debentures, whether as principal or agent, shall not be deemed an offer to the public for the purposes of this section.

(5) A person who is knowingly responsible for the issue, circulation or distribution of any prospectus, or for the issue of a form of application for shares or debentures, in contravention of the provisions of this section shall be liable to a fine not exceeding ten thousand taka.

(6) In this section and in section 389, the expression "prospectus" "shares" and "debentures" have the same meaning as and when used in relation to a company incorporated under this Act.

389. Requirements as to prospectus.-- In order to comply with this Part a prospectus, in addition to complying with the provisions of sub-clauses (ii) and (iii) of clause(a) of sub-section (1) of section 388, must--

(a) Contain particulars with respect to the following matters, namely--

(i) the objects of the company;

(ii) the instrument constituting or defining the onstitution of the company;

(iii) the enactments, or provisions having the force of an enactment, by or under which the incorporation of the company was effected;

(iv) an address in Bangladesh where the said instrument, enactments or provisions, or copies thereof, and if the same are in a foreign language other than English a translation thereof in the Bengali or English certified in the prescribe manner can be inspected;

(v) the date on which and the country in which the company was incorporated.

(vi) whether the company has established a place of business in Bangladesh:

Provided that the provisions of sub-clause (i), (ii), and (iii) of this clause shall not apply in the case of a prospectus issued more than two years after the date at which the company is entitled to commence business;

(b) subject to the provisions of this section, state the matters specified in sub-section (1) of section 135 and set out the reports specified in that section :

Provided that--

(i) where any prospectus is published as a newspaper advertisement, it shall be a sufficient compliance with the requirements that the prospectus must specify the objects of the company if the advertisement specified the primary objects with which the company was formed; and

(ii) in section 135 of this Act, a reference to the article of the company shall be deemed, to be a reference to the constitution of the company.

(2) Any condition requiring or binding any applicant for shares or debenture shall be void, if the acceptance thereof has the effect of--

(a) waiving compliance with any requirements of this section; or

(b) serving him with notice of any contract, document or matter not specifically referred to in the prospectus.

(3) In the event of non-compliance with or contravention of any of the requirements, of this section, a director or other person responsible for the prospectus shall not incur any liability by reason of the non-compliance or contravention, if--

(a) as regards any matter not disclosed, he proves that he was not congnizant thereof; or

(b) he proves that the non-compliance or contravention arose from an honest mistake of fact on his part; or

(c) the non-compliance or contravention was in respect of matter which, in the option of the court dealing with the case, were immarterial or were otherwise such as ought, in the option of that Court, having regard to all the circumstances of the case, reasonably to be excused.

Provided that in the event of failure to include in a prospectus a statement with respect to the matters specified in clause 18 of the Part-I of Schedule-III or in pursuance of sub-section (1) of section 135, no director or other person shall insure any liability in respect of the failure unless it be proved that he had knowledge of the matters not disclosed.

(4) Nothing in this section limit or diminish any liability which any person may incur under the general law or this Act, apart from this section.

390. Restriction on canvassing for sale of shares.--(1) It shall be an oftence of any person goes from house to house of the public or any member of public offering shares of a company incorporoated outside Bangladesh for subscription to or sale of such shares.

(2) In this sub-section the expression `house" shall not include an office used for business purposes.

(3) Any person acting in contraventions of this section shall be liable to a fine not exceeding five hundred taka.

391. Provisions regarding charges.-- The provisions of section 159 to 168- both inclusive, and 171 to 176, both inclusive, shall extend to charge on properties in Bangladesh which are created and to charges on property in Bangladesh which us acquired, by a company incorporated outside Bangladesh which has an established place of business in Bangladesh :

Provided that, were a charge is created outside Bangladesh or the completion of the equisition of property takes place outside Bangladesh, sub-clause (i) of the proviso to sub-section (1) of section 159 and the proviso to sub-section (1) of section 160 shall apply as if the property wherever situated were situated tside Bangladesh.

392. Notice of appointment of receiver etc.--(1) The provisions of section 169 and 170 share apply to the case of all companies incorporated outside Bangladesh but having an established place of business in Bangladesh.

(2) The provisions of section 181 shall apply to such companies to the extent of requiring them to keep at their principal place of business in Bangladesh the books of account required by that section with respect to money received and expended, sales and purchases made, and assets and liabilities in relation to its business in Bangladesh.

FOREIGN PRIVATE INVESTMENT (PROMOTION AND PROTECTION) ACT, 1980

ACT, NO. XI OF 1980

An Act to provide for the promotion and protection of foreign private investment in Bangladesh.

WHEREAS it is expedient to provide for the promotion and protection of foreign private investment in Bangladesh;

It is hereby enacted as follows:-

1. Short title - This act may be called the Foreign Private investment (Promotion and Protection) Act, 1980.

2. Definitions. - (1) In this Act, unless there is anything repugnant in the subject or context,-

(a) **"foreign capital"** means capital invested in Bangladesh in any industrial undertaking by a citizen of any foreign country or by a company incorporated outside Bangladesh, in the form of foreign exchange, imported machinery and equipment, or in such other form as the Government may approve for the purpose of such investment;

(b) **"foreign private Investment"** means investment of foreign capital by a person who is not a citizen of Bangladesh or by a company incorporated outside Bangladesh, but does not include investment by a foreign Government or an agency of foreign Government;

(c) **"industrial undertaking"** means an industry, establishment or other undertaking engaged in the production or processing of any goods, or in the development and extraction of such mineral resources or products, or in the providing of such services, as may be specified in this behalf by the Government.

(2) Words and expressions used but not defined in this act shall have the same mean-ing as in the Companies Act, 1913 (VII of 1913).

3 Foreign private investment.-(1) The Government may, for the promotion of foreign private investment, sanction establishment with foreign capital of any industrial undertaking-

(a) Which does not exist in Bangladesh and the establishment whereof, in the opinion of the Government, is desirable; or

(b) Which is not being carried on in Bangladesh on a scale adequate to the economic and social needs of the country; or

(c) Which is likely to contribute to-

(I) the development of capital, technical and managerial resources of Bangladesh ; or

(ii) the discovery mobilisation or better utilization of the natural resources ; or

(iii) the strengthening or the balance of payment of Bangladesh ; or

(iv) increasing employment opportunities in Bangladesh ; or

(v) the economic development of the country in any other manner.

(2) Sanction of the establishment with foreign capital of an industrial undertaking under sub-section (1) may be subject to such condition as the Government may deem fit to impose.

4. PROTECTION AND EQUITABLE TREATMENT.-

The Government shall accord fair and equitable treatment to foreign private investment which shall enjoy full protection and security in Bangladesh.

5. Terms of sanction, etc.-The terms of sanction, permission or licence granted by Government to an industrial undertaking having foreign private investment shall not be unilaterally changed so as to adversely alter the conditions under which the establishment of such undertaking was sanctioned; nor shall foreign private investment be accorded a less favourable treat-ment than what is accorded to similar private investment by the citizens of Bangladesh in the application of relevant rules and regulations.

6. Idemnification, etc.-In the event of losses of foreign investment owing to civil commotion, insurrection, or riot, foreign private investment shall be accorded the same treatment with regard to indemnification, compensation, restitution, or other settlement as is accorded to investment by the citizens of Bangladesh.

7. EXPROPRIATION AND NATIONALISATION.-

(1) Foreign private investment shall not be expropriated or nationalised or be subject to any measures having effect of expropriation or nationalisation except for a public purpose against adequate compensation which shall be paid expeditiously and be freely transferable.

2. Adequate compensation for the purpose of sub-section (1) shall be an amount equivalent to the market value of investment expropriated or nationalised immediately before the expropriation or nationalisation.

8. REPATRIATION OF INVESTMENT.-

(1) In respect of foreign private investment, the transfer of capital and the returns from it and, in the event of liquidation of industrial undertaking having such investment, of the proceeds from such liquidation is guaranteed.

(2) The guarantee under sub-section (1) shall be subject to the right which, in circumstances of exceptional financial and economic difficulties, the Government may exercise in accordance with the applicable laws and regulations in such circumstances.

9. Removal of difficulty.-If any difficulty arises in giving effect to any provision of this Act, the Government may make such order, not inconsistent with the provisions of this Act, as may appear to it to be necessary for the purpose of removing the difficulty.

PROCEDURE FOR OBTAINING FACILITIES AND SERVICES PROVIDED FOR SETTING UP INDUSTRIES IN BANGLADESH

The Industrial Policy 1991 (revised in 1992) has clearly emphasized importance on the role of the private sector in industrial development. The role of the government has been changed from regulatory to promotional. As a result of this policy, sanctioning and other procedures for obtaining different facilities and services have been simplified.

Industrial Policy ensures equal treatment for local and foreign investment. According to the policy no formal permission of the government is required to set up industries and for BMR/BMRE of the existing industries with the entrepreneurs' own fund or with the fund from private banks or private financing institutions. Industries set up under foreign loan, suppliers' credit, Pay-As-You-Earn (PAYE) scheme and non-repatriable foreign exchange are deemed to have been set up with own fund.

However, for availing institutional facilities such as, import entitlement for raw materials under restricted list, infrastructure facilities (industrial plot, electric, gas, telephone, water & sewerage connection, etc.) industries are required to be registered with the concerned sponsoring agency.

To avail of the facilities and services provided by the BOI for setting up of industries the procedures mentioned below are to be followed by the entrepreneurs.

Registration of joint venture/100% foreign investment proposals in the private sector

No prior approval or No-Objection Certificate is required for setting up of a joint venture/100% foreign direct investment.

To avail of facilities and the institutional support services provided by the govt. entrepreneurs/investors are advised to apply for registration to BOI in a simple prescribed form.

(Specimen of application form for registration at Appendix-B)

Registration of self financed local investment proposals including industries sanctioned/financed by financial institutions or commercial banks

The entrepreneurs of such projects are to fill up a simple prescribed application form and submit to BOI for registration. After a first hand scrutiny of the information, BOI issues registration letter.

PERMISSION FOR SETTING UP JOINT VENTURE INDUSTRIAL UNITS WITH THE PUBLIC SECTOR CORPORATIONS

An entrepreneur, either local or foreign, can set up an industry with public sector corporation. Such joint venture is required to be registered with the BOI if the private sector's contribution is more than 50% of the project cost and in such case it is treated as private sector project. For any public sector which makes contribution out of their own fund needs approval of the concerned ministry. If the contribution of the corporation is 50% or above, it is treated as a public sector project. The public sector project is processed by the concerned ministry for approval of the Planning Commission.

PROCEDURE FOR IMPORT OF RAW & PACKING MATERIALS AND SPARE PARTS BY INDUSTRIAL UNITS

No permission is required for import of free list items. For items in the restricted list, BOI, BEPZA and BSCIC are responsible for issuance of import entitlement. Import Registration Certificate (IRC) will be issued by the concerned authority in favour of the industrial enterprises within 30 days of receiving applications.

Items included in the banned list cannot be imported unless otherwise specified.

(Banned and Restricted list items are at Appendix-C & Appendix-D)

In case of import of raw and packing materials of the pharmaceutical industry, the Drugs Administration Directorate under Ministry of Health & Family Welfare prepares Block Lists on half yearly basis. BOI/BEPZA/BSCIC provides all other assistance relating to imports in the private sector in their respective jurisdictions. In this connection procedure followed by BOI is as under:

On receipt of application in the prescribed form along with copies of (1) TIN certificate, (2) Trade Licence, (3) Membership Certificate of relevant trade association/chamber, (4) Certificate from the nominated bank regarding opening of account, (5) Incorporation Certificate, in case of limited companies and (6) Letter of registration with BOI, necessary field inspection is done to determine annual production capacity and half yearly/yearly import entitlement of raw & packing materials.

The entrepreneur is then advised to deposit IRC fees (on the basis of annual import entitlement) by Treasury Challan to the Bangladesh Bank/Treasury. On receipt of the copy of treasury challan, recommendation is referred to the office of the Chief Controller of Imports & Exports (CCI&E) for issuance of ad-hoc IRC.

The entrepreneur will then approach nominated bank for opening Letters of Credit for import. After starting commercial production the entrepreneur may apply to BOI for regularisation of the ad-hoc import entitlement. On receipt of application for regularisation of the entitlement, utilization of ad-hoc import entitlement is verified through field inspection and if found satisfactory BOI recommends to CCI&E for regularisation. Import entitlement may, however, be refixed on verification of the actual requirement.

GUIDE-LINES FOR REGISTRATION/APPROVAL OF FOREIGN LOAN, SUPPLIERS' CREDIT, PAYE SCHEME, ETC.

Entrepreneurs in the private industrial sector arranging foreign credit in the form of loan, suppliers' credit, PAYE scheme etc. falling within the following guide-lines are not required to obtain prior approval from BOI for contracting such credit:

. The effective rate of interest should not exceed LIBOR+4% (effective interest is the sum of the stated annual rate of interest and the annualized fees such as commitment fee, syndication fee, front-end fee, project appraisal fee etc.).

. The down payment, if any, in case of suppliers' credit should not exceed 10% of the credit amount.

. Repayment period should not be less than 7 years.

A copy of the foreign loan agreement signed by both parties should be submitted to BOI for registration.

Prior approval of BOI is required for the proposals which do not fall within the aforesaid guidelines.

Remittance of royalty, technical know-how and technical assistance fees Royalty: Royalty is a fee paid by the local manufacturer to its foreign collaborator in consideration of

. Licence to use the brand name and trade mark of the foreign manufacturer on the local product (s) and/or;

. Assignment of rights under inventions by the foreign company as well as current manufacturing experience.

TECHNICAL KNOW-HOW AND TECHNICAL ASSISTANCE FEES:

Technical know-how and technical assistance fee is a fee paid by the local unit to its foreign collaborator in consideration of preparation of factory layout, engineering specifications of the project, assistance in selecting machine, supervision of civil construction and installation of machinery and equipment, know-how and assistance in production, testing, safety and quality control, assistance by way of making available patented process and/or know-how and right to avail of the technical information resulting from research and development, training of local personnel, technical assistance in management and marketing in deserving cases and assistance in other technical matters etc.

No prior permission of BOI is required for entering into agreements for remitting fees for the purpose of royalty, technical know-how and technical assistance if the total fees and other expenses connected with technology transfer (service fee, marketing commission etc.) are within the following prescribed limits:

a. For new projects such fees and other expenses should not exceed an aggregate limit of 6% of the C&F value of imported machinery.

b. Recurrent annual fees for royalties and other expenses such as fees for technical know-how, technical assistance, operational services, marketing of products etc. should not exceed an aggregate limit of 6% of the previous year's sales of the firms as declared in the tax return.

Once the technology transfer agreements falling within the above limits are signed, these are required to be furnished to BOI for registration.

Proposals which are not covered under the prescribed limits will require prior approval of BOI for which application have to be submitted along with necessary documents and copy of the relevant draft agreement.

PROCEDURE FOR OBTAINING WORK PERMIT

Work permit for foreign nationals is a pre-requisite for employment in Bangladesh. Private sector industrial enterprises desiring to employ foreign nationals are required to apply in advance in the prescribed form of BOI. For expatriate employment the guide-lines followed are:

a. Nationals of the countries recognized by Bangladesh are considered for employment.

b. Employment of expatriate personnel be considered only in industrial establishments which are sanctioned/registered by the appropriate authority.

c. Employment of foreign nationals is normally considered for the job for which local experts/technicians are not available and persons below 18 years of age are not eligible for employment.

d. Decision of the Board of Directors of the concerned company for new employment/extension is to be furnished.

e. Number of foreign employees should not exceed 5% of the total employees including top management personnel.

f. Initially employment of any foreign national is considered for a term of 2 years which is extensible on the basis of merit of the case.

g. Necessary security clearance by the Ministry of Home Affairs.

PROCEDURE FOR OBTAINING INDUSTRIAL PLOT

Entrepreneurs requiring industrial plot for setting up of an industry in any industrial areas/estates apart from BEPZA and BSCIC, may approach BOI mentioning the size of plot required by them along with copies of sanction/registration letter and industrial layout plan for justifying actual requirement. After receiving the application BOI provides assistance to get the industrial plot.

Most of the industrial areas/estates are owned/controlled by city development authorities in three divisional head quarters, RAJUK in Dhaka, CDA in Chittagong and KDA in Khulna. Besides these, there are a few industrial estates owned and controlled by some other government agencies namely, (a) Public Works Department and (b) Housing and Settlement Directorate.

BOI also recommends for acquisition of land to the concerned authorities if required by the industrial units. In such cases the entrepreneurs are required to submit relevant papers and information in connection with the land to be acquired by the Deputy Commissioners (D.C.) concerned.

Procedure of obtaining electricity, gas, water, sewerage & telephone connection for industries

Entrepreneurs may apply either directly to the concerned authority for obtaining utility services or approach BOI for assistance along with copy of registration/sanction letter.

INCENTIVES AND FACILITIES FOR THE INVESTORS

Tax holiday: Tax holiday is allowed to industries for the following periods according to the location of the establishment:

. Dhaka, Sylhet and Chittagong Division: 5 Years
(excluding 3 hill districts)

. Other Division: 7 Years

. 3 Hill districts of Chittagong Division: 7 Years

The period of tax holiday is calculated from the month of commencement of commercial production or operation of the industrial undertaking. The eligibility of tax holiday is to be determined by the NBR.

Tax holiday facility can be availed by industries set up in Bangladesh within June 30, 2000 A.D.

Accelerated depreciation: Accelerated depreciation in lieu of tax holiday is allowed at the rate of 80% of actual cost of machinery or plant for the year in which the unit starts commercial production and 20% for the following years. The rate of depreciation is 100% for areas specified by the NBR.

CONCESSIONARY DUTY ON IMPORTED CAPITAL MACHINERY:

Import duty at the rate of 7.5 percent ad valorem is payable on capital machinery and spares imported for initial installation or BMR/BMRE of the existing industries. The value of spare parts should not, however, exceed 10 percent of the total C & F value of the machinery. Out of this 7.5 percent rate of duty payable, export - oriented industries and industries located in the under developed areas, may enjoy a further concession of the import duty in the following manner:

100 per cent export oriented industries:
No import duty is charged in case of capital machinery and spares listed in NBR's relevant notification. However, import duty @ 7.5% is secured in the form of a bank guarantee or an indemnity bond to be returned after installation of the machinery.
Minimum 70 per cent export oriented industries outside developed areas:
Import duty @ 2.5% is charged in case of of capital machinery and spares listed in NBR's relevant notification. Additional import duty @ 5% is secured in the form of a bank guarantee or cash deposit to be returned after installation of the machinery.
Minimum 70 per cent export oriented industries in developed areas:
Import duty @ 5% is charged in case of
capital machinery and spares listed in NBR's relevant notification. Additional import duty @ 2.5% is secured in the form of a bank guarantee or cash deposit to be returned after installation of the machinery.
Other industries outside developed areas:
Import duty @ 5% is charged in case of
capital machinery and spares listed in NBR's relevant notification. Additional import duty @ 2.5% is secured in the form of a bank guarantee or cash deposit to be returned after installation of the machinery.
Other industries in developed areas:
Import duty @ 7.5% is charged in case of
capital machinery and spares listed in NBR's relevant notification.

Value Added Tax (VAT) is not payable for imported capital machinery and spares. Please see at Appendix - E for list of different areas (developed/under developed).

Rationalisation of import duty: Duties and taxes on import of goods which are produced locally will be higher than those applicable to import of raw materials for producing such goods.

Incentives to non-resident Bangladeshis : Special incentives are provided to encourage non-resident Bangladeshis for investment in the country. Non-resident Bangladeshi investors will enjoy facilities similar to those of foreign investors. Moreover, they can buy newly issued shares/debentures of Bangladeshi companies. A quota of 10 % has been fixed for non-resident Bangladeshis in primary public shares. Furthermore, they can maintain foreign currency deposits in the Non-resident Foreign Currency Deposit (NFCD) Account.

OTHER INCENTIVES

. Tax exemption on royalties, technical know - how fees received by any foreign collaborator, firm, company and expert.

. Tax exemption on the interest on foreign loans under certain conditions.

. Avoidance of double taxation in case of foreign investors on the basis of bilateral agreements.

. Exemption of income tax up to 3 years for the foreign technicians employed in industries specified in the relevant schedule of income tax ordinance.

. Tax exemption on income of the private sector power generation company for 15 years from the date of commercial production.

. Facilities for repatriation of invested capital, profit & dividend.

. Six months' multiple entry visa for the investors.

RE-INVESTMENT OF REPATRIABLE DIVIDEND TREATED AS NEW INVESTMENT.

. Citizenship by investing a minimum of US$ 5,00,000 or by transferring US$ 10,00,000 to any recognized financial institution (non repatriable).

. Permanent resident ship by investing a minimum of US$ 75,000 (non-repatriable)

. Tax exemption on dividend income of non - resilient shareholders during tax exemption period of an industry set up in export processing zone and also after the expiry of tax exemption period if the dividend is re-investment in the same project.

. Exemption of tax on income from industrial undertaking set up in export processing zone for 10 years from the date of commercial production.

. Tax exemption on capital gains from the transfer of shares of public limited companies listed with a stock exchange.

ADDITIONAL INCENTIVES TO EXPORT ORIENTED AND EXPORT LINKAGE INDUSTRIES

Encouraging export oriented industries is one of the major objectives of the Industrial Policy, 1991 and as such the government ensures allsupport and co-operation to the exporters as per Export Policy. Some of the facilities and incentives offered are as follows :

. Concessionary duty as per SRO is allowed on the import of capital machinery and spare parts for setting up export-oriented industries or BMRE of existing industries. For 100% export-oriented industriesno import duty is payable.

. Facilities such as special bonded warehouse against back-to-back letters of credit or notional import duty and non payment of Value Added Tax (VAT) facilities are available as per SRO of the government.

. System for duty drawback is being simplified and concised. The exporter will be able to get back the duty draw-back directly from the concerned commercial bank.

. Bank loan up to 90 percent of the value against irrevocable and confirmed letters of credit/sales agreement is available.

. For granting export performance benefit, the list of export products and the rate of Export Performance Benefit (XPB) is reviewed from time to time.

. With a view to ensuring backward linkage, export-oriented industries including export-oriented ready-made garment industries using indigenous raw materials instead of imported one are given additional facilities and benefits at prescribed rates. Similar incentives are extended to the suppliers of raw materials to export-oriented industries.

. Export-oriented industries are allocated foreign exchange for publicity campaign and for opening offices abroad.

. Entire export earning from handicrafts and cottage industries is exempted from income tax. In case of all other industries, proportional income tax rebate on export earnings is given between 30 and 100 percent. Industries which export 100 percent of their products are given tax exemption up to 100 percent.

. Facility for importing raw materials is given for manufacturing exportable commodities under banned/restricted list.

. Import of specified quantities of duty-free samples for manufacturing exportable products is allowed. The quantity and value of samples is determined jointly by the concerned sponsoring agency and the National Board of Revenue (NBR).

. Local products supplied to local projects against foreign exchange under international tender are treated as indirect exports and the producer is entitled to avail all export facilities.

. Export oriented industries like toys, luggage & fashion articles, electronic goods, leather goods, diamond cutting & polishing, jewellery, stationery goods, silk cloth, gift items, cut & artificial flowers & orchid, vegetable processing and engineering consultancy services identified by the government as thrust sectors are provided special facilities in the form of cash incentives, venture capital and other facilities.

. Export oriented industries are exempted from paying local taxes (such as municipal taxes.

. Leather industries exporting at least 80% manufactured products will be treated as 100% export oriented industries.

. Manufacturers of indigenous fabrics (such as woven, knit, hosiery, grey, printed, dyed, grament check, handloom, silk and other specialized fabrics) supplying their products to 100% export oriented garment industries are entitled to avail a cash subsidy equivalent to 25% of the value of the fabrics provided the manufacturers of the fabrics do not enjoy duty draw back or duty free bonded ware house facility.

Apart from the above mentioned facilities, other facilities as announced and provided in the Export Policy are also applicable for export-oriented and export-linkage industries.

RELAXATION/LIBERALISATION OF EXCHANGE CONTROL REGULATIONS

On March 24, 1994 Bangladesh `Taka' was declared convertible for current external transactions. Consequently, individuals/firms resident in Bangladesh may conduct all current external transactions, including trade and investment through banks authorised to deal in foreign exchange (Authorised Dealers) without prior approval of Bangladesh Bank. Non-resident direct investment in industrial enterprises and non-resident portfolio investment through stock exchanges also do not require prior approval of Bangladesh Bank. Remittance of post-tax dividends/profits on non-resident direct or portfolio investments do not require prior approval, sale proceeds, including capital gains on non-resident portfolio investments may also be remitted abroad without prior approval. Investors may obtainrelevant procedural details by contacting any Authorised Dealer bank in Bangladesh. The salient points on liberalisation measures intendedfor investment facilitation and for encouragement of exports are as below.

To facilitate investment:

Prior approval of the Bangladesh Bank is no longer required for :

. Remittance of profits to their head offices by foreign firms and companies operating in Bangladesh.

. Issuance of shares to non-residents against investments for setting up industries in Bangladesh.

. Remittance of dividends on such shares to the non-resident investors.

. Portfolio investment by non-residents including foreign individuals/enterprises in shares and securities through stock exchanges in Bangladesh.

. Remittance of dividend on portfolio investment by non-residents through stock exchanges in Bangladesh.

. Remittance of sale proceeds including capital gains of portfolio investments of non-residents through stock exchanges in Bangladesh.

. Opening of letters of credit by banks against suppliers' credit and other foreign borrowings contracted by industrial enterprises in the private sector in accordance with general guidelines prescribed by BOI (subject to a maximum effective rate of interest of LIBOR + 4%,repayment period not less than 7 years) or with specific approval of BOI.

. Remittance in repayment of principal and payment of interest of such loans.

. Remittance of technical fees and royalties against technical assistance/royalty agreements in conformity with BOI guidelines.

. Remittance of savings of expatriate personnel at the time of their leaving Bangladesh out of the salaries and benefits stated in their employment contracts as approved by BOI.

.Extension of term loans by banks on normal banking considerations to foreign firms operating in Bangladesh.

. Extension of working capital loans to all foreign owned/controlled industrial and trading firms/companies by banks on the basis of banker customer relationship and normal banking practice.

. Obtaining of interest free repatriable short terms foreign currency loans by foreign firms investing in Bangladesh from their head officesor any other sources through any authorised dealer.

TO ENCOURAGE EXPORT:

. Annual foreign exchange retention quota of exporters in general has been refixed at 40% of FOB export earnings.

. For exports of items with high import content (such as naphtha, furnace oil and bitumen, ready made garments, electronic goods etc.) the retention quota is 7.5% of FOB export earnings. Service
exporters are allowed to retain in foreign exchange 5% of their earnings.

. Exporters may keep their foreign exchange quota in foreign currency accounts in US Dollar, Pound Sterling, Duetch Mark or Japanese Yen with a bank in Bangladesh dealing in foreign exchange. Balances in these foreign currency accounts can be used by the exporters for bonafide business purposes such as business visits abroad, participation in export fairs and seminars, import of raw materials,
machinery and spares etc. Funds from these accounts may also be used to set up offices abroad without prior permission of Bangladesh Bank.

INVESTMENT GUARANTEES/AGREEMENTS/PROTECTIONS

Legal protection : The Foreign Private Investment (Promotion &Protection) Act, 1980 ensures legal protection to foreign investment in Bangladesh against nationalisation and expropriation. It also
guarantees repatriation of capital & dividend and equitable treatment with local investors at (Appendix - F).

Bilateral agreements for avoidance of double taxation : Bilateralagreements have been concluded by the Government of the People's Republic of Bangladesh with the following countries for avoidance of double taxation :

Belgium Pakistan

Canada	Poland
China	Romania
Denmark	Singapore
France	South Korea
Germany	Sri Lanka
India	Sweden
Italy	Thailand
Japan	The Netherlands
Malaysia	United Kingdom (Including Northern Ireland)

Negotiations are going on with U.S.A., Iran, Philippines, Qatar, Australia, Nepal, Turkey, Indonesia, Cyprus, Norway, Finland and Spain.

TRAVEL TO BANGLADESH

US STATE DEPARTMENT SUGGESTIONS FOR TRAVELERS

COUNTRY DESCRIPTION: Bangladesh has a developing economy. Tourist facilities outside major cities and tourist areas are minimal.

ENTRY REQUIREMENTS: A passport and onward/return ticket are required. A visa is not required for a tourist stay of up to 15 days. Visas (landing permits) are available for a fee upon arrival by air. Further information on entry requirements can be obtained from the Embassy of the Peoples' Republic of Bangladesh, 2201 Wisconsin Avenue N.W. Suite 300, Washington, D.C. 20007, telephone 202-342-8373, Internet: http://members.aol.com/banglaemb/main.htm or from the Bangladesh consulates in New York, 211 E. 43rd Street, Suite 502, New York, NY 10017, telephone 212-599-6767, or Los Angeles, 10850 Wilshire Boulevard, Suite 1250, Los Angeles, CA 90024, telephone 310-441-9399.

SAFETY/SECURITY/AREAS OF INSTABILITY: Public demonstrations, marches and labor strikes are widely used means of political expression in Bangladesh. A number of general strikes, or "hartals," have been called by the political opposition over the past several years, resulting in the virtual shutdown of transportation and commerce, and attacks on individuals who do not observe the "hartals." Clashes between rival political groups have resulted in deaths and injuries to participants. Violence is a particular problem on university campuses. Visitors to Bangladesh should check with the Consular Section at the U.S. Embassy in Dhaka for updated information on planned political activities.

CRIME INFORMATION: Crime rates in Bangladesh have traditionally been low compared to those in other areas of the world. However, crime in Dhaka and Chittigong is increasing, as are reports of crimes involving weapons. Foreigners have not been especially targeted. The loss or theft of a U.S. passport abroad should be reported immediately to local police and to the U.S. Embassy in Dhaka. U.S. citizens can refer to the Department of State's pamphlets *A Safe Trip Abroad* and *Tips for Travelers to South Asia* to promote a more trouble-free journey. The pamphlets are available by mail from the Superintendent of Documents, U.S. Government Printing Office, Washington, D.C. 20402, via the Internet at http://www.access.gpo.gov/su_docs, or via the Bureau of Consular Affairs home page at http://travel.state.gov.

MEDICAL FACILITIES: Medical facilities in Bangladesh do not approach U.S. standards, even in tourist areas. Doctors and hospitals often expect immediate cash payment for health services. The Medicare/Medicaid program does not provide for payment of medical services outside the United States. U.S. medical insurance is not always valid outside the United States. Travelers have found that, in some cases, supplemental medical insurance with specific overseas coverage, including provision for medical evacuation has proven useful.

MEDICAL INSURANCE: Uninsured travelers who require medical care overseas may face extreme difficulties. Check with your own insurance company to confirm whether your policy applies overseas, including provision for medical evacuation. Ascertain whether payment will be made to the overseas hospital or doctor or whether you will be reimbursed later for expenses you incur. Some insurance policies also include coverage for psychiatric treatment and for disposition of remains in the event of death. Useful information on medical emergencies abroad, including overseas insurance programs, is provided in the Department of State's Bureau of Consular

Affairs brochure *Medical Information for Americans traveling Abroad*, available via the Bureau of Consular Affairs home page or autofax: 202-647-3000.

OTHER HEALTH INFORMATION: Information on vaccinations and other health precautions may be obtained from the Centers for Disease Control and Prevention's international traveler's hotline at telephone: 1-877-FYI-TRIP (1-877-394-8747); fax: 1-888-CDC-FAXX (1-888-232-3299), or via their Internet site at http://www.cdc.gov.

TRAFFIC SAFETY AND ROAD CONDITIONS: While in a foreign country, U.S. citizens may encounter road conditions that differ significantly from those in the United States. The information below concerning Bangladesh is provided for general reference only, and may not be totally accurate in a particular location or circumstance.

Safety of Public Transportation: poor
Urban Road Conditions/Maintenance: poor
Rural Road Conditions/Maintenance: poor
Availability of Roadside Assistance: poor

The Bangladesh road network is in generally poor condition, in part due to the difficulty of building and maintaining a transportation infrastructure across a vast river delta. The streets of Dhaka are congested, with hundreds of thousands of bicycle rickshaws competing with three-wheeled taxis, cars and trucks for limited road space. Because intercity roads are narrow and in poor condition, driving outside urban areas at night may be dangerous.

AVIATION SAFETY OVERSIGHT: The U.S. Federal Aviation Administration (FAA) has assessed the Government of Bangladesh's Civil Aviation Authority as Category 2--not in compliance with international aviation safety standards for oversight of Bangladesh's air carrier operations. While consultations to correct the deficiencies are ongoing, Bangladesh's air carriers are permitted to conduct limited operations to the U.S. subject to heightened FAA surveillance. For further information, travelers may contact the Department of Transportation within the U.S. at 1-800-322-7873, or visit the FAA's Internet website at http://www.faa.gov/avr/iasa/index.htm. The U.S. Department of Defense (DOD) does not permit its personnel to use air carriers from Category 2 countries for official business except for flights originating from or terminating in the U.S. For information regarding the DOD policy on specific carriers, travelers may contact DOD at 618-256-4801.

CUSTOMS REGULATIONS: There are restrictions on importing currency and weapons. Contact the Embassy of Bangladesh for specific information.

CRIMINAL PENALTIES: While in a foreign country, a U.S. citizen is subject to the country's laws and regulations, which sometimes differ significantly from those in the United States and may not afford the protections available to the individual under U.S. law. Penalties for breaking the law can be more severe than in the United States for similar offenses. Persons violating Bangladesh's laws, even unknowingly, may be expelled, arrested or imprisoned. Penalties for possession of, use of, or trafficking in illegal drugs in Bangladesh are strict. The death penalty or life imprisonment can be imposed for some drug-related crimes. At a minimum, convicted offenders can expect jail sentences and fines.

CHILDREN'S ISSUES: For information on international adoption of children, international parental child abduction, and international child support enforcement issues, please refer to our Internet site at http//travel.state.gov/children's_issues.html or telephone 202-736-7000.

REGISTRATION/EMBASSY LOCATION: Americans living in or visiting Bangladesh are encouraged to register at the Consular Section of the U.S. Embassy in Dhaka and obtain updated information on travel and security within Bangladesh. The U.S. Embassy is located at Diplomatic Enclave, Madani Avenue, Baridhara, Dhaka, telephone (880-2) 884700-22. Their Internet home page is http://www.citechco.net/usdhaka.

BUSINESS TRAVEL

CUSTOMS

Bangladeshi business executives are usually very courteous, and try to make their foreign guests feel at ease. Business visitors should be aware that in Bangladesh, men and women do not usually shake hands with each other, and may avoid doing so with a visitor of the opposite sex. Foreign visitors often find that hosting meals for their Bangladeshi agents or business contacts helps to smooth business negotiations. Visitors may also be invited to share meals as guests of their Bangladeshi hosts.

TRAVEL ADVISORY AND VISAS

Updated travel advisory information on Bangladesh is available from the State Department's Bureau of Consular Affairs in several formats. For a line of recorded information, call (202) 647-5225. To access the Consular Affairs Bulletin Board, call (202) 647-9225. For information by fax, call (202) 547-3000. In addition, the Internet/World Wide Web homepage maintained by the State Department's Bureau of Consular Affairs has Bangladesh travel advisory information at http://travel.state.gov.

All United States citizens are required to have visas for entry into Bangladesh. Business travelers should request visas with five-year duration and multiple entries. Should a business traveler be unable to arrange for a visa in advance, immigration officials at Zia International Airport in Dhaka are authorized to issue limited visas for up to 90 days for a $ 45 fee. Visa extensions are possible; a $ 45 fee must be paid to the Department of Immigration and Passports, 17 Segun Bagicha, Dhaka 1000, telephone (880 2) 9553332, fax 9562787, contact: Assistant Director.

Generally extensions are granted for 3-6 months (short-term) with a single entry. For 1 year or more (long-term) extensions for an expatriate working on a government project, a letter from the relevant ministry of the BDG is required, along with the prescribed visa extension application form. One passport size photograph is also required.

For further information concerning entry requirements for Bangladesh, travelers can contact the Embassy of the People's Republic of Bangladesh, 2201 Wisconsin Ave., N.W., Suite 300-325, Washington, DC 20007, telephone: (202) 342-8372, 342-8373, 342-8374, 342-8375, and 342-8376, or the Consulate General of the People's Republic of Bangladesh, 211 East 43rd St., Suite 502, NY, NY 10017, telephone: (212) 599-6767 and 599-6850, fax (212) 682-9211.

The International Certificate of Vaccination is no longer required for travel to Bangladesh, but typhoid immunization and malaria suppressants are recommended, particularly for those traveling outside Dhaka.

TRAVEL FEES

Business travelers departing on domestic and international flights must pay an Embarkation Fee/Departure Tax, currently TK 50 for domestic flights and TK 300 for international flights. Foreigners are not required to pay other local travel taxes.

CURRENCY AND EXCHANGE REGULATIONS

There is no limit on the amount of foreign or U.S. dollar instruments (travelers checks, money orders, etc.) that may be brought into Bangladesh, but all foreign exchange exceeding $5,000 must be declared upon entry, and visitors should be prepared to account for it upon departure. Visitors should only make financial transactions through authorized channels.

Commercial exchange facilities are available through both domestic and foreign commercial banks or through local hotel cashiers. The banking sector can carry out most international transactions, but efficient service varies greatly among banks and individual branches.

HOLIDAYS

January 23 (Jumatul Bida)
January 29, 30, 31 (Eid-ul-Fitr)
February 21 (Martyrs' Day)
March 17 (Birthday of the Founder of Bangladesh)
March 26 (Independence Day)
April 7,8,9 (Eid-ul-Azha)
May 1 (May Day)
May 11 (Buddha Purnima)
July 7 (Eid Miladunnabi)
August 14 (Janmasthami)
August 15 (National Mourning Day)
October 1 (Durga Puja)
December 16 (Victory Day)
December 25 (Christmas Day).

BUSINESS INFRASTRUCTURE

Transportation: Zia International Airport is located at Kurmitola, about 12 kilometers north of Dhaka city. The national air carrier, Biman Bangladesh Airlines, currently is the major domestic air travel provider. GMG, a private STOL (short takeoff and landing) flight operator, has flights from Dhaka to Chittagong, Barisal, Jessore and Sylhet.

Language: Although Bangla (Bengali) is the official language of Bangladesh, English is widely spoken and used in official and business circles. U.S. business people may greet their Bangladeshi counterparts with normal English salutations. The usual greeting among Bangladeshis is the Arabic phrase "as-salaam-alaikum" (meaning "peace be with you"). The cordial esponse is "walaikum salaam" ("peace to you as well"). A polite parting phrase is "Khoda haafez" ("God preserve").

Communications: Telex, telephone, fax, Internet e-mail and airmail postal services are available for business correspondence. Most international telephone calls must be booked through an operator, usually after some delay. Collect telephone calls or toll-free calls cannot be made from Bangladesh.

International direct dialing telephones and fax machines are increasingly available in major cities and hotels in Bangladesh. Cellular phone service is available in Dhaka and Chittagong. Bangladesh is six hours ahead of Greenwich Mean Time (GMT) (11 hours ahead of Eastern standard time or 10 hours during daylight savings time). Airmail correspondence takes two weeks to arrive from the United States. Registration of all letters sent by international mail is recommended.

Express Mail Service (EMS) is available to the major cities. International courier services, including Airborne, DHL, Federal Express, TNT Skypack, and United Parcel Service, operate to and from Bangladesh.

Lodging: Two international class hotels are located in Dhaka, the Dhaka Sheraton and the Sonargaon Pan Pacific Hotel. A more moderately priced but older hotel, the Hotel Purbani, is also used by business visitors to Dhaka. In Chittagong, business visitors usually stay at the Hotel Agrabad. For longer stays, guest-house accommodations are available in upper-class neighborhoods in Dhaka and Chittagong.

Health: Medical facilities are inadequate in Bangladesh. Most diseases are water-borne. Water must be boiled for safety; bottled water is increasingly widely available. Certain vaccinations are essential. There are foreign-trained doctors in Dhaka and other cities. However, hospital/clinic support services are usually sub-standard. Travelers are advised to get medevac insurance and to establish contact with a doctor upon arrival. The following western-trained physicians/facilities are present in Dhaka:

Dr. M.A. Wahab: 881454
British High Commission Medical Unit, Elizabeth House: 884345
DR. TIMOR NAWAZ: 872871

Food: Restaurants in Dhaka and Chittagong serve mainly local (Bengali) and other Asian cuisines. Continental food is available at Dhaka's internationally operated hotels. Local food is spicy to American tastes. The main components of local food are boiled rice and fish, or curry of mutton, beef, or chicken. Vegetables and lentils are also popular. There is no effective system of health inspection of restaurants. A number of restaurants have opened in the last several years that are popular with expatriates.

DESEASES PREVENTION

Food and waterborne diseases are the number one cause of illness in travelers. **Travelers' diarrhea** can be caused by viruses, bacteria, or parasites, which are found throughout the region and can contaminate food or water. Infections may cause diarrhea and vomiting (*E. coli*, *Salmonella*, cholera, and parasites), fever (typhoid fever and toxoplasmosis), or liver damage (hepatitis). Make sure your food and drinking water are safe. (See below.)

Malaria is a preventable infection that can be fatal if left untreated. Prevent infection by taking prescription antimalarial drugs and protecting yourself against mosquito bites (see below). Malaria risk in this region exists in some urban and many rural areas, depending on elevation. For specific locations, see **Malaria Information for Travelers to the Indian** Subcontinent. Most travelers to the Indian Subcontinent at risk for malaria should take mefloquine to prevent malaria.

A certificate of yellow fever vaccination may be **required** for entry into certain of these countries if you are coming from countries in tropical South America or sub-Saharan Africa. (There is no risk for yellow fever in the Indian Subcontinent.) For detailed information, see Comprehensive Yellow Fever Vaccination Requirements.

Filariasis, Japanese encephalitis, leishmaniasis, and plague are diseases carried by insects that also occur in this region. Protecting yourself against insect bites (see below) will help to prevent these diseases.

If you visit the Himalayan Mountains, ascend gradually to allow time for your body to adjust to the high altitude, which can cause insomnia, headaches, nausea, and altitude sickness. In addition, use sunblock rated at least 15 SPF, because the risk of sunburn is greater at high altitudes.

Because motor vehicle crashes are a leading cause of injury among travelers, walk and drive defensively. Avoid travel at night if possible and always use seat belts.

CDC Recommends the Following Vaccines (as Appropriate for Age):
See your doctor at least 4–6 weeks before your trip to allow time for shots to take effect.

- Hepatitis A or immune globulin (IG).
- Hepatitis B, if you might be exposed to blood (for example, health-care workers), have sexual contact with the local population, stay longer than 6 months, or be exposed through medical treatment.
- Japanese encephalitis, only if you plan to visit rural areas for 4 weeks or more, except under special circumstances, such as a known outbreak of Japanese encephalitis.
- Rabies, if you might be exposed to wild or domestic animals through your work or recreation.
- Typhoid vaccination is particularly important because of the presence of *S. typhi* strains resistant to multiple antibiotics in this region.
- As needed, booster doses for tetanus-diphtheria and measles, and a one-time dose of polio for adults. Hepatitis B vaccine is now recommended for all infants and for children ages 11–12 years who did not receive the series as infants.

To Stay Healthy, Do:

- Wash hands often with soap and water.
- Drink only bottled or boiled water, or carbonated (bubbly) drinks in cans or bottles. Avoid tap water, fountain drinks, and ice cubes. If this is not possible, make water safer by BOTH filtering through an "absolute 1-micron or less" filter AND adding iodine tablets to the filtered water. "Absolute 1-micron filters" are found in camping/outdoor supply stores.
- Eat only thoroughly cooked food or fruits and vegetables you have peeled yourself. Remember: boil it, cook it, peel it, or forget it.
- If you are going to visit areas where there is risk for malaria, take your malaria prevention medication before, during, and after travel, as directed. (See your doctor for a prescription.)
- Protect yourself from insects by remaining in well-screened areas, using repellents (applied sparingly at 4-hour intervals) and permethrin-impregnated mosquito nets, and wearing long-sleeved shirts and long pants from dusk through dawn.
- To prevent fungal and parasitic infections, keep feet clean and dry, and do not go barefoot.
- Always use latex condoms to reduce the risk of HIV and other sexually transmitted diseases.

To Avoid Getting Sick:

- Don't eat food purchased from street vendors.
- Don't drink beverages with ice.
- Don't eat dairy products unless you know they have been pasteurized.
- Don't share needles with anyone.
- Don't handle animals (especially monkeys, dogs, and cats), to avoid bites and serious diseases (including rabies and plague).
- Don't swim in fresh water. Salt water is usually safer.

What You Need To Bring with You:

- Long-sleeved shirt and long pants to wear while outside whenever possible, to prevent illnesses carried by insects (e.g., malaria, dengue, filariasis, leishmaniasis, and onchocerciasis).
- Insect repellent containing DEET (diethylmethyltoluamide), in 30%–35% strength for adults and 6%–10% for children. Travelers who are not in air-conditioned or well-screened housing should purchase a bed net impregnated with the insecticide permethrin. (Bed nets can be purchased in camping or military supply stores.)
- Over-the-counter antidiarrheal medicine to take if you have diarrhea.
- Iodine tablets and water filters to purify water if bottled water is not available. See Do's above for more detailed information about water filters.
- Sunblock, sunglasses, hat.
- Prescription medications: make sure you have enough to last during your trip, as well as a copy of the prescription(s).

After You Return Home:
If you have visited an area where there is risk for malaria, continue taking your malaria medication weekly for 4 weeks after you leave the area.
If you become ill after travel—even as long as a year after your trip—tell your doctor the areas you have visited.

For More Information:
Ask your doctor or check the CDC web sites for more information about how to protect yourself against diseases that occur in the Indian Subcontinent, such as:

DISEASES– CARRIED BY INSECTS

- Dengue
- Japanese encephalitis
- Malaria
- Plague

CARRIED IN FOOD OR WATER

- Cholera
- *Escherichia coli* diarrhea
- Hepatitis A
- Typhoid Fever

PERSON-TO-PERSON CONTACT

- Hepatitis B
- HIV/AIDS

GENERAL INFORMATION

Wearing apparel :
Tropical in summer na dlight- woolen in winter.

Currency :
Taka (Ta) is the unit of currency. The Taka is equal to 100 paisa (smallest unit). Notes of 1,2, 5,10,20,50,100,500,taka and coins of 5,10,25,50 and 100 paisa are in circulation.

Banking hours :
09:00 am-3 p.m. on Sunday- Wednesday, Thursday 09:00 a.m. 1.00 p.m. and closed on Friday & Saturday.

Time difference: 06 hours GMT

Working Hours :
Office Hours: 09:00 a.m-05:00 a.m. on Sunday-Thursday, Friday and Saturday closed.

Newspapers :
Dhaka are published from Dhaka, Chittagong and other important cities and towns both in Bangla and English, Main English newspaper are Bangladesh Observer, The Bangladesh Times, The Daily Star, The New Nation, The Independent, The Financial Express and the Holiday (Weekly).

Radio Stations :
Dhaka, Chittagong, Rajshahi, Sylhet, Rangpur, Khulna, Rangamati, Comilla, News is broadcast in Bangla and English.

Television :
Dhaka, Chittagong, Khulna, Natore, Sylhet, Mymensingh, Rangpur, Noakhali, Satkhira, Cox's Bazar, Rangamati. CNN and BBC international Service have started telecast recently.

Electricity : L 220 Volts A.C

Airport :
International: Dhaka (ZIA), Chittagong (Patenga)

Domestic :
Dhaka, Chittagong, Jessore, Saidpur, Rajshahi, Cox's Bazar and Sylhet.

Sea Ports:
Chittagong & Mongla.

River Ports :
Dhaka, Chandpur, Barisal, Khulna, Patuakhali, Baghabari, Serajgonj, Narayangonj and Bhairab Bazar.

Best Tourist Season : October to March.

TOURIST INFORMATION CENTRES

Dhaka:
Parjatan Head Office (Ph: 819192, 817855-9)
Sheraton Hotel (Ph: 509479, 863391,/566),
Zia International Airport (Ph: 894416).

Chittagong:
Motel Shaikat (Ph: 619845, 619514),

Cox's Bazar:
Parjatan Holiday Complex (Ph: 4202, 3274, 3275, 3211, 4246),

Rajshahi:
Parjatan Motel (Ph: 775492),

Rangamati:
Parjatan Holiday Complex (Ph: 3126),

Bogra:
Parjatan Motel (Ph: 6759),

Rajshahi :
Parjatan Motel (Ph: 775492)
Rangpur:
Parjatan Motel (Ph: 3681),
Sylhet :
Parjatan Motel (Ph: 712426).

POST, TELEGRAPH, FAX, TELEPHONE

Facilities are available every where including big Hotels Telex, Cable and Phone connections are easily made to any part of the World. Direct dialing system is available for all major towns and cities. Public telephones available at important market places, Police boxed and POs in the cities and important towns. Fax services is also available at important towns and big hotels.
General Post Office is near Baitul Mokarram Mosque and main Telegraph Office is just behind Gulstan Building (west) in Dhaka.

EMBASSIES AND CONSULATES

Bangladesh High Commission in Australia	< http://users.cyberone.com.au/bdeshact/ >
Bangladesh High Commissioner in Canada	< http://www.iosphere.net/%7Ebhc/ >
Bangladesh High Commissioner in Singapore	< http://www.bangladesh.org.sg/ >
Embassy of Bangladesh in Germany	< http://www.bangladeshembassy.org/emb-e.html >
Embassy of Bangladesh in Morocco	< http://users.mtds.com/~bdoot/bangladesh_ang.htm >
Embassy of Bangladesh in the United States	< http://www.bangladoot.org/consular.asp >
Permanent Mission of Bangladesh to the United Nations	< http://www.un.int/bangladesh >

SOURCES OF INFORMATION

AgriNet Bangladesh	< http://members.tripod.com/~UTTAMDEB/ >
Association of Development Agencies in Bangladesh (ADAB)	< http://www.sdnbd.org/adab_profile.htm >
Association for Economic and Development Studies of Bangladesh	< http://www.aedsb.org/ >
Bangla2000, Directory	< http://www.bangla2000.com/ >
Bangladesh Business Directory and Services	< http://www.sonalibangla.com/ >
Bangladesh Centre for Advanced Studies	< http://www.bcas.net/ >
Bangladesh Development Gateway	< http://www.bangladeshgateway.org/index.php >
Bangladesh International Community	< http://bicn.com/ >
Bangladesh Institute for Development Studies	< http://www.bids-bd.org/ >
Bangladesh Rural Advancement Committee	< http://www.brac.net/ >
Business Information Bangladesh	< http://www.bizinfo-bd.com/index.php >
Centre for Environmental and Geographic Information	< http://www.cegisbd.com/ >
Centre for Policy Dialogue	< http://www.cpd-bangladesh.org/ >

Dhaka Calling, a monthly guide	< http://www.dhakacalling.com/ >
Drik Net	< http://www.drik.net/ >
Grameen Bank	< http://www.grameen-info.org/ >
Proshika, Centre for Human Development	< http://www.proshika.org/ >
South Asia Research Network	< http://sarn.ssrc.org/ >
Sustainable Development Networking Programme	< http://www.sdnbd.org/ >
TRACE, Trade Cooperation and Economic Policy Reform Programme	< http://www.tracebd.org/ >
United Nations Development Programme-Bangladesh	< http://www.un-bd.org/undp/ >
Virtual Bangladesh	< http://www.virtualbangladesh.com/ >
Yellow Pages Bangladesh	< http://www.bgyellowpages.com/ >

SUPPLEMENT

IMPORTANT EXPORT-IMPORT REGULATIONS

LIST OF GOODS BANNED FOR IMPORT

HS Heading	HS Code	Description
01.03	All HS codes	Live swine
01.05	All HS codes	Chicks, except "parent stock" and "grandparent stock"
02.09	0209.00	All items
03.02	0302.70	Eggs of shrimps and prawns
03.06	0306.23	Larva of shrimps and prawns
04.07	0407.00	Eggs except "hatching eggs"
05.02	All H.S codes	All items
05.11	0511.10	Deep frozen semen of oxen, except deep frozen semen of Frisian, Frisian Cross, Shahiwal, Shahiwal Cross, A.F.S., A.F.S. Cross variety domestic cows
12.07	All HS codes	Poppy seeds and "dried Postadana" ("Postadana" is not importable as spices or in any other way)
12.11	All HS codes	Ghas (Andropogen SPP) and Bhang (Channabis Sativa)
13.02	All HS codes	Opium
14.04	1404.901	Tendu leaves (Biri leaves)
15.01	1501.00	All items including lard
15.03	1503.001 1503.009	All items including lard stearing except "inedible tallow and RBD palm stearing"
22.07	All HS codes	All items except "Ethanol (ethyl alcohol) analar grade (undernatured)"
23.07	2307.00	All items
25.20	2520.10	Gypsum
27.11	All HS codes	Petroleum gas and other gaseous hydrocarbons
27.13	All HS codes	All items including petroleum coke, petroleum betumin and petroleum oil residues
29.30	2930.909	Allyl isothlicyonate (artificial mustard oil)
31.03	3103.10	Coloured and granular SSP and power SSP, i.e. any kind of coloured SSP and all types of granular SSP and power SSP fertilizer
38.08	All HS codes	Insecticides namely heptachlore-40WP, DDT, bidrin Brand in the generic name, dicrotopes, methyle bromide, clorden-40WP and daildrin
48.19	All HS codes	All cartons except (1) outer carton system which is used for State Express 555 cigarettes; (2) laminated inner carton used for export of all frozen food including shrimps
50.07	All HS codes	Woven fabrics of silk or silk waste
51.02 to 51.05 and	All HS codes	Hair of swine and yarn made thereof

51.08; 51.09		
52.08 to 52.012	All HS codes	All items except (1) long cloth (white only) up to 33s counts and width up to 36"; (2) poplin including shirting white, dyed, printed, striped and checks up to 40s counts and width up to 36"; (3) cambric including shirting white, dyed, printed, striped and checks up to 40s counts and width up to 36"; (4) serge and gabardine of width up to 45" of all constructions; (5) twill and corduroy of width up to 45" of all constructions; (6) mull, organdie, lawn, voil white, dyed or printed up to 65s counts and width 35"; (7) flannel white, dyed and printed up to 45" width; (8) cotton synthetic blended suiting of all constructions up to 60" width; (9) cotton synthetic blended shirting white, dyed and printed up to 45" width; (10) umbrella cloth
54.07 and 54.08	All HS codes	(1) Shirting and suiting of 85% or more by weight of synthetic or man-made fibre (synthetic, regenerated or blended yarn of both) or similar fabrics in any form, including fents and cut pieces except polyester shear of mesh 80-150 required for screen printing machine/table and saree fabric of 85% or more by weight, of synthetic of man-made fibre (synthetic, regenerated or blended yarn of both) in pieces of 5½ yards to 6 yards not in thaan or rolls; (2) fents, cut pieces, fabrics cut into sizes of piece goods; (3) cotton synthetic blended suiting of all constructions above 60" width
55.12 to 55.16	All HS codes	The following except polyester shear of mesh 80-150 required for screen printing machine/table: (1) shirting and suiting of 85% or more by weight of synthetic or man-made fibre (synthetic, regenerated or blended yarn of both) and similar fabrics in any form; (2) fents, cut pieces, fabrics cut into sizes and piece goods; (3) cotton and synthetic blended suiting white, dyed, printed above 45" width; (4) cotton synthetic blended suiting of all constructions above 60" width
56.07	5607.41 to 5607.90	Ropes made of nylon and polythene except nylon cord for V-belt
56.08	All HS codes	Fishing nets (Gillnet) with meshes of 4.5 centimetres or less in width or length
60.01; 60.02	All HS codes	All items except knit fabrics, mesh fabrics, pocketing cloth, ribbing materials, nylon shirting and knit fabric brassiere pad
81.11	All HS codes	All types of second-hand motorcycles more than 3 years old
89.06	All HS codes	Second-hand ships more than 15 years old except warships of all kinds (both new and second-hand)
90.28	9028.30	Single phase electric meter (in completely built-up condition)

Source: Bangladesh, Import Policy Order 1997–2002.

Note: The following goods shall not be importable:

Maps, charts and geographical globes which indicate the territory of Bangladesh in conflict with the maps published by the Department of Survey, Government Bangladesh;

Horror comics, obscene and subversive literature including such pamphlets, posters, newspapers, periodicals, photographs, films, gramophone records, audio cassettes, video cassette tapes, etc.;

Books, newspapers, periodicals, documents and other papers, posters, photographs, films, gramophone records, audio cassettes and video cassette tapes, etc. containing matters likely to outrage the religious feelings and beliefs of any class of the citizens of Bangladesh;

Old, second-hand and reconditioned goods, factory rejects and goods of job-lot/stock-lot of secondary/substandard quality, unless otherwise specified in this order;

Reconditioned office equipment, photocopier, typewriter machine, telex, phone, computer, fax;

All kind of wastes, unless otherwise specified in this order;

Goods, including their containers, bearing any words or inscriptions of a religious connotation the use or disposal of which may injure the religious feelings and beliefs of any class of the citizens of Bangladesh;

Goods, including their containers, bearing any obscene picture, writing inscription or visible representation.

LIST OF GOODS RESTRICTED FOR IMPORT

HS heading	HS code	Description of items	Conditions of import
01.05	All HS codes	Chicks	Only "parent stock" and "grandparent stock" one day-old chicks shall be importable and a certificate issued by the authorized officer of the responsible department of the exporting country, to the effect that the importable chicks are free from contagious disease, shall be obtained. In addition, the importer must show to the bank, at the time of letter of credit opening, a certificate from an authorized officer of the responsible directorate that she/he has either a hatchery or breeder firm.
02.03	All HS codes	All items	Importable only by foreign exchange earning hotels as per conditions in para. 24(1) of the Import Policy Order (IPO).
02.06	All HS codes	All items	Importable only by foreign exchange earning hotels as per conditions in para. 24(1) of IPO.
04.02	All HS codes	Milk food	Importable subject to fulfillment of conditions in paras. 26(1). 26(2), 26(3) and 24(9) of IPO.
04.07	0407.00	Egg	"Hatching eggs" shall be importable. For import of "hatching eggs" the importer shall obtain a certificate from the concerned government department of the exporting country to the effect that the eggs are suitable for hatching and a certificate from the director, Livestock Department of Bangladesh, to the effect that the importer requires to import such quantity of hatching eggs.
05.11	0511.10	Deep frozen semen of oxen	Deep frozen semen of Frisian, Frisian Cross, Shahiwal, Shahiwal Cross, Frisian-Shahiwal Cross, A.F.S., A.F.S. Cross variety domestic cows shall be importable. A certificate shall be obtained from the authorized officer of the responsible department of the exporting country regarding the variety of semen and to the effect that it is free from any contagious and venereal disease.
07.01	0701.10	Potato seeds	Potato seeds shall be importable subject to the following conditions: (a) The importer shall submit, along with import documents, a quarantine certificate furnished by the original supplier and a phytosanitary certificate, along with export documents from the government agency of the seed exporting country; (b) A quarantine certificate shall also be obtained from the plant protection authority before clearing imported potato seeds from the customs authority.
13.02	All HS codes	All items	All items except opium, agar and pectin are importable with prior clearance from the Director. Drugs

			Administration.
15.11	All HS codes	Refined palm olein	(a) Import of refined palm olein shall be subject to production of a separate certificate from the health authorities and the chambers of commerce and industry of the exporting countries to the effect that the consignment of the palm olein is fit for human consumption (edible). This certificate shall be submitted to the customs authorities at the time of clearance of consignments; (b) The following items shall not be permissible for import as edible oil: - Solid or semi-solid palm oil which looks like vegetable ghee; - Refined, bleached and deodorized (RBD) palm stearin; - Crude palm stearin and refined and crude palm oil. The Office of the chief controller of import and export will give permission on a case by case basis only to the edible oil producing industries which have fractionation plants to import refined and crude palm oil on the basis of the recommendation of the Board of Investment. The BOI will monitor the matter.
15.13	All HS codes	Coconut oil	Coconut oil shall be importable, by the recognized industrial units, for use in hair oil up to acid value 0.5 and the soap industry up to acid value 10.0. It shall be also importable for commercial purposes, in which case acid value will not exceed 0.5.
16.01	1601.00	Sausages of meat of swine	Importable only by foreign exchange earning hotels as per conditions in para. 24(1) of IPO.
17.01	All HS codes	(a) raw sugar (white crystal sugar or refined crystal sugar with polarization not less than 99.7 in either case). Unrefined sugar/gur; (b) Other sugars (beet sugar and cane sugar in solid form); (c) Sucrose, chemically pure sugar and refined sugar.	(a) Import of sugar is normally banned. However, a limited quantity of sugar shall be imported subject to the specific procedure on fulfilment of the condition prescribed by the Government; (b) Importable only by the recognized pharmaceutical units in limited quantity on specific recommendation of the Director, Drug Administration and with prior permission from the Chief Controller; (c) Imported by recognized industries as raw materials according to the approved block-list of the Drug Administration and prescribed specification.
19.01	All HS codes	Baby food (with cream)	Importable, subject to fulfilment of conditions in paras. 26(1), 26(2), 26(3) and 24(9) of IPO.
22.03 to 22.06	All HS codes	All items	Beer and wine of all categories shall be importable only by foreign exchange earning hotels as per conditions in para. 24(1) of IPO. In special cases, such items may be imported with approval of Ministry of Commerce and prior permission from the Chief controller subject to specified conditions. However, in all cases, the concerned importer shall first obtain licence/permission from the Director General, Narcotics Control Department. The conditions

			mentioned above shall be equally applicable for the import of alcoholic and non-alcoholic beer.
22.07	All HS codes	All items	Only "ethanol (ethyl alcohol) analar grade (indenatured)" is importable by recognized pharmaceutical units with clearance from the Director, Drug Administration and subject to prescribed conditions.
22.08	All HS codes	All items	Importable only by foreign exchange earning hotels as per conditions inpara. 24(1) of IPO.
25.01	All HS codes	(a) Common salt except table salt; (b) Table salt.	(a) Importable subject to conditions prescribed by the Government as and when required; (b) Importable only by foreign exchange earning hotels subject to prescribed conditions in para. 24(1) of IPO.
25.03	All HS codes	Sulfur	Importable subject to prescribed conditions for import of explosives in para. 26(4) of IPO.
25.23	All HS codes	Cement	Forimport of cement in the private sector, the proportional standard of cement must be 232:1993 (specified by BSTI). In addition, as per BSTI specification, the standard of portland polarized fuel ash cement should be as BDS 1557:1997 and the standard of portland blast furnace slag cement should be as BDS 1958:1997. In all cases, a pre-shipment inspection certificate shall be obtained from an internationally reputed surveyor to the effect that the declared quantity, weight and proportional standard of cement are as per the specified standard and in all cases the name of the cement must be mentioned on each bag of cement.
27.01 27.04	All HS codes	Coal/hard coke	For import of coal and hard coke in both the private and public sectors, a pre-shipment certificate shall be obtained from an internationally reputed surveyor to the effect that the quantity, weight and quality (standard) of the item are found as declared.
27.05		Gas in cylinder	Importable only with the clearance certificate from the chief inspector of explosives.
27.09		(a) Petroleum oil and all kinds of oil obtained from bituminous mineral crude and Liquefied Petroleum Gas. (b) Ethylene oxide gas.	(a) Importable by the Bangladesh Petroleum Corporation. However, in the private sector, it is importable with the approval of the Ministry of Power, Energy and Mineral Resources and prior permission from the Ministry of Commerce; (b) Importable by recognized industries as raw materials according to the approved block-list of Drug Administration and prescribed specification.
27.10	All HS codes	All petroleum products except liquid paraffin	Importable only by the Bangladesh Petroleum Corporation. However, electric transformer manufacturing units shall be allowed to import transformer oil only as raw materials up to the required quantity for their own use subject to the clearance form the Bangladesh Petroleum Corporation and by fulfilling other conditions imposed by that Corporation.
28.02	2802.00	Sulfur	Importable subject to prescribe conditions for import of explosives in para. 26(4) of IPO.
28.04	2804.70	Phosphorus	Importable subject to prescribed conditions for import of explosives in para. 26(4) of IPO.
28.29	2829.19	Potassium chlorate	Importable subject to prescribed conditions for import of explosives in para. 26(4) of IPO.

28.34	2834.21 2834.299 2834.299	(a) Potassium nitrate; (b) Barium nitrate; (c) Thorium nitrate.	(a) Importable subject to prescribed conditions for import of explosives of IPO. (b) Importable subject to prescribe conditions for import of explosives of IPO. (c) Importable only with prior permission from the Bangladesh Atomic Energy Commission.
28.44 to 28.46	All HS codes	All items including radioactive chemical/element and isotopes	Importable only with prior permission from the Bangladesh Atomic Energy Commission.
29.04	All HS codes	Trinitrotoluene (TNT)	Importable subject to prescribed conditions for import of explosives in para. 26(4) of IPO.
29.35	2935.00	Sulphonamides	Importable only with clearance from the Director, Drug Administration and subject to prescribed conditions in paras. 26(7) and 24(3) of IPO.
29.36	All HS codes	All items	Importable by drug importers and drug manufacturing industries only with clearance from the Director, Drugs Administration and subject to prescribed conditions in paras. 26(7) and 24(3) of IPO. However, Vitamins A and D (food grade) arefreely importable by other importers.
29.37 to 29.39	All HS codes	All items	Importable with clearance from the Director, Drug Administration and subject to prescribed conditions in paras. 26(7) and 24(3) of IPO.
29.41	All HS codes	Antibiotics	Importable with clearance from the Director, Drug Administration and subject to prescribed conditions in paras. 26(7) and 24(3) of IPO.
30.01	All HS codes	All items	Importable with clearance from the Director, Drugs Administration and subject to prescribed conditions in paras. 26(7) and 24(3) of IPO.
30.02	All HS codes	All items including "live vaccines"	Importable with clearance from the Director, Drugs Administration and subject to prescribed conditions in paras. 26(7) and 24(3) of IPO.
30.03	All HS codes	All items	Importable with clearance from the Director, Drugs Administration and subject to prescribed conditions in paras. 26(7) and 24(3) of IPO.
30.04	All HS codes	All items	Importable with clearance from the Director, Drugs Administration and subject to prescribed conditions in paras. 26(7) and 24(3) of IPO.
31.02 to 31.04	All HS codes	Chemical fertilizer	(a) A list of ingredients of the imported fertilizer certified by the manufacturer shall be submitted along with the shipping documents. The importer must be a member of the Bangladesh Fertilizer Association (BFA); (b) A pre-shipment certificate from an internationally recognized inspection company shall be submitted with the shipping documents and the specification of the imported fertilizer mentioned in that certificate must coincide with the specification approved by the Ministry of Agriculture. Fertilizer shall be importable only from the manufacturer or from the manufacturer's representative; (c) Specification as well as information regarding physical and chemical properties of the imported fertilizer shall be furnished in the invoice of the shipping documents.

			Mentioned specification and properties must coincide with those approved by the Ministry of Agriculture; (d) Other information according to the international rules shall be furnished in the bill of lading; (e) By fulfilling the above-mentioned conditions, imported fertilizer can be released without post-landing inspection but on condition that both the supplier and importer will be simultaneously responsible for detection of harmful material in any later examination.
35.07	All HS codes	Enzymes	For import by pharmaceutical industries clearance from Director, Drug Administration is required subject to prescribed conditions in paras. 26(7) and 24(3) of IPO. However, "enzymes (foodgrade)" are freely importable.
36.01 to 36.04	All HS codes	All items including explosives	Importable only with clearance from the concerned ministry and subject to prescribed conditions in para. 25(4) of IPO.
37.06	All HS codes	Cinematograph film exposed and developed whether or not incorporating sound track	(a) Cinematographic film (exposed) in the English language without subtitles and in other languages (except subcontinental languages) with subtitles in Bangla or in English shall be permissible for import; (b) Import of film in subcontinental languages with or without subtitles shall not be permissible. However, an import or export permit, as considered necessary, may be issued on the basis of specific recommendations of the Film Development Corporation for import or export of the print/negative of such cinematographic film produced as a joint venture; (c) Import of all cinematographic films shall be subject to censorship rule codes.
38.08	All HS codes	All items except items mentioned in banned list.	(a) Importable subject to the prescribed conditions in para. 26(5) of IPO. (b) Dettramethrine of synthetic pyrithroid group shall be importable with the prior permission of the Ministry of Commerce but only by those firms who will be certified and guaranteed by the Ministry of Health that the item will be used only for public health purpose.
52.08 to 52.12	All HS codes	(a) Grey cloth, all sorts; (b) Indigo denim (jeans fabrics) 100% cotton fabrics above 36" width (in thaan or rolls) not in cut pieces or cut to size; (c) Combat cloth; (d) Drill and cellular dyed including mineral khaki.	(a) Importable subject to prescribed conditions in para. 24(70) of IPO; (b) Importable against back-to-back letters of credit by export-oriented ready-made garment units operating under bonded a warehouse system; (c) Importable only by the Defence Services; (d) Importable by public sector agencies only on the basis of recommendation of Ministry of Textiles.
55.12 to 55.16	All HS codes	(a) Grey cloth, all sorts	(a) Importable subject to prescribed conditions in para. 24(7) of IPO.

		(b) Combat cloth	24(7) of IPO. (b) (ii) Importable only by the Defence Services.
56.08	All HS codes	Fishing nets	With the prior permission from the Director General, Fisheries Department only deep-sea fishing vessels shall be allowed to import nets with meshes of 4.5 cm or above under the Sea Fish Ordinance, 1983. The Director General, Fisheries Department shall give permission for an importer to import 4.5 cm radius/mesh-net up to a maximum of 8 (eight) bags/sacks per year per trawler.
60.01 and 60.02	All HS codes	Knit fabrics, mesh fabrics, pocketing cloth, ribbing materials and nylon satin	Importable against back-to-back letters of credit only by the export-oriented ready-made garment industry operating under a bonded warehouse system.
63.09	All HS codes	Second-hand clothing	Importable subject to prescribed conditions and procedure in para. 26(6) of IPO.
72.07	All HS codes	MS billets	Recognized industrial units shall import only prime qualities MS billets irrespective of the source of finance. Import of MS billets shall be subject to pre-shipment inspection by an internationally reputed surveyor. Necessary certificate regarding pre-shipment inspection shall be produced to the customs authority at the time.
72.10	All HS codes	CI sheet	CI sheet of 0.457 mm or more thickness containing a zinc coating of 381.45 gr or more per square metre will be freely importable. In addition, CI sheets, coloured or non-coloured, of 0.35 mm or more thickness containing a coating of alloy of zinc aluminium, etc. of 150 gr or more per square metre shall be importable.
84.01	All HS codes	Nuclear reactors and parts	Importable by the Bangladesh Atomic Energy Commission only with the clearance of the sponsoring ministry.
84.02 and 84.04	All HS codes	Boiler	Importable with the certificate from an internationally recognized and also government-approved pre-shipment inspection agent.
84.07 and 84.08	All HS codes	Second-hand engines and gearboxes	(a) Commercial import of second-hand/reconditioned engines and gear boxes of buses, trucks, minibuses and microbuses will be permissible, but such engines and gear boxes shall not be permissible for import if they are more than five years old. In this case a certificate regarding age limit, either from the exporting country's recognized chamber of commerce and industry or from an internationally reputed surveyor, shall be submitted to the customs authority at the time of release of the goods; (b) Second-hand/reconditioned marine diesel engines above 35 (thirty-five) horsepower used in coasters, launches and self-propelled barges and other watercrafts of this type will be commercially importable.
84.23	All HS codes	Weighing machines	Only weighing machines based on the metric system (in built-up or knocked-down condition) and the spares, metric system weights and measures shall be importable.
85.25	All HS codes	Radio transmitters and trans-receiver wireless equipment, walkie-talkie and other radio broadcast receivers, including	Importable by Radio Bangladesh and Bangladesh Television with clearance from the sponsoring ministry. Also importable by other government, semi-government and autonomous agencies on the basis of clearance from

		receivers incorporating sound recorders, or reproducers	the concerned administrative ministry and NOC from the Ministry of Posts and Telecommunications. Telecommunication equipment is also importable bythe private sector on the basis of NOC from the Ministry of Posts and Telecommunications.
85.26	All HS codes	Radio navigational aid apparatus, radar apparatus and radio remote control apparatus.	Importable by user agencies with clearance from the sponsoring ministry.
87.01 to 87.04	All HS codes	All types of motor vehicles and trucks	(a) Manufacturing age of the used reconditioned vehicles must not be more than five years at the time of shipment. In case of determining the date/age of the concerned vehicles, the age of the vehicle shall start counting from the first day of the next year of manufacture. In case of vehicles made in Japan, the date of manufacture shall be determined from the chassis book, published by the Japan Automobile Association. For the import of vehicles made in other countries where a chassis book is not published, the importer shall submit a certificate regarding the date of manufacture of the vehicle from an internationally reputed surveyor firm.
87.10	All HS codes	All items including tanks and armoured fighting vehicles	Importable only by the Ministry of Defence.
87.11	All HS codes	Less than 3 (three) years old motorcycles	(a) This three-year period will be calculated from the first day of the next calendar year of the manufacturing year. To determine the age of old motorcycles, a certificate from an internationally recognized and NBR approved inspection company may be accepted as an alternative to the registration cancellation certificate.
89.01 and 89.02	All HS codes	Seagoing ships, oil tankers and fishing trawlers	Ships, oil tankers and fishing trawlers more than 20 years old shall not be importable.
89.06	All HS codes	Warships of all kinds (both new and second-hand)	Importable only by the Ministry of Defence.
90.16	All HS codes	Weights and measures	Only metric system weights and measures and measuring instruments shall importable.
90.28	9028.90	Parts and components of electric meter and parts and components of single phase electric meter in CKD, SKD condition	Importable only by the recognized electric meter manufacturing industrial units as per their entitlement for the items.
93.01	9301.00	All items including military weapons	Importable only by the Ministry of Defence.
93.02	All HS codes	All items including revolvers and pistols	Importable by firearms dealers with the approval of Ministry of Home Affairs. Also importable as passenger baggage by a person holding a valid firearm licence and the prior permission from the Ministry of Commerce. Any person or private sector firm can import firearms through the TCB.
93.03 to 93.05	All HS codes	All items including firearms (excluding prohibited bores)	Importable by firearms dealers with the approval of Ministry of Home Affairs. Also importable as passenger baggage by a person holding a valid firearms licence and prior permission from the Ministry of Commerce. Any person or private sector firm can import firearms through the TCB.

93.06	All HS codes	(a) Ammunitions for spots, hunting etc. (b) Others	(a) Importable by firearms dealers with the approval of Ministry of Home Affairs Also importable as passenger baggage by a person holding a valid firearms licence and prior permission from the Ministry of Commerce. Any person or private sector firm can import firearms through the TCB. (b) Importable only by the Ministry of Defence.
93.07	All HS codes	All items including swords and bayonets	Importable only by user agencies with clearance from the sponsoring/administrative Ministry.

The following multiple HS heading items are importable on fulfilment of the conditions mentioned against each item.

Sl No.	Description	Application conditions
(1)	Animals plants and plant products	Quarantine conditions shall be applicable.
(2)	Second-hand/reconditioned machineries	Importable without any price limit. However, a certificate from an established internationally reputed surveyor to the effect that each machine has at least 10 (ten) years of economic life must be submitted along with a bill of lading.
(3)	Tyre cord fabric (secondary quality)	Tire cord fabric of secondary quality fit for making fishing nets shall be freely importable on commercial basis.
(4)	Food and beverage	In case of imports of all kinds of food and beverages, the date of manufacture and the date of expiry shall be clearly mentioned on each package/container of such items. However, it shall not be necessary to mention the date of expiry for the import of wine/liquor.
(5)	Pesticides and insecticides	In case of import of pesticides and insecticides, conditions mentioned in para. 26(5) of IPO shall be complied with. Moreover, pesticides will be determined as per the Pesticides Ordinance, 1971 (Ordinance No. 11 of 1971).

Source: Bangladesh, Import Policy Order 1997–2002.

LIST OF IMPORTS EXEMPTED FROM IMPORT LICENCE FEE

• Imports by any Department of the Government

• Imports by any local authority

•Imports by any recognized educational institution • Imports by any hospital financed or aided by or under the supervision of the Government or any local authority

Imports of phosphate

• Imports under the export promotion scheme or the export industries special licensing scheme

Imports for or on behalf of the President or under order of the Government Imports by the following officials or organizations

– United Nations officials

– Colombo Plan experts

- Ford Foundation personnel

- Bangladesh Red Cross Society

• Imports of vehicles, office equipment and spare parts by the International Rice Research InstituteDhaka

• Imports of equipment, machinery, vehicles, spare parts, chemicals under different aid anprogrammes by the Bangladesh Agricultural Research Institute

• Imports of goods exported from Bangladesh for purposes of exhibition,replacement free of charge Imports on a returnable basis, for bonded goods or for goods in transit Imports by oil production companies with which the Government has a profit-sharing in respect of such machinery and equipment that are only subject to a concessionary rate of customs duty not exceeding 51 per cent

• Imports of CKD components of one hand radios and CKD components of PO TV by approvedradio and TV manufacturing units

Imorts of capital machinery and spares for industrialization of areas other than those falling in the following police stations and upazilas (*subdistricts*), namely:

- Kotwali, Sutrapur, Laling, Dhanmondi, Ramna, Motjheel, Teignon, Damra,

Gulshan, Mirpur and Mohannadpur police stations and Savar and Keraniganj Upay

Dhaka district

- Tongi police station and gazipur and Kaliganj Upazilas of Gasipur district - Narayanganja, Bander, Fatulla and Siddhirganj Upazilas of Narayangonj district

- Narsin di Upazila of Narsingdi district

- Kotwali, Doublemooring, Chittagong Port and Panchlaish police stations and Hathazari, Sitakunda, Rangunia and Raozen Upayilas of Chittagong district

- Kotwali police station and Doulatpur and Phutala Upazilas of Khulna district • Imports of capital machineries along with initial spares for export-oriented industries, subject to a certificate issued by the Department of Industry

• Imports of any goods under specific agreem

Imorts under the following Heading Nos. and HS codes of the First Schedule to the Customs Ac 1969 (IV of 1969), namely: Headin

- g No. 12.09 - Heading Nos. 23.01 to 23.06 and HS code No. 2309.90.00

- HS code Nos. 2922.41.00, 2923.10.00, 2930.40.00, 2935.00.00, 2941.9030.02

LIST OF GOODS PROHIBITED FOR EXPORT

- Petroleum and petroleum products except naphtha, furnace oil, lubricant oil and bitumen. However, this prohibition shall not be applicable to the export of petroleum and LNG by foreign firms operating in Bangladesh under producti their share as agreed upon.

- Oil seeds and edible oil except Kapokthe country out of oil seeds and crude oil imported for export purposes may be exported subject to permission of the Ministry of Commerce. Jute seeds and sun hem seeds. Wheat.

- Molasses and Khandseri sugar.

- Live animals, all sorts and sLife (Preservation) Ordinance, 1973 (President's Ordinance No. 23 of 1973, as amen1974), except the species listed in the First Schedule of the Ordinance.

- Firearms, ammunitions, explosives and ingredien- Fissionable materials.

- Rare archaeological items. - Human skeleton, blood plasma or any other material produced out of human blood. Pulses, all sorts.

- Unfrozen and unprocessed prawns and shrimps. - Onions.

- Saline water shrimps of 71/90 counts or below except "harina" and "chaka" variety and fresh water shrimps of 61/70 counts or below. Rice bran except de-oiled rice bran. - Bamboo and cane in whole form and

LIST OF GOODS RESTRICTED FOR EXPORT

The following items are exportable under special permission of the Ministry of Commerce:

- Molasses: permissible on case-by-case basis

- De-oiled rice bran: permissible on a case-by-case basis only in instances where the Ministry/Directorates of Fisheries and Livestock fails to purchase the available stock within a reasonable time and price.

- Wheat bran: permissible only on a case-by-case basis only in instances where the Ministry/Directorates of Fisheries and Livestock fails to purchase the available stock within a reasonable time and price.

- Urea fertilizer: Export of urea fertilizer produced in the factories of the Bangladesh Chemical Industries Corporation (except Kanaphuli Fertilizer Company) is permissible only on the recommendation of the Ministry of Industries on a case-by-case basis.

- Cow and buffalo horns and hooves: permissible only on a case-by-case basis.

- Date-gur: half of the quantity produced in a year shall be exportable on a case-by-case basis.

Source: Bangladesh, Export Policy

TERMS OF INTELLECTUAL PROPERTY RIGHTS PROTECTION IN BANGLADESH

IPR	Main legislation	Duration of protection	Minimum duration of protection under the TRIPS	Comments
Copyrights	Copyright Ordinance, 1962, as amended by Copyright (Amendment) Act, 1974 and Copyright (Amendment) Ordinance, 1978	Life of author plus 50 years	Life of author plus 50 years	

- related rights		50 years from year of performance or fixation; 25 years from year of broadcast	50 years from year of performance or fixation; 20 years from year of broadcast	
Patents	Patents and Designs Act, 1911 and Patents and Designs Rules, 1933	16 years from date of application; renewable for 5 or 10 years	20 years from date of filing	Amendments extend to 20 years
Industrial designs	Patents and Designs Act, 1911 and Patents and Designs Rules, 1933	5 years; renewable for two successive 5-year periods	10 years	
Geographical indications	None	None	Unlimited	
Trademarks	Trade Marks Act, 1940, as amended by Trade Marks Rules, 1963	7 years from date of registration; renewable for periods of 15 years	At least 7 years; renewable indefinitely	
Layout designs of integrated circuits	None	None	10 years from first commercial exploitation	Amendments provide for 15 years
Undisclosed information	None	None	No specific period	

Source: **WTO, *Trade Policy Report: Bangladesh,* WT/TPR/S/68, (Geneva, WTO, July 2000, and based on information provided by the authorities of Bangladesh.**

LIST OF PERMITTED IMPORT ITEMS FOR EPZ INDUSTRIES

1	Woven dyed and printed fabrics
2	Knitted dyed and printed fabrics
3	Terry towels. Shop towels, surgical towels
4	Sewing yarn
5	Sweater yarn
6	Hand bag. School bag, luggage
7	Label, poly bag and other garments accessories
8	Padding and quilting material
9	Zipper
10	Carton box
11	Sports shoes, leather shoes
12	Electronic items
13	Electrical items
14	Circuit board
15	Audio and video tapes
16	Electronic ballasts
17	Software
18	Floppy diskette
19	Fan motor
20	Artificial flowers
21	Plastic bags
22	Printed jute bags and ropes
23	Vinyl belts
24	Toys

25	Chair, table, basket, folding and compact chair
26	Plywood
27	Aluminium ingots
28	Fishing reel and golf shaft
29	Metallic vehicle parts/machinery
30	Metallic pipe fittings
31	Steel marine chain
32	Bicycles
33	Bicycles parts
34	Dye cast parts
35	Marine/industrial mechanical parts
36	Plastic granules
37	Parts of optical instruments
38	Crystal blanks
39	Quartz crystal
40	Hanger and hanger accessories
41	Gloves

Source: Metropolitan Chamber of Commerce and Industry

AIRLINES REPRESENTATIVES

Air France 54, Motijheel C/A, Dhaka PABX : 9563050, 9561338, 9561337	Aeroflot Dhaka Sheraton Hotel, Dhaka Tel : 506636, 863391, 503056, 831422
Air India Dhaka Sheraton Hotel, Dhaka Tel : 505367, 602675, 863868	Biman Bangladesh Airlines Biman Balaka Bhaban, Kurmitola, Dhaka PABX : 897410-20
British Airways PLC Sena Kalyan Bhaban (8th floor) 195, Motijheel C/A, Dhaka PABX: 9564869-72, 9564840 FAX : 880-2-9564839, 894264	Emirates 64, Motijheel C/A, Dhaka Tel : 9563830, 9563825-9, 9563797, 9563813
Gulf Airways 10, Kawran Bazar, Dhaka Tel : 9563830, 9563825-9, 9563797, 9563813	Korean Airlines 64, Motijheel C/A, Dhaka Tel : 9563817-19
Japan Airlines 9E, Motijheel C/A, Dhaka Tel : 9559340, 9551334	KLM Royal Dutch Airlines 10, Kawran Bazar, Dhaka Tel : 813005, 815354, 815839
Lufthansa-German Airlines Dhaka Sheraton Hotel, Dhaka Tel :868995, 865913, 861191	Singapore Airlines Gulshan Tower (7th floor) Plot No. 31, Road No. 53 Gulshan-2, Gulshan, Dhaka Tel :871250-1, 871369-70, 871362
Pakistan International Airlines Dhaka Sheraton Hotel, Dhaka Tel : 832985, 883023, 502668, 863391/501112, 501155	Saudi Arabian Airlines (Saudia) Dhaka Sheraton Hotel, Dhaka Tel : 834720, 834711-19 FAX : 888-2-832984
Air France (AF) GSA Bengal Airlift Ltd. Ph: 9886634-7	Al Italia (AZ) GSA QC Shipping Ltd. BCIC Building (Ground Floor) 30-31, Dilksha C.A, Dhaka. Ph: 9558144
Myanmar Airlines Internationals	Cathay Pacific (CX)

GSA Wings Travels & Tours Ltd. SWH 4, Gulshan Avenue Gulshan-1, Dhaka Ph: 870579-80 Fax: 870274	GSA Vintage International Ltd. 57, Dilkusha C/A, Dhaka Ph: 9559721, 9557117
Ethiopian Airlines (ET) GSA MAAS travel & Tours Ltd. 16, Motijheel C/A, Dhaka Ph: 869976, 868663 Fax: 880-2-866983	Trans World Airline INC. (TWA) GSA HAC Enterprises Ltd. 5 Motijheel C/A, Dhaka Ph: 9552491, 9552208
United Airlines GSA United Link Ltd. Sena Kalyan Bhaban (18th Floor) 195, Motijheel C/A, Dhaka Ph: 862488, 9567379 Fax: 880-2-868697	KLM (KL) Royal Dutch Airlines GSA Travel Time Ltd. Kawran Bazar, Dhaka Ph: 813005, 81536-4 Fax: 880-2-813639
Korean Air (KE) GSA-ABC Air Ltd. 64, Motijheel C/A, Dhaka Ph: 8639845 Fax: 880-2-863252	Lufthansa- Germen Airlines (LN) GSA- Vantage Aviation Ltd. Dhaka Sheraton Hotel, Dhaka Ph: 868995, 865913
Malaysian Airlines System (MH) GSA Shahjalal Aviation System Sonargaon Hotel, Dhaka. Ph: 813112, 815113 811641 Extn: 4268	Philippine Airlines (Pr) GSA Maks (Pvt.) Ltd. 82, Kakrail, VIP Road, Dhaka Ph: 413339, 409126 Fax: 880-2-831751
Qantas (QF) GSA Bengal Airlift Ltd. Ph: 9886634-7	Japan Airlines Ltd. GSA Travel Ways Ltd. 9/E. Motijheel C/A, Dhaka Ph: 9550950, 9550340 Fax: 880-2-835265
Swiss Air (SR) GSA Thai Airways International Ltd. Dhaka Sheraton Hotel, Dhaka. Ph: 834711-19	Tour operators Bangladesh Parjatan Corporation (Nations Tourism Organization) 233, Airport Road, Tejgaon, Dhaka. Ph: 817855-9 Fax: 880-2-817235
Travel House Ltd. 8, Kamal Ataturk Avenue GPO Box # 3831, Banani, Dhaka Ph: 881726, 881825	The Guide Sector-7, Road-14, House 468 Rabindra Sarani, Uttra Model Town, Dhaka. Ph: 980365
Tour Bangla Ltd. 5/A, Eskaton Garden Road, Dhaka Ph: 831186	Sundarbands Tourist Complex 59, Kazi Nazrul Islam Avenue Airport Road, Dhaka Ph: 9118892
Unique Tours & Travels 51-b, Kamal Ataturk Avenue Banani, Dhaka Ph: 9885116-23	Vintage Tours & Travels Sonargaon Hotel Kawran Bazar, Dhaka Ph: 326920, 323986, 811005/4147
A. Intraco (BD) Ltd. 114, Motijheel C/A Red Crescent Building (2nd Flood), Dhaka Ph: 9554810, 9551313	Chittagong: Sute No 200, Hotel Agrabad Agrabad C/A, Chittagong Ph: 500111-10
Tour Planners Mohammadi Super Market (2nd Floor) 4, Sobhanbag, Dhaka-1207 Ph: 329897	Disover Tourism Ltd. 4 New Circular Road (3rd Floor) Malibagh, Dhaka Ph: 416788

Fax: 880-2-881986	
Eu-BA Tours (Bangladesh) Ltd. 35/1, Sonargaon Road, Dhaka Ph: 864094	Disover Toursm Ltd. 4 New Circular Road (3rd Floor) Malibagh, Dhaka Ph: 416788
EU-BA Tours (Bangladesh) Ltd. 35/1, Sonargaon Road, Dhaka Ph: 864094	

LONG DISTANCE AREA CODES FOR BANGLADESH

Barisal	0431	Bagerhat	0401
Bogra	051	Brahmanbaria	0851
Bhola	0491	Bandarban	0361
Barguna	0446	Chandpur	0841
Chittagong	031	Cox's Bazar	0341
Choumuhani	0321	Chuadanga	0321
Chapaninawabganj	0781	Chuadanga	0761
Comilla	081	Dhaka	02
Dinajpur	0531	Feni	0331
Faridpur	0631	Gopalganj	0423
Gazipur	0681	Hobiganj	0831
Ishwardi	0732	Jessore	0421
Jamalpur	0981	Khulna	041
Kurigram	0581	Kushtia	071
Khagrachari	0371	Moulavi Bazar	0861
Mongla	0402	Noakhali	0321
Natore	0771	Pabna	0731
Patuakhali	0441	Rangamati	0351
Sirajganj	0751	Shantahar	0741
Sylhet	0821	Tangail	0921
Lalmonirhat	0591	Magura	0611
Mymensingh	091	Naogaon	0741
Narayanganj	0671	Narshingdi	0621
Rajshahi	0721	Rangpur	0521
Thakurgaon	0561	Madaripur	0661
Manikganj	0651	Panchagar	0562
Nilphamari	0551	Satkhira	0471
Pirojpur	0461	Narail	0481
Joypurhat	0571	Meherpur	0791
Saidpur	0552	Rajbari	0641
Munshiganj	0691	Sherpur	0951

Netrakona	0951	Jhenaidah	0451
Jhalokathi	0496		

DIPLOMATIC MISSIONS IN BANGLADESH

AFGHANISTAN Houe No. CWN ©-2A Road No. 24, Gulshan Dhaka-1212 Phone : 603232, 600394	AUSTRALIA 184, Gulshan Avenue Gulshan, Dhaka-1212 Tel : 873101-5 Fax : 880-2-871125, 883794
BELGIUM 22 Gulshan Avenue Dhaka-1212 Tel : 600138, 604249 Fax : 880-2-883939	BRAZIL House No. CEN(D) 14 Road No. 101 Dhaka-1212 Tel : 605390, 606911 Fax : 880-2-883330
CANADA House No. 16A, Road 48 Gulshan, Dhaka-1212 Tel : 607071-7, 883639 Fax : 880-2-883043	CHINA Plot No. 2 & 4, Road No. 3 Block-1, Banani, Dhaka Tel : 884862, 884164 Fax : 880-2-830004
DENMARK House NW(H)1, Raod 51 Gulshan, Dhaka-1212 Tel : 881799 Fax : 880-2-883638	EGYPT House No. New 9 Road No. 90, Gulshan Dhaka-1212 Tel : 882766-7 Fax : 880-2-884883
EUROPEAN COMMUNITIES (EC) Plot No. 7, Road No. 84 Gulshan, Dhaka-1212 Tel : 884730-2, 607017 Fax : 880-2-883118	FRANCE Road No. 18, House No. 108 Gulshan, Dhaka-1212 Tel : 607083-4 Fax : 880-2-883612
GERMANY 178 Gulshan Avenue Dhaka- 1212 Tel : 884735-7 Fax : 880-2-883574	HOLY SEE (VATICAN) United Nations Road No.2 Baridhara, Dhaka Tel : 882018, 882143 Fax : 880-2-883574
HUNGARY 80, Gulshan Avenue Dhaka Tel : 608101-12 Fax : 880-2-883117	INDIA House No. 120, Road No. 2 Dhanmondi R/A, Dhaka Tel : 503606, 504166 Fax : 880-2-863662
INDONESIA 75, Gulshan Avenue Dhaka-1212 Tel : 9881640-1 Fax : 880-2-885391	IRAN House No. 7, Road No. 6 Baridhara, Dhaka Tel : 885948,885896, 603948 Fax : 880-2-883167
IRAQ 112, Gulshan Avenue Dhaka-1212 Tel : 600298, 600299 Fax : 880-2-882377	ITALY Plot No. 2 & 3 Road No. 74/79 Gulshan, Dhaka-1212 Tel : 882781-3 Fax : 880-2-882578
JAPAN	KOREA. DPR

Plot No. 5 & 7 Dutabash Road Baridhara, Dhaka Tel : 870087 Fax : 880-2-886737	House No. 6, Road No. 7 Baridhara, Dhaka Tel : 601250, 606358 Fax : 880-2-80813
KOREA, REPUBLIC House No. New(E)17 Road No. 55 Gulshan, Dhaka-1212 Tel : 872088-90 Fax : 880-2-883871	KUWAIT House - SE(D) (5,26) South Link Road Gulshan, Dhaka-1212 Tel : 882700-3 Fax : 880-2-883753
LIBIYA 4 (CWN © Gulshan Avenue, Dhaka-1212 Tel : 600148(9) Fax : 880-2-883417	MALAYSIA House No. 4, Road No. 118 Gulshan, Dhaka-1212 Tel : 887759-61 Fax : 880-2-883115
MOROCCO House No. 44 United Nations Road Baridhara, Dhaka Tel : 9880329, 883176 Fax : 880-2-870018	MAYANMAR (BURMA) 106 Gulshan Avenue Dhaka-1212 Tel : 601915, 601461
NEPAL United Nations Road No. 2 Baridhara, Diplomatic Enclave Dhaka Tel : 602091, 601790, 601890 Fax : 880-2-886401	NETHERLANDS House No. 49, Road No. 90 Gulshan, Dhaka-1212 Tel : 882715-8 Fax : 880-2-883326
NORWAY House No. 9, Road No. 111 Gulshan, Dhaka-1212 Tel : 883880, 870563, 883065 Fax : 880-2-883661	PAKISTAN House No. NE© 2 Roa dNo. 71 Gulshan, Dhaka Tel : 885388(9) Fax : 880-2-883677
PHILIPPINES House - 7, Block-21 Baridhara, Dhaka Tel : 600077, 605945, 883686 Fax : 880-2-883097	POLAND House No. 11, Road No. 77 Gulshan, Dhaka-1212 Tel : 606098, 608503 Fax : 880-2-8713458
QATAR House No. 23, Road No. 108 Gulshan, Dhaka-1212 Tel : 604477-8 Fax : 880-2-883950	RUSSIAN FEDERATION House No. NE(J)9, Road - 79 Gulshan, Dhaka-1212 Tel : 601050, 888147, 888142 Fax : 880-2-883735
ROMANIA House - 33, Road No. 74 Gulshan, Dhaka-1212 Tel : 600128, 882502	SAUDI ARABIA House No. 12 (New) Road No. 92 Gulshan, Dhaka-1212 Tel : 889123-31, 889133-35 Fax : 880-2-883616.
SRILANKA House 22, Road No. 56 Gulshan, Dhaka-1212 Tel : 870779, 603048 Fax : 880-2-883971	SWEDEN House No. 1, Road No. 31 Gulshan, Dhaka-1212 Tel : 884761-4 Fax : 880-2-883948
SWITZERLAND	TURKEY

House No. 31B, Road No. 18 Banani, Dhaka Tel : 872874-6 Fax : 880-2-883872	House No. 7, Road 62 Gulshan, Dhaka-1212 Tel : 882198, 883536 Fax : 880-2-883873
THAILAND House No. NW(D)12 Road No. 58/62 Gulshan, Dhaka-1212 Tal : 873261 Fax : 880-2-883588	UAE House No. CEN(H) 41 Road No. 113 Gulshan, Dhaka Tel : 9882244, 9882255
UK United Nations Road Baridhara, Dhaka Tel : 882705-9 Fax : 880-2-883437, 882666, 883474	USA Madani Avenue, Baridhara Dhaka Tel : 884700-22 Fax : 880-2-883744
BANGLADESH MISSIONS ABROAD (Cable addresses for all mission BANGLADOOT)	AUSRTARLIA 35, Endeavour Street Canberra A.C.T. 2603 Tel (06) 2953328 Fax : 006-6-2953351, 2950032
BAHRAIN House No. 159, Road No. 2004 Block No. 320 Area Hoora, Manama, Bahrain Tel : 293371-2, 293374 Fax : (0973) 291272	KINGDOM OF BELGIUM 29-31 Rue Jacques Jordaens 1050 Brussels Tel : (02) 6405500, 6405606 Fax : 32-2-6465998
THE KINGDOM OF BHUTAN Plot No. HIG G-3, Upper Chubachu Thimphu, Bhutan Tel : 22539 Fax : 975-22629	FERDERATIVE REPUBLIC OF BARAZIL SHIS QL-10, Conj, 01, Casa-17 Brasila-DF Barzil CEP : 70468-900 Tel : 248-4820, 248-4905 Fax : 55-61-2484, 609
CANADA 275 Bank Street Suite-302 Ottawa, Ontaria K2P2L6 Tel : (613) 236-0138 & 236-0139 Fax : (613) 567-3213	REPUBLIC OF FRANCE 5, Square Petraque 75016 Paris, France Tel : 47049435, 45534120 Fax : (33-1) 47047241
REPUBLIC OF GERMANY Bonner Stress 48, 53173 Bonn Tel : 0228-352525, 362940 Tix : 885640 Bangd Fax : 0228-354142	HONG KONG Room 3807, Chian Resources Building 26, Harbour Road, wanchai, Hong Kong Tel : 8274278-9 Fax : (852) 8271916
PEOPLE'S REPUBLIC OF CHINA 42, Guang Hua Lu, Beijing-100600 Tel : 65322521, 65323706 Fax : 65324346	ARAB REPUBLIC OF EGYPT 47, Ahmed Heshma St. Zamalek, Cairo Tel : 3412645, 3402401 Fax : 002-02-3612951
REPUBLIC IF INDIA 56, Ring Road, Laipat Nagar III New Delhi-110024 Tel : 6824065, 6834668 Fax : 91-11-6839237 E. Mail. Bdoot.del@smv.	CALCUTA 9, Circus Avenue Calcutta-700 017 Tel : 247-5208, 247-0341 Fax : 91-33-2470941 Email : BDHC@CIRRUS.

F. Springtrpg. Ems.usne.net.in	WBBLS.Com.
AGARTALA (VISA OFFICE) Kunjaban Road Agartala-799006 West Tripura Tel : 224807, 225260	REPUBLIC OF INDONESIA Jalan Denpasar Raya No. 3 Block A-13 Kav 10, Kuningan Jakarta Tel : 5251986, 5221574 Fax : 62-21-5261807
ISLAMIC REPUBLIC OF IRAN Ave, Gandhi, Street No. 5 Building No. 14, Tehran, Iran Tel : 8772979-80 Fax : 009821-8778295	REPUBLIC OF IRAQ House No. 6, Road Np. 14 Sector 929, Hai Al Babel Meshah, Bangdad Tel : 719667, 7190063 Fax : 7186045
ITALY Via Antonio Bertoloni-14 Rome - 00197 Tel : 8083595, 8078541 Fax : (396) 8084853	MALAYSIA 204-1, JALAN AMPANG 50450 KUALA LAMPUR Tel : 2423271, 2422505 & 2487940 Fax : 82-2-790-5313
JAPAN 4-15-15, Meguor Meguro-Ku tokyo, 153, Japan Tel : 5704-0216-8 Fax : 5704-1669	KENYA Ole Odume Road P.O. Box 41645 Nairobi, Kenya Tel : 562815-6 Fax : 254-2-901866
LIBYA Hadba El-Khadra, Vill Oman El-Wershafani P.O. Box No. 5086, Tripoli Tel : 903807, 900856 Fax : 218-21-901866	THE UNION OF MYANMAR 56, Kaba Aya Pagoda Road Yangoon, Myanmar Tel : 549556-7 Fax : 095-1-548745
SITTWE (MYANMAR) Main Road, South Lanmadaw Quarters Rakhine State Sittwee Myanmar Tel : 21126, 21968	KUWAIT House No. 3, Block 1 Street 14, Khaldia Tel : 4834078, 48113669 Fax : (965) 4831603
MOROCCO 25, Avenue Tarik Lbn Ziad Rabat, Morocco Tel : (212)-7-760963 7-766711, 7-766713 Fax : 212-7-766729	KINGDOM OF NEPAL Maharajganj Ring Road Kathmondu Municipality Work No. 22 Shanti Ashram, Kitta No. 9 Kathmandu Twl : 414943, 414265 Fax : 977-1-414265
SULTANATE OF OMAN Plot No. 181, Momtaz Area, P.O. Box. No. 3959, Rawi, Muscat Tel : 707462, 708756, 703155 Fax : 0098-708495	THE ISLAMIC REPUBLIC OF PAKISTAN House No. 1, Street No. 5 F-6/3, Islamabad Tel : 279267 Fax : 279266
KARACHI PAKISTAN 9 Choudhury Khaliaquzzaman Road Karachi 0401, Pakistan Tel : 5683984, 5660702, 5683537 Fax : 92-21-5682303	REPUBLIC OF PHILIPPINES 106, Paseo de resas Universal Re Building (2nd floor) Makati Metro Manila Tel : 817-5001, 817-5010 Fax : 00632-816-4941

REPUBLIC OF POLAND Hl Rejtna 15, m-2021 02516 Warsaw Tel :480637,483200,480540 Fax : 48-22-484974	STATE OF QATAR Villa. No.13, St No. 810 42 Ibn Bajah, Opp: Doha Cinema P.O. Box No. 2080, Doha Tel: 673471, 671927 Fax: (0974) 671190
RUSSAIN FEDERATION Zemledel si Pereulok-6 Moskow-119121 Tel: 246-79-00 Fax: 248-3185	KINGDOM OF SAUDI ARABIA, RIYADH Sulaimaniya, al-waroud Quarter North of Aruba Street, House No 50 Sulamaniya, Riyadh Tel: 4655300, 46419554, 4641594 Fax: 4633555
JEDDAH Kilo 3, Makkah Road, (Behind Mitsubrish Car Office) Jeddah, KSA Tel: 6878456, 6894712 Fax: 6800392	SENEGAL Immeuble Kebe, 7th Floor Avenue Andre Peytavin Dakar Tel: 216881 Fax: 221-225017
SINGAPORE 06-07 United Square, 101 Thomson Road, Singapore 1120 Tel: 2550075, 2545797 Fax: (065) 2551824	SOUTH AFRICA 410, Farendern Street, Sunnyside Pretoria 00002 Tel: (012) 3432105-7 Fax: (012) 3435222
DEMOCRATIC SOCIALIST REPUBLIC OF SRILANKA 286, Bauddhaloka Mawata Colombo-7, Srianka Tel: 502198, 502397 Fax: 00941-508123	SWEDEN Sturegatan 6 (3rd Floor) 114-35 Stockholm Tel: 08-679 9555, 679 9560, 679 9565 Fax: 08-611-9817
SWITZERLAND UN OFFICES GENEVA 65, Rau de Lausanne 1202 Geneva Tel: 7325940, 7325949, 732139 Fax: (41-22) 738-4616	THAILAND House No. 727, Thonglor, Soi-55 Sukhvit Road, Bangkok, Thailand Tel: 392-9437, 392-9438 Fax: (662) 391-8070
REPUBLIC OF TURKEY 78/7-10 Cinnah Caddesi, Cankaya, Ankara Tel: 432750, 4392751 Fax: (312) 4392408	UNITED ARAB EMIRATES Vill No. 32. Khalidya Abu Dhabi, U.A.E. Tel: 668375 Fax: 667324 (Abu Dhabi)
DUBAI Vill No. 32. Khalidya Abu Dhabi, U.A.E. Tel: 668375 Fax: 667324 (Abu Dhabi)	UNITED KINGDOM 28, Quee's Gate London SW 7 5JA Tel: 01-1-584-0081 Fax: 071-225-2130
BIRMINGHAM (U.K) 31-33 Guildhall Building 12, Navigation Street, Birmingham, B2 4BT Tel : 0121-643-2386 Fax : 0121-643-9004	MANCHESTER (U.K.) 28-32 Princess Street Manchester, M1 4LB Tel : 0161-236-4853 Fax : 0161-236-1064
UNITED STATES OF AMERICA 2201 Wisconsin Avenue N.W.	UZBEKISTAN 12 Khlopkouborochnaya

Suite 300-325 Washington-D.C. 2007 Tel : (202) 342 8372-76 Fax : (212) 972-4038	Dist. M. Ulugbeg Taskent, 700007 Tel : (703712) 891712, 689929 Fax : (7-3712) 891711
VIETNAM House no. 1D Appartment 101-104 Van Phuc Diplomatic Area-1, Hanol Tel : 84-48231625 Fax : 84-4-231628	ZIMBABWE 44 Dowine Avenue Belgravia Tel : 263-4-4307714 Fax : 263-4-4336389

LARGEST BANKS

Sonali Bank
Head Office, Mitijheel C.A, Dhaka
Tel: 9550426-34, Fax: 9561410

Agrani Bank
Head Office, Motijheel C.A, Dhaka
Tel: 9566160-69, 9566153-54, Fax: 9562346, 9563662

Janata Bank
Head Office, Motijheel C.A, Dhaka
Tel: 9560000, 9560027-30, Fax: 9564644

Bangladesh Shilpa Bank
BSB Bhaban, 8, Rajuk Avenue, Dhaka
Tel: 9555151-59, 9560013-15, Fax: 880-2-9562061, E-Mail: bsblink@citechco.net

Investment Corporation of Bangladesh
BSB Bhaban (12-15 Floor), 8, Rajuk Avenue, Dhaka- 1000,
Tel: 9563455-57, 9563495-97, Fax: 880-2-9563313

Bangladesh Krishi Bank
Head Office, 83-85, Motijheel C.A, Dhaka- 1000,
Tel: 9560021-25, Fax: 880-2-9561211

Rupali Bank Ltd
Head Office, Rupali Bhaban, 34, Dilkusha C.A, Dhaka- 1000,
Tel: 9551624-25, 9554122, Fax: 880-2-9564148

Pubali Bank Ltd
Head Office, 26, Dilkusha C.A, Dhaka- 1000
Tel: 9569050-52, 9551614-17, Fax: 880-2-9564009

Uttara Bank Ltd
Head Office, 90, Motijheel C.A, Dhaka- 1000,
Tel: 9551162, 9565732, Fax:880-2-863539, 9553081

International Finance Investment and Commerce Bank Limited
BSB Building (17th & 19th Floor), 8, Rajuk Avenue, Dhaka- 1000
Tel: 9563020, 9562062, Fax: 880-2- 9562015

Southest Bank Limited
1, Dilkusha C.A, (3rd Floor), Dhaka- 1000
Tel: 9550081-85, 9567271-72, Fax: 880-2-9550093

National Bank Limited
18, Dilkusha C.A, Dhaka- 1000
Tel: 9563081-85, Fax: 880-2- 9563953 & 9569404

The City Bank Ltd
10, Dilkusha C.A, Dhaka- 1000
Tel: 9565925-34, Fax: 880-2- 9562347

United Commercial Bank Ltd
59-60, Motijheel C.A, Dhaka- 1000
Tel: 9555075-77, Fax: 880-2-9560587

Islami Bank Bangladesh Ltd
71, Dilkusha C.A, Dhaka- 1000
Tel: 9563046-49, Fax: 880-2-9564532, E-Mail: ibbl@ncll.com

Prime Bank Limited
Adamjee Court Annex Building
119-120, Motijheel C.A, Dhaka- 1000, Tel: 9567265-70,

Bank of Small Industries and Commerce (Bangladesh) Ltd
Sena Kalyan Bhaban (6th Floor), 195, Motijheel C.A, Dhaka- 1000
Tel: 9568190, 9567910, Fax: 880-2-9564829

Grameen Bank
Mirpur, Section-2, Dhaka, Tel: 805755-58

Eastern Bank Ltd
10, Dilkusha C.A, Dhaka- 1000
Tel: 9556360-70, Fax: 880-2-9562364

National Credit and Commerce Bank Limited

7-8, Motijheel C.A, Dhaka- 1000,
Tel: 867857-61, Fax: 880-2-9566290

Dhaka Bank limited
Adamjee Court, 115-120, Motijheel C/A, Dhaka-1000,
Tel: 9556587-94, Fax: 880-2-9556584

INSURANCE COMPANIES

Bangladesh National Insurance Co. Ltd
21, Rajuk Avenue, Motijheel C/A,Dhaka-1000.
Tel: 9559547

Bangladesh Co-Operative Insurance Ltd.
Sena Kalyan Bhaban, 195, Motijheel C/A, Dhaka-1000
Tel: 9561121, 9555645

Bangladesh Genaral Insurance Co. Ltd.
42, Dilkusha C/A, Dhaka-1000.
Tel: 9550379, 9564213

Central Insurance Co. Ltd.
Uttara Bank Bhaban, 90-91, Motijheel C/A, Dhaka-1000.
Tel: 9560254, 9567421-2

City General Insurance Co. Ltd.
Baitul Hossain Building (3rd Floor), 27, Dilkusha C/A, Dhaka- 1000
Tel: 9564033

Eastern Insurance Co. Ltd.
44, Dilkusha C/A, Dhaka-1000.
Tel: 9552759, 9563033-4

Eastland Insurance Co. Ltd.
13, Dilkusha C/A, Dhaka-1000.
Tel: 9563928, 9560048-9

Federal Insurance Co. Ltd.
122-124, Motijheel C/A, Dhaka-1000.
Tel: 9562877, 9560003-4

Green Delta Insurance Co. Ltd.
Hadi Mansion(4th Floor), 2, Dilkusha C/A, Dhaka-1000.
Tel: 9552188, 9560005-6

Janata Insurance Co. Ltd.
125, Motijheel C/A, Dhaka-1000.
Tel: 9560141, 9563438

Karnaphuli Insurance Co. Ltd.
Sena Kallyan Bhaban, 195, Motijheel C/A, Dhaka-1000.
Tel: 9561150, 9564808-9

Mercantile Insurance Company Ltd.
61, Motijheel C/A, Dhaka- 1000
Tel: 9557662-4, 9557665

Meghna Insurance Co. Ltd.
73, Motijheel C/A, Dhaka- 1000
Tel: 9554989, 9557796

Northern General Insurance Co. Ltd.
128, Motijheel C/A, Malek Mansion (2nd Floor), Dhaka-1000.
Tel: 9559077

People's Insurance Co. Ltd.
Senakalyan Bhaban, 195, Motijheel C/A, Dhaka-1000.
Tel: 9564797-8

Pragati Insurance Limited
Uttara Bank Bhaban, 90-91, Motijheel C/A, Dhaka-1000.
Tel: 9561385

Phoenix Insurance Co. Ltd.
Purbani Annexe Building, 1/A, Dilkusha C.A, Dhaka 1000
Tel: 9563608

Purabi General Insurance Co. Ltd.
23 Motijheel C.A., Dhaka- 1000
Tel: 9566006-7

Prime Insurance Company Ltd.
63 Dilkusha C.A., Dhaka 1000
Tel: 9552742

Provati Insurance Co.Ltd.
Khan Mansion, (11th floor), 107 Motijheel C.A, Dhaka 1000
Tel: 9559561-3

Pioneer Insurance Co. Ltd
Jiban Bima Tower,(6th floor), 10 Dilkusha C.A.,Dhaka 1000
Tel: 9557674-5

Rupali Insurance Co. Ltd.
Rupali Bima Bhaban, 7 Rajuk Avenue,Dhaka-1000
Tel: 9565628

Reliance Insurance Limited
BSB Building, 8 Rajuk Avenue, Dhaka-1000.
Tel: 9560105-6

United Insurance Co. Ltd.
Camellia House, 22 Kazi Nazrul Islam Avenue, Dhaka-1000
Tel: 862159

Leasing Companies

International Development Leasing Comany of Bangladesh Ltd. (IDLC)
Hadi Mansion (6th Floor), 2, Dilkusha C/A, Dhaka-1000
Tel: 9560111-3, 9563619, Fax: 9563620

Phoenix Leasing Company
Shadhinata Bhaban, (1st Floor), 88, Motijheel C/A, Dhaka- 1000
Tel: 9569007-10, Fax: 813417, E-Mail: phoenix@bangla.net

United Leasing Company (ULC)
Camilia House, (Gr. Floor), 22, Kazi Nuzrul Islam Avenue, Dhaka- 1000
Tel: 869336-8, Fax: 863570

Industrial Promotion and Development Company of Bangladesh Limited (IPDC)
Chamber Building (6th Floor), 122-124, Motijheel C/A, Dhaka- 1000
Tel: 9559311-2, 9553254, Fax: 9565493

Micro Industrial Development Assistance Security (MIDAS)
House No. 5, Road No. 16, Dhanmondi R/A, Dhaka- 1205
Tel: 9110335-6, 9110680

Industrial Finance Ltd.
79, Green Road , Dhaka- 1205
Tel: 814253, Fax: 811449

United Leasing Co. Ltd.
Camilia House, 22, Kazi Nuzrul Islam Avenue, Dhaka- 1000
Tel: 869366, 869336-8, Fax: 863576

Prime Finance & Investment Ltd.
63, Dilkusha C/A, Dhaka- 1000
Tel: 9563678, 9563860, 9563868, Fax: 880-2-9563692

LEADING CHAMBERS AND TRADE PROMOTION ORGANIZATIONS IN BANGLADESH

CHAMBERS

The Federation of Bangladesh Chambers of Commerce and Industry
"Federation Bhaban", 60 Motijheel C/A, 3rd Floor, G P O Box: 2079, Dhaka –1000
Tel: 864760, 282880, 257734, PABX: 240102-3, Fax : 880-2-863213
Cab: FEDCOMERCE, Dhaka, Tlx: 632412 FBCCI BJ

The Dhaka Chamber of Commerce and Industry
65-66, Motijheel C/A, Dhaka-1000, Bangladesh
Tel : 9552562 (Hunting Line), Fax : 880-2-9560830, e-mail : dcci@bangla.net

Metropolitan Chamber of Commerce and Industry,(MCCI)
Chamber Building,
122-124, Motijheel C/A., Dhaka-1000,
Tel: 9565208-10, Fax : 880-2-9565212

Bangladesh Chamber of Industries
BCIC Building, 30-31, Dilkusha C/A, (3RD FL.) Dhaka-1000,
G.P.O. Box: 3988, Dhaka -1000, Tel: 9566704, 9567120

International Chamber of Commerce – Bangladesh
National Secretariat : DCCI Building, 65-66 Motijheel C/A, Dhaka- 1000
Tel: 9557478, 9667273, Fax : 9557429, E-mail : iccb@citechco.net

Foreign Investors Chamber of Commerce and Industry, (FICCI)
"Mahbub Castle" (4th Fl), 35-1, Purana Paltan Line, Inner Circular Road, Dhaka
Tel: 839448, 412877, Fax: 880-2-839449

Chittagong Chamber of Commerce and Industry (CCCI)
Chamber House, P.O. Box: No. 481, Agrabad C/A, Chittagong,
Tel: 880-31-713366-9, 711356, 711355

Rajshahi Chamber of Commerce & Industry (RCCI)
P.O. Ghoramara, Station Road, Rajshahi
Tel: (0721) 772412, 772115

Sylhet Chamber of Commerce and Industry (SCCI)
Chamber Building, P.O. Box: No. 97, Jail Road, Sylhet,
Tel: (0821) 714403, 716069, 715110,

Khulna Chamber of Commerce & Industry (KCCI)
"Chamber Mansion" 5 K. D. A. Commercial Area, P.O.Box: 26, Khan A. Sobur Road, Khulna
Tel: (041) 21745, 24135, 20186, 21695.

Barisal Chamber of Commerce and Industry (BCCI)
Shaw Road (Nazirer Pool), P.O. Box: 30, Barisal,
Tel: (0431) 3064

TRADE PROMOTION ORGANISATIONS

Ministry of Industries
Shilpa Bhaban, Motijheel C/A, Dhaka- 1000
Tel: 9567024, Fax: 860588

Board of Investment
Jiban Bima Tower (1st Floor)
10, Dilkusha C/A, Dhaka- 1000
Tel: 9563570, 9567541, Fax: 9562312
E-mail: ecby@bdmail.net

Ministry of Commerce
Bangladesh Secretariat
Dhaka- 1000
Tel: 869006

Ministry of Finance
Bangladesh Secretariat
Dhaka- 1000
Tel: 860406

Ministry of Science and Technology
Bangladesh Secretariat
Dhaka-1000

National Board of Revenue
Segun Bagicha, Dhaka
Tel: 838120-26 & 838101-08, Fax: 836143

Export Promotion Bureau (EPB)
122-124, Motijheel C/A, Dhaka- 1000
Tel: 9552245-9, Fax: 9568000
E-mail: epd.tic@pradeshta.net

Tariff Commission
12-Storied Building (9th Floor)
New Secretariat
Segun Bagicha, Dhaka
Tel: 834542, 9335933

Bangladesh Small & Cottage Industries Corporation
137-138, Motijheel C/A, Dhaka- 1000
Tel: 9556191-92 & 9553293

Bangladesh Handicrafts Manufacturers & Exporters Association (Banglacrafts)
13, Gaus Nagar, New Eskaton Road
Dhaka- 1000
Tel: 889123, 887260, Fax: 888564

Bangladesh Export Processing Zones Authority
222, New Eskaton Road, Dhaka
Tel: 832553, 9348455

HOTELS

Dhaka: (NWD Code: 02)Shonargaon (Five Star: Ph: 811005, 812011, 811641), Sheraton (Three Star: Ph: 863391, 861191), 864065, Abakash (Ph : 607085-9, 881548), Purbani (Ph : 9552229, 9563624), Sundarban (Ph : 505055-9, 503982), Zakaria (Ph : 885003-4), Al-Helal (Ph. 406533, 409002-5), Blue Nile (Ph : 509416), Metropolitan (Ph. 9554683-7), Park International (Ph : 405191-2), YMCA (Ph : 417621, 418939), Hotel Midway International (Ph : 407568, 9331 086), White House (Ph : 834020), Hotel Pritom (Ph : 9564339), Hotel Nidmohal (Ph : 9111576), Dhaka Hotel (Ph : 9553430), Hotel Midtown (Ph: 883698)

Chittagong : (NWD Code: 031)Agrabad (Ph : 713311-8), Shaikat (Ph : 619845, 611046-8), Shahjahan (Ph : 615643), Miska, Safina (Ph : 614318-9) Meridian (Ph : 210371, 212538).

Rangamati : (NWD Code : 0351)Parjatan Motel (Ph :3126), Parjatan Cottages (Ph : 3126), Shapla (Ph:3393), Hiramon (Ph:3390)

Cox's Bazar: (NWD Code: 0341)Parjatan Hotels : Shaibal (Ph : 3275), Upal (Ph : 4258), Probal (Ph : 3211), Cottages (Ph : 4246), Youth Inn (Ph. 3403), Saymon (Ph : 4231, 4075, 3255), Hotel Sea Queen (Ph :3789) Hotel Palanky (Ph : 3667), Hotel Panwa (Ph : 3282), Hotel Shagargaon (Ph : 4248), Hotel S.K. International (Ph : 3830, 3874), Hotel Marmed (Ph : 3683), Hotel Al-Amin (Ph : 3480), Hotel Tajsheba (Ph : 4583) Hotel Niribily (Ph: 3279), Hotel Nishitha (Ph : 4014), Hotel Holiday (Ph : 3875), Hotel Coxwan (Ph : 3566), Hotel United (Ph : 3471), Hotel Bilkis (Ph : 3962, 3942), Hotel Kohinur (Ph : 3470)

Sylhet: (NWD Code: 0821)Parjatan Motel (Ph : 712426), Hiltown (Ph : 713390), Anurag (Ph: 716716, 715717), Hotel Palash (Ph 718811)

Bogra : (NWD Code: 051)Parjatan Motel (Ph :6753)
Rajshahi : (NWD Code: 0721)
Parjatan Motel (Ph : 775492, 775237)

Rangpur : (NWD Code : 0521)
Parjatan Motel (Ph : 2111, 3900, 3784, 2911).
Khulna : (NWD Code: 041)
Royal (Ph: 21638-9), Rupsha (Ph: 60563), Park (Ph: 20990, 24077, Selim (Ph: 20191, 24711)
Jessore : (NWD Code: 0421)
Midtown (Ph: 6501)
NWD = Nationwide Dialing
ISD Code for Bangladesh = 880

AIR LINES

AEROFLOT
Dhaka Sheraton Hotel, Dhaka, Tel: 506636, 863391, 861191

AIR FRANCE
54, Motijheel C/A, Dhaka- 1000, Tel: 9563050, 9561338, 9561337

AIR INDIA
Dhaka Sheraton Hotel, Dhaka, Tel: 505367, 863868, 863391/8562

BIMAN BANGLADESH AIRLINES
100, Motijheel C/A, Dhaka- 1000, Tel: 9560151-89, 894771-79 (Airport)

BRITISH AIRWAYS PLC
Sena Kalyan Bhaban (8th Floor), 195, Motijheel C/A, Dhaka- 1000
Tel: 9564869-72, 9664840, Fax: 9564839, 894264

EMIRATES
64, Motijheel C/A, Dhaka- 1000, Tel: 9563830, 9563825-9

GULF AIRWAYS
10,Kawran Bazar, Dhaka, Tel: 813236, 813238-39

KOREAN AIRLINES
64, Motijheel C/A, Dhaka- 1000, Tel: 9563817, 9563818-9

INDIAN AIRLINES
Dhaka Sheraton Hotel, Dhaka, Tel: 863613, 861191/665

JAPAN AIRLINES
9/E, Motijheel C/A, Dhaka- 1000, Tel: 9559340, 9551334

KLM ROYAL DUTCH AIRLINES
10, Kawran Bazar, Dhaka, Tel: 813005, 815354, 815839

LUFTHANSA-GERMAN AIRLINES
Dhaka Sheraton Hotel, Dhaka, Tel: 868995, 865913, 861191/ 8671

SINGAPORE AIRLINES
Gulshan Tower (7th Floor), Plot No. 31, Road No. 53, Gulshan-2, Dhaka
Tel: 871250-1, 871369-70

PAKISTAN INTERNATIONAL AIRLINES
Dhaka Sheraton Hotel, Dhaka, Tel: 832985, 883023, 863391/ 8595

SAUDI ARABIAN AIRLINES (SAUDIA)
Sonargaon Hotel, Dhaka, Tel: 816859, 816860, 811641/ 4252

THAI AIRWAYS INTERNATIONAL LTD
Dhaka Sheraton Hotel, Dhaka, Tel: 834711-19, 834720, Fax: 880-2-832984

SHIPPING COMPANIES

AQUAMARINE LTD. (AQM)
Ahmed Mansion (1st Fl), 24, Santinagar, Chamelibagh, Dhaka-1217, P.O.Box: No. 3241, Tel: 836548, 836401-2 (DH), Tlx: 642854, 632416 AML BJ, Fax: 833929

ATLAS SHIPPING LINES LTD. (ASLL)
Hadi Mansion (9th Floor), 2, Dilkusha C/A, Dhaka- 1000,
Tel: 9556332, 9557465, 9557025, Tlx: 632461, 671078 ASLL BJ

BANGLADESH SHIPPING CORPORATION (BSC)
BSC Bhaban,Saltgola Road, P.O. Box No. 641, Chittagong,
Tel: 505061-9, 501053-56, 502290, 501855 (Direct), Tlx: 66277, 66359 & 66253 BSC BJ,Cable: BANGLASHIP CTG. Fax: 031-710506 & 501288
Dhaka Office: 28/1, Toyenbee Circular Road, Motijheel C/A, Dhaka- 1000
Tel: 9553524, 9553521, 9553585, Tlx: 632204, 642231 BSC BJ. Fax: 9565589

BANGLADESH SHIPPING AGENCIES (PVT) LTD. (BAS)
C/o. Shatabdi Aviation (Pvt) Ltd. 53/3, DIT Extension Road
(2nd Floor) Naya Paltan, Dhaka. Tel: 411882

BIRDS BANGLADESH AGENCIES LTD. (BBA)
103, Motijheel C/A, Dhaka- 1000, Tel: 955-2997, 9556347
Tlx: 642670 BIRDS BJ, 632135 HISPD BJ, Fax: 880-2-9566343, 9560140

BANGLADESH SHIPPING LINES LTD. (BD SHIP)
Sena Kalyan Bhaban, 195, Motijheel C/A, Dhaka- 1000, Tel: 9565184, 9115183-4, Tlx: 632666 BDSHIP BJ, 632656 HRC BJ, Fax: 880-2-863734, 866446

K LINE BANGLADESH LTD.
239, New Circular Road, (2nd Floor) Moghbazar, Dhaka- 1217
Tel: 402645, 416531, 416562, Tlx: 632153 KLB BJ, Fax: 880-2-836886

MARINERS (BD) LTD.
Sena Kalyan Bhaban (12th Floor),Room No. 1203,195, Motijheel C/A, Dhaka- 1000
Tel: 956-4349, 9551238, 9564934, Fax: 880-2-9564935

MARITIME SERVICES LTD. (MSL)
Ispahani Building (8th Floor), 14-15, Motijheel C/A, Dhaka- 1000
Tel: 9550361, 9550912, Tlx: CTG. 633274 MUNZU BJ, Fax: 880-2-9565316

OMNITRANS INTERNATIONAL LTD.
National Scouts Bhaban,(4th Floor),70/1,Inner Circular Road, Kakrail, Dhaka- 1000
G. P. O. Box: No. 4215,Tel: 834401-4, 834737-8,Tlx: 632254 SHIP BJ
Fax: 880-2-831910, 834959

QC SHIPPING LTD.
Sharif Mansion (4th Floor), 56-57,Motijheel C/A,G. P. O. Box No.3718,Dhaka-1000
Tel: 9551408, 9551455, 9551649, Fax: 880-2-9560666, Tlx: 675631 QCDA BJ.

R. R. SHIPPING LTD.
28, Dilkusha C/A, P.O. Box No.7211 (Dilkusha), Suite No. 801, Dhaka- 1000
Tel: 9563887, Fax: 9560830

SAMUDRAJATRA SHIPPING LINES (SSLL)
Eastern Plaza (9th Floor), Dhaka, Tel: 867088, 866917, Fax: 867044

SHAW WALLACE BANGLADESH LTD. (SW)
BSEC Bhaban (7th Floor), 102, Kazi Nazrul Islam Avenue, Kawran Bazar,
P.O. Box No. 672, Dhaka- 1215, Tel: 810511, 810601-2, Fax: 880-2-810510

MAERSK BANGLADESH LTD.
Jahangir Tower (3rd Floor), 10,Kazi Nazrul Islam Avenue, Kawran Bazar, Dhaka1215 Tel: 815985, 817847, Fax: 880-2-813352

SINGAPORE EASTERN AGENCY LTD.
56, Dilkusha C/A (1st Floor), Dhaka- 1000 Tel: 9551974, 9552515, 9557019, Fax: 880-2-863168

BASIC TITLES ON BANGLADESH

IMPORTANT!
All publications are updated annually!
Please contact IBP, Inc. at ibpusa3@gmail.com for the latest ISBNs and additional information

TITLE
Bangladesh A "Spy" Guide - Strategic Information and Developments
Bangladesh A Spy" Guide"
Bangladesh Agriculture Investment and Business Guide - Strategic and Practical Information
Bangladesh Agriculture Investment and Business Guide - Strategic and Practical Information
Bangladesh Air Force Handbook
Bangladesh Air Force Handbook
Bangladesh Army Weapon Systems Handbook
Bangladesh Army Weapon Systems Handbook
Bangladesh Army Weapon Systems Handbook
Bangladesh Army, National Security and Defense Policy Handbook
Bangladesh Army, National Security and Defense Policy Handbook
Bangladesh Banking & Financial Market Handbook
Bangladesh Banking & Financial Market Handbook
Bangladesh Business and Investment Opportunities Yearbook
Bangladesh Business and Investment Opportunities Yearbook
Bangladesh Business and Investment Opportunities Yearbook Volume 1 Strategic Information and Opportunities
Bangladesh Business and Investment Opportunities Yearbook Volume 2 Leading Export-Import, Business, Investment Opportunities and Projects
Bangladesh Business Intelligence Report - Practical Information, Opportunities, Contacts
Bangladesh Business Intelligence Report - Practical Information, Opportunities, Contacts
Bangladesh Business Law Handbook - Strategic Information and Basic Laws
Bangladesh Business Law Handbook - Strategic Information and Basic Laws
Bangladesh Business Law Handbook - Strategic Information and Basic Laws
Bangladesh Business Law Handbook - Strategic Information and Basic Laws
Bangladesh Business Law Handbook Volume 2 Investment and Trade Laws Volume 2 Investment and Trade Laws
Bangladesh Business Success Guide - Basic Practical Information and Contacts
Bangladesh Clothing & Textile Industry Handbook
Bangladesh Clothing & Textile Industry Handbook
Bangladesh Company Laws and Regulations Handbook
Bangladesh Company Laws and Regulations Handbook - Strategic Information and Basic Laws
Bangladesh Constitution and Citizenship Laws Handbook - Strategic Information and Basic Laws

TITLE
Bangladesh Country Study Guide - Strategic Information and Developments
Bangladesh Country Study Guide - Strategic Information and Developments
Bangladesh Country Study Guide - Strategic Information and Developments Volume 1 Strategic Information and Developments
Bangladesh Criminal Laws, Regulations and Procedures Handbook - Strategic Information, Regulations, Procedures
Bangladesh Customs, Trade Regulations and Procedures Handbook
Bangladesh Customs, Trade Regulations and Procedures Handbook
Bangladesh Diplomatic Handbook - Strategic Information and Developments
Bangladesh Diplomatic Handbook - Strategic Information and Developments
Bangladesh Ecology & Nature Protection Handbook
Bangladesh Ecology & Nature Protection Handbook
Bangladesh Ecology & Nature Protection Laws and Regulation Handbook
Bangladesh Economic & Development Strategy Handbook
Bangladesh Economic & Development Strategy Handbook
Bangladesh Education System and Policy Handbook
Bangladesh Electoral, Political Parties Laws and Regulations Handbook - Strategic Information, Regulations, Procedures
Bangladesh Energy Policy, Laws and Regulation Handbook
Bangladesh Energy Policy, Laws and Regulations Handbook
Bangladesh Energy Policy, Laws and Regulations Handbook
Bangladesh Export-Import Trade and Business Directory
Bangladesh Export-Import Trade and Business Directory
Bangladesh Fishing and Aquaculture Industry Handbook - Strategic Information, Regulations, Opportunities
Bangladesh Foreign Policy and Government Guide
Bangladesh Foreign Policy and Government Guide
Bangladesh Government and Business Contacts Handbook
Bangladesh Government and Business Contacts Handbook
Bangladesh Immigration Laws and Regulations Handbook - Strategic Information and Basic Laws
Bangladesh Industrial and Business Directory
Bangladesh Industrial and Business Directory
Bangladesh Insolvency (Bankruptcy) Laws and Regulations Handbook - Strategic Information and Basic Laws
Bangladesh Internet and E-Commerce Investment and Business Guide - Strategic and Practical Information: Regulations and Opportunities
Bangladesh Internet and E-Commerce Investment and Business Guide - Strategic and Practical Information: Regulations and Opportunities
Bangladesh Investment and Business Guide - Strategic and Practical Information
Bangladesh Investment and Business Guide - Strategic and Practical Information
Bangladesh Investment and Business Guide - Strategic and Practical Information
Bangladesh Investment and Business Guide - Strategic and Practical Information
Bangladesh Investment and Business Guide Volume 2 Business, Investment Opportunities and Incentives
Bangladesh Investment and Business Profile - Basic Information and Contacts for Succesful

TITLE
investment and Business Activity
Bangladesh Investment and Trade Laws and Regulations Handbook
Bangladesh Investment, Trade Strategy and Agreements Handbook - Strategic Information and Basic Agreements
Bangladesh Justice System and National Police Handbook
Bangladesh Justice System and National Police Handbook
Bangladesh Labor Laws and Regulations Handbook - Strategic Information and Basic Laws
Bangladesh Land Ownership and Agriculture Laws Handbook
Bangladesh Medical & Pharmaceutical Industry Handbook
Bangladesh Medical & Pharmaceutical Industry Handbook
Bangladesh Mineral & Mining Sector Investment and Business Guide - Strategic and Practical Information
Bangladesh Mineral & Mining Sector Investment and Business Guide - Strategic and Practical Information
Bangladesh Mining Laws and Regulations Handbook
Bangladesh Oil & Gas Sector Business & Investment Opportunities Yearbook
Bangladesh Oil & Gas Sector Business & Investment Opportunities Yearbook
Bangladesh Oil and Gas Exploration Laws and Regulation Handbook
Bangladesh Parliament Guide
Bangladesh Parliament Guide
Bangladesh Prime Minister Handbook
Bangladesh Prime Minister Handbook
Bangladesh Privatization Opportunities Handbook
Bangladesh Privatization Opportunities Handbook
Bangladesh Privatization Programs and Regulations Handbook
Bangladesh Privatization Programs and Regulations Handbook
Bangladesh Recent Economic and Political Developments Yearbook
Bangladesh Recent Economic and Political Developments Yearbook
Bangladesh Recent Economic and Political Developments Yearbook
Bangladesh Research & Development Policy Handbook
Bangladesh Research & Development Policy Handbook
Bangladesh Research & Development Policy Handbook
Bangladesh Starting Business (Incorporating) in....Guide
Bangladesh Tax Guide Volume 1 Strategic Information and Basic Regulations
Bangladesh Taxation Laws and Regulations Handbook
Bangladesh Telecom Laws and Regulations Handbook
Bangladesh Telecommunication Industry Business Opportunities Handbook
Bangladesh Telecommunication Industry Business Opportunities Handbook
Bangladesh Traders and Investors Handbook
Bangladesh Traders and Investors Handbook
Bangladesh Traders Manual: Export-Import, Trade, Investment
Bangladesh Transportation Policy and Regulations Handbook
Bangladesh: How to Invest, Start and Run Profitable Business in Bangladesh Guide - Practical Information, Opportunities, Contacts

BASIC LAWS AND REGULATIONS AFFECTING BUSINESS[3]

COUTRY	LAW TITLE
Bangladesh	Animals Slaughter(Restriction) and Meat Control Act, 1957
Bangladesh	Anticorruption Commission Law, 2004 & Anticorruption Commission Rules, 2007.
Bangladesh	Anti-dumping Rules for Bangladesh
Bangladesh	Anti-terrorism Act (Bangla)
Bangladesh	Bangladesh Energy Regulatory Commission Act, 2003
Bangladesh	Bangladesh Energy Regulatory Commission Electricity Distribution Tariff Regulation, 2008.
Bangladesh	Bangladesh Energy Regulatory Commission Gas Transmission Tariff Regulation, 2008.
Bangladesh	Bangladesh Payment and Settlement Systems regulations 2009
Bangladesh	Canals Act 1864
Bangladesh	Constitution of the People's Republic of Bangladesh
Bangladesh	Countervailing Rules for Bangladesh
Bangladesh	Customs Act 1969
Bangladesh	Electric Generation Regulation & Methodology 2007
Bangladesh	Embankment & Drainage Act, 1952
Bangladesh	Financial Institutions Act
Bangladesh	Foreign Exchange Regulation Act, 1947
Bangladesh	Forest Act 1927
Bangladesh	General Financial Rules
Bangladesh	Labor Law 2006
Bangladesh	Labor Welfare Foundation Law-2006
Bangladesh	Margin Rules, 1999
Bangladesh	Member of Parliament (Determination of Dispute) Act, 1980
Bangladesh	Microcredit Regulatory Authority Act (Bangla)
Bangladesh	Minimum Wages Board Laws
Bangladesh	Money Laundering Prevention Act (Bangla)
Bangladesh	National University Act, 1992.
Bangladesh	President Election Rules, 1991
Bangladesh	Public Procurement Act 2006
Bangladesh	Public Procurement Regulations 2003
Bangladesh	Public Procurement Rules, 2008
Bangladesh	Representation of the People Order, 1972
Bangladesh	Sale of Goods Act, 1930
Bangladesh	Tax Law
Bangladesh	Telecommunication Act 2001
Bangladesh	Telegraphy Act 1885
Bangladesh	The Acting Judges Act, 1867
Bangladesh	The Administrative Tribunals Act, 1980

[3] For ordering tests of specific laws in English or French, Please contact Global Investment Center USA at ibpusa3@gmail.com

Bangladesh	The Administrator General's Act, 1913
Bangladesh	The Agricultural and Sanitary Improvement Act, 1920
Bangladesh	The Agricultural Census Act, 1958
Bangladesh	The Agricultural Debtors Act, 1935
Bangladesh	The Agricultural Labor (Minimum Wages) Ordinance, 1984
Bangladesh	The Agricultural Produce (Grading and Marking) Act, 1937
Bangladesh	The Agricultural Produce Cess Act, 1940
Bangladesh	The Air Force Act, 1953
Bangladesh	The Aircraft (Removal of Danger to Safety) Ordinance, 1965
Bangladesh	The Alienation of Land (Distressed Circumstances) (Restoration) Ordinance, 1976
Bangladesh	The Alluvial Lands Act, 1920
Bangladesh	The Amusements Tax Act, 1922
Bangladesh	The Anand Marriage Act, 1909
Bangladesh	The Animals Slaughter (Restriction) and Meat Control Act, 1957 (East Pakistan Act)
Bangladesh	The Antiquities Act, 1968
Bangladesh	The Arya Marriage Validation Act, 1937
Bangladesh	The Asian Development Bank Order, 1973 (President's Order)
Bangladesh	The Attia Forest (Protection) Ordinance, 1982
Bangladesh	The Bangladesh Civil Service (Agriculture: Fisheries) Composition and Cadre Rules, 1980
Bangladesh	The Bangladesh Energy Regulatory Commission Act 2003
Bangladesh	The Bangladesh Environment Conservation Act, 1995
Bangladesh	The Bangladesh Oil, Gas and Mineral Corporation Ordinance, 1985
Bangladesh	The Bangladesh Passport Order, 1973 (President's Order).
Bangladesh	The Bangladesh Petroleum Act, 1974
Bangladesh	The Bangladesh Petroleum Corporation Ordinance, 1976
Bangladesh	The Bangladesh Power Development Boards Order, 1972 (President's Order)
Bangladesh	The Bangladesh Rifles (Special Provisions) Ordinance, 1976
Bangladesh	The Bangladesh Rural Development Board Ordinance, 1982
Bangladesh	The Bangladesh Taxation Laws (Adaptation) Order, 1972 (President's Order)
Bangladesh	The Bangladesh Telegraph and Telephone Board Ordinance, 1979
Bangladesh	The Bangladesh Transfer of Immovable Property (Temporary Provisions) Order, 1972
Bangladesh	The Bangladesh Veterinary Practitioners Ordinance, 1982
Bangladesh	The Bangladesh Wild Life (Preservation) Order, 1973 (President's Order)
Bangladesh	The Bankers' Book Evidence Act, 1891
Bangladesh	The Banks and Financial Institutions Laws Amendment Act, 1980
Bangladesh	The Bengal Cruelty to Animals Act, 1920
Bangladesh	The Bills of Lading Act, 1856
Bangladesh	The Births, Deaths and Marriages Registration Act, 1886
Bangladesh	The Borstal Schools Act, 1928
Bangladesh	The Building Construction Act, 1952
Bangladesh	The Business Profits Tax Act, 1947
Bangladesh	The Canals Act, 1864
Bangladesh	The Cantonments Act, 1924

Bangladesh	The Carriage by Air (International Convention) Act, 1966
Bangladesh	The Carriage By Air Act, 1934
Bangladesh	The Carriage of Goods by Sea Act, 1925
Bangladesh	The Carriers Act, 1865
Bangladesh	The Cattle (Prevention of Trespass) Ordinance, 1959 (East Pakistan Ordinance)
Bangladesh	The Cattle-trespass Act, 1871
Bangladesh	The Censorship of Films Act, 1963
Bangladesh	The Charitable and Religious Trusts Act, 1920
Bangladesh	The Child Marriage Restraint Act, 1929
Bangladesh	The Children Act, 1974
Bangladesh	The Chittagong Port Authority Ordinance, 1976
Bangladesh	The Chittagong University Act, 1973
Bangladesh	The Christian Marriage Act, 1872
Bangladesh	The Cinematograph Act, 1918
Bangladesh	The Citizenship Act, 1951
Bangladesh	The Civil Aviation Authority Ordinance, 1985
Bangladesh	The Civil Aviation Ordinance, 1960
Bangladesh	The Civil Courts Act, 1887
Bangladesh	The Civil Defense Act, 1952
Bangladesh	The Code of Civil Procedure, 1908
Bangladesh	The Code of Criminal Procedure, 1898
Bangladesh	The Commercial Documents Evidence Act, 1939
Bangladesh	The Companies (Foreign Interests) Act, 1918
Bangladesh	The Companies Act 1994
Bangladesh	The Conservator of Ports, Lands and Buildings (Recovery Of Possession) Act, 1967 (East Pakistan Act)
Bangladesh	The Consumer Rights Protection Act, 2009
Bangladesh	The Contempt of Courts Act, 1926
Bangladesh	The Contract Act, 1872
Bangladesh	The Control of Entry Act, 1952
Bangladesh	The Control of Essential Commodities Act, 1956 (East Pakistan Act)
Bangladesh	The Cotton Act, 1957
Bangladesh	The Cotton Cess Act, 1923
Bangladesh	The Cotton Cloth Act, 1918
Bangladesh	The Cotton Ginning and Pressing Act, 1957 (East Pakistan Act)
Bangladesh	The Cotton Industry (Statistics) Act, 1926
Bangladesh	The Cotton Transport Act, 1923
Bangladesh	The Court of Wards Act, 1879
Bangladesh	The Court-fees Act, 1870
Bangladesh	The Credit Rating Companies Rules, 1996
Bangladesh	The Criminal Law (Amendment) Act, 1948 (East Bengal Act)
Bangladesh	The Criminal Law (Industrial Areas) Amendment Act, 1942 (Bengal Act)
Bangladesh	The Criminal Law Amendment Act, 1938
Bangladesh	The Criminal Law Amendment Act, 1958
Bangladesh	The Criminal Law Amendment Ordinance, 1944

Bangladesh	The Cruelty to Animals Act, 1920
Bangladesh	The Culturable Waste Land (Utilization) Ordinance, 1959 (East Pakistan Ordinance)
Bangladesh	The Customs Act, 1969
Bangladesh	The Dangerous Cargoes Act, 1953
Bangladesh	The Destruction of Records Act, 1917
Bangladesh	The Development Act, 1935
Bangladesh	The Dhaka Metropolitan Police Ordinance, 1976
Bangladesh	The Diplomatic Immunities (Commonwealth Countries Representatives) Act, 1957
Bangladesh	The Diplomatic Immunities (Conferences with Commonwealth Countries) Act, 1963
Bangladesh	The Dissolution of Muslim Marriages Act, 1939
Bangladesh	The Districts Act, 1836
Bangladesh	The Divorce Act, 1869
Bangladesh	The Drugs (Control) Ordinance, 1982
Bangladesh	The Drugs (Supplementary Provisions) Ordinance, 1986
Bangladesh	The Drugs Act, 1940
Bangladesh	The East Pakistan Government Fisheries (Protection) Ordinance, 1959
Bangladesh	The Electoral Roles Act, 2009 (Bangla)
Bangladesh	The Electricity Act, 1910
Bangladesh	The Embankment and Drainage Act, 1952 (East Bengal Act)
Bangladesh	The Emigration Ordinance, 1982
Bangladesh	The Environment Conservation Rules 1997
Bangladesh	The Environment Court Act 2000
Bangladesh	The Environment pollution control ordinance 1977
Bangladesh	The Epidemic Diseases Act, 1897
Bangladesh	The Essential Articles (Price Control and Anti-Hoarding) Act, 1953 (East Bengal Act)
Bangladesh	The Essential Commodities Act, 1957 Act No Iii Of 1957
Bangladesh	The Evidence Act, 1872
Bangladesh	The Excess Profits Tax Act, 1940
Bangladesh	The Excise (Malt Liquors) Act, 1890
Bangladesh	The Excise Duty on Minerals (Labor Welfare) Act, 1967
Bangladesh	The Excises and Salt Act, 1944
Bangladesh	The Explosive Substances Act, 1908
Bangladesh	The Explosives Act, 1884
Bangladesh	The Extradition Act, 1974
Bangladesh	The Family Courts Ordinance, 1985
Bangladesh	The Film Clubs (Registration and Regulation) Act, 1980
Bangladesh	The Film Development Corporation Act, 1957 (East Pakistan Act)
Bangladesh	The Finance Act, 1981
Bangladesh	The Financial Institutions Laws Amendment Ordinance, 1977
Bangladesh	The Fish and Fish Products (Inspection and Quality Control) Ordinance, 1983
Bangladesh	The Food (Special Courts) Act, 1956 (East Pakistan Act)
Bangladesh	The Food grains Supply (Prevention of Prejudicial Activity) Ordinance, 1979
Bangladesh	The Foreign Exchange Regulation Act, 1947
Bangladesh	The Foreign Marriage Act, 1903
Bangladesh	The Foreigners Act, 1946

Bangladesh	The Forest Act, 1927
Bangladesh	The Forest Industries Development Corporation Ordinance, 1959 (East Pakistan Ordinance)
Bangladesh	The Government Buildings Act, 1899
Bangladesh	The Government Savings Banks Act, 1873
Bangladesh	The Grameen Bank Ordinance, 1983
Bangladesh	The Ground Water Management Ordinance, 1985
Bangladesh	The Highways Act, 1925
Bangladesh	The Identification of Prisoners Act, 1920
Bangladesh	The Import of Goods (Price Equalization Surcharge) Act, 1967
Bangladesh	The Import Policy Order 2006-2009
Bangladesh	The Imports and Exports (Control) Act, 1950
Bangladesh	The Income-tax and Excess Profits Tax (Emergency) Ordinance, 1942
Bangladesh	The Income-tax Ordinance, 1984
Bangladesh	The Indecent Advertisements Prohibition Act, 1963
Bangladesh	The Inland Shipping Ordinance, 1976
Bangladesh	The Inland Water Transport Authority Ordinance, 1958 (East Pakistan Ordinance)
Bangladesh	The Insurance Act, 1938
Bangladesh	The Insurance Corporations Act, 1973
Bangladesh	The International Crimes (Tribunals) Act, 1973
Bangladesh	The Irrigation Act, 1876
Bangladesh	The Islamic Development Bank Act, 1975
Bangladesh	The Islamic University Act, 1980
Bangladesh	The Jahangirnagar University Act, 1973
Bangladesh	The Land Development Tax Ordinance, 1976
Bangladesh	The Land Reforms Ordinance, 1984
Bangladesh	The Limitation Act, 1908
Bangladesh	The Local Government (Union Parishads) Ordinance, 1983
Bangladesh	The Marine Fisheries Ordinance, 1983
Bangladesh	The Marine Fisheries Rules, 1983
Bangladesh	The Medical and Dental Council Act, 1980
Bangladesh	The Medical Degrees Act, 1916
Bangladesh	The Merchandise Marks Act, 1889
Bangladesh	The Micro-Credit regulatory Authority Act
Bangladesh	The Mines Act, 1923
Bangladesh	The Mining Settlements Act, 1912
Bangladesh	The Ministers, Ministers of State and Deputy Ministers (Remuneration and Privileges) Act, 1973
Bangladesh	The Money-Lenders Act, 1933
Bangladesh	The Motor Vehicles Ordinance, 1983
Bangladesh	The Motor Vehicles Tax Act, 1932
Bangladesh	The Narcotics Control Act 1990
Bangladesh	The National Guard Act, 1950
Bangladesh	The Naturalization Act, 1926
Bangladesh	The Ombudsman Act, 1980

Bangladesh	The Partnership Act, 1932
Bangladesh	The Passport (Offences) Act, 1952
Bangladesh	The Passport Act, 1920
Bangladesh	The Patents And Designs Act, 1911
Bangladesh	The Penal Code, 1860
Bangladesh	The Petroleum Act, 1934
Bangladesh	The Petroleum Products (Development Surcharge) Ordinance, 1961
Bangladesh	The Poisons Act, 1919
Bangladesh	The Police Act, 1861
Bangladesh	The Political Parties Ordinance, 1978
Bangladesh	The Ports Act, 1908
Bangladesh	The Post Office Act 1898
Bangladesh	The President's (Remuneration and Privileges) Act 1975
Bangladesh	The Prevention of Corruption Act, 1947
Bangladesh	The Prevention of Cruelty to Animals Ordinance, 1962
Bangladesh	The Prevention of Malaria (Special Provisions) Ordinance, 1978
Bangladesh	The Prime Minister's (Remuneration and Privileges) Act, 1975
Bangladesh	The Prisoners Act, 1900
Bangladesh	The Prisons Act, 1894
Bangladesh	The Private Fisheries Protection Act, 1889
Bangladesh	The Protection and Conservation of Fish Act, 1950
Bangladesh	The Public Procurement Act 2006
Bangladesh	The Railways Act, 1890
Bangladesh	The Rajshahi University Act, 1973
Bangladesh	The Registration Act, 1908
Bangladesh	The Registration of Foreigners Act, 1939
Bangladesh	The Sale of Goods Act, 1930
Bangladesh	The Securities Act, 1920
Bangladesh	The Securities and Exchange Ordinance, 1969
Bangladesh	The Securities and Exchange Rules,1987
Bangladesh	The Seeds Ordinance, 1977
Bangladesh	The Small Cause Courts Act, 1887
Bangladesh	The Societies Registration Act 1860
Bangladesh	The Tanks Improvement Act, 1939
Bangladesh	The Territorial Waters and Maritime Zones Act, 1974
Bangladesh	The Town Improvement Act, 1953
Bangladesh	The Trade Marks Act, 1940
Bangladesh	The Trade Organization Ordinance, 1961
Bangladesh	The University Laws Amendment Act, 1980
Bangladesh	The Vaccination Act, 1880
Bangladesh	The water pollution control act
Bangladesh	Trade Marks Act, 2009 (Bangla)
Bangladesh	Water Development Board Act 2000
Bangladesh	Wireless Telegraphy Act 1933

WORLD HOW TO INVEST, START AND RUN PROFITABLE BUSINESS LIBRARY

Strategic political, geographic, economic, business information, contacts and important developments

Price: $99.95 each

COMPLETE FULL TITLE	ISBN
How to Invest, Start and Run Profitable Business in Afghanistan Guide - Practical Information, Opportunities, Contacts	978-1-4330-8269-6
How to Invest, Start and Run Profitable Business in Aland Guide - Practical Information, Opportunities, Contacts	978-1-4330-8270-2
How to Invest, Start and Run Profitable Business in Albania Guide - Practical Information, Opportunities, Contacts	978-1-4330-8271-9
How to Invest, Start and Run Profitable Business in Algeria Guide - Practical Information, Opportunities, Contacts	978-1-4330-8272-6
How to Invest, Start and Run Profitable Business in Andorra Guide - Practical Information, Opportunities, Contacts	978-1-4330-8273-3
How to Invest, Start and Run Profitable Business in Angola Guide - Practical Information, Opportunities, Contacts	978-1-4330-8275-7
How to Invest, Start and Run Profitable Business in Anguilla Guide - Practical Information, Opportunities, Contacts	978-1-4330-8276-4
How to Invest, Start and Run Profitable Business in Antigua and Barbuda Guide - Practical Information, Opportunities, Contacts	978-1-4330-8277-1
How to Invest, Start and Run Profitable Business in Antilles (Netherlands) Guide - Practical Information, Opportunities, Contacts	978-1-4330-8278-8
How to Invest, Start and Run Profitable Business in Argentina Guide - Practical Information, Opportunities, Contacts	978-1-4330-8279-5
How to Invest, Start and Run Profitable Business in Armenia Guide - Practical Information, Opportunities, Contacts	978-1-4330-8280-1
How to Invest, Start and Run Profitable Business in Aruba Guide - Practical Information, Opportunities, Contacts	978-1-4330-8281-8
How to Invest, Start and Run Profitable Business in Australia Guide - Practical Information, Opportunities, Contacts	978-1-4330-8282-5
How to Invest, Start and Run Profitable Business in Austria Guide - Practical Information, Opportunities, Contacts	978-1-4330-8283-2
How to Invest, Start and Run Profitable Business in Azerbaijan Guide - Practical Information, Opportunities, Contacts	978-1-4330-8284-9
How to Invest, Start and Run Profitable Business in Bahamas Guide - Practical Information, Opportunities, Contacts	978-1-4330-8285-6
How to Invest, Start and Run Profitable Business in Bahrain Guide - Practical Information, Opportunities, Contacts	978-1-4330-8286-3
How to Invest, Start and Run Profitable Business in Bangladesh Guide - Practical Information, Opportunities, Contacts	978-1-4330-8287-0
How to Invest, Start and Run Profitable Business in Barbados Guide - Practical Information, Opportunities, Contacts	978-1-4330-8288-7
How to Invest, Start and Run Profitable Business in Belarus Guide - Practical Information, Opportunities, Contacts	978-1-4330-8289-4

COMPLETE FULL TITLE	ISBN
How to Invest, Start and Run Profitable Business in Belgium Guide - Practical Information, Opportunities, Contacts	978-1-4330-8290-0
How to Invest, Start and Run Profitable Business in Belize Guide - Practical Information, Opportunities, Contacts	978-1-4330-8291-7
How to Invest, Start and Run Profitable Business in Benin Guide - Practical Information, Opportunities, Contacts	978-1-4330-8292-4
How to Invest, Start and Run Profitable Business in Bermuda Guide - Practical Information, Opportunities, Contacts	978-1-4330-8293-1
How to Invest, Start and Run Profitable Business in Bhutan Guide - Practical Information, Opportunities, Contacts	978-1-4330-8294-8
How to Invest, Start and Run Profitable Business in Bolivia Guide - Practical Information, Opportunities, Contacts	978-1-4330-8295-5
How to Invest, Start and Run Profitable Business in Bosnia and Herzegovina Guide - Practical Information, Opportunities, Contacts	978-1-4330-8296-2
How to Invest, Start and Run Profitable Business in Botswana Guide - Practical Information, Opportunities, Contacts	978-1-4330-8297-9
How to Invest, Start and Run Profitable Business in Brazil Guide - Practical Information, Opportunities, Contacts	978-1-4330-8298-6
How to Invest, Start and Run Profitable Business in Brunei Guide - Practical Information, Opportunities, Contacts	978-1-4330-8299-3
How to Invest, Start and Run Profitable Business in Bulgaria Guide - Practical Information, Opportunities, Contacts	978-1-4330-8300-6
How to Invest, Start and Run Profitable Business in Burkina Faso Guide - Practical Information, Opportunities, Contacts	978-1-4330-8301-3
How to Invest, Start and Run Profitable Business in Burundi Guide - Practical Information, Opportunities, Contacts	978-1-4330-8302-0
How to Invest, Start and Run Profitable Business in Cambodia Guide - Practical Information, Opportunities, Contacts	978-1-4330-8303-7
How to Invest, Start and Run Profitable Business in Cameroon Guide - Practical Information, Opportunities, Contacts	978-1-4330-8304-4
How to Invest, Start and Run Profitable Business in Canada Guide - Practical Information, Opportunities, Contacts	978-1-4330-8305-1
How to Invest, Start and Run Profitable Business in Cape Verde Guide - Practical Information, Opportunities, Contacts	978-1-4330-8306-8
How to Invest, Start and Run Profitable Business in Cayman Islands Guide - Practical Information, Opportunities, Contacts	978-1-4330-8307-5
How to Invest, Start and Run Profitable Business in Central African Republic Guide - Practical Information, Opportunities, Contacts	978-1-4330-8308-2
How to Invest, Start and Run Profitable Business in Chad Guide - Practical Information, Opportunities, Contacts	978-1-4330-8309-9
How to Invest, Start and Run Profitable Business in Chile Guide - Practical Information, Opportunities, Contacts	978-1-4330-8310-5
How to Invest, Start and Run Profitable Business in China Guide - Practical Information, Opportunities, Contacts	978-1-4330-8311-2
How to Invest, Start and Run Profitable Business in Colombia Guide - Practical Information, Opportunities, Contacts	978-1-4330-8312-9
How to Invest, Start and Run Profitable Business in Comoros Guide - Practical Information, Opportunities, Contacts	978-1-4330-8313-6
How to Invest, Start and Run Profitable Business in Congo Guide - Practical Information, Opportunities, Contacts	978-1-4330-8314-3
How to Invest, Start and Run Profitable Business in Congo, Democratic Republic Guide - Practical Information, Opportunities, Contacts	978-1-4330-8315-0
How to Invest, Start and Run Profitable Business in Cook Islands Guide - Practical Information, Opportunities, Contacts	978-1-4330-8316-7
How to Invest, Start and Run Profitable Business in Costa Rica Guide - Practical Information, Opportunities, Contacts	978-1-4330-8317-4
How to Invest, Start and Run Profitable Business in Cote d'Ivoire Guide - Practical Information, Opportunities, Contacts	978-1-4330-8318-1
How to Invest, Start and Run Profitable Business in Croatia Guide - Practical Information, Opportunities, Contacts	978-1-4330-8319-8
How to Invest, Start and Run Profitable Business in Cuba Guide - Practical Information,	978-1-4330-8320-4

COMPLETE FULL TITLE	ISBN
Opportunities, Contacts	
How to Invest, Start and Run Profitable Business in Cyprus Guide - Practical Information, Opportunities, Contacts	978-1-4330-8321-1
How to Invest, Start and Run Profitable Business in Czech Republic Guide - Practical Information, Opportunities, Contacts	978-1-4330-8322-8
How to Invest, Start and Run Profitable Business in Denmark Guide - Practical Information, Opportunities, Contacts	978-1-4330-8323-5
How to Invest, Start and Run Profitable Business in Djibouti Guide - Practical Information, Opportunities, Contacts	978-1-4330-8324-2
How to Invest, Start and Run Profitable Business in Dominica Guide - Practical Information, Opportunities, Contacts	978-1-4330-8325-9
How to Invest, Start and Run Profitable Business in Dominican Republic Guide - Practical Information, Opportunities, Contacts	978-1-4330-8326-6
How to Invest, Start and Run Profitable Business in Ecuador Guide - Practical Information, Opportunities, Contacts	978-1-4330-8327-3
How to Invest, Start and Run Profitable Business in Egypt Guide - Practical Information, Opportunities, Contacts	978-1-4330-8328-0
How to Invest, Start and Run Profitable Business in El Salvador Guide - Practical Information, Opportunities, Contacts	978-1-4330-8329-7
How to Invest, Start and Run Profitable Business in Equatorial Guinea Guide - Practical Information, Opportunities, Contacts	978-1-4330-8330-3
How to Invest, Start and Run Profitable Business in Eritrea Guide - Practical Information, Opportunities, Contacts	978-1-4330-8331-0
How to Invest, Start and Run Profitable Business in Estonia Guide - Practical Information, Opportunities, Contacts	978-1-4330-8332-7
How to Invest, Start and Run Profitable Business in Ethiopia Guide - Practical Information, Opportunities, Contacts	978-1-4330-8333-4
How to Invest, Start and Run Profitable Business in Falkland Islands Guide - Practical Information, Opportunities, Contacts	978-1-4330-8334-1
How to Invest, Start and Run Profitable Business in Faroes Islands Guide - Practical Information, Opportunities, Contacts	978-1-4330-8335-8
How to Invest, Start and Run Profitable Business in Fiji Guide - Practical Information, Opportunities, Contacts	978-1-4330-8336-5
How to Invest, Start and Run Profitable Business in Finland Guide - Practical Information, Opportunities, Contacts	978-1-4330-8337-2
How to Invest, Start and Run Profitable Business in France Guide - Practical Information, Opportunities, Contacts	978-1-4330-8338-9
How to Invest, Start and Run Profitable Business in Gabon Guide - Practical Information, Opportunities, Contacts	978-1-4330-8339-6
How to Invest, Start and Run Profitable Business in Gambia Guide - Practical Information, Opportunities, Contacts	978-1-4330-8340-2
How to Invest, Start and Run Profitable Business in Georgia Republic Guide - Practical Information, Opportunities, Contacts	978-1-4330-8341-9
How to Invest, Start and Run Profitable Business in Germany Guide - Practical Information, Opportunities, Contacts	978-1-4330-8342-6
How to Invest, Start and Run Profitable Business in Ghana Guide - Practical Information, Opportunities, Contacts	978-1-4330-8343-3
How to Invest, Start and Run Profitable Business in Gibraltar Guide - Practical Information, Opportunities, Contacts	978-1-4330-8344-0
How to Invest, Start and Run Profitable Business in Greece Guide - Practical Information, Opportunities, Contacts	978-1-4330-8345-7
How to Invest, Start and Run Profitable Business in Greenland Guide - Practical Information, Opportunities, Contacts	978-1-4330-8346-4
How to Invest, Start and Run Profitable Business in Grenada Guide - Practical Information, Opportunities, Contacts	978-1-4330-8347-1
How to Invest, Start and Run Profitable Business in Guam Guide - Practical Information, Opportunities, Contacts	978-1-4330-8348-8
How to Invest, Start and Run Profitable Business in Guatemala Guide - Practical Information, Opportunities, Contacts	978-1-4330-8349-5
How to Invest, Start and Run Profitable Business in Guernsey Guide - Practical Information, Opportunities, Contacts	978-1-4330-8350-1

COMPLETE FULL TITLE	ISBN
How to Invest, Start and Run Profitable Business in Guinea Guide - Practical Information, Opportunities, Contacts	978-1-4330-8351-8
How to Invest, Start and Run Profitable Business in Guinea-Bissau Guide - Practical Information, Opportunities, Contacts	978-1-4330-8352-5
How to Invest, Start and Run Profitable Business in Guyana Guide - Practical Information, Opportunities, Contacts	978-1-4330-8353-2
How to Invest, Start and Run Profitable Business in Haiti Guide - Practical Information, Opportunities, Contacts	978-1-4330-8354-9
How to Invest, Start and Run Profitable Business in Honduras Guide - Practical Information, Opportunities, Contacts	978-1-4330-8355-6
How to Invest, Start and Run Profitable Business in Hungary Guide - Practical Information, Opportunities, Contacts	978-1-4330-8356-3
How to Invest, Start and Run Profitable Business in Iceland Guide - Practical Information, Opportunities, Contacts	978-1-4330-8357-0
How to Invest, Start and Run Profitable Business in India Guide - Practical Information, Opportunities, Contacts	978-1-4330-8358-7
How to Invest, Start and Run Profitable Business in Indonesia Guide - Practical Information, Opportunities, Contacts	978-1-4330-8359-4
How to Invest, Start and Run Profitable Business in Iran Guide - Practical Information, Opportunities, Contacts	978-1-4330-8360-0
How to Invest, Start and Run Profitable Business in Iraq Guide - Practical Information, Opportunities, Contacts	978-1-4330-8361-7
How to Invest, Start and Run Profitable Business in Ireland Guide - Practical Information, Opportunities, Contacts	978-1-4330-8362-4
How to Invest, Start and Run Profitable Business in Israel Guide - Practical Information, Opportunities, Contacts	978-1-4330-8363-1
How to Invest, Start and Run Profitable Business in Italy Guide - Practical Information, Opportunities, Contacts	978-1-4330-8364-8
How to Invest, Start and Run Profitable Business in Jamaica Guide - Practical Information, Opportunities, Contacts	978-1-4330-8365-5
How to Invest, Start and Run Profitable Business in Japan Guide - Practical Information, Opportunities, Contacts	978-1-4330-8366-2
How to Invest, Start and Run Profitable Business in Jersey Guide - Practical Information, Opportunities, Contacts	978-1-4330-8367-9
How to Invest, Start and Run Profitable Business in Jordan Guide - Practical Information, Opportunities, Contacts	978-1-4330-8368-6
How to Invest, Start and Run Profitable Business in Kazakhstan Guide - Practical Information, Opportunities, Contacts	978-1-4330-8369-3
How to Invest, Start and Run Profitable Business in Kenya Guide - Practical Information, Opportunities, Contacts	978-1-4330-8370-9
How to Invest, Start and Run Profitable Business in Kiribati Guide - Practical Information, Opportunities, Contacts	978-1-4330-8371-6
How to Invest, Start and Run Profitable Business in Korea, North Guide - Practical Information, Opportunities, Contacts	978-1-4330-8372-3
How to Invest, Start and Run Profitable Business in Korea, South Guide - Practical Information, Opportunities, Contacts	978-1-4330-8373-0
How to Invest, Start and Run Profitable Business in Kosovo Guide - Practical Information, Opportunities, Contacts	978-1-4330-8374-7
How to Invest, Start and Run Profitable Business in Kurdistan Guide - Practical Information, Opportunities, Contacts	978-1-4330-8375-4
How to Invest, Start and Run Profitable Business in Kuwait Guide - Practical Information, Opportunities, Contacts	978-1-4330-8376-1
How to Invest, Start and Run Profitable Business in Kyrgyzstan Guide - Practical Information, Opportunities, Contacts	978-1-4330-8377-8
How to Invest, Start and Run Profitable Business in Laos Guide - Practical Information, Opportunities, Contacts	978-1-4330-8378-5
How to Invest, Start and Run Profitable Business in Latvia Guide - Practical Information, Opportunities, Contacts	978-1-4330-8379-2
How to Invest, Start and Run Profitable Business in Lebanon Guide - Practical Information, Opportunities, Contacts	978-1-4330-8380-8
How to Invest, Start and Run Profitable Business in Lesotho Guide - Practical Information,	978-1-4330-8381-5

COMPLETE FULL TITLE	ISBN
Opportunities, Contacts	
How to Invest, Start and Run Profitable Business in Liberia Guide - Practical Information, Opportunities, Contacts	978-1-4330-8382-2
How to Invest, Start and Run Profitable Business in Libya Guide - Practical Information, Opportunities, Contacts	978-1-4330-8383-9
How to Invest, Start and Run Profitable Business in Liechtenstein Guide - Practical Information, Opportunities, Contacts	978-1-4330-8384-6
How to Invest, Start and Run Profitable Business in Lithuania Guide - Practical Information, Opportunities, Contacts	978-1-4330-8385-3
How to Invest, Start and Run Profitable Business in Luxembourg Guide - Practical Information, Opportunities, Contacts	978-1-4330-8386-0
How to Invest, Start and Run Profitable Business in Macao Guide - Practical Information, Opportunities, Contacts	978-1-4330-8387-7
How to Invest, Start and Run Profitable Business in Macedonia Guide - Practical Information, Opportunities, Contacts	978-1-4330-8388-4
How to Invest, Start and Run Profitable Business in Madagascar Guide - Practical Information, Opportunities, Contacts	978-1-4330-8389-1
How to Invest, Start and Run Profitable Business in Madeira Guide - Practical Information, Opportunities, Contacts	978-1-4330-8390-7
How to Invest, Start and Run Profitable Business in Malawi Guide - Practical Information, Opportunities, Contacts	978-1-4330-8391-4
How to Invest, Start and Run Profitable Business in Malaysia Guide - Practical Information, Opportunities, Contacts	978-1-4330-8392-1
How to Invest, Start and Run Profitable Business in Maldives Guide - Practical Information, Opportunities, Contacts	978-1-4330-8393-8
How to Invest, Start and Run Profitable Business in Mali Guide - Practical Information, Opportunities, Contacts	978-1-4330-8394-5
How to Invest, Start and Run Profitable Business in Malta Guide - Practical Information, Opportunities, Contacts	978-1-4330-8395-2
How to Invest, Start and Run Profitable Business in Man Guide - Practical Information, Opportunities, Contacts	978-1-4330-8396-9
How to Invest, Start and Run Profitable Business in Marshall Islands Guide - Practical Information, Opportunities, Contacts	978-1-4330-8397-6
How to Invest, Start and Run Profitable Business in Mauritania Guide - Practical Information, Opportunities, Contacts	978-1-4330-8398-3
How to Invest, Start and Run Profitable Business in Mauritius Guide - Practical Information, Opportunities, Contacts	978-1-4330-8399-0
How to Invest, Start and Run Profitable Business in Mayotte Guide - Practical Information, Opportunities, Contacts	978-1-4330-8400-3
How to Invest, Start and Run Profitable Business in Mexico Guide - Practical Information, Opportunities, Contacts	978-1-4330-8401-0
How to Invest, Start and Run Profitable Business in Micronesia Guide - Practical Information, Opportunities, Contacts	978-1-4330-8402-7
How to Invest, Start and Run Profitable Business in Moldova Guide - Practical Information, Opportunities, Contacts	978-1-4330-8403-4
How to Invest, Start and Run Profitable Business in Monaco Guide - Practical Information, Opportunities, Contacts	978-1-4330-8404-1
How to Invest, Start and Run Profitable Business in Mongolia Guide - Practical Information, Opportunities, Contacts	978-1-4330-8405-8
How to Invest, Start and Run Profitable Business in Monserrat Guide - Practical Information, Opportunities, Contacts	978-1-4330-8406-5
How to Invest, Start and Run Profitable Business in Morocco Guide - Practical Information, Opportunities, Contacts	978-1-4330-8407-2
How to Invest, Start and Run Profitable Business in Mozambique Guide - Practical Information, Opportunities, Contacts	978-1-4330-8408-9
How to Invest, Start and Run Profitable Business in Myanmar Guide - Practical Information, Opportunities, Contacts	978-1-4330-8409-6
How to Invest, Start and Run Profitable Business in Namibia Guide - Practical Information, Opportunities, Contacts	978-1-4330-8410-2
How to Invest, Start and Run Profitable Business in Nauru Guide - Practical Information, Opportunities, Contacts	978-1-4330-8411-9

COMPLETE FULL TITLE	ISBN
How to Invest, Start and Run Profitable Business in Nepal Guide - Practical Information, Opportunities, Contacts	978-1-4330-8412-6
How to Invest, Start and Run Profitable Business in Netherlands Guide - Practical Information, Opportunities, Contacts	978-1-4330-8413-3
How to Invest, Start and Run Profitable Business in New Caledonia Guide - Practical Information, Opportunities, Contacts	978-1-4330-8414-0
How to Invest, Start and Run Profitable Business in New Zealand Guide - Practical Information, Opportunities, Contacts	978-1-4330-8415-7
How to Invest, Start and Run Profitable Business in Nicaragua Guide - Practical Information, Opportunities, Contacts	978-1-4330-8416-4
How to Invest, Start and Run Profitable Business in Niger Guide - Practical Information, Opportunities, Contacts	978-1-4330-8417-1
How to Invest, Start and Run Profitable Business in Nigeria Guide - Practical Information, Opportunities, Contacts	978-1-4330-8418-8
How to Invest, Start and Run Profitable Business in Niue Guide - Practical Information, Opportunities, Contacts	978-1-4330-8419-5
How to Invest, Start and Run Profitable Business in Northern Mariana Islands Guide - Practical Information, Opportunities, Contacts	978-1-4330-8420-1
How to Invest, Start and Run Profitable Business in Norway Guide - Practical Information, Opportunities, Contacts	978-1-4330-8421-8
How to Invest, Start and Run Profitable Business in Oman Guide - Practical Information, Opportunities, Contacts	978-1-4330-8422-5
How to Invest, Start and Run Profitable Business in Pakistan Guide - Practical Information, Opportunities, Contacts	978-1-4330-8423-2
How to Invest, Start and Run Profitable Business in Palau Guide - Practical Information, Opportunities, Contacts	978-1-4330-8424-9
How to Invest, Start and Run Profitable Business in Palestine Guide - Practical Information, Opportunities, Contacts	978-1-4330-8425-6
How to Invest, Start and Run Profitable Business in Panama Guide - Practical Information, Opportunities, Contacts	978-1-4330-8426-3
How to Invest, Start and Run Profitable Business in Papua New Guinea Guide - Practical Information, Opportunities, Contacts	978-1-4330-8427-0
How to Invest, Start and Run Profitable Business in Paraguay Guide - Practical Information, Opportunities, Contacts	978-1-4330-8428-7
How to Invest, Start and Run Profitable Business in Peru Guide - Practical Information, Opportunities, Contacts	978-1-4330-8429-4
How to Invest, Start and Run Profitable Business in Philippines Guide - Practical Information, Opportunities, Contacts	978-1-4330-8430-0
How to Invest, Start and Run Profitable Business in Pitcairn Islands Guide - Practical Information, Opportunities, Contacts	978-1-4330-8431-7
How to Invest, Start and Run Profitable Business in Poland Guide - Practical Information, Opportunities, Contacts	978-1-4330-8432-4
How to Invest, Start and Run Profitable Business in Polynesia French Guide - Practical Information, Opportunities, Contacts	978-1-4330-8433-1
How to Invest, Start and Run Profitable Business in Portugal Guide - Practical Information, Opportunities, Contacts	978-1-4330-8434-8
How to Invest, Start and Run Profitable Business in Qatar Guide - Practical Information, Opportunities, Contacts	978-1-4330-8435-5
How to Invest, Start and Run Profitable Business in Romania Guide - Practical Information, Opportunities, Contacts	978-1-4330-8436-2
How to Invest, Start and Run Profitable Business in Russia Guide - Practical Information, Opportunities, Contacts	978-1-4330-8437-9
How to Invest, Start and Run Profitable Business in Rwanda Guide - Practical Information, Opportunities, Contacts	978-1-4330-8438-6
How to Invest, Start and Run Profitable Business in Saint Kitts and Nevis Guide - Practical Information, Opportunities, Contacts	978-1-4330-8439-3
How to Invest, Start and Run Profitable Business in Saint Lucia Guide - Practical Information, Opportunities, Contacts	978-1-4330-8440-9
How to Invest, Start and Run Profitable Business in Saint Vincent and The Grenadines Guide - Practical Information, Opportunities, Contacts	978-1-4330-8441-6
How to Invest, Start and Run Profitable Business in Samoa (American) A Guide - Practical	978-1-4330-8442-3

COMPLETE FULL TITLE	ISBN
Information, Opportunities, Contacts	
How to Invest, Start and Run Profitable Business in Samoa (Western) Guide - Practical Information, Opportunities, Contacts	978-1-4330-8443-0
How to Invest, Start and Run Profitable Business in San Marino Guide - Practical Information, Opportunities, Contacts	978-1-4330-8444-7
How to Invest, Start and Run Profitable Business in Sao Tome and Principe Guide - Practical Information, Opportunities, Contacts	978-1-4330-8445-4
How to Invest, Start and Run Profitable Business in Saudi Arabia Guide - Practical Information, Opportunities, Contacts	978-1-4330-8446-1
How to Invest, Start and Run Profitable Business in Scotland Guide - Practical Information, Opportunities, Contacts	978-1-4330-8447-8
How to Invest, Start and Run Profitable Business in Senegal Guide - Practical Information, Opportunities, Contacts	978-1-4330-8448-5
How to Invest, Start and Run Profitable Business in Serbia Guide - Practical Information, Opportunities, Contacts	978-1-4330-8449-2
How to Invest, Start and Run Profitable Business in Seychelles Guide - Practical Information, Opportunities, Contacts	978-1-4330-8450-8
How to Invest, Start and Run Profitable Business in Sierra Leone Guide - Practical Information, Opportunities, Contacts	978-1-4330-8451-5
How to Invest, Start and Run Profitable Business in Singapore Guide - Practical Information, Opportunities, Contacts	978-1-4330-8452-2
How to Invest, Start and Run Profitable Business in Slovakia Guide - Practical Information, Opportunities, Contacts	978-1-4330-8453-9
How to Invest, Start and Run Profitable Business in Slovenia Guide - Practical Information, Opportunities, Contacts	978-1-4330-8454-6
How to Invest, Start and Run Profitable Business in Solomon Islands Guide - Practical Information, Opportunities, Contacts	978-1-4330-8455-3
How to Invest, Start and Run Profitable Business in Somalia Guide - Practical Information, Opportunities, Contacts	978-1-4330-8456-0
How to Invest, Start and Run Profitable Business in South Africa Guide - Practical Information, Opportunities, Contacts	978-1-4330-8457-7
How to Invest, Start and Run Profitable Business in Spain Guide - Practical Information, Opportunities, Contacts	978-1-4330-8458-4
How to Invest, Start and Run Profitable Business in Sri Lanka Guide - Practical Information, Opportunities, Contacts	978-1-4330-8459-1
How to Invest, Start and Run Profitable Business in St. Helena Guide - Practical Information, Opportunities, Contacts	978-1-4330-8460-7
How to Invest, Start and Run Profitable Business in St. Pierre & Miguel Guide - Practical Information, Opportunities, Contacts	978-1-4330-8461-4
How to Invest, Start and Run Profitable Business in Sudan (North) Guide - Practical Information, Opportunities, Contacts	978-1-4330-8462-1
How to Invest, Start and Run Profitable Business in Suriname Guide - Practical Information, Opportunities, Contacts	978-1-4330-8463-8
How to Invest, Start and Run Profitable Business in Swaziland Guide - Practical Information, Opportunities, Contacts	978-1-4330-8464-5
How to Invest, Start and Run Profitable Business in Sweden Guide - Practical Information, Opportunities, Contacts	978-1-4330-8465-2
How to Invest, Start and Run Profitable Business in Switzerland Guide - Practical Information, Opportunities, Contacts	978-1-4330-8466-9
How to Invest, Start and Run Profitable Business in Syria Guide - Practical Information, Opportunities, Contacts	978-1-4330-8467-6
How to Invest, Start and Run Profitable Business in Taiwan Guide - Practical Information, Opportunities, Contacts	978-1-4330-8468-3
How to Invest, Start and Run Profitable Business in Tajikistan Guide - Practical Information, Opportunities, Contacts	978-1-4330-8469-0
How to Invest, Start and Run Profitable Business in Tanzania Guide - Practical Information, Opportunities, Contacts	978-1-4330-8470-6
How to Invest, Start and Run Profitable Business in Thailand Guide - Practical Information, Opportunities, Contacts	978-1-4330-8471-3
How to Invest, Start and Run Profitable Business in Togo Guide - Practical Information, Opportunities, Contacts	978-1-4330-8472-0

COMPLETE FULL TITLE	ISBN
How to Invest, Start and Run Profitable Business in Tonga Guide - Practical Information, Opportunities, Contacts	978-1-4330-8473-7
How to Invest, Start and Run Profitable Business in Trinidad and Tobago Guide - Practical Information, Opportunities, Contacts	978-1-4330-8474-4
How to Invest, Start and Run Profitable Business in Tunisia Guide - Practical Information, Opportunities, Contacts	978-1-4330-8475-1
How to Invest, Start and Run Profitable Business in Turkey Guide - Practical Information, Opportunities, Contacts	978-1-4330-8476-8
How to Invest, Start and Run Profitable Business in Turkmenistan Guide - Practical Information, Opportunities, Contacts	978-1-4330-8477-5
How to Invest, Start and Run Profitable Business in Turks & Caicos Guide - Practical Information, Opportunities, Contacts	978-1-4330-8478-2
How to Invest, Start and Run Profitable Business in Tuvalu Guide - Practical Information, Opportunities, Contacts	978-1-4330-8479-9
How to Invest, Start and Run Profitable Business in Uganda Guide - Practical Information, Opportunities, Contacts	978-1-4330-8480-5
How to Invest, Start and Run Profitable Business in Ukraine Guide - Practical Information, Opportunities, Contacts	978-1-4330-8481-2
How to Invest, Start and Run Profitable Business in the United Arab Emirates Guide - Practical Information, Opportunities, Contacts	978-1-4330-8482-9
How to Invest, Start and Run Profitable Business in United Kingdom Guide - Practical Information, Opportunities, Contacts	978-1-4330-8483-6
How to Invest, Start and Run Profitable Business in United States Guide - Practical Information, Opportunities, Contacts	978-1-4330-8484-3
How to Invest, Start and Run Profitable Business in Uruguay Guide - Practical Information, Opportunities, Contacts	978-1-4330-8485-0
How to Invest, Start and Run Profitable Business in Uzbekistan Guide - Practical Information, Opportunities, Contacts	978-1-4330-8486-7
How to Invest, Start and Run Profitable Business in Vanuatu Guide - Practical Information, Opportunities, Contacts	978-1-4330-8487-4
How to Invest, Start and Run Profitable Business in Vatican City Guide - Practical Information, Opportunities, Contacts	978-1-4330-8488-1
How to Invest, Start and Run Profitable Business in Venezuela Guide - Practical Information, Opportunities, Contacts	978-1-4330-8489-8
How to Invest, Start and Run Profitable Business in Vietnam Guide - Practical Information, Opportunities, Contacts	978-1-4330-8490-4
How to Invest, Start and Run Profitable Business in Virgin Islands, British Guide - Practical Information, Opportunities, Contacts	978-1-4330-8491-1
How to Invest, Start and Run Profitable Business in Wake Atoll Guide - Practical Information, Opportunities, Contacts	978-1-4330-8492-8
How to Invest, Start and Run Profitable Business in Wallis & Futuna Guide - Practical Information, Opportunities, Contacts	978-1-4330-8493-5
How to Invest, Start and Run Profitable Business in Western Sahara Guide - Practical Information, Opportunities, Contacts	978-1-4330-8494-2
How to Invest, Start and Run Profitable Business in Yemen Guide - Practical Information, Opportunities, Contacts	978-1-4330-8495-9
How to Invest, Start and Run Profitable Business in Zambia Guide - Practical Information, Opportunities, Contacts	978-1-4330-8496-6
How to Invest, Start and Run Profitable Business in Zimbabwe Guide - Practical Information, Opportunities, Contacts	978-1-4330-8497-3
How to Invest, Start and Run Profitable Business in Sudan (South) Guide - Practical Information, Opportunities, Contacts	978-1-4330-8498-0

To order and for additional analytical and marketing information, please contacts
International Business Publications, USA at:
P.O. Box 15343, Washington, DC 20003, USA. Phone: (202) 546-210 Fax: (202) 546-32
E-mail: ibpusa3@gmail.com

www.ingramcontent.com/pod-product-compliance
Ingram Content Group UK Ltd.
Pitfield, Milton Keynes, MK11 3LW, UK
UKHW051457290926
15471UKWH00008B/1261